American
Foreign Policy
Since World War II

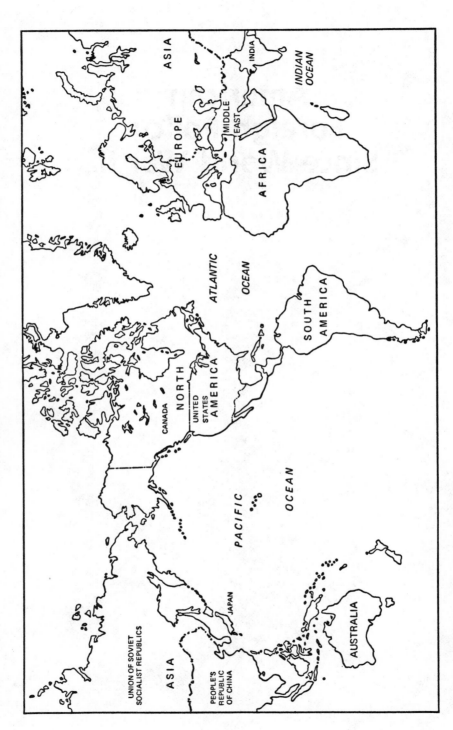

The United States of America/World

American Foreign Policy Since World War II

TENTH EDITION

JOHN SPANIER

University of Florida

HOLT, RINEHART AND WINSTON

New York   Chicago   San Francisco   Philadelphia
Montreal   Toronto   London   Sydney   Tokyo
Mexico City   Rio de Janeiro   Madrid

To
David
for being
and
for being himself

Library of Congress Cataloging in Publication Data

Spanier, John W.
   American foreign policy since World War II.

   Bibliography: p. 336
   Includes index.
   1. United States—Foreign relations—1945–
I. Title.
E744.S8   1985   327.73   84-25190

ISBN 0-03-001093-4

CBS COLLEGE PUBLISHING
Holt, Rinehart and Winston
The Dryden Press
Saunders College Publishing

PREFACE

The purpose of this tenth edition is to present an account of American foreign policy from the closing days of World War II to the beginning of the second Reagan administration. Why did the Cold War start? Why has it continued for four decades and why does it look as if it will go on well into the twenty-first century? How and where has this rivalry between the United States and the Soviet Union been conducted? What in particular has been the impact of nuclear weapons on the pattern of American-Soviet relations? These are but some of the questions examined. The focus of this study is on the superpower rivalry because it has dominated international politics; but this focus does not exclude the actions of other states or ignore other key areas and problems, such as the Third or Underdeveloped World and its relations with the First or Western Industrial World.

This book is *not* a diplomatic history—a detailed presentation of American actions in the world since 1945. It is rather an interpretation of the roles the United States has played on the world stage since it became a nuclear superpower. While some analyses of past events have been cut or reduced in length, the assumption remains that the present cannot be understood on its own terms; the powerful influence of the Vietnam War on the conduct of American foreign policy remains, to be sure, but insight both into that war and contemporary policy can only be gained by a better grasp of the causes and evolution of the American-Soviet conflict since the two powers were allies in the common struggle against Hitler's Germany.

The framework of this book remains the same as that of the previous editions. The analysis continues to focus on what I call the "American approach to foreign policy." For reasons explained below, this approach is unlike that of any other nation in its distaste for "power politics" and the desire on the one hand to escape it or on the other to moralize it by crusading against the enemy. The constancy of this style, from Truman and Eisenhower to Carter and Reagan, is really amazing and testifies to its tenacity. President Nixon was perhaps the major exception. Whether this American "national style" has served the country well or ill is a matter of individual judgment. That is remains an excellent way of understanding and explaining American foreign policy can hardly be doubted.

Every country's style is a product of its history, geography, political organization, and culture. Each nation's experience is unique and so, therefore, is how it sees the world. For each learns—or mislearns—from its past, but applies the lessons it has learned to the present and the future. The American experience has profoundly shaped the nation's perceptions of the fundamental nature of international politics: whether to expect conflict or harmony, the character of political opponents, and how they may be coped with in order to create a world consistent with American values and expectations. In the book's last chapter, which reappraises the containment policy and looks to some extent into its future, I sum up my own evaluation of the effects of this style on the conduct of American foreign policy over the last four decades.

J.S.

Contents

Maps

U.S. Administrations Since World War II

Dates	President	Secretary of State	Secretary of Defense	National Security Assistant
1945–1952	Harry S Truman	Edward Stettinius James Byrnes George Marshall Dean Acheson	James Forrestal Louis Johnson Robert Lovett George Marshall	
1953–1960	Dwight D. Eisenhower	John Dulles Christian Herter	Charles Wilson Neil McElroy Thomas Gates	
1961–1963	John F. Kennedy	Dean Rusk	Robert McNamara	McGeorge Bundy
1963–1968	Lyndon B. Johnson	Dean Rusk	Robert McNamara Clark Clifford	McGeorge Bundy W. W. Rostow
1969–1974	Richard M. Nixon	William Rogers Henry Kissinger	Melvin Laird Elliot Richardson James Schlesinger	Henry Kissinger
1974–1976	Gerald Ford	Henry Kissinger	James Schlesinger Donald Rumsfeld	Henry Kissinger Brent Scowcroft
1977–1980	Jimmy Carter	Cyrus Vance Edward Muskie	Harold Brown	Zbigniew Brzezinski
1981–1984	Ronald Reagan	Alexander Haig George Shultz	Caspar Weinberger	Richard Allen William P. Clark Robert McFarlane

Chapter 1

THE AMERICAN
APPROACH
TO FOREIGN POLICY

THE STATE SYSTEM

American foreign policy since World War II is the story of the interaction between the state system and the American style of conducting foreign policy. In the state system, each member—especially the Great Powers, its principal actors—tends to feel a high degree of insecurity. In the absence of a world government that could govern and safeguard it, each state knows that it can depend on no one but itself for its own preservation and safety. Self-protection is the only protection in an essentially anarchical system; understandably, states tend to regard one another as potential adversaries, menaces to one another's territorial integrity and political independence. In short, the very nature of the state system breeds feelings of insecurity, distrust, suspicion, and fear.

This atmosphere produces a constant scramble for power. Enhancing one's power relative to that of a possible foe becomes a principal means of reducing one's own insecurity. When a state perceives its neighbor as a potential enemy, it will try to deter a possible attack by becoming a little stronger than its neighbor; the latter, in its turn, will also fear an attack and, therefore, will perceive its own best interest to lie in sufficient strength to forestall such a contingency, or, failing that, to win the resulting war. Thus, it is not man's alleged aggressive instinct as a "naked ape" or man's presumed desire for acquiring ever greater power that accounts for what is popularly called "power politics"; rather, power politics stems from each state's continuous concern with its security. Because the external environment is perceived by states as menacing to their security—the prerequisite for the enjoyment by each one of them of its particular way of life—they are naturally prone to reacting fearfully against what they believe to be threats. And in such a context it does not take much for one state to arouse and confirm another state's apprehensions and thereby stimulate reciprocal images of hostility, which each state will find it easy to substantiate by the opponent's behavior. Indeed, this enmity will in most instances be maintained despite contradictory evidence and even avowedly friendly acts. Conciliatory behavior is likely to be dismissed as an indicator of weakness or as a trick to relax one's guard and, therefore, not to be accepted at face value but exploited or guarded against.

In any event, it is easy to understand why in these circumstances states pursue a balance-of-power policy. A balance or equilibrium would make victory in a war less probable for an opponent and certainly very costly in comparison with any possible gains. Logically, therefore, a balance is presumed to be that distribution of power most likely to deter an attack. By contrast, possession of disproportionate power might tempt a state to undertake aggression by making it far less costly to gain a predominant position and impose its will upon other states. In other words, the fundamental assumption underlying the state system is that its members cannot be trusted with power, since they will be tempted to abuse it. Unrestrained power in the system constitutes a threat to all states; power is, therefore, the best antidote to power. As one close observer of international politics, Arnold Wolfers, has noted:

> Under these conditions of anarchy the expectation of violence and even of annihilation is ever-present. To forget this and thus fail in the concern for enhanced power spells the doom of a state. This does not mean open constant warfare; expansion of power at the expense of others will not take place if there is enough counterpower to deter or to stop states from undertaking it. Although no state is interested in a mere balance of power, the efforts of all states to maximize power may lead to equilibrium. If and when that happens, there is "peace" or, more exactly, a condition of stalemate or truce. Under the conditions described here, this balancing of power process is the only available "peace" strategy.

Power thus elicits countervailing power. The basic rule of the "international game" is to resist attempts by any state to expand and seek a predominant position in the international system. Therefore, when the balance is disturbed, equilibrium will tend to be restored by the emergence of counterpower. States ignore at their peril this rule to maintain a balance of power; policymakers need to be equally careful that they judge correctly the necessary countervailing power.

What all this means is that we can to a very significant degree explain any state's behavior in terms of the ever-changing distribution of power. As that distribution changes, so does a state's foreign policy. For example, the impact of a shift in the distribution of power is evident in America's involvements in the two world wars of this century. During most of the nineteenth century and early twentieth century the United States was able to preserve its historical isolation from "power politics" and enjoy an unprecedented degree of security thanks to the balance of power on the European continent maintained by Britain to protect its own security. No one state or coalition of states was able to conquer most of Europe, organize its vast resources in manpower and industrial strength, and then use these to menace the United States. Britain's opposition to any state's seeking such hegemony therefore made it possible for the United States to remain what today is called "nonaligned."

However, after 1870, when Germany was unified and launched a massive program of industrialization, British power declined relative to Germany's growing capability. The early years of World War I showed clearly that even British and French power together could not contain Germany. With the collapse of Tsarist Russia in the East and the transfer of almost 2 million German soldiers to the Western Front, a German victory became a distinct possibility. It was at that point that Germany's unrestricted submarine warfare, which included attacks on American shipping, precipitated U.S. intervention, and this was what made it possible to contain the German spring offensive of 1918, leading to Germany's defeat.

After victory America retreated into isolationism again, only to be compelled just over two decades later once more to concern itself with the European balance of power. The unexpected German defeat of France in 1940 again confronted the United States with the specter of an invasion and defeat of Britain. President Franklin D. Roosevelt therefore undertook a number of measures to strengthen Britain to withstand any Nazi assault. He sent fifty old destroyers to help defend the English Channel, and he set up the Lend-Lease program, which made the United States the "arsenal of democracy." The balance of power had made this increasing commitment to Britain necessary, even though such actions increased the risk of war with Germany. In fact, by the time of Pearl Harbor, the United States was already engaged in an undeclared naval war with Germany in the Atlantic, and full-scale war with Germany was merely a matter of time: sooner or later, German submarines would have started sinking American merchant ships carrying war supplies to Britain in order to compel its surrender. The German invasion of the Soviet Union in 1941 briefly postponed the Battle of the Atlantic, and when it did take place the United States was already at war. But had Adolf Hitler, in 1940–1941, given the order to sink all ships bound for Britain, President Roosevelt, like President Woodrow Wilson before him, would have had to ask Congress for a declaration of war.

One further point is worth noting about these two examples, namely, that the issue in neither case was whether the American people wished to go to war against Germany. The isolationist mood was still far too strong. Nevertheless, the United States did intervene in both cases; in neither instance, furthermore, was there any existing commitment, legal or moral, that obligated the nation to intervene. The issue in 1917 and in 1941 was not whether the nation preferred peace and domestic preoccupation to foreign involvement, but what self-preservation obliged it to do. The shifting balance of power left the country little choice if it wished to preserve its security. To sum up: The strategy of any nation in the state system is—or should be—to oppose any state that seeks predominance since this would constitute a threat to its security and national independence. Power is the best antidote to power and a balance of power in the state system provides the best protection for all of its members.

THE AMERICAN NATIONAL STYLE

The particular style that characterized the American approach to World War II and later the cold war—that is, the distinctive set of national perceptions and repetitive patterns of behavior—was the product of domestic experiences. The priority of internal political and economic tasks, all of which were reinforced by the opening of the West and the subsequent transcontinental drive to the Pacific, led to the depreciation of the importance of foreign policy and the role that power plays in protecting the nation's interests. The ability of the United States to live in isolation during the nineteenth century and a good part of the twentieth century was attributed not to the nation's geographic distance from Europe or to the Royal Navy as the protector of the *Pax Britannica*, but to the nature of democracy. The United States was more than just the world's first "new nation"; it was also the world's first democracy and, as such, the first country in history that would devote itself to improving the lot of the common man, granting each individual the opportunity to enrich and ennoble his life. ("Give me your tired, your poor, your huddled masses yearning to breathe free," reads the inscription on the Statue of Liberty.) The more perfect union was to be an egalitarian society. European concepts of social hierarchy, nobility and titles, and bitter class struggles were not to be planted in its democratic soil. "Here the free spirit of mankind, at length, throws its last fetters off," exclaimed one writer. America was to be a "beacon lighting for all the world the paths of human destiny," wrote Ralph Waldo Emerson.

From the very beginning of their national life, Americans believed strongly in their destiny—to spread, *by example*, freedom and social justice to all men and to lead mankind away from its wicked ways to the New Jerusalem on earth. The massive immigration of the nineteenth century—particularly after 1865— was to reinforce this sense of destiny. "Repudiation of Europe," as John Dos Passos once said, "is, after all, America's main excuse for being." Europe stood for war, poverty, and exploitation; America, for peace, opportunity, and democracy. But the United States was not merely to be a beacon of a superior democratic domestic way of life. It was also to be an example of a morally superior democratic pattern of international behavior. The United States would voluntarily reject power politics as unfit for the conduct of its foreign policy. Democratic theory posits that man is a rational and moral creature and that differences among men can be settled by rational persuasion and moral exhortation. Indeed, granted this assumption about man, the only differences that could arise would simply be misunderstandings, and, since man is endowed with reason and a moral sense, what quarrels could not be settled, given the necessary goodwill? Peace—the result of harmony among men—was thus considered the natural or normal state.

Conversely, conflict was considered a deviation from this norm, caused primarily by wicked statesmen whose morality and reason had been corrupted by the exercise of uncontrolled authority. Power politics was an instrument of selfish and autocratic rulers—that is, men unrestrained by democratic public opinion—who loved to wield it for their own personal advantage. To them, war was a grand game. They could remain in their palatial homes, continuing to eat well and to enjoy the luxuries of life. They suffered none of the hardships of war. These hardships fell upon the ordinary people; it was they who had to leave their families to fight, to endure the higher taxes made necessary by the costs of war, possibly to see their homes destroyed and their loved ones maimed or killed. It was only the despot who thought of war as a sport, as a sort of "bully" fox hunt; the common man, who had to endure all the cruelties of war, was therefore by his very nature peaceful. The conclusion was clear: Undemocratic states were inherently warlike and evil; democratic nations, in which the people controlled and regularly changed their leaders, were peaceful and moral.

American experience seemed to support this conclusion. The United States was a democracy, and it was at peace. Furthermore, peace seemed to be the normal state of affairs. It was therefore logical that democracy and peaceful behavior and intentions should be thought of as synonymous. Americans never asked themselves whether democracy was really responsible for the peace they enjoyed, or whether this peace they assumed to be a natural condition was the product of other forces. The constant wars of Europe appeared to provide the answer: European politics was power politics, and this was because of the undemocratic nature of European regimes. Americans therefore had cut themselves off from Europe and its class conflicts and power politics after the Revolutionary War. America had to guard its democratic purity and abstain from any involvement in the affairs of Europe lest it be soiled and corrupted. Nonalignment or isolationism was therefore the morally correct policy, for it allowed the United States to quarantine itself from Europe's hierarchical social structures and immoral international habits. At the same time, by confusing the results of geography—the width of the Atlantic—and Europe's focus on Asia, the Middle East, and Africa with the virtues of American democracy, Americans could smugly enjoy their self-conferred moral superiority as the world's first democracy. It was the Monroe Doctrine, proclaimed in 1823, that first stressed, officially and explicitly, this ideological difference between the New and Old Worlds. It declared specifically that the American political system was "essentially different" from that of Europe, whose nations were constantly engaged in warfare. The implication was very clear: Democratic government equals peace, and aristocratic government—which was identified with despotism—means war.

But this association of peace with democracy was not the only reason for the American depreciation of power politics. Another was that the United States was an overwhelmingly one-class society—one in which most shared a common set of middle-class, capitalistic, and democratic values or beliefs. America was unique among nations in this respect. The European countries were, by contrast, three-class societies. In addition to the middle class, they contained in their bodies politic an aristocratic class, whose energies were devoted either to maintaining itself in power or to recapturing power in order to return to the glorious days of a feudal past. Moreover, European urbanization and industrialization during the nineteenth century gave birth to a proletariat, which, because it felt it did not receive a fair share of the national income, became a revolutionary class. The nations of the Old World were, in short, a composite of three elements: a reactionary aristocracy, a democratic middle class, and a revolutionary proletariat. Or, to put it another way, these nations had, in an intellectual as well as a political sense, a right, a center, and a left.

The United States had only a center, both intellectually and politically. It had never experienced a feudal past and therefore possessed no large and powerful aristocratic class on the right; and because it was, by and large, an egalitarian society, it also lacked a genuine left-wing movement of protest, such as Socialism and Communism. America was, as Alexis de Tocqueville had said, "born free" as a middle-class, individualistic, capitalistic, and democratic society. It was not divided by the kind of deep ideological conflicts that in France, for instance, set one class of Frenchmen against another. No one class was ever so afraid of another that it preferred national defeat to domestic revolution—as in France in the late 1930s, when the *haute bourgeoisie* was so apprehensive of a proletarian upheaval that its slogan became "Better Hitler than Blum [Leon Blum, the French Socialist leader]."

Americans in the past have been so in accord on basic values that whenever the nation has been threatened externally the public has become fearful of internal disloyalty. It is one of the great ironies of American society that, while Americans possessed this unity of shared beliefs to a greater degree than any other people, their apprehension of external danger led them, first, to insist upon a general and somewhat dogmatic reaffirmation of loyalty to the "American way of life," and then to hunt for internal groups that might betray this way of life. Disagreement tended to become suspect as disloyalty; men were accused of "un-American" thinking and behavior and labeled "loyalty or security risks." Perhaps only a society so overwhelmingly committed to one set of values could have been so sensitive to internal subversion and so fearful of internal betrayal; perhaps only a society in which two or more ideologies have long since learned to live together can genuinely tolerate diverse opinions. Who has ever heard of "un-British" or "un-French" activities? The United States has often been called a "melting pot" because of the many different nationality groups it comprises, but, before each generation of immigrants has been fully accepted into American society, it has had to be "Americanized." Few Americans have ever accepted diversity as a value. American society has, in fact, taken great pride in destroying diversity through assimilation.

It was precisely this overwhelming agreement on the fundamental values of American society and Europe's intense class struggles that reinforced the American misunderstanding of the nation and functions of power on the international scene. Dissatisfied groups never developed a revolutionary ideology because the growing prosperity spread to them before they could translate their grievances against the capitalist system into political action. (The black American, of course, represents a clear and important exception.) With the exception of the Civil War, America—politically secure, socially cohesive, and economically prosperous—was able, therefore, to resolve most of its differences peacefully. Living in isolation, this country could therefore believe in an evolutionary, democratic, economically prosperous, historical process; revolution and radicalism were considered bad. In sharp contrast, because of their internal class struggles and external conflicts among themselves, the nations of Europe fully appreciated the role of power politics.

Politics did not, in any event, seem very important to Americans. The United States matured during the nineteenth century, the era of *laissez-faire* capitalism whose basic assumption was that man was economically motivated. It was self-interest that governed the behavior of man; it might be referred to as "enlightened self-interest," but it was nevertheless self-interest. Each individual, seeking to maximize his wealth, responded to the demand of the free market. In an effort to increase his profit, he supplied the product the consumers wanted. The laws of supply and demand therefore transformed each person's economic selfishness into socially beneficial results. The entire society would prosper. The free market was thus considered the central institution that provided "the greatest good for the greatest number." Politics mattered little in this self-adjusting economic system based upon individuals whose combined efforts resulted in the general welfare. The best government was the government that governed least. Arbitrary political interference with the economic laws of the market would only upset the results these laws were intended to produce. Private property, profit, and the free market were thus the keys to ensuring the happiness of man by providing him with abundance. Capitalism, in short, reflected the materialism of the age of industrialization.

To state the issue even more bluntly: Economics was good, politics was bad. This simple dichotomy came naturally to the capitalist middle class. Were the benefits of economic freedom not as "self-evident" as the truths stated in the Declaration of Independence? And had this economic freedom not been gained only by a long and bitter struggle of the European middle class to cut down the authority of the powerful monarchical state, and finally to overthrow it by revolution in France? The middle class, as it had grown more prosperous and numerous, had become increasingly resentful of paying taxes from which the aristocracy was usually exempt, of the restrictions placed upon trade and industry, of the absence of institutions in which middle-class economic and political interests were represented, of the class barriers to the social status that came with careers in the army and in the bureaucracy, and of the general lack of freedom of thought and expression. Since the middle class identified the power of the state with its own lack of freedom, its aim was to restrict this power. Only by placing restraints upon the authority of the state could it gain the individual liberty and, above all, the right to private enterprise it sought. Democratic philosophy stated these claims in terms of the individual's "natural rights" against the state. The exercise of political authority was thus equated with the abuse of that authority and the suppression of personal freedoms. The power of the state had therefore to be restricted to the minimum to ensure the individual's maximum political and economic liberties. It was with this purpose in mind that the American Constitution divided authority between the states and the federal government, and, within the latter, among the executive, legislative, and judicial branches. Federalism and the separation of powers were deliberately designed to keep all governments—and especially the national government—weak. Man's secular problems would be resolved not by the state's political actions but by the individual's own economic actions in society in peacetime.

Again, both man's economic motivation and the benefits of a government that acts least were considered to be reflected in the American experience. Millions came to the United States from other lands to seek a better way of life. America was the earthly paradise where all men, no matter how poor or humble they had been in the old country, could earn a respectable living. A virgin and underdeveloped land, America presented magnificent opportunities for individual enterprise. First, there was the Western frontier with its rich soil; later, during the Industrial Revolution, the country's bountiful natural resources were exploited. The environment, technology, individual enterprise, and helpful governmental policies enabled the American people to become the "people of plenty." But to earn money was not only economically necessary in order to attain a comfortable standard of living; it was also psychologically necessary in order to gain social status and to earn the respect of one's fellow citizens.

It follows logically that, if material gain confers social respect and position upon men, everyone will preoccupy himself with the pursuit and accumulation of the "almighty dollar." If men in an egalitarian society are judged primarily by their economic achievements, they will concentrate on "getting ahead." It is not surprising, therefore, that money comes closer to being the common standard of value in the United States than in any other country. For money is the symbol of power and prestige; it is the sign of success, just as failure to earn enough money is a token of personal failure. It has been said, not without some justice, that the American prefers two cars to two mistresses.

It was hardly surprising that in these circumstances the solution to international problems should be thought of in economic terms. Economics was identified with social harmony and the welfare of all peoples; politics was equated with conflict and war and death. Just as the "good society" was to be the product of free competition, so the peaceful international society would be created by free trade. An international *laissez-faire* policy would benefit all states just as a national *laissez-faire* policy benefited each individual within these states. Consequently, people all over the world had a vested interest in peace in order to carry on their economic relations. Trade and war were incompatible. Trade depended upon mutual prosperity (the poor do not buy much from one another). War impoverishes and destroys and creates ill will among nations. Commerce benefits all the participating states; the more trade, the greater the number of individual interests involved. Commerce was consequently nationally and individually profitable and created a vested interest in peace. War, by contrast, was economically unprofitable and therefore obsolete. Free trade and peace, in short, were one and the same cause.

One result of this American depreciation of power was that the United States has historically drawn a clear-cut distinction between war and peace in its approach to foreign policy. Peace was characterized by a state of harmony among nations; power politics, on the other hand, was considered abnormal and war a crime. In peacetime, one needed to pay little or no attention to foreign problems; indeed, to do so would have diverted men from their individual, materialistic concerns and upset the whole scale of social values. The effect of this attitude was clear: Americans turned their attention toward the outside world with reluctance and usually only when they felt provoked—that is, when the foreign menace had become so clear that it could no longer be ignored. Or, to state it somewhat differently, the United States rarely initiated policy; the stimuli that were responsible for the formulation of American foreign policy came from beyond America's frontiers.

Once Americans were provoked, however, and the United States had to resort to force, the employment of this force was justified in terms of the universal moral principles with which the United States, as a democratic country, identified itself. Resort to the evil instrument of war could be justified only by presuming noble purposes and completely destroying the immoral enemy who threatened the integrity, if not the existence, of these principles. American power had to be "righteous" power; only its full exercise could ensure salvation or the absolution of sin. A second result of the depreciation of power was, therefore, that the national aversion to violence became transformed into a national glorification of violence, and wars became ideological crusades to destroy whatever state had provoked the United States and then send its people to democratic reform school. Making the world safe for democracy—the stated objective during World War I—was to be achieved by democratizing the populace of the offending nation, making its new rulers responsible to the people they governed and thereby converting the formerly authoritarian or totalitarian state into a peaceful democratic state and banishing power politics for all time. Once that aim had been achieved, the United States could again withdraw into itself, secure in the knowledge that American works had again proved to be "good works." In this context, foreign affairs were an annoying diversion from more important domestic matters. But such diversions were only temporary, since maximum force was applied to the aggressor or warmonger to punish him for his provocation and to teach him that aggression was immoral and would not be rewarded. As a result, American wars were total wars to end war itself, but once the wars were over the United States would once more withdraw from international politics. Normalcy having been restored, the pendulum would swing back.

This is the pattern of American foreign policy: from isolationism to interventionism, from withdrawal to crusading and back again. As a self-proclaimed morally and politically superior country, the United States could remain uncontaminated only by abstaining from involvement in a corrupt world or, if the world would not leave it alone, destroying the source of evil. In short, both the isolationist and the crusading impulses sprang from the same moralism. These swings tended, moreover, to be accompanied by radical shifts of mood: from one of optimism, which sprang from the belief that America was going to reform the world, to one of disillusionment as the grandiose objectives the United States had set for itself proved beyond its capacity to reach. Feeling too good for this world, which clearly did not want to be reformed, preferring its old corrupt habits, the nation retreated into isolationism to perfect and protect its way of life. Having expected too much from the use of its power, the U.S. then also tended to feel guilty and ashamed about having used its power at all.

Third, not only did the American approach to international politics consider peace and war as two mutually exclusive states of affairs; it also divorced force from diplomacy. In peacetime, diplomacy unsupported by force was supposed to preserve the harmony among states. But, in wartime, political considerations were subordinated to force. Once the diplomats had failed to keep the peace with appeals to morality and reason, military considerations became primary. During war, the soldier was placed in charge. Just as the professional medical man had the responsibility for curing his patients of their several maladies, so the military "doctor" had to control the curative treatment of the international society when it was infected with the disease of power politics.

The United States, then, had traditionally rejected the concept of war as a political instrument and the Clausewitzian definition of war as the continuation of politics by other means. Instead, it had regarded war as a politically neutral operation that should be guided by its own professional rules and imperatives. The military officer was a nonpolitical man who conducted his campaign in a strictly military, technically efficient manner. And war was a purely military instrument whose sole aim was the destruction of the enemy's forces and of his despotic regime so that his people could then be democratized. Policy and strategy were unrelated; strategy began where policy ended. After the Japanese attack on Pearl Harbor, the secretary of state turned to the secretary of war (as he was then called) and said the situation was now out of his hands; it was all up to the latter. As the war in Europe was coming to a close, General Marshall, architect of the Western allies' victory, responded to the British plea to send U.S. forces to liberate Prague and as much of Czechoslovakia as possible before the Soviet army arrived by saying that he would not risk American lives for "purely political purposes"—a commendable sentiment, but what is war about if not the achievement of political purposes?

War was thus a means employed to abolish power politics; war was conducted to end all wars. This same moralistic attitude, which was responsible for the Americans' all-or-nothing approach to war—either to abstain from the dirty game of power politics or to crusade for its complete elimination—also militated against the use of diplomacy in its classical sense: to compromise interests, to conciliate differences, and to moderate and isolate conflicts. While, on the one hand, Americans regarded diplomacy as a rational process for straightening out misunderstandings between nations, they were, on the other hand, extremely suspicious of diplomacy. If the United States was by definition moral, it obviously could not compromise; for a nation endowed with a moral mission could hardly violate its own principles. That constituted appeasement and national humiliation. The nation's principles would be transgressed, the nation's interests improperly defended, the national honor stained. For to compromise with the immoral enemy was to be contaminated with evil. Moreover, to reach a settlement with him, rather than wiping him out in order to safeguard those principles, would be to acknowledge American weakness. This attitude toward diplomacy, which, in effect, made its use as an instrument of compromise difficult, thus reinforced the predilection for violence as a means of settling international problems. For war allowed the nation to destroy its evil opponent while permitting it to keep its moral mission intact and unsullied by any compromises that might infect its purity.

THE CONTRAST BETWEEN SYSTEMIC AND NATIONAL BEHAVIOR

Thus, on the eve of the eruption of the cold war, the American approach to foreign policy contrasted sharply in a number of important respects with the conduct required by the state system. For example, having historically given precedence to domestic affairs, the United States, not surprisingly, has found it difficult to attain and maintain a balance between foreign and domestic priorities. On the whole, American foreign policy has tended to swing from an isolationist position in which the country served as an example of democratic brotherhood and social justice on earth to a posture of massive and violent intervention once provoked. Level-headed, consistent participation in the international system has been difficult; all-or-nothing swings have been the more common pattern.

Furthermore, the American perception of an international harmony of interests stood in stark contrast to the state system's emphasis on the inevitability of conflict and differences of interests among states. The former view regarded conflict as an abnormal condition, the latter perceived harmony as an illusion. The United States, long isolated from Europe and therefore not socialized into the state system, did not accept the reality and permanence of conflicts among its members. Differences between states were not considered natural, and certainly not deep and long-range; rather, they were attributed to wicked leaders (who could be eliminated), authoritarian political systems (which could be reformed), or misunderstandings (which could be straightened out if the adversaries approached each other with sincerity and empathy). Once these obstacles had been removed, peace, harmony, and goodwill would reign supreme.

Above all, America had always considered itself a morally and politically superior society due to its democratic culture. This meant that its attitude toward the use of power internationally had been dominated by the belief that the struggle for power did not exist or could be avoided by isolating oneself from it or could be eliminated by crusading against those countries indulging in power politics. Moralism in foreign policy proscribed the use of power in peacetime lest one became tainted; it could be employed only in confrontations with unambiguous aggression, transformed then into an obligation to fight on behalf of righteous causes. In short, power, internationally just as domestically, could be legitimated only by democratic purposes; otherwise, its exercise would be evil and would necessarily arouse guilt feelings.

The great American compulsion to feel moral about the nation's behavior reinforced the cyclical swings from isolationism to crusading and back again. The perception of power as simply the raw material of international politics— its use as an instrument of compromise, conciliation, and moderation of interstate politics, its discriminating application toward achievement of specific and less-than-total objectives—was clearly antithetical to the American understanding of power. The term "power politics" was itself kind of "dirty," an anathema, a reminder of a way of doing things that the New World had hopefully left behind, and a potential threat to its virtue if the nation were to indulge in that kind of immoral Old World behavior.

One of the most telling symptoms of America's national style in conducting foreign policy is that after every major war the reasons for the country's participation in struggle and bloodshed have been reinterpreted. These revisionist histories have certain common themes: The conflicts in which the nation had become entangled did not in fact threaten its security interests; it became involved because the politicians saw a menace where none existed, and this illusion had been promoted by propagandists who aroused and manipulated public opinion, by soldiers with bureaucratic motives, and, above all else, by bankers and industrialists—the "merchants of death" of the 1930s, the "military industrial complex" of the 1960s—whose economic interests benefited from the struggle. America's engagements in the two world wars of this century (as in the cold war later) were mistakes; they were really unnecessary or im-moral, if not both. The evil enemy yesterday identified as the aggressor and *provocateur* thus apparently did not represent a threat to American security at all; to the contrary, the threat turns out to have come from within, not from without. But for certain *domestic forces* the United States could have continued to isolate itself from international politics; note also that these internal groups propelling the nation into war were, in characteristic American fashion, said to be motivated by profit.

The fundamental revisionist assumption, then, has been that the nation had a choice whether it wanted to employ "power politics." Conversely, revisionism rejected the idea that the distribution of power in the state system left the United States—or any other country, for that matter—with a choice only of whether it would help maintain the balance of power or not. Power was equated with its abuse. Abstention from its use and creating a truly just society at home were considered wiser and more moral policies. Crusading, allegedly for the reform of the world, risked corrupting America's very soul, since it diverted attention and resources from reform at home to military preparation and war. Revisionism, then, was essentially an argument for continued isolation from world politics.

But if one could no longer avoid power politics or crusade against it in order to abolish it, there was yet another solution: to escape from it, to flee the troublesome and divisive world of power into the more peaceful and united world of economics. The belief that political conflict among states could be transformed into cooperation among nations when they focused on what was truly important—the improvement of man's material and social life—was an-other major characteristic of American style. Whereas power was rather nega-tively associated with strife, destruction, and loss of life, economics was by contrast positively viewed because it was concerned with creating prosperity and improving man's welfare. Politics was bad and economics good, it is worth repeating, because by the logic of the free market international trade would benefit all states and this, in turn, would give each of them a vested interest in peace. If power politics and concern for security led to conflict and war, eco-nomics with its concern for raising everyone's standard of living bound all men, regardless of nationality or race, together. They had to cooperate for the com-mon good in which they all shared. The post-Vietnam revulsion against the balance of power and emphasis on "interdependence" was hardly novel. Even while the republic was still young there were already those who felt that

The [national political] barriers that existed seemed artificial and ephemeral in comparison with the fine net by which the merchants tied the individuals of the different nations together like "threads of silk." . . . [T]he merchants—whether they are English, Dutch, Russian, or Chinese—do not serve a single nation; they serve everyone and are citizens of the whole world. Commerce was believed to bind the nations together and to create not only a community of interests but also a distribution of labor among them—a new comprehensive principle placing the isolated sovereign nations in a higher political unit. In the eighteenth century, writers were likely to say that the various nations belonged to "one society"; it was stated that all states together formed "a family of nations," and the whole globe a "general and unbreakable confederation."*

The United States after World War II, therefore, confronted a world with attitudes and behavior patterns inherited from its long period of isolationism from Europe. But the situation that faced the United States in 1945 no longer allowed it to abstain from this political struggle. The need to contain the Soviet Union by establishing and maintaining the balance of power required long-range policies that would effectively combine the political, military, and economic components of power. American security interests demanded no less. It remained to be seen whether a nation, inwardly oriented and temperamentally impatient, with little experience in international politics, could adjust to the sudden demands of "power politics," switching quickly from isolationism to involvement first in the eastern Mediterranean, then Western Europe, and shortly after that, Asia.

*Felix Gilbert, To The Farewell Address (Princeton, N.J.: Princeton University Press, 1961), p. 57.

Chapter 2

THE BEGINNING
OF THE COLD WAR

AMERICAN WARTIME ILLUSIONS

Before one of the wartime conferences between Prime Minister Winston Churchill and President Franklin Roosevelt, an American intelligence forecast of the Soviet Union's postwar position concluded that the Soviet Union would be the dominant power on the continent of Europe: "With Germany crushed, there is no power in Europe to oppose her tremendous military forces. . . . The conclusions from the foregoing are obvious. Since Russia is the decisive factor in the war, she must be given every assistance, and every effort must be made to obtain her friendship. Likewise, since without question she will dominate Europe on the defeat of the Axis, it is even more essential to develop and maintain the most friendly relations with Russia."

The importance of this estimate lies less in its prediction of the Soviet Union's postwar position—which was, after all, fairly obvious—than in its reflection of American expectations about future Soviet-American relations. American policymakers were apparently unable to conceive of the Soviet Union, the acknowledged new dominant power in Europe, replacing Nazi Germany as a grave threat to the European and global balance of power. Yet the United States had already twice in this century been propelled into Europe's wars at exactly those moments when Germany became so powerful that it menaced—indeed, almost destroyed—this balance. The lessons of history—specifically, the impact of any nation's domination of Europe upon American security—had not yet been absorbed. President Roosevelt and the American government did not aim at reestablishing a balance of power in Europe to safeguard the United States; they expected this security to stem from mutual Soviet-American goodwill, unsupported by any power considerations. This reliance upon mere goodwill and mutual esteem was to prove foolish at best and, at worst, might have been fatal.

Indeed, the expectation of a postwar "era of good feeling" between the Soviet Union and the United States was characteristic of the unsuspecting and utopian nature of American wartime thinking, which held that war was an interruption of the normal state of harmony among nations, that military force was an instrument for punishing the aggressor or war criminals, that those who cooperated with their country in its ideological crusade were equally moral and selfless, and that, once the war was finished, the natural harmony would be restored and the struggle for power ended. The implication was clear: The United States need take no precautionary steps against its noble wartime allies in anticipation of a possible disintegration of the alliance and potential hostility among its partners. Instead, it was hoped that the friendly relations and mutual respect that American leaders believed had matured during the war would preserve the common outlook and purposes and guarantee an enduring peace.

These optimistic expectations of future Soviet-American relations made it necessary, however, to explain away continuing signs of Soviet hostility and suspicion. Throughout the war, the Soviets constantly suspected the United States and Britain of devious intentions. This was particularly true with regard to the Western delay in opening up a second front. When the front was postponed from 1942 to 1943 to 1944, Joseph Stalin, dictator of the Soviet Union, became very bitter. He brusquely rejected Allied explanations that enough invasion barges for such an enormous undertaking were not available, and he especially denounced Prime Minister Churchill for declaring that there would be no invasion until the Germans were so weakened that Allied forces would not have to suffer forbiddingly high losses. To Stalin, this was no explanation, for the Soviets accepted huge losses of men as a matter of course. "When we come to a minefield," Marshall G. K. Zhukov explained to General Dwight Eisenhower after the war, "our infantry attacks exactly as if it were not there. The losses we get from personnel mines we consider only equal to those we would have gotten from machine guns and artillery if the Germans had chosen to defend that particular area with strong bodies of troops instead of with minefields."

It was no wonder, then, that the Soviets should dismiss these Allied explanations and fasten instead upon what was for them a more reasonable interpretation of American and British behavior. From the Marxist viewpoint, the Allies were doing exactly what they should be doing—namely, postponing the second front until the Soviet Union and Germany had exhausted each other. Then the two Western powers could land in France, march bloodlessly into Germany, and dictate the peace to both Germany and the Soviet Union. The Western delay was, in short, apparently seen as a deliberate attempt by the world's two leading capitalist powers to destroy both of their two major ideological opponents at one and the same time. Throughout the war, the Russians displayed again and again this almost paranoid fear of hostile Western intentions.

American leaders found a ready explanation for these repeated indications of Soviet suspicion. They thought of Soviet foreign policy not in terms of the internal dynamics of the regime and its enmity toward all non-Communist nations, but solely in terms of Soviet reactions to Western policies. The Soviet attitude was viewed against the pattern of prewar anti-Soviet Western acts: the Allied intervention in Russia at the end of World War I in order to overthrow the Soviet regime and, after the failure of that attempt, the establishment by France of the *cordon sanitaire* in Eastern Europe to keep the Soviet virus from infecting Europe; the West's rejection of Soviet efforts in the mid- and late 1930s to build an alliance against Hitler; and especially, the Munich agreement in 1938, which, by destroying Czechoslovakia, in effect opened Hitler's gateway to the East. In short, Western efforts to ostracize and ultimately destroy the Soviet Union, as well as attempts to turn the Hitlerian threat away from the West and toward Russia, were considered the primary reasons for the existence of Soviet hostility.

To overcome this attitude, the West had only to demonstrate its good intentions and prove its friendliness. The question was not *whether* Soviet cooperation could be won for the postwar world, only *how* it could be gained. And if Western efforts did bear fruit and create goodwill, what conflicts of interest could not be settled peacefully in the future? Various Soviet policies and acts during the war—the disbanding of the Comintern (the instrument of international Communism), the toning down of Communist ideology and new emphasis placed on Soviet nationalism, the relaxation of restrictions upon the Church, the praise of the United States and Britain for also being democratic, and, above all, the statement of Soviet war aims in the same language of peace, democracy, and freedom used by the West—all seemed to prove that if the Western powers demonstrated their friendship they could convert the Soviets into friends.

President Roosevelt and his advisors certainly believed that they had firmly established such amicable relations with the Soviet Union at the Yalta Conference in February 1945. Stalin had made concessions on a number of vital issues and promised goodwill for the future. He had accepted the United Nations on the basis of the American formula that the veto in the Security Council should be applied only to enforcement action, and not to peaceful attempts at the settlement of disputes. Moreover, in the "Declaration on Liberated Europe," he had promised to support self-government and allow free elections in Eastern Europe. And regarding the Far East, he had responded to the wishes of the American military and promised to enter the war against Japan. Finally, he had repeatedly expressed his hope for fifty years of peace and "big power" cooperation.

It is little wonder that at the end of the conference the American delegation felt a mood of "supreme exultation." The new era of goodwill was to be embodied in the United Nations. Here the peoples of the world could exercise vigilance over the statesmen in their dealings with one another and prevent them from striking any wicked bargains that might erupt into another global war. The United Nations was regarded as an example of democracy on an international scale: Just as the people within democratic states could constantly watch their representatives and prevent them from effecting compromises injurious to their interests, so the people of all countries would now be able to keep an eye on their statesmen, making it impossible for them to arrange any secret deals that would betray the people's interests and shatter the peace of the world. Peace-loving world public opinion, expressing itself across national boundaries, would maintain a constant guard over the diplomats and hold them accountable. Covenants were to be open, and "openly arrived at," as President Woodrow Wilson had once expressed it.

Power politics would be banned once and for all. In the words of Secretary of State Cordell Hull: "There will no longer be need for spheres of influence, for alliances, balance of power, or any other of the special arrangements through which, in the unhappy past, the nations strove to safeguard their security or promote their interests." Reliance would instead be placed upon sound principles and good fellowship. Again, in Hull's words: "All these principles and policies [of international cooperation] are so beneficial and appealing to the sense of justice, of right and of the well-being of free peoples everywhere that in the course of a few years the entire international machinery should be working fairly satisfactorily." The Advisory Commission on Postwar Foreign Policy had been even more emphatic in its stress on the subordination of power politics to principles: "International security was regarded as the supreme objective, but at the same time the subcommittee held that the attainment of security must square with principles of justice in order to be actual and enduring . . . the vital interests of the United States lay in following a 'diplomacy of principle'—of moral disinterestedness instead of power politics." No comment could more aptly have summed up the American habit of viewing international politics in terms of abstract moral principles instead of clashes of interest and power. And no institution could have embodied more fully the immediate postwar hope for a return to "normalcy," the desire for minimum international involvement, and the expectation that the wartime cooperation with the Soviet Union would continue than the United Nations, which was essentially seen as a *substitute* for the vigorous, self-reliant, national conduct of foreign policy.

SOVIET POSTWAR EXPANSION

The American dream of postwar peace and Big Three cooperation was to be shattered as the Soviet Union expanded into Eastern and Central Europe, imposing its control upon Poland, Hungary, Bulgaria, Romania, and Albania. (Yugoslavia was already under the Communist control of Marshal Tito, and Czechoslovakia was living under the shadow of the Red Army.) In each of these nations of Eastern Europe where the Soviets had their troops, they unilaterally established pro-Soviet coalition governments. The key posts in these regimes—

the ministries of the interior, which usually controlled the police, and defense, which controlled the army—were in the hands of the Communists. With this decisive lever of power in their grasp, it was an easy matter to extend their domination and subvert the independence of these countries. Thus, as the war drew to a close, it became clear that the words of the Yalta Declaration, in which the Soviets had committed themselves to free elections and democratic governments in Eastern Europe, meant quite different things to the Soviets and to the Americans. For the Soviet Union, control of Eastern Europe, and especially Poland, was essential. This area constituted a vital link in its security belt. After two German invasions in less than thirty years, it was perhaps inevitable that the Soviet Union would try to establish "friendly" governments throughout the area. To the Soviets, "democratic governments" meant Communist governments, and "free elections" meant elections from which parties not favorable to the Communists were barred. The peace treaties with the former German satellite states (Hungary, Bulgaria, Romania), which were painfully negotiated by the victors in a series of foreign ministers' conferences during 1945 and 1946, could not therefore loosen the tight Soviet grip on what were by now Soviet satellite states.

In terms of the state system, this Soviet behavior is understandable. Each state must act as its own guardian against potential adversaries in a system characterized by conflict among states and a sense of insecurity and fear on the part of its members. Thus, as the alliance against the common enemy came to an end, the Soviet Union would predictably strengthen itself against the power most likely to be its new opponent. As Russia, with a long history of invasions from the West, it had learned the basic rules of the international game through bitter experience; as *Soviet* Russia, its sense of peril had been intensified by an ideology that posited capitalist states as implacable enemies. Hence, the establishment of anti-Communist regimes in Eastern Europe was unacceptable. The American insistence upon free elections was seen as an attempt to establish such anti-Communist and therefore anti-Soviet regimes and thereby push the Soviet Union out of Europe. The assumption was that a non-Communist government would be an anti-Communist one.

This assumption was doubtful on at least two scores: First, the Eastern European non-Communist opposition represented mainly the forces of reform and democracy, which opposed a return to the prewar type of reactionary governments; second, while great powers have historically been dominant in the areas close to their borders, smaller neighbors have usually accommodated themselves to this fact because they have recognized the wisdom of doing so. The equation of non-Communist with anti-Communist was, therefore, more of a commentary on the Soviet leaders' subjective perceptions than on objective reality. Yet obviously, how they saw reality was how they defined it. This, plus the fact that the Soviet Union lacked natural protective barriers, such as the English Channel or the Atlantic Ocean, led her to push outward to keep enemies as far away as possible.

President Roosevelt, however, acted precisely upon the assumption that non-Communist did not necessarily mean anti-Soviet. During the war, he had been all too aware of the consequences of a possible Soviet-American clash in the wake of Germany's defeat. As the leader of a nation that had *not* been socialized by the state system, he accurately represented American attitudes and expectations when he so single-mindedly pursued his policy of friendship toward the Soviet Union to reduce its suspicions of the West and lay a foundation of mutual trust and goodwill upon which the postwar peace could be built. Roosevelt, as we have seen, explained Soviet behavior almost exclusively as a reaction to such interwar Western steps as the establishment of the *cordon sanitaire* in Eastern Europe. Thus, he did not view free elections in that area in terms of the creation of a new anti-Soviet belt. For him, free elections, non-Communist coalition governments in which Communists might participate if they gained a sizable vote, and a friendly attitude toward both West *and* East were quite compatible.

The model he had in mind was Czechoslovakia. As the only democracy in that area, Czechoslovakia had had close ties with the West since its birth after World War I. But it had also become friendly with the Soviet Union since France and Britain had failed to rescue Czechoslovakia at Munich and betrayed it by appeasing Hitler in 1938. Thus after 1945 Czechoslovakia, like the other Eastern European states, knew that it lay in the Soviet sphere of influence and that its security depended upon getting along with, not irritating, its powerful neighbor. Czech leaders expressed only amicable feelings for the Soviet Union and they signed a security treaty with it; and in one of the rare free elections the Soviets allowed in Eastern Europe the Communist Party received the largest vote of any party and thus held key posts in the government. To share power in a coalition government, however, was to share power with class enemies. A "friendly" state, to the Soviets, was one totally controlled by the Communist Party. A "friendly" state, in Roosevelt's eyes, was one that was sensitive to Soviet security interests while retaining autonomy domestically; a Communist Party monopoly of power was not a prerequisite for a pro-Soviet foreign policy. In Eastern Europe, however, Soviet bayonets ensured that Moscow's view prevailed.

The power vacuum created by Germany's defeat, which permitted Soviet power to extend into the center of Europe and which precipitated the cold war, was virtually a replay of the struggle that erupted after the end of the war against Napoleon. The tsar's troops on that occasion entered Paris; his alliance with Prussia and his control over what then constituted Poland presented Russia's allies—Austria-Hungary and England—with the possibility of Russian continental hegemony. These two states plus the former enemy, France, therefore signed a secret alliance threatening to go to war with Russia if the tsar remained adamantly opposed to a peace treaty that distributed power in such a manner that all the principal states could feel reasonably secure. When the news of this secret arrangement was leaked, the tsar became more compliant. In brief, *the post-World War II conflict*—with Stalin taking Tsar Alexander's place and the United States playing the role of England in rearranging the new balance of power—*was not fundamentally due to the personalities of leaders or to the principal contestants' domestic political or economic systems; it was essentially due to the nature of the state system and the emergent bipolar distribution of power, which led each state to see the other as the principal threat to its security and to take appropriate steps that each deemed essentially defensive but was seen by the other as offensive, expansionist, and aggressive.* In a real sense, the cold war was structurally or systemically determined and its unfolding contained elements of a Greek tragedy. There was one further element of continuity. As in the two world wars, in which Britain had led the effort to contain Germany, London—not Washington—took the first steps in opposing the Soviet Union after 1945. Indeed, the United States attempted initially to play the role of mediator between the Soviet Union and Britain! Only as British power proved to be insufficient did the United States, as before but more quickly, take over the task of balancing Soviet power.

American initiative came about gradually in the 1946–1947 period and was precipitated mainly when Stalin turned from consolidating his grip in Eastern Europe to seeking to extend Soviet influence beyond the lines drawn by Allied armies during the war. The United States had accommodated itself to Soviet control over Eastern Europe, especially Poland, the corridor through which German armies had marched on Russia twice in a quarter-century. Moscow's security interests were understandable, and Washington, despite its disappointments over the Soviet nonfulfillment of its Yalta obligations in Poland, quickly recognized the new Polish government as well as the other Soviet-installed regimes in Eastern Europe. Only when the Soviets attempted to effect a major breakthrough into the Middle East did American opposition become genuinely aroused. Greece, Turkey, and Iran were the first states to feel Soviet pressure.

The pressure on Iran began in early 1946, when the Soviets refused to withdraw their troops from that country. These troops had been there since late 1941, when the Soviet Union and Britain had invaded Iran in order to forestall increased Nazi influence and to use Iran as a corridor for the transportation of military aid shipped by the West to the Persian Gulf for transit to the Soviet Union. The Soviets had occupied northern Iran, the British the central and southern sections. When the latter withdrew their troops after the war, the Soviets sought to convert Iran into a Soviet satellite. Oil concessions offered in return for Soviet permission to let Iran exercise its sovereign authority over northern Iran were rejected.

During this period, the Soviet Union also put pressure on Turkey. Indeed, the Soviets had begun to do this as early as June 1945, when they suddenly demanded the cession of several Turkish districts lying on the Turkish-Soviet frontier, the revision of the Montreux Convention governing the Dardanelles Straits in favor of a joint Soviet-Turkish administration, Turkey's severance of ties with Britain and the conclusion of a treaty with the Soviet Union similar to those that the Soviet Union had concluded with its Balkan satellites, and finally, the leasing to the Soviet Union of bases for naval and land forces in the Dardanelles for its "joint defense." This time Moscow rejected a compromise proposal that would have given the Soviet Union a veto over any non-Black Sea powers' warships seeking passage through the straits. In August 1946, the Soviet Union renewed its demand, in a note to the United States and Britain, for a new administration of the straits. In effect, this would have turned Turkey into a Soviet satellite.

In Greece, too, Communist pressure was exerted on the government through wide-scale guerrilla warfare, which began in the fall of 1946. Civil war in Greece was actually nothing new. During the war, the Communist and anti-Communist guerrillas fighting the Germans had spent much of their energy battling each other. When the British landed in Greece and the Germans withdrew from the country, the Communists had attempted to take over the capital city of Athens. Only after several weeks of bitter street fighting and the landing of British reinforcements was the Communist control of Athens dislodged and a truce signed in January 1945. Just over a year later—in March 1946—the Greeks held a general election in which right-wing forces captured the majority of votes.

The Greek situation did not improve, however. The country was exhausted from the Italian and German invasions, the four years of occupation, and the Germans' scorched-earth policy as they retreated. Moreover, Greece had always been dependent upon imports that were paid for by exports, but its traditional market in Central Europe was now closed. While the masses lived at a bare subsistence level, the black market flourished. The inability of any government to deal with this situation aroused a good deal of social discontent. And the large, 100,000-man army that Greece needed to protect itself from its Communist neighbors (Albania, Yugoslavia, and Bulgaria) had brought the country to near-bankruptcy. If Britain had not helped finance—as well as train and equip—the army and kept troops in the country to stabilize the situation, Greece would in all probability have collapsed. It was in these circumstances that in August 1946 the Communist forces began to squeeze Greece by renewing the guerrilla warfare in the north, where the guerrillas could be kept well supplied by Greece's Communist neighbors.

In all these situations, the American government was suddenly confronted with the need for action to support Britain, the traditional guardian of this area, against encroachment. In the case of Iran, the United States and Britain delivered firm statements that strongly implied that the two countries would use force to defend Iran. The Soviet response in late March 1946 was the announcement that the Red Army would be withdrawn during the next five to six weeks. In the Turkish case, the United States sent a naval task force into the Mediterranean immediately after the receipt of the Soviet note on August 7. Twelve days later, the United States replied to the note by rejecting the Soviet demand to share exclusive responsibility for the defense of the straits with Turkey.

Britain sent a similar reply. The Greek situation had not yet come to a head, and the need for American action could be postponed for a while longer. But it should be pointed out that the Truman administration's actions in Iran and Turkey were merely swift reactions to immediate crises. They were not the product of an overall American strategy. Such a coherent strategy came only after a new assessment of Soviet foreign policy had occurred.

THE STRATEGY OF CONTAINMENT

A period of eighteen months passed before the United States undertook that reassessment—from the surrender of Japan on September 2, 1945, until the announcement of the Truman Doctrine on March 12, 1947. Perhaps such a reevaluation could not have been made any more quickly. Public opinion in a democratic country does not normally shift drastically overnight. It would have been too much to expect the American public to change suddenly from an attitude of friendliness toward the Soviet Union—inspired largely by the picture of Soviet wartime bravery and endurance and by hopes for peaceful postwar cooperation—to a hostile mood. The United States wished only to be left alone to preoccupy itself once more with domestic affairs. The end of the war signaled the end of power politics and the restoration of normal peacetime harmony among nations.

In response to this expectation, the public demanded a speedy demobilization. In May 1945, at the end of the war with Germany, the United States had an army of 3.5 million men organized into 68 divisions in Europe, supported by 149 air groups. By March 1946, only ten months later, the United States had only 400,000 troops left, mainly new recruits; the homeland reserve was 6 battalions. Further reductions in army strength followed. Air force and navy cuts duplicated this same pattern. This deliberate reduction of military strength, as a symptom of America's psychological demobilization, could not have failed to encourage Soviet intransigence in Europe and attempts to extend Soviet influence. American diplomacy and force retained their traditional separation. America's large and powerful armed forces and its enormous industrial strength, which could have provided the basis for serious negotiations about Eastern Europe—which Stalin satellized only gradually as he saw that his consolidation of Soviet power in the area elicited only protest notes from Washington—were respectively dismantled and converted to the production of consumer goods. American policy, supported by sufficient conventional military power, was impotent. (And "atomic diplomacy," despite later revisionists, was not used either in the immediate postwar period. If it had been, as was claimed, it certainly did not frighten Stalin nor deter him from strengthening his grip on Eastern Europe or trying to expand beyond the areas where World War II had ended.)

It was these Soviet efforts that finally provoked the United States and led to a reevaluation of American policy. Three positions became clear during this period. At one extreme stood that old realist Winston Churchill. At the end of the European war, he had counseled against the withdrawal of American troops. He had insisted that they stay, together with British troops, in order to force the Soviet Union to live up to its Yalta obligations regarding free elections in Eastern Europe and the withdrawal of the Red Army from eastern Germany. The United States had rejected Churchill's plea. In early 1946, at Fulton, Missouri, Churchill took his case directly to the American public. The Soviet Union, he asserted, was an expansionist state. "From Stettin in the Baltic to Trieste in the Adriatic, an iron curtain has descended across the continent. Behind that line lie all the capitals of the ancient states of Central and Eastern Europe. Warsaw, Berlin, Prague, Vienna, Budapest, Belgrade, Bucharest, and Sofia, all the famous cities and populations around them lie in the Soviet sphere and all are subject in one form or another, not only to Soviet influence but to a very high and increasing measure of control from Moscow." Churchill did not believe that the Soviets wanted war: "What they desire is the fruits of war and the indefinite expansion of their power and doctrines." This could be prevented only by the opposing power of the British Commonwealth and the United States.

Churchill, in short, said bluntly that the cold war had begun, that Americans must recognize this fact and give up their dreams of Big Three unity in the United Nations. International organization was no substitute for the balance of power. "Our difficulties and dangers will not be removed by closing our eyes to them. They will not be removed by mere waiting to see what happens; nor will they be relieved by a policy of appeasement." An alliance of the English-speaking peoples was the prerequisite for American and British security and world peace.

At the other extreme stood Secretary of Commerce Henry Wallace, who felt it was precisely the kind of aggressive attitude expressed by Churchill that was to blame for Soviet hostility. The United States and Britain had no more business in Eastern Europe than had the Soviet Union in Latin America; to each, the respective area was vital for national security. Western interference in nations bordering on the Soviet Union was bound to arouse Soviet suspicion, just as Soviet intervention in countries neighboring on the United States would. "We may not like what Russia does in Eastern Europe," said Wallace. "Her type of land reform, industrial expropriation, and suspension of basic liberties offends the great majority of the people of the United States. But whether we like it or not, the Russians will try to socialize their sphere of influence just as we try to democratize our sphere of influence (including Japan and Western Germany)." The tough attitude that Churchill and other "reactionaries" at home and abroad demanded was precisely the wrong policy; it would only increase international tension. "We must not let British balance-of-power manipulations determine whether and when the United States gets into a war . . . 'getting tough' never bought anything real and lasting—whether for schoolyard bullies or world powers. The tougher we get, the tougher the Russians will get." Only mutual trust would allow the United States and the Soviet Union to live together peacefully, and such trust could not be created by an unfriendly American attitude and policy.

The American government and public wavered between these two positions. The administration recognized that Big Three cooperation had ended, and it realized that the time when the United States needed to demonstrate goodwill toward the Soviet Union in order to overcome the latter's suspicions had passed. No further concessions would be made to preserve the surface friendship with the Soviet Union. America had tried to gain Soviet amity by being a friend; it was now up to Soviet leaders to demonstrate a similarly friendly attitude toward America as well. Paper agreements, written in such general terms that they actually hid divergent purposes, were no longer regarded as demonstrating such friendship. Something more than paper agreements was needed: Soviet words would have to be matched by Soviet deeds.

The American secretary of state, James Byrnes, called this new line the "policy of firmness and patience." This phrase meant that the United States would take a firm position whenever the Soviet Union became intransigent and that it would not compromise simply in order to reach a quick agreement. This change in official American attitude toward the Soviet Union was not, however, a fundamental one. A firm line was to be followed only on concrete issues. The assumption was that if the United States took a tougher bargaining position and no longer seemed in a hurry to resolve particular points of tension, the Soviet rulers would see the pointlessness of their obduracy and agree to fair compromise solutions of their differences with the United States and the West. In short, American firmness would make the Soviets "reasonable." For they were regarded as "unreasonable" merely on particular issues. The new American position, as one political analyst has aptly summed it up, "meant to most of its exponents that the Soviet Union had to be induced by firmness to play the game in the American way. There was no consistent official suggestion that the United States should begin to play a different game." The prerequisite for such a suggestion was that American policymakers recognize the revolutionary nature of the Soviet regime.

This recognition came with increasing speed as the Greek crisis reached a peak. By early 1947, it was obvious that the United States would have to play a different game. It was George Kennan, the Foreign Service's foremost expert on the Soviet Union, who first presented the basis of what was to be a new American policy. Kennan's analysis focused on the Communist outlook on world affairs. In the Soviet leaders' pattern of thought, he said, the Soviet Union had no community of interest with the capitalist states; indeed, they saw their relationship with the Western powers in terms of an innate antagonism. Communist ideology had taught them "that the outside world was hostile and that it was their duty eventually to overthrow the political forces beyond their borders. The powerful hands of Russian history and tradition reached up to sustain them in this feeling. Finally, their own aggressive intransigence with respect to the outside world began to find its own reaction. . . . It is an undeniable privilege for every man to prove himself right in the thesis that the world is his enemy; for if he reiterates it frequently enough and makes it the background for his conduct, he is bound to be right." According to Kennan, this Soviet hostility was a constant factor; it would continue until the capitalist world had been destroyed: "Basically, the antagonism remains. It is postulated. And from it flow many of the phenomena which we find disturbing in the Kremlin's conduct of foreign policy: the secretiveness, the lack of frankness, the duplicity, the war suspiciousness, and the basic unfriendliness of purpose. . . . These characteristics of the Soviet policy, like the postulates from which they flow, are basic to the *internal* nature of Soviet power, and will be with us . . . until the nature of Soviet power is changed [italics added]." Until that moment, he said, Soviet strategy and objectives would remain the same.

Kennan's analysis with its emphasis on Communist ideology and its effects on the Soviet leaders' perception of the nature of international politics suggests that one result of the ideology would be to reinforce the rules most leaders responsible for their nation's security had learned long ago: Protect yourself, be on guard at all times, remember that today's ally may be tomorrow's enemy, demonstrate a healthy skepticism about other countries' declarations of friendship, never forget that in the final analysis you can depend only on yourself and, therefore, keep strong, especially militarily. Most states feel insecure in a system of independent states but the Soviet Union was especially insecure because its ideology clearly defined the foe (the capitalist states), attributed total hostility to this enemy, and viewed the resulting struggle as long-term and irreconcilable. Thus conflict and an intense concern with power characterized the Soviet approach to international politics.

They also added an offensive element to Soviet foreign policy: a mission to save mankind from the wickedness of capitalism and establish a new postcapitalist international order in which social justice domestically and peace among nations would finally reign. For it was capitalism with its profit motive that was alleged to be the reason that within countries the few exploited the many and some men were rich while most were poor; and it was capitalist states searching for profits beyond their borders that were claimed to be responsible for international wars. Soviet foreign policy was, therefore, revolutionary; its aim was nothing less than the total and radical transformation of the international system.

The American-Soviet struggle would thus be a long one, but Kennan stressed that Soviet hostility did not mean that the Soviets would embark upon a do-or-die program to overthrow capitalism by a fixed date. They had no timetable for conquest. In a brilliant passage, Kennan outlined the Soviet concept of the struggle:

> The Kremlin is under no ideological compulsion to accomplish its purposes in a hurry. Like the Church, it is dealing in ideological concepts whicn are of a long-

term validity, and it can afford to be patient. It has no right to risk the existing achievements of the revolution for the sake of vain baubles of the future. The very teachings of Lenin himself require great caution and flexibility in the pursuit of Communist purposes. Again, these precepts are fortified by the lessons of Russian history: of centuries of obscure battles between nomadic forces over the stretches of a vast unfortified plain. Here caution, circumspection, flexibility, and deception are the valuable qualities; and their value finds natural appreciation in the Russian, or the Oriental mind. Thus the Kremlin has no compunction about retreating in the face of superior force. And being under the compulsion of no timetable, it does not get panicky under the necessity of such a retreat. Its political action is a fluid stream which moves constantly, wherever it is permitted to move, toward a given goal. Its main concern is to make sure that it has filled every nook and cranny available to it in the basin of world power. But if it finds unassailable barriers in its path, it accepts these philosophically and accommodates itself to them. The main thing is that there should always be pressure, increasing constant pressure, toward the desired goal. There is no trace of any feeling in Soviet psychology that the goal must be reached at any given time.

How could the United States counter such a policy—a policy that was always pushing, seeking weak spots, attempting to fill power vacuums? Kennan's answer was that American policy would have to be one of "long-term, patient, but firm and vigilant containment." The United States would find Soviet diplomacy both easier and more difficult to deal with than that of dictators such as Napoleon or Hitler. "On the one hand, it [Soviet policy] is more sensitive to contrary force, more ready to yield on individual sectors of the diplomatic front when that force is felt to be too strong, and thus more rational in the logic and rhetoric of power. On the other hand, it cannot be easily defeated or discouraged by a single victory on the part of its opponents. And the patient persistence by which it is animated means that it can be effectively countered not by sporadic acts which represent the momentary whims of democratic opinion, but only by intelligent long-range policies on the part of Russia's adversaries—policies no less steady in their purpose, and no less variegated and resourceful in their application, than those of the Soviet Union itself."

Kennan viewed containment as a test of American democracy to conduct an effective, responsible foreign policy *and* contribute to changes within the Soviet Union that might bring about a moderation of its revolutionary aims. The United States, he emphasized, "has it in its power to increase enormously the strains under which Soviet policy must operate, to force upon the Kremlin a far greater degree of moderation and circumspection than it has had to observe in recent years, and in this way to promote tendencies which must eventually find their outlet in either the breakup or the gradual mellowing of Soviet power. For no mystical, messianic movement—and particularly not that of the Kremlin—can face frustration indefinitely without eventually adjusting itself in one way or another to the logic of that state of affairs."

Why was the United States so favorably positioned for a long-term struggle with the Soviet Union? Because, Kennan argued, industry was the key ingredi-

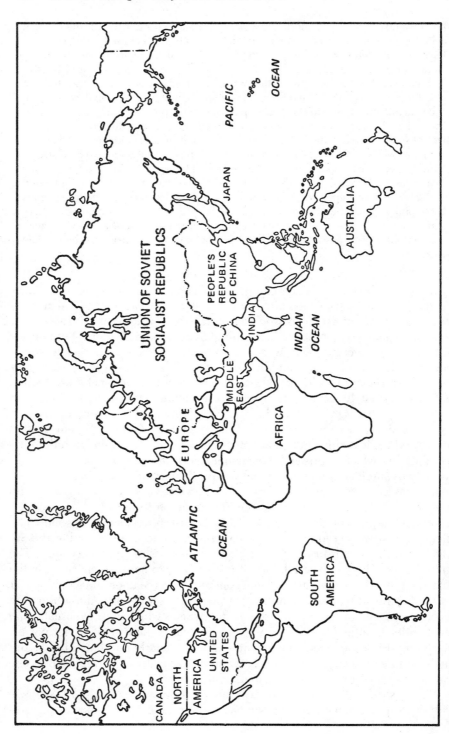

The Soviet Union as a Eurasian and World Power

ent of power and the United States controlled most of the centers of industry. There were five such centers in the world: the United States, Britain, West Germany, Japan, and the Soviet Union. The United States and its future allies possessed four of these centers, the Soviet Union just one. Containment meant confining the Soviet Union to that one. The question was not whether we had sufficient power to contain the Soviet Union but the patience and wisdom to do so.

Note the two courses of action that were implicitly rejected by the decision to adopt containment. One was preventive war. The United States had an atomic monopoly until late 1949; by then it had a fairly sizable atomic stockpile plus a sufficient number of bombers to deliver it. The Soviet Union had virtually none of either. In short, the United States briefly had the opportunity of establishing a *Pax Americana*, or world domination. But using this atomic monopoly was never seriously considered, for a "Pearl Harbor" on Soviet Russia was contrary to American tradition and morality. The other course implicitly rejected was a retreat back to America's historic isolationist posture.

THE TRUMAN DOCTRINE

Whether the United States could meet this Soviet challenge became a pressing question when, on the afternoon of February 21, 1947, the first secretary of the British Embassy in Washington visited the State Department and handed American officials two notes from His Majesty's government. One concerned Greece, the other Turkey. In effect, they both stated the same thing: that Britain could no longer meet its traditional responsibilities in those two countries. Since both were on the verge of collapse, the import of the British notes was clear: that a Soviet breakthrough could be prevented only by an all-out American commitment.

February 21 was thus a historic day. On that day, Great Britain, the only remaining power in Europe, acknowledged its exhaustion. It had fought Philip II of Spain, Louis XIV and Napoleon of France, Kaiser Wilhelm II and Adolf Hitler of Germany. It had preserved the balance of power that had protected the United States for so long that it seemed almost natural for it to continue to do so. But its ability to protect that balance had steadily declined in the twentieth century. Twice it had needed American help. Each time, however, it had fought the longer battle; on neither occasion had the United States entered the war until it became clear that Germany and its allies were too strong for Great Britain and that America would have to help in safeguarding its own security. Now, all of a sudden, there was no power to protect the United States but the United States itself; no one stood between that country and the present threat to its security. All the other major powers of the world had collapsed—except the Soviet Union. A bipolar world suddenly faced the United States.

The immediate crisis suddenly confronting the United States had its locale in the eastern Mediterranean. Direct Soviet pressure on Iran and Turkey had temporarily been successfully resisted. The Soviets had now turned to outflanking these two nations by concentrating their attention on Greece. If Greece collapsed—and all reports from that hapless country indicated that it would fall within a few weeks—it was thought in Washington that it would only be a question of time until Turkey and Iran would crumble before Soviet power. But the fall of Greece would not only affect its neighbors to the east; it would also lead to an increase of Communist pressure on Italy. For Italy would then be faced with two Communist states to its east—Yugoslavia and Greece—and with the largest Communist party in Western Europe in its own midst. And to the northwest of Italy lay France, with the second largest Communist party in the West. Thus, the security of all of Western Europe would be endangered as well.

Consequently, the United States felt it had no choice but to act in this situation. On March 12, 1947, President Harry Truman went before a joint session of Congress to deliver a speech that must rank as one of the most important in American history. After outlining the situation in Greece, he spelled out what was to become known as the Truman Doctrine. The United States, he emphasized, could survive only in a world in which freedom flourished. And it would not realize this objective

> . . . unless we are willing to help free peoples to maintain their institutions and their national integrity against aggressive movements that seek to impose upon them totalitarian regimes. *This is no more than a frank recognition that totalitarian regimes imposed on free peoples, by direct or indirect aggression, undermine the foundations of international peace and hence the security of the United States* [italics added]. . . .
>
> At the present moment in world history nearly every nation must choose between alternative ways of life. The choice is often not a free one.
>
> One way of life is based upon the will of the majority, and is distinguished by free institutions, representative government, free elections, guarantees of individual liberty, freedom of speech and religion, and freedom from political oppression.
>
> The second way of life is based upon the will of a minority forcibly imposed upon the majority. It relies upon terror and oppression, a controlled press and radio, fixed elections, and the suppression of personal freedoms.
>
> I believe it must be the policy of the United States to support free peoples who are resisting attempted subjugations by armed minorities or by outside pressure.
>
> I believe that we must assist free peoples to work out their own destinies in their own way.
>
> I believe that our help should be primarily through economic and financial aid which is essential to economic stability and orderly political processes.

Stressing the impact of Greece's collapse upon Turkey and the Middle East, as well as upon Europe, the president asked Congress to appropriate $400 million for economic aid and military supplies for both countries and to authorize the dispatch of American civilian and military personnel in order to help the two nations in their tasks of reconstruction and provide their armies with appropriate instruction and training.

Thus the United States began the policy of containment. A number of points about this initial commitment need special emphasis. First, the Soviet threat to the balance of power left the United States no choice but to adopt a countervailing policy. With the war over, the United States would have much preferred to concentrate on domestic affairs; the massive postwar demobilization clearly demonstrated this preference. But the external environment intervened: the bipolar distribution of power molded the nation's policy course. Such a distribution of power is the most sensitive of all because the two states are bound to be alert to the slightest shift in the balance lest one adversary gain the power he needs to assert and impose his will upon the other. For a gain of power and security by one tends to be seen as a loss of power and security for the other. A bipolar balance is therefore very dangerous, for it produces, among its effects, constant confrontations and crises that could spark a military clash. Yet they are also an indication that the balance is being kept. As one side pushes, his opponent pushes him back.

The second point to stress is that anti-Communism was not the major ingredient of American policy during and immediately after World War II. During the war, the United States had constantly sought to overcome the Kremlin's suspicions of the West in order to lay the foundation for postwar harmony and peace. And as the war drew to its conclusion, the principal concern of American policymakers was not to eliminate the self-proclaimed bastion of world revolution and enemy of Western capitalism, nor to push the Soviet Union out of Eastern Europe and convert that area into a market for American corporations (even had the desire existed, poverty-stricken Eastern Europe would not have been a very profitable market for American goods), but to forestall a complete return to the historic position of isolationism. The public mood was all too evident in the hasty military demobilization, the riots of some overseas units that felt that their demobilization was not rapid enough, and the cries of America's children heard both in Congress and the White House: "We want our daddies." For the United States to have pursued the assertive foreign policy complete with atomic threats that the revisionists have claimed it did would have required a dictatorial disregard for the wide-spread demands of public opinion.

It was not until a year and a half after World War II ended that the Truman Doctrine was enunciated. Only after further attempts to reconcile differences with Moscow, after continued Soviet pressure, denunciations, and vilifications, was containment launched. Hostile Soviet behavior was the reason for the gradual shift of American policy and public opinion from amity to enmity; American policy was not the product of a virulent and preexisting anti-Communist ideology. Rather, it was activated by the same concern for preventing a major nation from achieving dominance in Europe that had already twice in this century led the United States into war. Thus, post–1945 American policy was consistent with United States behavior in 1917 and 1940–1941; in both cases, the nation had gone to war to prevent such an outcome. This was not fundamentally an ideological issue. In World Wars I and II, the enemy was Germany; in the initial engagement, it was led by a conservative monarchy, in the second, by an extreme right-wing fascist regime. In the cold war, the adversary was Soviet Russia, a radical left-wing regime. American action, however, remained the same, regardless of the ideological nature of the opponent.

Third, the role of anti-Communism in American policy was essentially to mobilize Congressional and public support for the policy once it had been decided upon. A nation that had historically condemned power politics as immoral and as a corruption of the democratic ideal needed a moral basis for its new use of power. Anti-Communism fitted into the familiar dichotomy of a peaceful and democratic New World confronted by a warlike and dictatorial Old Europe. For a people weary after four years of war, who identified the termination of war with the end of power politics, who were used to isolation from Europe's wicked affairs, and who were preoccupied with the pursuit of happiness, success, and the dollar at home, anti-Communism was like the cavalry's bugle call to charge; it fitted neatly into the traditional American dichotomy of the world into extremes of evil and morality, thereby arousing the nation for yet another foreign policy mission. Until Vietnam, anti-Communism served the policymakers' purposes; the policy of containment received long and widespread public and Congressional support from both Democrats and Republicans. (Asian policy was to be the major exception to this rule, as we shall see.)

The fourth point worth noting is that, despite the universalism of the Truman Doctrine, its application was intended to be specific and limited, not global. American policymakers were well aware that the United States, though a Great Power, was not omnipotent; therefore, national priorities—which interests were vital and which were not—had to be decided carefully and power applied discriminately. American responses would depend, then, both on where the external challenges occurred and on how Washington defined the relationship of such challenges to the nation's security. Under the guise of a crusading rhetoric, containment was to be implemented only where the Soviet state appeared to be seeking to expand its power. The priority given to balance-of-power considerations was evident from the very beginning since, despite the declared democratic purposes stated by the Truman Doctrine, the first application of the doctrine was to Greece and Turkey, neither of whom were democratic.

Their strategic location was given precedence over their domestic nature. In Western Europe, of course, America's strategic and power considerations were compatible with its democratic values. The containment of the Soviet Union could be equated with the defense of democracy. But outside of Western Europe, strategy and values were often incompatible with one another, thus confronting the United States with a classic dilemma: To protect strategically located, undemocratic regimes might fortify containment (in the short run, at least) but stain America's reputation and weaken the justification for United States policy; on the other hand, to align itself only with democratic states, of which there were all too few, might make it impossible to carry out the containment policy. The cause might thus be kept pure, but the security of democracy would be weakened. This dilemma was to plague this nation's policy in subsequent years and often make the declared aim that the United States was seeking to protect the democratic way of life appear as hypocritical.

Chapter 3

CONTAINMENT IN EUROPE

THE MARSHALL PLAN

The commitment to Greece and Turkey was only the first act under the new American policy of containing Soviet expansion. Britain's state of near-collapse was symptomatic of all of Europe's collapse. Basically, Britain's crisis was an economic one. As an island-nation, it was dependent for its livelihood upon international trade. It had to export or die, for the Industrial Revolution it had undergone during the nineteenth century had almost completely urbanized it. Less than 5 percent of Britain's population was engaged in agriculture. This meant that it had to import much of its food: meat, wheat, butter, tea, cocoa, coffee, and sugar. Except for coal, Britain also had to import most of the raw materials needed by its industries: cotton, rubber, wool, iron ore, timber, and oil.

Before 1939, Britain had paid for these foods and raw materials by one of three means: services such as shipping, income from foreign investments, and manufactured exports. But the war had crippled its merchant marine, liquidated most of its investments, and destroyed many of its factories. With the first two means of financing its imports all but gone, it had to increase its export drive. Just to maintain the 1939 standard of living, it had to raise its exports by 75 percent. By December 1946, despite an American loan and a severe austerity program that included the rationing of bread, Britain had only reached its prewar level of production. It was in these circumstances that nature delivered what almost proved to be a knockout blow. In the winter of 1946–1947, Europe suffered one of its severest cold periods in history; temperatures went below zero. In Britain, the transportation system came to a virtual standstill. Industries could not be supplied with the fuel to keep them running, and factories

34

were closed. By February 1947, more than half of Britain's factories lay idle. Coal was not even mined, and gas and electricity were in short supply. When the thaw finally arrived, Britain was beset by floods.

The export drive thus completely collapsed, and Britain had come to the end of its rope. The financial editor of Reuter's saw the true measure of the winter disaster: "The biggest crash since the fall of Constantinople—the collapse of the heart of an Empire—impends. This is not the story of a couple of snowstorms. It is the story of the awful debility in which a couple of snowstorms could have such effects." The future looked bleak and ominous: Millions of Britons were unemployed, cold and hungry, worn out by the long years of war and the determined postwar efforts to recover. Despite all the personal and uncomplaining sacrifices they had made, their efforts had come to nothing. Britain's fate could have been worse only if the war had been lost.

In Germany, postwar conditions were truly horrible. The war had been carried into the heart of Germany. Few German cities or towns had escaped Allied bombing, street fighting, or willful destruction by the Nazis themselves as they retreated. To aggravate this situation, 10 million additional Germans came into these ruins from former German territory annexed by Poland. There was only one word to describe Germany in 1945—chaos. Millions of people were faced with the basic necessity of finding food, shelter, and work.

The measure of Germany's collapse was indicated by the fact that the cigarette had replaced money as the prevailing unit of exchange. Cigarettes could buy almost anything. The black market flourished. Even as late as 1947, a package of cigarettes was equivalent to a working man's entire wages for a month. The Allied target ration of 1550 calories per day, which was hardly sufficient to sustain a healthy human being, was rarely reached. Everywhere people were hungry. It was a desperate situation. Respectable girls sold their bodies for one or two cigarettes, a pair of nylons, or an army ration; dishonor was preferable to death. Juvenile delinquency increased and stealing became as respectable a way of earning a living for boys as did prostitution for girls. Along with this economic, social, political, and moral breakdown came the cold weather. There was no fuel for heating. Three-quarters of the factories still standing in the American and British zones of occupation were closed. In January 1947, production fell to 31 percent of the 1936 level, Germany's best year; by February, it had declined to 29 percent. Even before this industrial shutdown German steel production during 1946 had reached only 2 million tons—approximately only one-third of Allied authorization.

Allied policy was not designed to alleviate this situation. The Allies were still primarily engaged with Germany's disarmament and demilitarization, and with the elimination of all industries whose output could be used for military production. America and Britain were not particularly anxious to rebuild Germany's industrial power. They recalled only too vividly that it had taken the combined efforts of three world powers to bring the Nazi war machine to a halt and defeat it. Nor were the Allies especially concerned with the lot of the

German people during the immediate postwar days. After six years of war, such concern could hardly have been expected. The memories of Nazi atrocities and crimes, of wanton destruction, and of millions of innocent people slaughtered in concentration camps were still very much alive. The hatred the Nazis had engendered could not be erased overnight. After six years of brutal warfare, the Allies were unlikely to display much forgiveness and chivalry toward the Germans.

The French, above all others, were not likely to forget the Nazis. Though their economy had been badly damaged during the war, by late 1946 the French had made a remarkable recovery. But iron and steel production had reached only half the prewar total. Here, too, coal was the key factor, since the iron and steel industries were dependent upon imported coal. But European coal production was still well below the pre–1939 annual average. German production was low, and Britain needed for itself all the coal it mined. Therefore, scarce dollars had to be spent for the purchase of high-cost American coal. The result was a vivid demonstration of the division of labor in the modern economy. France's industry was unable to produce sufficient goods to exchange for food. The farmer thereupon withdrew fields from crop cultivation and used them for grazing. He kept more food for himself and his family, and also fed his livestock more grain. Meanwhile, the urban population was short of food, and the government had to spend its few remaining dollars—which it needed for reconstruction—to buy food from abroad. The winter of 1946–1947 aggravated this situation even further by destroying an estimated 3 to 4 million acres of wheat.

This situation was made to order for the large and well-organized French Communist Party. One-quarter of France's electorate—practically the entire working class—voted for the Party. (In Italy, the figure was one-third of the electorate.) The reason for this was simple: Capitalism had alienated these people. The workers were, in effect, internal *émigrés* who voted Communist in protest against a system they felt had long mistreated them; unlike workers in Britain and in the United States, they had suffered all the hardships of capitalism while enjoying few of its benefits, such as good wages and social opportunities. As a result, the Communist Party in France was placed in a powerful position in political and trade union life. The Party was the largest in France and could prevent any reforms from being adopted, thereby preserving its *raison d'être*. The Party also controlled the largest French trade union, which had a membership of 80 percent of the workers in the immediate postwar years. In 1947, as United States-Soviet tensions increased, the Party used this control to initiate or exploit strikes in order to paralyze the entire economy and bring the republic to its knees.

With Europe on the verge of collapse, everything seemed to force it into dependence upon America. Most of the items needed for reconstruction— wheat, cotton, sulphur, sugar, machinery, trucks, and coal—could be obtained in sufficient quantities only from the United States. Yet Europe, with a stagnating economy, was in no position to earn the dollars needed to pay for these goods. Moreover, the United States was so well supplied with everything that it did not have to buy much from abroad. Thus, the European countries were unable to obtain enough dollars for the purchase of the commodities required for their recovery. The result was the ominous "dollar gap"—a term that frightened the Europeans as much as the "cold war."

Europe's collapse thus posed a fundamental question to the United States: Is Europe vital to American security? The answer was never in doubt: American independence and security required that the United States establish a balance of power in the interior of Europe. This was necessary to check any nation with designs on the sea-bordering states as a prerequisite to the elimination of Britain and eventual world conquest. During most of the nineteenth century, this balance had been maintained by the British navy. Now that Britain's power had declined drastically, the United States would have to carry out the task alone. Western Europe possessed the largest aggregation of skilled workers, technicians, and managers outside the United States. It maintained the second greatest concentration of industrial power in the world. A healthy and strong Europe could help shore up the balance of power.

The role of the United States toward Europe, therefore, had to be that of a doctor toward an ill patient—and the prescribed cure was a massive injection of dollars. A large-scale program of economic aid was to be administered in the form of grants rather than loans, which could only intensify Europe's dollar problems. Only such a program could help Europe restore and surpass its prewar agricultural and industrial production, close the dollar gap, and lead Europe to the recovery of its *élan vital*, political stability, and economic prosperity, thereby possibly allowing France and Italy to reintegrate their working classes into their bodies politic.

American aid was made conditional, however, upon economic cooperation among the European states. In this respect, the United States clearly held itself up as a model for the Europeans. The Economic Cooperation Act of 1948 called specifically for European economic integration. America, it stated, was "mindful of the advantage which the United States has enjoyed through the existence of a large-scale domestic market with no internal trade barriers and [believed] that similar advantages can accrue to the countries of Europe." Thus, in official American opinion, European integration became both the prerequisite for Europe's recovery and the necessary basis for Europe's long-range prosperity. It is not difficult to see why American policymakers, with their belief in low-cost mass production, should have felt that Europe's economic recovery and health were dependent upon the creation of a mass market. For decades, the European nations living together on a continent one-fourth the size of the United States had shut their markets off from one another with tariff walls, quota systems, and import and export licenses. By this means, national manu-

Europe

facturers assured themselves of the lion's share of their national markets. Sheltered from external competition, they had little incentive to modernize their equipment or techniques, for they minimized domestic competition by dividing their relatively small domestic markets among themselves. The American aim was to modernize this machinery, to overcome the cartelization of industry and the inefficiency of small family enterprises (as in France), and to destroy the artificial national divisions. Europe's industries were to be compelled to become large-scale and competitive by the creation of a "united states" of Europe.

The economic cooperation required by the United States was first stressed by Secretary of State George C. Marshall's call upon the European states to present his country with a plan for their *common* needs and *common* recovery.

The result was the Organization for European Economic Cooperation (OEEC), whose seventeen members pledged themselves to "cooperate with one another and with other like-minded countries in reducing tariffs and other barriers to trade" and "to promote with vigor the development of productivity through [the] efficient use of the resources at their command." OEEC's estimate of the cost of Europe's recovery over a four-year period was $33 billion. Congress was to cut this figure down to $17 billion, and the amount actually used by the Economic Cooperation Administration (ECA) between 1948 and 1952 was just over $12 billion. Britain, France, and West Germany received more than half of this amount.

The original invitation by the United States to the nations of Europe to plan their joint recovery was deliberately extended to *all* European countries, including the Soviet Union and the nations of Eastern Europe. If the United States had invited only the nations of Western Europe, it would have placed itself in a politically disadvantageous position in which it would have been blamed for the division of Europe and the intensification of the cold war. Actually, if the Soviets had participated, it seems unlikely that Congress would have supported the Marshall Plan: first, because the costs of the plan would have risen astronomically as a result of the very heavy damage suffered by the Soviet Union during the war; and second, because of the growing anti-Soviet feeling that the Soviet Union had engendered. The risk had to be accepted, however; it had to be the Soviets, who, by their rejection of Marshall Plan aid, would be responsible for the division of Europe. And the chances that the Soviets would do precisely that were very good. For European cooperation would mean that the Soviet Union would have to disclose full information about its economy and allow the United States to have some control in its economic planning, as well as in that of its satellites. This was unthinkable to a totalitarian state; a Communist state could hardly permit capitalists to have a voice in its economic development. Soviet participation would also have required the Soviet Union and its satellites to contribute toward Europe's recovery with food and raw materials, in return for the help they were receiving from the United States. Thus, the Soviets would actually be helping to stabilize the European situation. But if they did not participate —preferring to exploit Europe's misery—they would be blamed for continuing and aggravating the cold war. In either case, the United States could not lose by invoking Karl Marx's slogan, "From each according to his ability, to each according to his need." Actually, Soviet Foreign Minister V. M. Molotov did arrive in Paris with a large delegation of experts, and he gave American policymakers a scare. But only for a moment. Molotov soon denounced the plan as an attempt to interfere with Soviet sovereignty and withdrew. Western Europe could now plan the use of America's dollars for its recovery.

Was the Marshall Plan a success? The results tell their own story. By 1950— when the Korean War broke out—Europe was already exceeding its prewar production by 25 percent; two years later, this figure was 200 percent higher.

British exports were doing well, the French inflation was being slowed down, and German production had reached Germany's 1936 level. The dollar gap had been reduced from $12 billion to $2 billion. The Marshall Plan had been a massive success, and at a cost that represented only a tiny fraction of the U.S. national income over the same four-year period; it was, indeed, smaller than America's liquor bill for these same years!

THE NORTH ATLANTIC TREATY ORGANIZATION

Soon after the Marshall Plan was launched, however, it became clear that the plan by itself would not suffice. For in February 1948, the Soviets engineered a *coup d'état* in Prague, and—ten years after Munich and Hitler's subsequent seizure of that hapless nation—Czechoslovakia disappeared behind the iron curtain. A few months later, in June, the Soviets imposed a blockade on Berlin in an effort to dislodge the Western powers from that city. It is hardly surprising that the Europeans, who lived closer to these events than Americans, felt extremely jittery at these overt signs of Soviet hostility and aggressive intent. In this atmosphere of tension and insecurity, in which comparisons of Joseph Stalin's Russia with Hitler's Germany seemed all too valid, it became obvious that Europe's economic recovery was impossible; people do not make the necessary sacrifices and work hard to recuperate today if they feel that tomorrow they will be conquered and that their efforts will all have been in vain. In short, it suddenly became crystal clear that a prerequisite for Europe's recovery was military security.

The Europeans had already made some moves in this direction. In March 1947, France and Britain had signed the Treaty of Dunkirk to provide for their mutual defense against a threat to their security. Exactly a year later, in March 1948, Great Britain, France, the Netherlands, Belgium, and Luxembourg signed the Brussels Pact of collective self-defense. This Brussels Pact was established as a military counterpart to OEEC. Just as OEEC represented an organization dedicated to economic cooperation, the Brussels Pact represented one dedicated to military cooperation. And just as the vitality of OEEC had depended upon American capital for its success, the Brussels Pact members expected their alliance to attract American military support.

They were not to be disappointed. In April 1949, Belgium, Canada, Denmark, France, Great Britain, Iceland, Italy, Luxembourg, the Netherlands, Norway, Portugal, and the United States signed the North Atlantic Treaty Organization (NATO). The U.S. Senate ratified the treaty in July after extended hearings and debates, and the other ratifications were completed by August 1949. For the United States, this NATO commitment set a precedent: For the first time in its history, the country had committed itself to an alliance in peacetime. Europe had become "Our first line of defense." It was precisely this knowledge that the United States would fight to preserve Europe's freedom that was supposed to prevent a Soviet attack. Two world wars had proved

Europe's vital importance to American security. Instead of again allowing the balance of power to be upset and thereby once more becoming drawn into war, the United States now expected to eliminate this contingency by committing itself to the preservation of the European balance in peacetime—that is, *before* the enemy attack took place. The presumption was that the fear of meeting American resistance and fighting an all-out war with the United States would deter the potential aggressor from launching his attack.

This strategy of deterrence relied almost exclusively upon American strategic air power—that is, upon the ability of the Strategic Air Command (SAC) to destroy completely the Soviet Union with atomic bombs. This strategy was based upon two assumptions: first, that the only form of future war would be a total war, which would be precipitated by a direct Soviet attack upon the United States or Western Europe, and second, that deterrence could be achieved by air power and its ability to inflict such heavy damage upon an enemy that he would, in effect, be committing suicide if he launched an attack.

Two events were to change this reliance upon air power alone to deter or destroy the enemy. The first was the explosion of the first Soviet atomic bomb in late 1949. This foreshadowed a time when the Soviet Union, too, would possess an atomic stockpile; in short, it portended a significant increase in Soviet capability. The second event was the North Korean attack upon South Korea in June 1950. Since it was presumed that this attack could not have occurred without Soviet permission, the North Korean aggression suggested a change in Soviet intentions. And this possibility was strengthened in Washington's view by Communist China's intervention in North Korea in late November. The Western response was large-scale rearmament.

This involved three tasks for NATO: the establishment of a command structure, the formulation of a strategy by which to defend Europe on the ground, and the rebuilding of its ground forces. These efforts received their initial impetus when, in the dark days after Communist China's entry into the Korean War, President Harry Truman appointed General Dwight D. Eisenhower to serve as Supreme Allied Commander in Europe. Eisenhower, in turn, strove to make his command operational. His first move was to establish three commands under him: a Central Europe Command, a Northern Europe Command, and a Southern Europe Command. The first of these commands presided over the most important front—militarily because here was the plane upon which the Soviet Army could apply its full force and be met with full counterforce, and politically because Germany, France, and Great Britain lay on this axis.

The strategy NATO adopted was known as the "forward strategy"—that is, a defense at the Elbe. Politically, the Europeans wanted no part of a strategy that called for a withdrawal and would bring the Soviet Army to their borders, and most probably into their countries. They had no desire to provide battlefields again; they wanted the Soviet Army to be kept far from their frontiers. And liberation in a war in which atomic bombs would be dropped was no liberation at all: One could not liberate a corpse. Indeed, if the first Soviet onslaught were to drive the Allies completely out of Europe, the continent would fall permanently under Soviet control. The atomic bomb forbade a Normandy-type landing. Thus, from a political standpoint, Allied forces could not retreat. Europe would have to be defended as far east in Western Germany as possible.

Such a defense required troops and proper logistical support. When Eisenhower arrived in Europe, he found only twelve divisions—including the American ones—none of which was at full strength, properly trained, or fully equipped with the latest weapons. Nor were there any effective reserves to back them up. Perhaps neither of these facts was surprising: The European powers had greater needs and more important things to do in the immediate postwar days than to maintain or rebuild sizable military forces. In addition, because of America's atomic monopoly, it had seemed quite safe to rely solely upon SAC for deterrence and to use the troops in Germany solely for occupation duties.

But Eisenhower needed more ground forces for two purposes: The first would be to act as a "tripwire." In case the Soviets had any delusion that the United States would not go to war to defend Europe, the tripwire troops were to remove this belief. An attack by the Red Army would be bound to run into American troops, some of whom would obviously be killed. This would ensure American retaliation against the Soviet Union. The second function of the NATO army was to act as a "shield" by holding the Soviet Army at the point of attack, the Elbe River, while SAC laid waste the Soviet Union. Military planners believed that such shield forces would have to be quite large because of the size of the Soviet army.

But the need for an ample number of divisions faced the European states with a dreadful dilemma. They were unable and unwilling to mobilize the necessary troops. They were still in the midst of economic recovery and unprepared to devote too large a share of national budgets to rearmament. The American answer was the rearmament of Germany. If France and Britain could not supply the necessary troops, Germany would serve to supply them. Moreover, this decision seemed an eminently correct one. For the forward strategy meant that NATO would try to hold West Germany. It was only fitting that the Germans should contribute to their own defense. In turn, of course, German rearmament reinforced the need for a forward strategy. For the West Germans could hardly be persuaded to rearm if they could not be assured that West Germany would not be turned into a battlefield and that German troops would not be used merely for the defense of France and Britain. Thus, the German question once more raised its head. It was not a new question—but this time it received new answers.

GERMAN RECOVERY AND REARMAMENT

Ever since the middle of the nineteenth century—if not since the Congress of Vienna in 1815—Germany has held the key to the European balance of power.

This was true of Germany even in defeat in 1945. Almost from the cessation of hostilities, the Soviet Union and the United States began their contest over Germany. East Germany had fallen into Soviet hands; West Germany was occupied by the Western powers. Actually, the Allies were lucky, for West Germany contained the great majority of Germany's population and held the heart of its industrial power. West Germany, in short, was the chief prize in Europe.

During the war, Stalin, Churchill, and Roosevelt had decided to govern Germany through a four-power Allied Control Commission (with France as the fourth power), which would administer the entire country as a single economic unit. In practice, this task proved impossible. The Soviets, the British, and French, as well as the smaller European nations, had been promised reparations payments in compensation for the widespread destruction the Germans had caused in their countries. The Soviet sum was to consist of all the industrial equipment in the Soviet zone, plus one-quarter of the far greater industrial complex in West Germany (it was assumed during the war that Germany's industrial power would be intact at the end of the war). But—and these were to be the decisive points—the United States and Great Britain had insisted upon two restrictions on these reparations payments. First, Germany was to be left enough of its nonmilitary industries to maintain its standard of living at the same level as the rest of Europe (but definitely not higher); and second, no reparations were to be paid out of current production until Germany had earned enough money with its exports to pay for the imports it needed. Germany was to support itself. The Allies had no desire to spend their money supporting their former enemy.

The Soviets quickly began demolishing the industry in their zone without informing the Western powers how much they were taking. The Soviets also cut off the regular food supply from East Germany, which had traditionally been Germany's breadbasket; under the original agreement, they were to furnish this food in return for the three-fifths of capital equipment they were allowed to remove from the Western zones. These Soviet actions led to trouble. Almost exactly a year after V-E Day, the United States announced that it was suspending all further West German reparations payments to the Soviet Union. They were not to be resumed until the Soviet Union operated its zone as part of Germany under the original terms of agreement. The reason for this American action was clear: If East Germany no longer furnished the supplies of food that West Germany needed, West Germany would have to increase its exports to buy food from abroad; and if it had to increase exports, it had to increase production. The British agreed. Thus, the wartime agreement to hold German industrial production down for fear that Germany would again use its heavy industry in a secret rearmament program—as it had during the years between the two world wars—collapsed. The American and British purpose was to make Germany pay for its own needs.

But the two powers also had another and more important aim in mind: As Europe's economic collapse became clearer and the cold war intensified, it became necessary to lift Germany out of its economic stagnation and make its industry contribute to the general economic recovery of Europe. In July 1946, the United States offered to merge its zone with those of Britain and France; Germany was to be decompartmentalized in order to speed up its industrial recovery. The French, fearing Germany's reviving strength, refused to participate. The result was that in January 1947, an embryonic German state known as Bizonia (France was to join later) formally emerged. But this fusion would not by itself suffice to achieve Germany's economic recovery. The willing cooperation of the Germans themselves was needed. America and Britain therefore decided to let the Germans begin to take a more active part in running their own country; this, in effect, foreshadowed the eventual establishment of a West German government. Lastly, Germany needed a sound currency; without it, its economy could not recover. The subsequent currency reform carried out by the U.S. military government became the basis of West Germany's amazing economic recovery.

The Soviets reacted by blockading Berlin. The issue at stake was more than just Berlin: It was Germany itself. Berlin, as the old capital of Germany, was the symbol of the conflict over Germany. The Soviets certainly did not want to see West Germany become a partner of the West. Germany and Russia had fought two wars in forty years. Germany had beaten Russia the first time and almost defeated it again on the second occasion. Moreover, Germany was not a *status quo* power but a revisionist state eyeing territory now controlled by the Soviet Union and Poland. Whether these defensive reasons, springing from the Soviet Union's fear of Germany, were primary in precipitating the Berlin crisis, however, is rather doubtful. For if Soviet fear of Germany was so deep, it is difficult to understand why the Soviets had not earlier accepted an American proposal, offered them by Secretary James Byrnes, of an alliance of twenty-five or even forty years to neutralize Germany. In any case, whereas the Soviet Union had been much weaker than Germany before World War II, it emerged from that conflict far stronger—a superpower, in fact—while Germany, in spite of its potential strength, was now only a second-class power. The Soviet-German balance of power had decisively changed in the Soviet Union's favor, and another German attack upon the Soviet Union was unlikely in these circumstances. In any war, whether it acted unilaterally or as an ally of the United States, Germany would be the battlefield and therefore the first country to be destroyed. Fear of this consequence was a sufficient deterrent. The real danger to the Soviet Union of a revived Germany came from the fact that, once Germany's power had been added to that of the United States and its allies, the American position in Europe would obviously be greatly consolidated. This, in turn, stood in the way of two Soviet objectives: one, the withdrawal of American forces and the neutralization of Western Europe; and two, the long-term aim of winning Germany's participation in a subservient partnership. Germany's recovery, in short, would block Soviet expansionist purposes in Europe.

In order to forestall Germany's revival, therefore, the Soviets resorted to a test of strength. If the Allies could be forced out of Berlin, German confidence in American strength would be undermined. The Germans would hardly attach themselves to a friend too weak to protect them. Indeed, if American will power would crumble under Soviet pressure, France and Britain also might reconsider their adherence to NATO. The Berlin crisis, then, if it were not met, would disintegrate the entire American position in Europe and nullify America's postwar efforts to rebuild Europe as a partner in the struggle against the Soviet Union.

The method of conflict was decided at the outset by the unwillingness of either the United States or the Soviet Union to risk a total war. Thus, the Western powers ruled out almost at the start an attempt to reopen the corridor to Berlin by sending troops and tanks to challenge the Soviet army. Instead, they limited themselves to an airlift to supply the city with all its needs. The Soviets did not challenge this effort, for they were aware that in doing so they would leave the West no alternative but to fight a total war. Instead, they decided to wait and see whether the Western powers could take care of the needs of Berlin's 2.5 million citizens. It would take a minimum of 4000 tons of food and fuel daily—an enormous amount of tonnage to ship in by air. After 324 days of waiting, the Soviets were convinced that the Americans and the British were more than equal to the task. While the total supplies did not immediately attain the 4000-ton target, Allied planes were eventually to fly in as much as 13,000 tons daily. Planes landing at three-minute intervals flew in 60 percent more than the 8000 tons that had previously been sent each day by ground transport. By the spring of 1949, West Berliners were eating more than at the beginning of the blockade—and considerably more than the East Berliners! Faced with this colossal Allied achievement, the Soviets called off the blockade in May.

America's determination to hold Europe and not to allow further Soviet expansion had been demonstrated. The West Germans clearly saw that they could count on America to protect them. Just as NATO had been the prerequisite for Europe's economic recovery, the Berlin airlift was the final American act that led to Germany's resurgence. America had laid the basis for Germany's economic recovery through Marshall Plan funds and the currency reforms; and now, it had given Germany the sense of military security without which its economic reconstruction could not have been completed.

EUROPEAN INTEGRATION

Ironically, it was the fear of Germany's rising strength that was now, in turn, to stimulate further efforts toward European integration. The specter of a fully revived Germany struck fear into most of Germany's neighbors. The French, with their memories of 1870, 1914, and 1940, were particularly alarmed. Germany's recovery—stimulated by America's response to the cold war—thus posed a serious problem for Germany's partners: How could they hold Germany, potentially the strongest nation in Europe outside of the Soviet Union, in check? Ever since Germany's unification in the late nineteenth century, France had attempted to deal with the inherently greater strength of its aggressive and militaristic neighbor by forming alliances that could balance Germany's power. Since Britain had usually preferred to retain a free hand, and since its interests were also at times opposed to those of France, the French had relied primarily upon Continental allies. Before World War I, they discovered such an ally in Russia, and between the two wars they found partners in Poland, Czechoslovakia, Romania, and Yugoslavia. None of these alliances had saved France, however; in both wars, British power and especially American power had been the decisive factors in defeating Germany (aided by Soviet power, of course, in World War II). But once saved, the French again responded in terms of their traditional reflex—despite the extension of Soviet power into the heart of Europe. For France, Germany was still the enemy, and in December 1944, the French signed a Treaty of Mutual Assistance with the Soviets, thus making an alliance which they considered necessary for their security. Soviet hostility soon disillusioned the French and deprived the treaty of any meaning, however, and in fact made it necessary to add Germany's power to that of the West.

The failure of the traditional balance-of-power technique, by which an inferior power had always sought to balance a stronger nation, led France to seek a new way of exerting some control over Germany's growing power. French statesmen found an imaginative means in European integration. It was through the creation of a supranational community, to which Germany could transfer certain sovereign rights, that German power could be controlled. Only in this manner could German strength be prevented from again causing harm to all of Europe, and at the same time be employed instead for Europe's welfare and security.

France made its first move in this direction of a united Europe in May 1950, when Foreign Minister Robert Schuman proposed the plan that has since borne his name: a European Coal and Steel Community (ECSC) composed of "Little Europe" (France, Germany, Italy, and the Benelux countries of Belgium, the Netherlands, and Luxembourg). The Schuman Plan was to interweave German and French heavy industry to such an extent that it would become impossible ever to separate them again. Germany would never again be able to use its coal and steel industries for nationalistic and militaristic purposes. The political and military power of the Ruhr, for purely German purposes, was to be destroyed for all time. War between Germany and France would become not only unthinkable but impossible under these circumstances.

But the new French technique of restraining Germany did not consist merely of fusing Germany's superior strength with France's own lesser strength and thereby subjecting Germany's power to a certain degree of French control. "Europeanization" was also a means for France to achieve a balance with Germany. The combination of the French and German coal and steel industries would strengthen French heavy industry and create a Franco-German equilibrium with ECSC. Economic integration would thus allow France to overcome its inferior industrial strength. One of the main reasons for France's industrial lag had been its lack of energy sources. It possessed Europe's largest iron ore deposits, in Lorraine—resources which during Germany's annexation of Alsace-Lorraine from 1871 to 1918 had added in considerable measure to making Germany the second greatest industrial power in the world before 1914. But even when it had regained Alsace-Lorraine after World War I, France still lacked the coal to heat the furnaces. Europe's largest coal deposits lay in the Ruhr, and to a lesser extent in the Saar—that is, in Germany.

The Schuman Plan now, in effect, held out a bargain to West Germany. France was to receive coal from Germany at the same price paid by German manufacturers—and not at the previously much higher prices that made French products more expensive than German ones. In return, France was to abandon its opposition to raising German production, and prevail upon Britain and the United States to lift *all* controls from Germany's heavy industry— which would mean that Germany could once more compete on the international market. Even more important for Germany, entry into ECSC would be the first step toward regaining equal status with its former Western enemies, recovering its sovereignty, and strengthening its ties with the Western powers so that they would eventually include Germany in NATO. Thus, the Schuman Plan had both an economic and a political appeal for the Germans as well as the French.

The French plan was not, however, devised only to control Germany's resurgent power or to give France a strength equal to that of Germany. It had a third and more ambitious goal in mind: a united Europe under French leadership. For only by creating Little Europe could France again play a major role in world affairs. France alone was too weak to pursue an active part in a world dominated by two superpowers. Even in the Western coalition, the most influential European nation was Britain, not France; and, with Germany's recovery, it was very likely that Bonn's voice and opinions would also outweigh those of Paris in Washington. By itself, France would remain dependent upon its American protector, powerless to affect major Western policy decisions. A united Europe, with Franco-German unity at its core, was therefore France's alternative to remaining subservient to the United States and without influence either in NATO or on the world stage. Only through a united Europe could France gain an equal voice with what Charles de Gaulle was later to call the "Anglo-Saxons" in NATO, and possibly even exert independent pressure upon the Soviet Union.

These, then, were the benefits the French expected to gain from the Schuman Plan, and their approach was a highly realistic one. For they clearly saw that the nucleus of a united Europe would have to be a Franco-German union. The antagonism between these two states, born of their traditional enmity, would first have to be healed. Moreover, the French scheme did more than just evoke the dream of a united Europe, hoping that its vision would so fire people's imagination that they would suddenly discard their narrow nationalistic loyalties for a wider European allegiance. Europe could not be created by sentiment alone. The French determined to erect the new Europe upon a solid foundation, building from the bottom upward. Europe, they knew, could be forged only by tying together the interests of politically powerful and economically important groups in the various nations *across* national boundaries. For instance, the removal of all trade barriers in the coal and steel sector of the economy would encourage the modernization of mines and plants, as well as the elimination of those mines and plants that continued to operate inefficiently. And once the efficient producers had adjusted to the wider market and witnessed its opportunities, they would want to remove national barriers in other areas. Further, as production increased, Europe's standard of living would rise, and as French and Italian workers received more of what they believed to be their share, labor would see that its goal of a welfare state could be achieved only at the European level.

The French showed great political astuteness in their selection of heavy industry as the first to be integrated. Coal and steel form the basis of the entire industrial structure—they represent a sector that cannot possibly be separated from the overall economy. Since the separation created by ECSC was to be an artificial one to begin with, this would create a "spillover" effect. Or to put it another way: This would exert pressure on the unintegrated sectors of the economy; and as the benefits of the pooling of heavy industry became clearly observable, these sectors would follow suit. The Coal and Steel Community was thus seen as the first stage of an attempt to create a wider market in one particular area of the economy; and it was expected that this approach would be gradually extended to other areas of the economy, such as agriculture, transportation, and electricity, eventually leading to the creation of a "united states" of Europe with a huge market and a mass-production system. In brief, this functional approach stressed supranational cooperation and institutions within a limited functional sphere and the creation of common interests within that particular area of activity before extending it to other fields.

The ECSC institutions, then, were the embryo of a united Europe. They were soon to be applied to an area that their initial planners had not expected to include—the military forces of the different nationalities. The French originated this idea, too. American insistence on German rearmament made it unavoidable. To the French, the rearmament of their old enemy was both distasteful and dangerous. But France was faced with the inevitable, since German rearmament was made necessary primarily by France's own inability to supply more troops itself. Yet the French remained determined that the world would never see another *German* army, *German* general staff, *German* war ministry, or *German* ministry of armaments. The solution they proposed was the formation of a European Defense Community (EDC). Just as the French had conceived of ECSC as a means for controlling Germany's growing economic strength and harnessing it to Europe's welfare, so they now proposed a European army, composed of army corps in which no more than two divisions could be of one nationality, as an instrument for checking Germany's rising military power and using it for Europe's defense. The EDC Treaty was signed in May 1952. NATO, of course, remained the supreme command. EDC and NATO were, however, formally linked. Since all EDC members except Germany were members of NATO, this link ensured that Germany was obligated to come to NATO's defense and vice versa.

For Germany, entry into EDC was another step toward regaining full equality with the other Western powers and asserting its political prestige. Most important, in return for providing EDC with 500,000 men organized into twelve divisions, Germany would recover its sovereignty, with certain limitations. The Allies would reserve their authority to take the necessary measures to protect the security of their forces in Germany (not only against external aggression, but also against possible attempts by the extreme left or right to subvert West Germany from within), to continue governing Berlin, and—in order to prevent any Soviet-German deal—to preserve their exclusive right to negotiate with the Soviet Union on the question of German reunification. The kind of Germany they would seek—the United States, Britain, and France declared—would be "a unified Germany enjoying a liberal-democratic constitution, like that of the Federal Republic, and integrated within the European community."

The likelihood of attaining this objective was very small indeed. Western proposals to unite Germany constantly included terms that the Soviet Union could not possibly accept. These terms included reunification via free elections in both halves of Germany and insistence upon allowing the government of this reunified Germany freedom to conduct its own foreign policy. The former proposal would have meant the end of the Soviet-imposed Communist regime in East Germany; and the latter would have allied a unified Germany, probably headed by the pro-Western government of Konrad Adenauer, with the West. NATO would thus be extended to the Polish frontier and the Eastern satellite belt. The Soviets were hardly likely to accept such a restriction of their sphere of influence or permit willingly such an advance of Western power.

Allied terms thus ensured a continuation of a divided Germany—which was precisely what they wanted. France did not want to integrate with a united Germany—only with a split Germany. A reunited Germany would tend to dominate Little Europe, for it would certainly be more powerful than France or Italy. These nations were therefore opposed to Germany's reunification; and they, together with the United States, paid verbal allegiance to this goal only to keep the West German government of Chancellor Adenauer in power. For the German people, reunification was of course a vital concern, and Adenauer's claim was that through the alliance with the United States, Britain, and France, West Germany and the Western powers would be placed in such a strong position that one day they could negotiate the Soviet Union's exit from East Germany. Yet it must also be noted that the Federal Republic between the Elbe and the Rhine is a Germany without Prussia, that South Germany has long been hostile to Protestant Prussia, and the Rhineland has been much influenced by Western (especially French) democratic thought. A reunified Germany would undoubtedly have stimulated a movement to resurrect Prussia. It might therefore be said that, if Germany had to be divided, the present division, which cuts Prussia off from the Western part of Germany, could not have been more aptly drawn. It is this latter half that was integrated with the West in defense against the Soviet pressure from the East.

THE SOVIET SHIFT TO ASIA

It seems a cruel twist of fate that this very success of American foreign policy in Europe should have brought about a shift in the focus of Soviet pressure from Europe to Asia—a shift that in June 1950, led to the outbreak of the Korean War. The Truman Doctrine had prevented a Soviet breakthrough into Southeast Europe and the Middle East and established Western Europe's flank in the eastern Mediterranean. The Marshall Plan had set Europe on the path to economic recovery and health. NATO had guaranteed Europe its security. The lessons of two world wars had been absorbed, and the NATO commitment was the proof of this.

The United States had transformed a position of great weakness and vulnerability into one of relative strength. It had drawn a clear line between the American and Soviet spheres of influence and had demonstrated, in both Greece and Berlin, that it was in Europe to stay. (The Greek crisis had passed when Yugoslavia was ejected from the Soviet bloc in 1948; the Yugoslavs no longer provided aid to the Greek guerrillas.) What all this meant was that Europe was no longer a profitable field for guerrilla warfare, *coups d'état*, or subversive attempts.

Opportunities for immediate expansion had disappeared. To cross the line drawn by the United States was to risk total war, and this risk was hardly one the Soviet Union was willing to assume during a period in which the United States held atomic superiority. The Soviet leaders, as George Kennan had said, did not believe in pursuing an "adventuristic" policy that gambled with the very existence of the Soviet state.

So they turned their attention to the Far East. Here was a much more attractive field for political and military exploitation. Most countries in this area had only recently emerged from Western colonialism, and their nationalistic and anti-Western feelings were very strong. Nationalist China's collapse and the establishment of a Communist government on the mainland in late 1949 had even further weakened the Western position in Asia, for it had gravely shifted the balance of power in the Far East against the United States. The United

States no longer confronted only the Soviet Union; it was now faced with the challenge of the combined power of the Sino-Soviet bloc. Moreover, whereas pressure in Europe united the Western powers, pressure in Asia divided them, because they were fundamentally split over the character and nature of the new Chinese regime. And finally, no expansionist move in the Far East would entail the risk of total war. In the American pattern of defense, Europe held strategic priority; Asia was of secondary interest. Europe was so vital to American defense that any Soviet move in Western Europe entailed the risk of an all-out clash with the United States; no single area in Asia was so immediately vital to American security that it was worth the cost of total war. The recovery of Europe and China's collapse, then, created a vacuum in the East and turned Soviet pressure toward Asia. It was here that the dramatic clashes of the cold war were to occur during the next four years. And it was these clashes that were to lead to a reaction within the United States itself against American foreign policy.

Chapter 4

CONTAINMENT
IN THE FAR EAST

THE FALL OF NATIONALIST CHINA

During World War II, the United States had a twofold purpose in the Pacific: to defeat Japan and to create a powerful and friendly China in its place. It was hoped that a strong and democratic China would play a leading role in protecting the postwar peace in the Far East. The United States took several actions to confer upon China the status of a Great Power. It renounced its extraterritorial rights in China, repealed the Chinese exclusion laws, established an annual Chinese immigration quota, and made it possible for legally admitted Chinese to become American citizens. At Cairo in 1943, together with Great Britain, the United States promised to return "all the territories Japan had stolen from the Chinese, such as Manchuria, Formosa, and the Pescadores." It also awarded to China one of the five permanent seats on the United Nations Security Council; China was thus granted equal status with the Soviet Union, Great Britain, France and the United States.

The belief of American statesmen that the mere pronouncement of China as a Great Power could actually convert it into one was typically American: One need only believe strongly enough in the desirability of an event for it to happen. Perhaps American policymakers also hoped that if China were admitted into the Great Power club, it would behave like one. But American faith without Chinese works was insufficient to accomplish the task. It would have taken a miracle to do that; and while statesmen at times delude themselves into thinking that they can perform miracles, such things happen only in storybooks.

The first obstacle to creating a strong China was the sharp division within the country. Quite apart from the Japanese occupation of large areas of the country during the war, the Chinese were deeply split among themselves. There was not one China; there were two—a Communist China and a Nationalist China. The Communists were not scattered throughout the whole population, as in Europe; already in control of large segments of northwest China, they extended their sphere during the war by infiltrating into north-central China. In this area, the Japanese held the cities and the major lines of communication, while the Communists organized the countryside. By 1945, they controlled 116 million people, one-fourth of China's entire population, within an area that constituted 15 percent of China's territory, exclusive of Manchuria (Heilonjiang). Communist China was, in short, a nation within a nation.

Thus, if the United States wanted to create a united China, it would have to end this internal split. The American aim was to achieve this objective by establishing a coalition government in which all parties would be represented. The desirability of such a government was not questioned. What possible harm could there be in uniting the Nationalists and the Communists? The United States and the Soviet Union were cooperating against the common enemy, and most leaders and officials of the American government looked forward to friendly postwar relations. If these two nations, each representing a totally different way of life, could overcome past differences and get along together, why should the two Chinese parties not be able to settle their conflict? There was also another and more immediate reason why the United States wished to end China's division as quickly as possible. A China torn apart by internal strife could not make an effective contribution to the winning of the war. Both the Nationalists and the Communists were concerned more with fighting each other than with fighting the Japanese. But the American attitude is that once war breaks out, the total effort must be directed toward the single goal of military victory; any diversion of strength—particularly for "extraneous" political purposes—is considered unjustifiable. The war had to be won in the quickest possible time and with the minimum number of casualties. This attitude, then, reinforced the American desire to establish a coalition government in China.

All efforts aimed at achieving this goal, both during the war and afterward, were, however, in vain. Neither the Nationalists nor the Communists trusted one another. Both sought a monopoly of power, and both were constantly aware of the important role their armies played in the struggle for power: The Nationalists recognized that they would have to deprive their enemy of his army in order to ensure their own survival; and the Communists were realists enough to know that they needed their army to defeat Jiang Gaishek (Chiang Kai-shek). At the end of the war, both parties—and particularly the Nationalists—believed that they had the capabilities to defeat their opponent; compromise was therefore unnecessary.

China was not, however, divided only between two irreconcilable parties. Its pro-American Nationalist government was losing popular support and disintegrating. Perhaps the Nationalists were merely the victims of fate. Except for the two years from 1929 to 1931, the government was constantly engaged in fighting for its very survival—against the Japanese (who attacked Manchuria in 1931, Shanghai in 1932, and China itself in 1937), as well as the Communists. Faced with both external and internal danger, Jiang had neither the time nor the resources to concern himself with formulating and implementing the political, social, and economic reforms China needed. His principal concern was military: to stem the Japanese advance and maintain himself in power. The problem of modernizing China—above all, of meeting peasant aspirations— was strictly a subsidiary one. Moreover, Japanese successes during the war changed the basis of Jiang's support and thereby rendered any agrarian reform impossible. By 1939, the Japanese had occupied the entire coastal area of China and had driven the Nationalists inland. This meant that Jiang's Kuomintang Party, which controlled the government, had lost the main pillar of its support, the progressive commercial and financial interests in the coastal cities. Instead, it was forced to rely upon the conservative landlord class.

No government ever likes to commit suicide, and the Nationalist government proved no exception. A government whose principal social and economic support came from the landlords was unlikely to carry out any land reforms. Probably a majority of peasants were independent landowners, but many of China's peasants were tenants. Both groups were, at any rate, profoundly dissatisfied. Those who rented their land had to pay excessive sums; after the war, these sometimes amounted to 50 to 90 percent of the peasant's crops. Those who owned their own land were handicapped by the small size of their holding and the lack of capital. The government's taxation policies further impoverished the peasant, who bore the main burden of the taxes. Since the peasant's crops were visible and easily appraisable, corrupt officials usually took more of the crops than the peasant could afford to spare. The result was that the peasant lived in a constant state of impoverishment and indebtedness. In order to survive, he had to seek funds from a moneylender, usually the local landlord, who charged him an extremely high rate of interest, often from 20 to 30 percent. Consequently, the peasant got himself deeper and deeper into debt.

The fact that the peasants constituted four-fifths of China's population also meant that they had to provide most of the conscripts for the Nationalist army. But the able-bodied and eligible sons of the rich avoided military service; there were always enough corrupt officials who could be bribed. In the same way, the rich tended to avoid paying taxes. Jiang, in short, seemed to be doing his best to earn the peasants' hatred.

After the war, the Nationalists even managed to alienate the business circles that had formerly supported them. As the Nationalists returned to the coastal cities, they took over all Japanese-owned industries and ran them as state enterprises. This incensed the business community. Some of the Japanese property had formerly belonged to the Chinese, but the government simply neglected to return such property to its owners. Even worse was the fact that private enterprise now found itself faced with the powerful competition of state industries, which were controlled by relatives and close friends of Jiang. Naturally, the American aid funds with which the government supported its enterprises provided great profits for these people. As the American commander in China during the war, General Albert C. Wedemeyer, observed in 1947 upon his return on a fact-finding mission for the American government: "Certain rich families, some of whom have relatives in high positions of the Government, have been greatly increasing their fortunes. Nepotism is rife . . . sons, nephews, and brothers of government officials have been put into positions within the government-sponsored firms or in private firms to enable them to make huge profits at the expense of their government and their people."

The Nationalist position deteriorated even further because of China's unchecked inflation. The most devastating impact of this hyperinflation was upon government officials at the lower level; it provided them with a massive incentive for corruption. Their salaries were wholly inadequate, and they had to find means of supplementing their meager incomes. Honesty in these circumstances simply did not pay. Corruption became rife throughout the government.

As Jiang's government lost popularity, it began to resort increasingly to force to hold its position. The resulting police and military measures only further alienated the people. Wedemeyer found this situation: "Secret police operate widely, very much as they do in Russia and as they did in Germany. People disappear. . . . No trials and no sentences. . . . Everyone lives with a feeling of fear and loses confidence in the government." This was particularly true of the intellectuals, who, together with the peasantry, have been the traditional supporters of China's governments. Professors were dismissed, even arrested, when they began to criticize the government for its policies. Students similarly inclined were also thrown into jail.

The behavior of the army also spread hatred of the government. The Manchurian episode was typical. In Manchuria, according to Wedemeyer,

the Central Government armies were [at the end of the war with Japan] welcomed enthusiastically by the people as deliverers from Japanese oppression. Today, after several months of experience with the Central Government armies, the people experience a feeling of hatred and distrust because the officers and enlisted men were arrogant and rude. Also, they stole and looted freely; their general attitude was that of conquerors instead of liberators.

To sum up the position of the Nationalists: The government had alienated important segments of the politically articulate minority, especially the businessmen and intellectuals. The more inarticulate and passive peasants were tired of the constant fighting, the high rents and taxes. All three groups had either lost confidence in the ability of the government to take care of the problems of postwar China or felt that the government was not interested in their welfare. But only minorities in each group turned to the Communists. The majority simply disengaged themselves from the Nationalists and became indifferent to the outcome of the civil war. They did not rise up against the government in a "popular revolution." If the Communists won the civil war—and the military conflict would play the decisive role in determining this issue—they did so because most Chinese were willing to give the Communists the benefit of the doubt and allow them to demonstrate that they could give China a more effective government.

One reason for this lack of popular hostility and suspicion toward the Communists was, of course, the reverse side of the widespread anti-Nationalist sentiment. But another was the favorable picture the Communists presented of themselves to the Chinese population. The policies they pursued in the areas under their control were responsible for this. They did not destroy the traditional tenure system and expropriate or eliminate the landlords and moneylenders. They only reduced the rents to a fixed maximum and lowered the interest rates that could be charged on borrowed money. They permitted private enterprise and allowed all factions to participate in local government. Though they did assure Communist control by retaining the power to approve all candidates, their activities nevertheless seemed to support their claim that they stood for democracy, freedom, and individual liberty. Certainly, their economic and political practices demonstrated little Marxist bias. They appeared, instead, in the guise of genuine democrats; and their pose as agrarian reformers was widely accepted—precisely because, as an agrarian-based party, they actually did act as agrarian reformers.

If the Communists acted as if their only wish was to reform China along democratic and capitalistic lines, this was, of course, a tactical device. But the point remains that it was effective and achieved its purposes: It attracted minority support among the various strata of China's population disaffected by Nationalist policies, and it gained extensive acquiescence among the rest of the population. Jiang had alienated most of his popular support. The Communists, by cleverly hiding their real intentions, exploited this feeling of neutrality. For their purposes, a large neutral public was almost as beneficial as positive majority support; the only thing that really mattered was that this support had been withdrawn from Jiang.

The Communist position for the final military struggle was further strengthened when, near the end of the Pacific war, the Soviet army marched into Manchuria. Once established, the Soviets did two things that badly hurt China. First, they dismantled Manchuria's industry and transported the machinery back to the Soviet Union to help restore their own badly destroyed industry; as a result, Manchuria, China's industrial heartland, was unable to contribute to the country's economic recovery. Second, the Soviets allowed the Chinese Communists to infiltrate the countryside and handed them large stocks of Japanese arms and ammunition. Conversely, the Soviets delayed the return of Nationalist troops, who had to launch a major offensive to establish their control over Manchuria. The government forces did capture the cities, but the Communists remained in control of the countryside. The Soviet invasion of Manchuria thus was a serious blow to the Nationalists.

The blame for these events has often been attributed to President Franklin D. Roosevelt and the Yalta "betrayal," which granted the Soviet Union, among other things, a restoration of the rights Russia had held in Manchuria before its defeat by Japan in 1904–1905; the lease of Port Arthur as a Soviet naval base; the internationalization of the commercial port Dairen, which, unlike the Soviet Union's own Siberian port of Vladivostok, was not icebound part of the year; and the joint Sino-Soviet operation of the Chinese-Eastern and South Manchurian Railroads, which served these three cities. To take this charge seriously, though, one has to deny certain clear facts of wartime military strategy: namely, that American military men were unsure that the atomic bomb would be a success; that they believed an invasion of Japan would be necessary to bring about Japan's surrender; that they expected to suffer at least 1 million casualties and feared even more if the Japanese reinforced the home-island garrison with troops from Manchuria and northern China; and that they therefore wanted the Red Army to tackle these mainland forces before their invasion. The American government was willing to pay the Soviets the price they demanded if this would help save the lives of American soldiers, and this willingness was further increased by its suspicion that the Soviets planned to restore their tsarist position in Manchuria by declaring war on Japan at the moment when the United States seemed on the verge of victory. The Soviet takeover would then be a practically bloodless operation, with a minimal contribution to Japan's defeat. American officials wanted the Soviet Union to pay some kind of price, at least, for what it could actually take for nothing.

Finally, they wanted to secure a promise from the Soviets that they would sign a treaty of alliance and friendship with the Nationalist government. The purpose of this treaty was to secure the Soviet Union's support for Jiang Gaishek and to isolate his Communist opponents; this would enable Jiang to consolidate his grip on China and perhaps allow him to defeat his domestic enemy. The Soviets did, in fact, sign such a treaty, but then proceeded to violate it by aiding their Chinese comrades. However, Joseph Stalin apparently did not believe that this help strengthened the Chinese Communists sufficiently to defeat the Nationalists. He is reported to have counseled Mao Zedong (Mao Tse-tung) to join Jiang in a coalition government and accept Jiang's supremacy; in this respect, Stalin's policy seemed to have been the same as Harry Truman's. Mao is said to have nodded his assent to Stalin's advice and then disregarded it; he was more confident than Stalin of a final victory.

Throughout 1946 and 1947, the Communists limited their operations largely to raiding supply depots and communication lines, ambushing Nationalist forces, engaging in skirmishes, and attacking isolated garrisons. These local tactical successes heightened the Communist forces' confidence and morale just as they added to their opponents' demoralization. By 1948, the Communists had so increased the strength of their forces and firepower that they no longer had to rely solely upon hit-and-run tactics; they now sought out the Nationalist forces in order completely to annihilate them by concentrating superior masses of troops against them and attacking without respite. Throughout the whole campaign, the Communists kept the initiative; it was they who constantly chose the time and place of attack. By February 1, 1949, they controlled Manchuria.

Nationalist strength had by then declined to 1.5 million men, including 500,000 service troops. Up until mid-September 1948, the Nationalists had been able to replace their combat losses and thereby maintain their army at a strength of 2.7 million men. In other words, in only four and a half months, the Nationalists had lost 45 percent of their troops. Meanwhile, Communist strength had risen to 1.6 million regular troops—partly as the result of defections from the Nationalist armies. Eighty percent of the American equipment furnished to the government forces during and after the war had been lost, with an estimated 75 percent of it falling into the Communists' hands. General David Barr, the head of the American military mission in China, summed up the situation succinctly: "No battle has been lost since my arrival due to lack of ammunition or equipment. Their [the Nationalists'] military debacle, in my opinion, can all be attributed to the world's worst leadership and many other morale-destroying factors that led to a complete loss of the will to fight." Nowhere was this more clearly demonstrated than in Jiang's failure, after his loss of northern China, even to attempt a defense of south China by making a stand along the Yangtze River. Jiang thereby forfeited the mainland, and he withdrew to Taiwan (in those days also often called Formosa), an island lying 100 miles off the mainland coast. In the fall of 1949, Mao Zedong proclaimed the People's Republic of China.

One question about Nationalist China's defeat remains: Could the United States have prevented it? The answer is "probably"—*if* American officers had taken over the command of the Nationalist armies; *if* the United States had been willing to commit large-scale land, air, and sea forces to fight in China; and *if* the United States had been willing to commit even greater financial aid than the approximately $2 billion it had already given in grants and credits since V-J Day. But these conditions could not have been met. America's helter-skelter demobilization left it with insufficient forces either for supplying the officers for the direction of the Nationalist forces or for intervention in China. The United States had only one and one-third divisions at home. Nor were the American people in any mood to rearm in 1947–1948, particularly to fight a war in China.

The problem of extending further economic aid to Jiang was equally vexing. His corrupt, inefficient, and reactionary government did not provide a politically effective instrument through which to carry out the social and economic reforms China needed. Aiding Jiang seemed to be "pouring money down the drain." In contrast, U.S. economic aid to Europe, which the administration considered the area most vital to American security, had a good chance of achieving its objective—the political and economic recovery for Britain and the Continent. It would probably have been unwise in these circumstances to divert a very large slice of the government's not unlimited funds to attempt to restore a government that had lost the confidence of its own people. The power of the United States was, after all, not infinite; it would have to be applied selectively. Hence, those areas of vital interest in which its use would be most effective were to be the prime focus. As Secretary of State Dean Acheson stated it: "Nothing that this country did or could have done within the reasonable limits of its capabilities could have changed that result; nothing that was left undone by this country has contributed to it. It was the product of internal Chinese forces, forces which this country tried to influence but could not. A decision was arrived at within China, if only a decision by default."

REEVALUATION OF AMERICAN FAR EASTERN POLICY

Despite Jiang's debacle and the disintegration of the Far Eastern balance of power, the U.S. government took an optimistic view of developments. Shortly after the Nationalist collapse, Secretary Acheson expressed his belief that despite the common ideological points of view of the Chinese and Soviet regimes, they would eventually clash with one another. Acheson predicted that Russia's appetite for a sphere of influence in Manchuria and northern China would alienate Chinese nationalism. The implications of this point of view are clear. The first is that if the Chinese Communists were genuinely concerned with the preservation of China's national interest, they would resist Soviet penetration. Mao Zedong might, therefore, be a potential Tito. On the other hand, if Mao proved himself to be subservient to the Soviet Union, he would lose the support of the Chinese people. Since he would have shown that he served not the interests of China but those of another power, his regime would be identified with foreign rule. Given time, Acheson declared, the Chinese people would throw off this "foreign yoke." Thus, whichever of these two developments occurred, the United States could only gain from the antithesis between Communism and Chinese nationalism.

This analysis of Sino-Soviet relations indicated that the United States must first disentangle itself from Jiang Gaishek. Until this disassociation had been completed, the United States would remain identified with the government rejected by the Chinese people. This could only foster the growth of anti-American sentiment in China. It was precisely this that had to be avoided, for the attention of the Chinese people should not be diverted from the Soviet Union's actions. Under no circumstances, Acheson emphasized, must America "seize the unenviable position which the Russians have carved out for themselves. We must not undertake to deflect from the Russians to ourselves the righteous anger, and the wrath, and the hatred of the Chinese people which must develop." Only by disengaging itself from Jiang Gaishek could the United States exploit the alleged clash of interests between China and the Soviet Union.

The first step taken by the Truman administration to implement this policy was the release of a White Paper which argued that the Nationalists had lost control of the mainland despite adequate American economic and military aid. The clear implication was that Jiang was no longer worthy of American support; hence, American recognition of Jiang's government as the official government of China should be withdrawn. Conversely, it was suggested that the Communists should be recognized as the official government of China, both as a matter of fact and as a gesture of friendship. A second act was an announcement that American forces would not be used to defend Taiwan, and that the administration would no longer provide the Nationalists with military aid or advice: "The United States Government will not pursue a course which will lead to involvement in the civil conflict in China." This opened the way for the Chinese Communists to take Taiwan—an event that was expected before the end of 1950. The Communist government would then be the only claimant to represent China, and the United States could extend it recognition. Jiang, through whom containment had been impossible because he had been not a container but a sieve, would have been eliminated; containment of the Soviet Union could then be implemented through "Mao Tse-tito." But before this could happen, war had broken out in another area in the Far East—Korea.

LIMITED WAR IN KOREA AND THE TRUMAN-MACARTHUR CONFLICT

Korea had been a divided nation since 1945. Soviet forces had entered Korea two days after Japan surrendered. The nearest American troops at the time were in Okinawa, 600 miles away, and in the Philippines, 1500 to 2000 miles away. Consequently, the two powers decided to divide the country temporarily at the thirty-eighth parallel; the Soviets would disarm the Japanese above the parallel, the United States below. With the beginning of the cold war, this division became permanent. All American attempts to negotiate an end to the division and establish a democratic and united Korea failed.

As a result, the United States took the problem to the United Nations in late 1947 and called upon that organization to sponsor a free election throughout all of Korea. The General Assembly thereupon established a temporary commission in Korea and charged it with the responsibility of holding and supervising such an election. The Soviets, however, refused to grant the commission access to North Korea, and the election was thus limited to South Korea. Afterward, the United States recognized South Korea as the official republic and the government of Syngman Rhee as its legitimate representative. The American government also extended to Rhee economic, technical, and military aid to bolster his non-Communist government and help Korea establish a democratic society.

Thus, while South Korea was not an ally of the United States, there could be little doubt that the young republic was America's protégé.

It was this country that the North Korean Communists attacked in late June 1950. The Communist aggression took the American government by complete surprise. American policymakers had believed that the Soviet leaders, like themselves, thought only in terms of all-out war. It was precisely this single-minded American preoccupation with total war that had accounted for Korea's being left outside the American Pacific defense perimeter, which ran from the Aleutians to Japan, through the Ryukyus (Okinawa) to the Philippines. This made Korea militarily dispensable within the pattern of American security, for in a global war its fate would be decided in other theaters of war. A Soviet occupation of Korea would not raise Korea's strategic significance, since the peninsula could be neutralized by American air and sea power. American troops had therefore been withdrawn from Korea, because in a major war they would be vulnerable to Soviet land power and would probably be trapped. The resulting absence of pledged American military support to resist North Korean aggression rendered South Korea highly vulnerable; indeed, it left South Korea as an attractive vacuum inviting Communist expansion. On June 25, the North Korean army struck.

Overnight, the survival of South Korea became identified with the survival of the United States itself. For North Korea's aggression, which in Washington's opinion could hardly have been launched without Soviet encouragement and support, altered the basis upon which Korea's strategic significance had been calculated. Korea's value could no longer be assessed in terms of its relative importance during a total war. The cold war focused attention upon the wide political and military implications of a Communist occupation of South Korea and upon the threat such an occupation would pose for the entire containment policy. If the principal purpose of containment was to prevent further Soviet expansion, American inaction in the face of Soviet aggression could only encourage further aggressive acts in the future. The appetites of dictators were believed to be insatiable. And if containment was possible only through an alignment of the United States' power with that of allies, then failure to respond to South Korea's pleas for help must result in the disintegration of the alliance system and the isolation of the United States. If the United States merely stood by while South Korea fell, it would demonstrate to the world that it was either afraid of Soviet power or unconcerned with the safety of its friends or allies. American guarantees to help preserve their national integrity and political independence would thereafter be regarded as valueless; and this would leave nations whose security depended upon U.S. willingness to live up to its commitments with no alternative but to turn to neutralism for protection—a state in which they would be subject to increasing Soviet pressure and possibly eventual domination.

This reasoning applied particularly to Japan. With the demise of Nationalist China and the disintegration of the Far Eastern balance of power, the United

States was about to turn Japan into an ally and rearm it in an effort to recreate some semblance of strength in the Pacific. The same rationale applied equally to the NATO countries in Europe. If NATO collapsed, the balance of power would shift drastically in favor of the Soviet Union. In these circumstances, the consequences of American inaction would be extremely grave. In fact, the United States had no choice in a bipolar world but to oppose force with force— if it wished to prevent an upset of the global balance of power and its own strategic isolation.

Nevertheless, the limited Soviet aggression did not fit American strategic doctrine, based on a one-sided concentration upon air-atomic striking power. The Soviets had cleverly faced the United States with the dilemma of either risking a total war for a limited objective or taking no action at all and thus surrendering South Korea. American policy was prepared to deal only with an all-out Soviet surprise attack upon the United States or Western Europe; such an attack would be met by the power of the Strategic Air Command. But American strategy was completely unprepared to deal with the kind of less than total challenge that the Soviets had now posed in Asia. The North Korean aggression, in effect, meant that massive retaliation outside of Europe was not an effective policy. For the deterrent effect of U.S. retaliatory power depended upon whether an enemy believed that the country would actually "unleash" this power if he committed aggression. The limited attack in Korea demonstrated that the Soviet leaders were not deterred by the policy of massive retaliation, despite America's far greater atomic stockpile and ability to deliver it. They did not believe that the United States would risk all-out war to save Korea. For the Korean type of challenge could be met only by local response and primarily through the commitment of American ground forces. Containment depended not just upon the capacity to deter total war with strategic air power; it required, in addition, an army to meet precisely this kind of limited incursion.

But it was the army forces that the administration had been cutting since the end of World War II. General George C. Marshall recalled in 1951 that the army had been so small in the years preceding the Korean War that there had been only one and one-third divisions in the United States. The Chiefs of Staff had had so few troops at their command that they had even been worried about obtaining enough men to guard airstrips at Fairbanks, Alaska. According to Marshall, "We had literally almost no military forces outside of our Navy and outside of an effective but not too large Air Force, except the occupation garrisons, and . . . even in Japan they were only at about 60 percent strength."

Yet, if the United States were to escape the dilemma of total war or surrender, the Japanese-occupation divisions—undermanned and undertrained but luckily near the scene of battle—had to be committed. For two days, on June 27 and 28, the United States tried to stem the North Korean advance with air and sea forces alone. But on June 29, General Douglas MacArthur, the commander-in-chief in the Far East, reported that Korea would be lost unless ground forces were employed to halt the enemy army. These forces were then sent in under the aegis of the United Nations. This was done for two reasons. First, by virtue of the free election it had sponsored in South Korea, the United Nations had been intimately concerned with the birth of the young state. Second, one of the aims of American foreign policy was to associate its cold war policies with the symbolic, humanitarian values of the United Nations. Though it is traditional for nations to attempt to justify their policies in such a manner, the United States has shown a marked propensity for doing so. American depreciation of power and reluctance to recognize it as a factor in human affairs makes it psychologically necessary to rationalize actions in the international arena in terms of ideological objectives and universal moral principles. American power must be "righteous" power used not for purposes of power politics and selfish national advantage but for the peace and welfare of all mankind. Inherent in this public self-image of the United States as a noble and unselfish crusader on behalf of moral principles was an extreme danger, however— namely, that if the enemy were not properly punished through total defeat, the reaction to the war would be one of frustration and disillusionment, which could only jeopardize the containment policy itself.

This was precisely what was to happen, although, after initial setbacks, the war went well for a while. In a daring operation on September 15, General MacArthur, now U.N. supreme commander, landed an army at the west coast port of Inchon, 150 miles behind the North Korean lines. These forces then drove northward, thereby trapping more than half the enemy army. The rest of the shattered Communist army was in flight. On September 30, the U.N. forces reached the thirty-eighth parallel.

The question now confronting the United States was whether to cross the parallel. The war had been fought to restore South Korea; this implied a negotiated settlement on the parallel. This goal was now abandoned. The military situation favored the fulfillment of an American goal of several years' standing: the unification of the whole of Korea. The U.S. government therefore shifted its emphasis from containing the expansion of Soviet power to the forceful liberation of a Soviet satellite. Inchon, in short, transformed the whole character of the war—from a defensive action seeking only to reestablish the *status quo*, to an offensive one designed to effect a permanent change in the *status quo*.

The U.S. government believed that it was politically safe to attempt this. The administration did not believe that the Chinese Communist leaders would consider the U.N. advance a threat to their security, because they were Chinese first and Communists second. Mao and his colleagues were already thought to be so involved in their struggle with the Soviet Union over the detachment of northern China, Manchuria (Heilonjiang), and Sinkiang (Xinjiang) that their eyes were fixed on their own northern provinces rather than on North Korea. In short there was nothing to fear. The new objective of a militarily unified Korea was sanctioned by a U.N. resolution on October 7.

But American policymakers miscalculated. The Chinese did view the American march to their border as threatening, just as Washington had perceived the North Korean march southward toward Japan as threatening. So Peking (Beijing City) sent its armies into North Korea under the guise of "volunteers," and in late November it launched a major offensive that drove the U.N. forces back below the thirty-eighth parallel. Throughout December 1950, and early January 1951, there was no certainty that U.N. troops could hold the peninsula; but the tired, defeated, and outnumbered troops managed to rally and stem the Chinese offensives. By March, they had once more advanced to the thirty-eighth parallel. The administration was again faced with a decision: whether to seek a militarily unified Korea or to accept a divided Korea.

There was no doubt about what the American field commander wanted to do. MacArthur insisted that the political aim of the war was the establishment of a unified Korea. He maintained that failure to prosecute the military campaign with the vigor necessary to achieve this objective would constitute rank appeasement. Above all, MacArthur felt that the United States should take advantage of China's intervention to weaken it before it became too strong. He wished to "severely cripple and largely neutralize China's capability to wage aggressive war and thus save Asia from the engulfment otherwise facing it." The strategy with which MacArthur expected to accomplish these objectives consisted of a naval blockade of the Chinese coast; air bombardment of China's industrial complex, communication network, supply depots, and troop assembly points; reinforcement of his forces with Chinese Nationalist troops; and "diversionary action possibly leading to counter-invasion" by Jiang against the mainland.

The Truman administration, however, rejected MacArthur's proposals because they were considered too risky. It was feared that bombing China and inflicting a defeat upon the Soviet Union's principal ally would probably precipitate World War III. The Sino-Soviet Treaty of February 1950 bound the Soviet Union to come to the aid of China if the latter were attacked by Japan "or any other state which should unite with Japan" (an obvious reference to the United States). But even without this treaty, China was the Soviet Union's largest and most important ally. Soviet self-interest in the Far East and the necessity of maintaining Soviet prestige in the Communist sphere would make it difficult for the Soviet Union to ignore a direct attack upon the Chinese mainland.

But even if the Soviet Union remained a spectator, the United States could not extend the war. A "war of attrition" waged by Chinese manpower in Korea would "bleed us dry" and make it impossible to build a strong military defense in Europe. A large-scale diversion of American power to Asia would expose Europe to Soviet armies and might very well incite an attack at a moment of maximum American weakness on the Continent. The United States had to conserve its strength to check its principal enemy, the Soviet Union; the country could not afford to dissipate its power in a peripheral area against a secondary enemy. MacArthur's strategy, in the opinion of General Omar Bradley, chairman of the Joint Chiefs of Staff, would therefore involve the United States in the wrong war, at the wrong place, at the wrong time, and with the wrong enemy.

This view was shared by Britain and France. America's chief allies were naturally reluctant to see American power diverted to the Far East before Europe was secure against Soviet attack; and they had no desire to risk such an early outbreak of World War III for an area that was of minor strategic significance to them. Thus, if the United States decided to carry the war to China, it would have to act unilaterally. But the objective of balancing Soviet might and deterring a total war was predicated on NATO's unity and combined strength.

Finally, the Joint Chiefs of Staff rejected MacArthur's proposals because they were judged militarily ineffective. All of China's essential supplies came overland from the Soviet Union. It was therefore decided to concentrate U.S. air power upon the 200 miles of supply line in North Korea in order to interdict the Chinese logistical system. The employment of Nationalist troops was rejected because they had already demonstrated their ineffectiveness in China. Moreover, the Chinese people were hardly likely to welcome Jiang back.

Inherent in the administration's rejection of MacArthur's recommendations was the reversal of its position of October 7, that its objective was a militarily unified Korea, and a reassertion of its original attitude that the aim of the war was to restore the *status quo*. The Communists had attempted to erase the thirty-eighth parallel and incorporate South Korea into the Communist bloc; neither the North Koreans nor the Chinese Communists had succeeded in achieving this objective. The Communists had also hoped to destroy the Western alliance and isolate the United States; in this, too, they had failed. NATO had been preserved and greatly strengthened by its rearmament program and the stationing of four new American divisions in Europe. And the primary purpose of U.N. action in Korea, to put the Communists on notice that the Western powers would not tolerate Communist expansion by force, had been achieved. Thus, the wisest course seemed to be to attempt to end the war where it had begun.

However, MacArthur refused to accept this dismissal of his strategy and limitation of the war to the Korean peninsula. He continued to urge the president and the Joint Chiefs of Staff to lift the restrictions they had imposed upon him; and when they refused, he attempted to force their hand by taking his case into the public arena and appealing over their heads to the opposition party in Congress and to the American people themselves. This produced an intolerable situation. The president is responsible for the formulation of foreign policy; he is the nation's chief diplomat and commander-in-chief. No government can allow a field commander to challenge its policies, to appeal to the public and the opposition for a change in these policies, thus undermining its control over the military. The soldier is expected to obey his orders. He is judged not by the nature of the policy he executes—only by how well he executes it. If he cannot accept this policy he must resign; otherwise, he must be dismissed. In early

April, President Truman did precisely that. The resulting furor brought to the surface the public's disillusionment with containment.

THE REACTION TO CONTAINMENT

MacArthur's dismissal was met with a storm of disapproval throughout the United States. The president received a flood of vituperous telegrams and letters informing him in no uncertain terms that his decision had been a mistake. In his first public appearance after MacArthur's dismissal, when President Truman attended the first baseball game of the season to throw out the opening ball, he was booed. Several state legislatures condemned him for his "irresponsible and capricious action." Republicans in Congress announced their intention of initiating impeachment proceedings against him and Secretary Acheson. Both Truman and Acheson were burned in effigy in many communities throughout the land. In contrast, MacArthur was received everywhere not as a man who had openly attempted to undermine the cherished American principle of civilian supremacy over the military, but as a great returning hero. In each of the cities he visited—San Francisco, Washington, Chicago, Boston— millions turned out to cheer him. In New York City alone, an estimated 7.5 million people lined the streets to see him—twice the number that had witnessed General Dwight D. Eisenhower's triumphal return from Europe in 1945; 2850 tons of ticker tape, confetti, and streamers were showered upon MacArthur; New York looked as if it had been hit by a snowstorm in April.

This almost hysterical reception was primarily the result of the nation's frustration with the containment policy, which was psychologically and emotionally in contradiction with American values and experience in foreign affairs. Traditionally, the United States had abstained from involvement in foreign affairs. Attention had, instead, been focused on domestic development. The business of America had been America—not foreign countries. When foreign affairs had occasionally interrupted this preoccupation with domestic concerns, such matters had been quickly settled: If a Latin American state "misbehaved," a few thousand marines soon "corrected" the misdeeds of the offender; or if—as did happen twice in this century—Germany set out to conquer continental Europe, the United States harnessed all its resources, maximized its military strength, and crushed the enemy in the shortest possible time. Whatever the technique employed, the main point was that the conflict was settled quickly and completely. Only if the external crisis were solved immediately and totally could the American people return to their more important tasks—the internal development of their country and earning their living. In this context, foreign affairs were merely an annoying but temporary diversion.

Containment ran directly contrary to this experience. The cold war did not draw a clear-cut line between peace and war. It allowed the United States neither to abstain from foreign entanglement nor to harness its giant strength for one quick and all-out military effort to "punish" the enemy who had forced it to divert its attention from more pressing domestic matters. The administration's aim was not the destruction of the Soviet Union and its satellites, but only the creation of a balance of power to effect the "containment" of further Soviet attempts to expand. The objective of the government was not to erase the Soviet Union with a swift blow, but to accept the basic fact of coexistence. Truman and Acheson sought only to strengthen the United States and its allies in order to improve the terms of coexistence and the possibility of survival, not to end the Soviet threat once and for all.

The frustrations of such a continued defensive and negative policy, which left the initiative to the Soviet Union, were bad enough; failures made it intolerable. This was especially the case with China. Americans had long regarded China as their special ward. Whereas American foreign policy toward Europe during the last fifty years had been limited to two short but decisive military interventions occasioned by Germany's threats to the European balance of power, American involvement in the Far East, and particularly in China, had been active since the turn of the century. The original interest in China had not been political but commercial: China was potentially a huge market for American products. But U.S. policy toward China had contained some elements of altruistic intent as well—a genuine interest in the welfare and Christian salvation of the Chinese people. In fact, the United States had long regarded itself as the protector of China from foreign exploitation and invasion. Through the Open-Door policy—aimed at preventing Great Britain, France, Russia, Germany, and Japan from shutting American commerce out of China and at obtaining an equal opportunity to sell on the Chinese market—the United States had become politically committed to preserving the territorial integrity and political independence of China.

Since the American people had never been prepared to fight for this objective, however, the United States had failed to protect China from external pressures and invasions: The Russians had established a sphere of influence in Manchuria about 1900, and the Japanese had replaced the Russians as the actual rulers of this strategic area after the Russo-Japanese War. During and after World War I, Japan had expanded its influence and control over China, and in 1931 Japan had initiated the Sino-Japanese War to consummate its ambition to turn China into a Japanese vassal or colony. The Open-Door policy, then, had been largely a verbal one. Indeed, the United States had never been prepared to support this policy militarily; it was one in which diplomacy was divorced from force, and what it meant was that the United States usually disregarded its commitment whenever Russia or Japan challenged it. But Americans, even in those days, believed that words were a substitute for an effective policy; out of this arose the illusion that the United States had long been China's protector and friend, extending to the Chinese people the bountiful benefits of Western Christianity, political ideals, science, and medicine. Americans were, therefore, shocked by Jiang Gaishek's collapse in 1949 and the establishment of Communist control of the Chinese mainland. Certainly, they were totally unprepared for, and deeply resentful of, the propaganda emanating from Peking accusing the United States of being "the Chinese people's implacable enemy . . . a corrupt imperialistic nation, the world center of reaction and decadence . . . a paper tiger and entirely vulnerable to defeat." They had expected that a "loyal" and fundamentally democratic China, grateful to America for past protection and help, would emerge from World War II as a strong friend of this country and as a powerful and reliable ally in the Far East. The failure of these expectations in late 1949 came as a blow to the American public. Suddenly, the relative security founded on the successful application of containment policies in Europe—the Truman Doctrine, the Marshall Plan, the Berlin airlift, and NATO—seemed to have disintegrated. It appeared that the United States had stemmed the Communist menace in Europe only to allow it to achieve a breakthrough in Asia. The resulting insecurity and anxiety were further heightened by two other events about the same time: the news that the Soviet Union had exploded its first atomic bomb, thereby shattering the American monopoly of the weapon widely regarded as the principal deterrent to a Soviet attack, and the conviction in early 1950 of Alger Hiss, followed shortly by the trial of Judith Coplon and the confession of Klaus Fuchs—which suggested continued Soviet espionage in high places. The outbreak of the Korean War and Communist China's subsequent intervention added more fuel to the fires of discontent.

The public did not understand the causes of its frustration; it could not comprehend the reasons for these alleged failures of American foreign policy. Whenever the United States had been drawn into the international arena in the past, its actions had met with quick success. It had beaten the British, the Mexicans, the Spaniards, the Germans, and the Japanese. America had never been invaded, defeated, or occupied, as most other nations had been; it had, to be sure, committed mistakes, but with its great power it had always been able to rectify these. To a nation in which one popular slogan expressed confidence in doing "the difficult today, the impossible tomorrow," failure was a new experience. America's history had been a witness to victories only; its unbroken string of successes seemed evidence of national omnipotence.

It was this unquestioned assumption that the United States was omnipotent that suggested the reason for America's political and military failures: treason within its own government! For if America was all-powerful, it could not be its lack of strength that accounted for its defeats. It could not be that there was a limit to its ability to influence events abroad, far away from its shores. America's setbacks must have been the result of its own policies. Ostensibly, the reason China fell was that the "pro-Communist" administrations of Franklin Roosevelt and Harry Truman had either deliberately or unwittingly "sold China down the river." This charge—made primarily by the dominant conservative wing of the Republican Party, and particularly by Senators Robert Taft, Joseph R. McCarthy, and Richard Nixon—was simplicity itself: America's China policy had ended in Communist control of the mainland; the administration leaders and the State Department were responsible for the formulation and execution of foreign policy; thus, the government must be filled with Communists and Communist sympathizers who "tailored" American policy to advance the global aims of the Soviet Union. In short, disloyal or grossly incompetent American statesmen were responsible for the "loss" of China; it was to them, not to China, that the collapse of Nationalist China was due. Low Nationalist morale, administrative and military ineptness, and repressive policies that had alienated mass support had nothing to do with it; nor did the superior Communist organization, direction, morale, and ability to identify with popular aspirations.

This conspiratorial interpretation thus bridged the gap between the public's illusion of American omnipotence and the limits of America's power. The belief that Communist victories were caused by the treachery or stupidity of American policymakers made it unnecessary both to recognize this fact and to reevaluate the traditional American approach to foreign policy. It was also highly flattering to the Americans' chauvinistic sense of pride, for it permitted the public to continue to believe in America's omnipotence—and in its opponent's inferiority. Secretary Acheson had once said: "Our name for problems is significant. We call them headaches. You can take a powder, and they are gone. These pains [brought on by the world situation] are not like that. They . . . will stay with us until death. We have got to understand that all our lives danger, the uncertainty, the need for alertness, for efforts, for discipline will be upon us. This is new to us. It will be hard for us." MacArthur's return demonstrated that it was still very hard for us. The American people were still looking for the aspirin that would dissolve all their foreign-policy problems.

It was precisely because MacArthur identified himself with this illusion of omnipotence that he received such a tumultuous welcome upon his return to the United States. He understood the public's frustration, and he gave voice to it in familiar—one might even say, in "American"—words, words of victory holding forth a view of a quick and successful end to the bloodshed on the battlefield, words of confidence and praise for an America strong enough to accomplish anything it had the mind to do in this world, and words of condemnation for those who, driven by fear of the Soviet Union and troublesome allies, chained the proud and invincible American giant to the rock of "weakness" and "appeasement." War, he said, indicated that "you have exhausted all other potentialities of bringing the disagreements to an end," and once engaged, "there is no alternative than to apply every available means to bring it to a swift end. War's very objective is victory—not prolonged indecision. In war there is no substitute for victory." The very term "resisting aggression" indicated "that you can destroy the potentialities of the aggressor to continually hit you" and not "go on indefinitely, neither to win or lose." One cannot fight a "half war." The administration's policy was based upon the assumption that "when you use force, you can limit that force." This introduced a "new concept into military operations—the concept of appeasement."

Here was the kind of language the public could understand. Once the diplomats had failed to keep the peace and war had erupted, the military expert took over and fought a technically efficient war. As a nonpolitical figure, he should not be burdened with extraneous political considerations. His sole aim was the complete destruction of the enemy's forces—in short, military victory. The enemy needed to be punished for provoking war. Only his total defeat would achieve this aim. Only in this way could the nation's principles be safeguarded. America's full power, if necessary, had to be applied to destroy the aggressor who threatened these principles. Deliberate self-restraint was, in these circumstances, a betrayal of America's national honor. Evil must be wiped out; to allow its continued existence was intolerable. Such compromise implied weakness or softness. To accept it was "un-American."

The reaction to the Korean War was thus twofold. On the one hand, the public demanded a return to an "American" policy, a "dynamic" or "positive" policy that would brook no compromises with the enemy and would withstand Allied pressure to "appease." Such a "tougher" policy, it was hoped, would restore America's dignity, prestige, and initiative on the world scene. On the other hand, the public wanted relief from the almost constant foreign-policy involvements and costs of the past few years. This meant a lowering of international tension, ending the Korean War, reducing U.S. commitments, and cutting expenditures. The contradictory nature of these aims was symptomatic of the intense desire to return to the traditional way of conducting foreign policy: either to concentrate on domestic affairs and to abstain from all foreign policy, or to assert America's power without fear or compromise. It was this double and paradoxical legacy that the Eisenhower administration inherited from the Truman administration.

Chapter 5

THE STRATEGY OF "FRONTIERSMANSHIP"

EISENHOWER LIBERATION

During the presidential election campaign of 1952, the Republicans cleverly exploited the public's frustration with containment—a frustration grounded in the popular illusion of national omnipotence. America's great insecurity and its present involvement in the Korean War, they asserted, were the result of the "tragic blunders" that Franklin Roosevelt and Harry Truman had committed at the Teheran, Yalta, and Potsdam conferences with the Soviets. It was there that the Democratic leaders had deliberately and stealthily paved the way for Communism's postwar expansion by selling out Eastern Europe and betraying Jiang Gaishek. The two presidents had, according to the Republican Party platform, "flouted our peace-assuring pledges such as the Atlantic Charter, and [they] did so in favor of despots, who, it was well known, consider that murder, terror, slavery, concentration camps, and the ruthless and brutal denial of human rights are legitimate means to their desired ends. Teheran, Yalta, and Potsdam were the scenes of those tragic blunders with others to follow. The leaders of the administration acted without the knowledge or consent of Congress or the American people. They traded our overwhelming victory for a new enemy and for new oppressions and new wars which were quick to come." In other words, America's wounds were self-inflicted.

Similarly, the Republicans charged that Truman's postwar foreign policy was self-defeating. It underwrote the false premise that American power was limited and committed the United States to continued coexistence and constant involvement in foreign policy. As John Foster Dulles, the chief Republican spokesman on foreign policy, put it: "We are not working, sacrificing, and spending in order to be able to live *without* this peril—but to be able to live

71

with it, presumably forever." The administration's policies were "treadmill policies, which, at best, might perhaps keep us in the same place until we drop exhausted." The failures of containment were many: It was a negative policy; it surrendered the initiative to the enemy; it merely reacted to counter the Communist danger wherever and whenever the latter chose to attack; it was so costly that it would bankrupt the country; and it aimed only at preserving the *status quo*. In short, Dulles condemned the policy of containment as "negative, futile, and immoral."

The aim of American foreign policy, Dulles stressed, should not be to coexist indefinitely with the Communist menace; it should be to eliminate the menace. The purpose of American policy should be a rollback of Soviet power. The United States had only to proclaim its stand for freedom and announce that it would never be a party to any "deal" that confirmed Soviet despotism over alien peoples. Such a declaration would preserve the courage and hope of the satellite peoples and prevent them from accepting the Soviet regime. In Dulles's words, the United States "should make it publicly known that it wants and expects liberation to occur. The mere statement of that wish and expectation would change, in an electrifying way, the mood of the captive peoples. It would probably put heavy new burdens on the jailers and create new opportunities for liberation."

Never had the illusion of American omnipotence received a greater tribute. America's cause was righteous, and in order to be victorious it need only publicize this cause by launching a moral crusade. Right would then again prevail over might. The Republican program of action apparently envisaged the future secretary of state, John "Joshua" Dulles, marching around the walls of the Kremlin empire, sounding the call of freedom upon his trumpet. The walls would then come tumbling down, the enslaved peoples would be liberated, and Soviet power would be forced to retreat. The world would once more be safe for democracy.

The Republicans thus appeared not only to promise an eventual end to the cold war—they also pledged themselves to do it at less cost. For they claimed that the Democrats' foreign policy of indefinite coexistence, with its vast outlay for armaments and economic aid, would undermine the nation's economy. The Republicans asserted that it was the Soviet Union's aim to destroy America by forcing the country to spend itself into bankruptcy—an aim furthered by Democratic policy. America's defense had to be provided with a healthy economic foundation. This would require a sharp cut in the present huge foreign aid and military expenditures. The Republicans, in brief, promised the nation at one and the same time an offensive strategy, a balanced budget, and reduction of taxes. They pledged a rollback of Soviet power on the one hand and, on the other, a cut in the appropriations for America's defense.

Such goals were not only incompatible; they were unattainable. The mere enunciation of the doctrine of liberation would not free any Soviet satellite; good intentions, unsupported by concrete political and military policies, possess a notorious impotence on the international scene. But perhaps this did not really matter, since the policy of liberation seems to have been devised primarily to roll back the Democrats in the United States, not the Red Army in Eastern Europe. And for this domestic purpose, liberation was a highly effective strategy.

The country desperately wanted a more vigorous and forthright anti-Communist policy that promised an end to the cold war. At the same time, it was unprepared to take the risks involved: That is, a policy that actively sought the liberation of the satellite states would have to accept the very definite risk of all-out war with the Soviet Union. In these circumstances, the only kind of dynamism the country could afford was a verbal dynamism. And this was all the people seemed to want. It allowed them to delude themselves that the United States once again pursued a vigorous and forthright policy that would defeat its opponent. Liberation was the Republican Party's therapy for a public that refused to accept the facts of America's limited power in the world and rejected any changes in its traditional approach to foreign policy. That this policy of liberation was probably never meant to be more than a verbal appeal to the American people was clearly demonstrated at the time of the anti-Communist revolt in East Berlin and other East German cities in June 1953, and during the national uprising in Hungary in late 1956. In neither case did the Eisenhower administration act—except to condemn the Soviet Union for its suppression of Germans and Hungarians and to express its sympathy for the victims of Soviet despotism. In Berlin, it substituted food packages to the East Berliners for liberation; and in Hungary, it even reassured the Soviet Union that it had no intention of intervening. The *status quo* was thereby reaffirmed. Liberation had returned to the "womb" of containment.

The administration did, however, carry out its promises of military and economic retrenchment. This involved three measures. The first of these was to end the Korean War, which would allow the administration to cut the size of the army and avoid the cost of maintaining large standing ground forces. The second was to draw a clear line, or "frontier," around the entire Sino-Soviet bloc. The Democrats had already drawn such a frontier from Norway to Turkey; the Republicans expected to strengthen and extend it to the Middle and Far East. The third measure was to preserve this global boundary around the Communist world with the deterrent power of the Strategic Air Command. The Soviets and Chinese could cross the line only at the risk of total war with the United States; the fear of total destruction was expected to deter them.

This reliance upon strategic air power was also expected to appeal to the American public. In the first place, "massive retaliation" simply sounded more dynamic than containment; at the same time, it made possible a reduction of overall military expenditures. It was obviously considerably cheaper to concentrate military spending upon a one-weapon system than to build up and maintain large balanced forces to meet any contingency. The second appealing feature of massive retaliation was that it, in fact, rejected the concept of limited war, or "half war," and reasserted the old American doctrine of either abstaining or fighting an all-out war. This return to the more traditional American approach to war was natural in 1952. The Republicans had been elected largely because of the deep popular revulsion against the Korean War; it was clear that the people wanted no more Koreas.

Basically, then, Dwight D. Eisenhower's policy was not to be very different from his predecessor's: containment of Communism by drawing a frontier around the Sino-Soviet periphery and supporting that frontier with nuclear air power. But in one essential aspect the new administration's policy was different—and this difference was crucial. Truman and Dean Acheson had also relied upon air-atomic striking power to deter a total attack upon either the United States or America's "first line of defense" in Europe. But in Asia, once the Communists had faced them with a limited aggression, they had met this challenge with local ground resistance. The Eisenhower administration also expected to deter an all-out war with the threat of massive retaliation. But, unlike the Truman administration, it would not fight local ground wars. It proposed to prevent any future limited attacks by threatening to retaliate against the Soviet Union or Communist China.

This basic policy decision reflected Secretary Dulles's own strong conviction that the only effective means of stopping a prospective aggressor was to give him an advance warning that if he committed aggression, he would be subjected to such overwhelming retaliatory blows that his possible gains would be far outweighed by the punishment he would suffer. Dulles believed strongly that Korea would never have been invaded if the Communists had known that their attack would have been met with retaliatory air strikes on Moscow. It was the absence of such a warning that had led the Communists to miscalculate. The Eisenhower administration did not intend to repeat this mistake. It meant to draw the line so clearly that the enemy could be left in no doubt whatsoever of what would happen to him if he crossed it. The expectation was that by going to the "brink of war," the United States would be able to deter future Koreas. This policy, which later became known as "brinkmanship," was to be applied first in an attempt to bring about a cease-fire in Korea.

ENDING THE KOREAN WAR

Truce talks in Korea had begun in the summer of 1951, but the negotiations had dragged on fruitlessly until they reached a deadlock. When the Eisenhower administration took office in January 1953, it decided that if its efforts to gain an armistice failed, it would bomb Chinese bases and supply sources in Manchuria and China, blockade the mainland coast, and possibly use tactical atomic weapons "to provide a tremendous beef-up in the United Nations punch." Dulles conveyed this decision to Prime Minister Jawaharlal Nehru of India in late May 1953, on the assumption that Nehru would pass the message on to the Chinese Communists.

In early June, the deadlocked negotiations were resumed, and in late July the armistice was signed. Whether the administration's decisions alone were primarily responsible for the Chinese Communists' willingness to conclude the war is difficult to say. Probably other factors did play a significant role. For instance, Joseph Stalin had died in 1953, and his successors were proclaiming their belief in "peaceful coexistence" and trying hard to convince the non-Communist world that they wanted to relax international tension. Agreement on an armistice and an end to the war would provide evidence of their earnestness. But in Dulles's own mind, it was his threat to unleash American air power against China that induced the Chinese Communists to agree to end the fighting; in turn, this reinforced his faith in the utility of the advance warning coupled with the threat of heavy punishment.

Thus, the Korean War concluded just about where it had begun—on the thirty-eighth parallel. It had taken three years of fighting to decide that this line was to become part of the global line dividing the Communist bloc from the non-Communist bloc. In August, the United States signed a mutual security pact with South Korea designed as a deterrent to another attack. This alliance had already been preceded by a declaration, signed by the fifteen nations that had fought in Korea, warning the Chinese Communists that, in the event of renewed aggression, it would probably be impossible to confine hostilities to Korea. And they added this significant warning: The armistice must not "result in jeopardizing the restoration or the safeguarding of peace in any other part of Asia." Events in Indochina were soon to prove the meaninglessness of this statement.

THE FIRST INDOCHINA WAR AND SEATO

After World War II, strong nationalist movements in colonies that had long been ruled by European powers demanded independence for their countries. The British met these demands in India, Burma, and Ceylon. The French did not meet them in Indochina. Returning to Indochina after its years of Japanese occupation, they refused to grant any meaningful concessions to the government which, under Ho Chi Minh, had proclaimed the independence of Vietnam after Japan's collapse. The French, determined to reestablish sovereignty over their colony, recognized Ho's "Democratic Republic of Vietnam" as a free state within the French Union; as a part of the agreement, the French would be allowed to maintain garrisons in Vietnam for five years. But within less than a year, as a result of actions taken by France that the Vietminh considered to be in violation of its agreements, there developed open conflict between the Vietminh and the French, and this soon was transformed into the First Indochina War.

When France established an "independent" state of Vietnam in 1949 under Emperor Bao Dai, the Communist-dominated Vietminh became, in effect, "rebels," but with the important difference that they were rebels identified as nationalists fighting for the independence of Vietnam. By contrast, Bao Dai, who spent much of his time on the French Riviera, was seen as a French puppet, and, in fact, he could not have survived one day in office without the support of French arms. Ho, like Mao Zedong in China, conducted guerrilla warfare and met with considerable success. The French, who generally held the cities, were at a disadvantage from the beginning, for in the absence of genuine independence, the Vietnamese identified themselves with the Vietminh and saw the French as colonial rulers. In the long run, France paid a very high price for the war in terms of manpower, material, and morale.

During the first years of the war, American public opinion was unsympathetic to France's attempt to reestablish its colonial control over Indochina. But two events were to lead to United States involvement in this conflict. The first one was the defeat of Jiang Gaishek. This was a blow to France, because it meant that the Chinese Communists could now provide assistance to the Vietminh. The second event was the outbreak of the Korean War, which led to an increased awareness of the strategic importance of Indochina as the gateway to the whole of Southeast Asia. In a bipolar world, Indochina could not be allowed to fall.

The administration began therefore to provide France with economic and military aid. By 1954, the United States was paying about 75 percent of the costs of the war. The French position continued to deteriorate, however, especially once the Korean armistice was signed. For despite American warnings, Communist China had now shifted its pressure from Korea to Indochina and was rendering increasing assistance to the Vietminh. On March 13, 1954, the entire French position in northern Vietnam suddenly threatened to disintegrate as the Vietminh forces launched an assault upon the French fortress at Dienbienphu. It became painfully clear that the French could not hold the position alone. Only American intervention could save Dienbienphu and the French hold on Vietnam. What was the United States to do?

President Eisenhower had already declared that the fall of Indochina "would be of a most terrible significance to the United States of America," and he had termed Southeast Asia of "transcendent importance" to American security. The secretary of state had issued several statements that rather strongly suggested that America would not stand idly by while Indochina fell. He had warned the Chinese Communists in the same terms he had used after the armistice in Korea: Any aggression—that is, open intervention—would incur "grave consequences which might not be confined to Indochina." This warning also applied to any indirect Chinese intervention—namely, supplying overt assistance in the form of military advisors, equipment, and training for the Vietminh forces. Of prime importance was the strategic significance of Indochina, not whether the Chinese expanded by direct or indirect means.

Dienbienphu was for the administration, therefore, the moment of decision. Eisenhower and Dulles had declared Indochina to be of strategic importance to American security and had cautioned China against direct or indirect intervention by threatening it with massive retaliation. The Chinese had ignored these warnings. The U.S. government now had to "put up or shut up." It shut up; its threats turned out to have been only bluffs.

The reason for this is fairly clear: Because of the nature of American domestic politics, the Eisenhower administration was unwilling to involve the United States in another Korea. Moreover, the administration was already cutting the size of the army, and apparently there were not sufficient divisions available for fighting in Indochina. The army chief of staff certainly counseled against intervention on that ground. Only two possible courses of action remained. The first was to stop the Communist advance with air power alone; but this was a wholly unfeasible proposition, since air strikes by themselves could not possibly have halted a ground advance. They had failed to do so during the opening days of the Korean War, and it had been this failure that had necessitated the commitment of the army. And even if such air strikes had been tried in an attempt to stop the Vietminh, they would have been ineffective; for quite apart from Indochina's topography, the Vietminh were fighting a guerrilla war. Thus, the use of ground troops would have been as mandatory in Indochina as in Korea.

The alternative strategy was, of course, to attack China itself. Everything indicates that this is what the administration should have done if it really believed in its own policy of massive retaliation. Its entire strategy was predicated upon two principles of action: first, issuing a clear warning that would allow no doubt of American intentions and no room for Communist miscalculation; and second, if the Communists deliberately ignored the American warnings, punishing the enemy so heavily that he would never again dare challenge the United States. Yet in Indochina the administration did not follow its warning with such punishment.

Why did this happen? The answer is simple: It is one thing to deliver a threat of massive retaliation to an opponent, and quite another for him to believe it. The Soviets had not believed it in Korea; nor did the Chinese in Indochina. Both apparently rejected the notion that the United States would risk a total war for anything less than an all-out attack on either the United States or Europe. Thus, the United States was faced for a second time with the terrible dilemma of either doing nothing or risking all-out war (since the Eisenhower administration shared the Truman administration's fear that an attack on China would precipitate Soviet intervention).

Truman's experience with Korea had clearly shown that containment could not be successful without the willingness and capability to fight a limited war. Reliance upon strategic air power and an all-or-nothing strategy paralyzed American diplomacy. The United States' ability to drop atom bombs on Moscow or Peking was less than useless to defeat limited incursions in areas that the Americans were unwilling to defend at the risk of total war. Ground forces were absolutely necessary if the United States was to escape either defeat or involvement in a total conflict. (Indochina should also have demonstrated—as Americans were to learn a decade later—that a limited war against guerrilla forces also required political, social, and economic measures to alleviate the popular grievances upon which the guerrillas feed.) The Eisenhower administration had ignored these lessons of the Korean War. It had persuaded itself that Korea had happened only because the enemy had not received a previous warning that an attack upon South Korea would bring retaliatory strikes. While such warnings were certainly desirable to prevent enemy miscalculation, Indochina now proved that warnings alone were not enough. It showed that containment was incompatible with heavy budget cutting.

The result of American inaction was the French government's decision to make the best of the situation by negotiating with the Communists directly for an end to the war. The French people were as weary of the fighting as the American public had been of Korea. Just as the latter had elected Eisenhower to end the war, the French National Assembly had elected Pierre Mendés-France premier to end the Indochina hostilities. The new premier announced that he was willing to conclude the war, and on July 20, 1954, an armistice agreement was reached that divided the country at the seventeenth parallel. The Communists were left in control of northern Indochina; it seemed only a matter of time until they would take over the rest of the country, for the collapse of the southern rump state seemed imminent.

But the United States prevented this by supporting the new government of Ngo Dinh Diem, a staunch anti-Communist nationalist appointed by Bao Dai after Dienbienphu (Diem later ousted Bao Dai). The Eisenhower administration extended him economic and military aid to help him stabilize the situation in Vietnam. The danger of collapse temporarily receded. The seventeenth parallel, like the thirty-eighth parallel in Korea, became part of the international frontier separating the Communist and non-Communist worlds. To ensure this, the United States, Britain, France, Australia, New Zealand, the Philippines, Pakistan, and Thailand in September 1954 signed the Southeast Asia Collective Defense Treaty (SEATO) to defend the area of the South Pacific, with the exception of Hong Kong and Taiwan. A protocol to the treaty extended SEATO's protection to Vietnam, Laos, and Cambodia. It also provided for joint action to meet aggression; an attack upon any of its members would be considered a danger to the security of all, and each would then act to meet the common danger in accordance with its constitutional processes. In case of subversion, the parties agreed to consult one another immediately and agree on common measures to meet this threat.

SEATO, unlike the North Atlantic Treaty Organization alliance, which it resembled, did not possess a unified command or joint forces. The principal force behind the alliance was American sea and air power. The crucial element— land power—would have to be supplied by the member nations if the occasion arose. Moreover—and again unlike NATO—SEATO did not contain within it most of the nations located in the area. India, Burma, Ceylon, and Indonesia would not join. They had just emerged from Western colonialism and were unwilling to be tied again to the West through a military alliance. They preferred to remain neutral in the struggle between the Western powers and the Sino-Soviet bloc. Of the Asian nations that did join the pact, the Philippines did so because of its traditional ties to the United States, and Pakistan because it wished to strengthen itself against India; only Thailand was genuinely concerned with Communist China's expansion, for the French collapse in Indochina had brought Chinese power closer to its borders. But if SEATO was primarily a non-Asian alliance for the defense of an Asian area—a weakness that was to plague the alliance, for the absence of indigenous concern and resistance to Communist expansion could only ensure its eventual failure—its chief purpose was to warn the Communists of the stake America perceived in an area of what it continued to define as a bipolar world. If the United States, therefore, felt its security threatened by direct or indirect Communist aggression, SEATO provided it with the opportunity for unilateral intervention to preserve this newly drawn land frontier.

THE TAIWAN STRAITS AND THE OFFSHORE ISLANDS

Another critical situation arose in the Taiwan Straits. During the summer of 1954, the Chinese Communists openly proclaimed their intention of taking Taiwan and began shelling the Nationalist-held offshore islands (Quemoy is only nine miles outside the harbor of Amoy; Matsu lies almost as close, blocking the harbor of Foochow [Fouzhou], and the Tachen islands are 200 miles north of Taiwan). In December, the United States and the Nationalists signed a Treaty of Mutual Defense, by which the former guaranteed the security of Taiwan and the nearby Pescadore islands. The Nationalists also pledged themselves not to attack the mainland or reinforce their offshore garrisons without United States consent.

The offshore islands were not included under the terms of the treaty. However, as the situation in the straits grew more tense in January 1955, the president requested and received from Congress the authority to employ American armed forces to protect Taiwan and the Pescadores. This authority extended to the protection of "such related positions and territories" as the president judged necessary. In Dulles's mind, Quemoy and Matsu had to be defended to maintain the Nationalist government's morale. It would seem, therefore, that in case of attack, the administration would have committed American armed forces to the defense of the offshore islands. The Communists certainly thought so, and they abstained from any invasion attempts on Quemoy and Matsu. (The Nationalists had, meanwhile, evacuated the Tachens.)

Three years later, in August 1958, the American position became clear when the Communists again began to shell the offshore islands. The Seventh Fleet— with orders to retaliate if fired upon—escorted Nationalist supply ships to within three miles of the beleaguered islands and helped them to break the

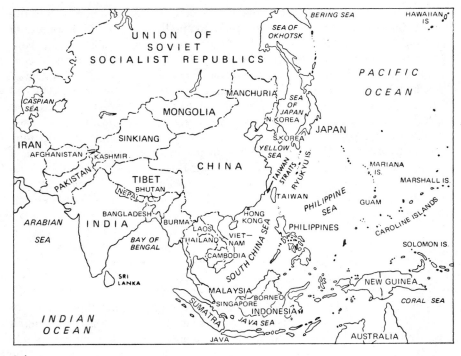

Asia

blockade; and the Nationalist air force, equipped by the United States with air-to-air missiles, defeated the Communist air force's attempt to establish air supremacy in the sky between the mainland and Quemoy.

Thus, the line remained where it had been before the two Taiwan crises—a few miles off Communist China's coast. Some months later, Dulles reaffirmed this line when he firmly rejected Jiang's calls for the reconquest of the mainland. American policy in the straits was committed to the preservation of the *status quo*. Each side should keep what it had and refrain from attacking the other. The Eisenhower administration had finally recognized what neither it nor its predecessor had been willing to admit openly before: that the Nationalist expectation of reconquering the mainland was a myth. At the same time, it tacitly acknowledged the Chinese Communist government as continental China's *de facto* government. It reconciled itself to the Communist conquest of the mainland. Containment had once more replaced liberation. The administration was, moreover, resolved to back up its "disengagement" policy with force. In the straits, it could support its political position with sea and air power; ground forces were not needed.

For the moment, the situation in the Far East had been stabilized. The "frontier" lines between the American and Soviet/Chinese spheres had been drawn at the thirty-eighth parallel in Korea, in the Taiwan Straits, at the seventeenth parallel in Indochina, and at the line drawn by SEATO. The Middle East, however, remained an area in turmoil.

THE MIDDLE EAST AND THE SUEZ WAR

In 1955, the United States completed its line around the Sino-Soviet periphery. Under its sponsorship, Britain, Turkey, Iraq, Iran, and Pakistan established the Middle East Treaty Organization (METO). Thus, the Baghdad Pact (as this treaty was called) extended the NATO line from Turkey to India. But this "northern tier," drawn—except for Iraq—along 3000 miles of the Soviet Union's southern frontier, drew a sharp reaction from the Soviet Union. Rebuffed in Iran and Turkey in 1946–1947 by America, the Soviet Union had not surrendered its ambitions in this area. The Middle East linked Europe, Africa, and Asia. For Britain, the area—and especially the Suez Canal—had traditionally been the lifeline of its old empire and of its present Commonwealth. Above all, Europe's economy was becoming increasingly dependent upon the Middle East for oil (America was still self-sufficient in oil); without oil, Europe would collapse. The power that could deny it this oil would be able to dictate its future. In short, for the Soviet Union the Middle East was the means to outflank and disintegrate NATO. Its opportunity to attempt to do this came as a result of the bitter Arab-Israeli conflict, the only slightly less bitter Anglo-Egyptian quarrel, Egypt's own expansionist ambitions, and the United States' attempt to draw the line of containment just south of the Soviet Union's border.

Arab antagonism toward Israel is understandable. In 1917, Britain had pledged itself in the Balfour Declaration to the establishment of a "national home" for the Jewish people in Palestine, while also promising the Arabs that the civil and religious rights of non-Jews would not be prejudiced. Zionists took this pledge as promising the conversion of Palestine into a Jewish state; they considered Palestine, a British mandate after the collapse of the Ottoman Empire during World War I, as their ancient and traditional homeland.

Britain's troubles became serious after Hitler's assumption of power in Germany—and impossible after World War II. Hitler had slaughtered 6 million Jews in his concentration camps; few of the survivors wished to remain in Europe, with its unhappy memories. Many emigrated to Palestine. The Jews were now determined to establish a Jewish state, while the Arabs feared that the Jewish immigration would crowd them out of what they also regarded as their rightful homeland. British troops were unable to keep the peace between the Arabs and Jews. Under these circumstances, Britain—already gravely weakened by the war and forced to curtail its commitments throughout the world—decided to end its burdensome mandate over Palestine.

In November 1947, the United Nations decided to partition Palestine into two independent states, one Jewish and the other Arab. The Arabs refused to accept this solution, however; they wanted Palestine to become an Arab state. On May 10, 1948, as Britain ended its mandate, the Jews proclaimed the state of Israel, and the armies of the Arab League (Egypt, Jordan, Syria, Lebanon, and Saudi Arabia) invaded the new state. In the ensuing war, the Israeli army defeated the larger Arab armies. The state of Israel became a fact of political life.

The Arabs, however, refused to recognize it as such. Though they did sign an armistice in February 1949, they refused to conclude a peace treaty. They continued to regard the Jews as infidels who had no right to be in Israel. Moreover, they felt deeply humiliated by their defeat. The Arabs awaited their day of revenge; meanwhile, they continued to proclaim their intention to destroy Israel. They conducted constant guerrilla warfare against Israel—sabotaging, pillaging, and murdering (so did the Israeli army when it intermittently took revenge by launching heavy assaults into Arab territory); they refused to allow Israeli shipping through the Suez Canal and blockaded the Gulf of Aqaba; and they tightened the ring around Israel. In April 1956, Egypt, Syria, Saudi Arabia, and Yemen formed a joint command against Israel under Egyptian leadership, and in October 1956, Egypt, Jordan, and Syria announced another joint command "the principal concern of which is the war of destruction against Israel." Earlier (in late September 1955), Egypt had concluded an arms deal with Czechoslovakia, although the actual agreement was signed with the Soviet Union; under this arrangement, Egypt received a large quantity of arms, including planes and tanks. Egypt now had the tools with which to achieve a decisive military superiority over Israel. This, in turn, raised a very vital question for Israel: Should it strike now or wait until Egypt and its allies were ready for the "second round"? As Egypt solidified the encirclement of Israel, grew increasingly aggressive, and began to absorb the Soviet arms, the Israelis decided to strike before it was too late. All that was needed was the right condition for launching their preventive attack.

This condition, which was to occur in October 1956, was the product of Anglo-Egyptian antagonism. Britain had controlled Egypt since 1881, when it had established a protectorate over Egypt in order to safeguard its own communications through Suez to India. The 1936 treaty between the two countries had converted this status into an alliance. By its terms, British troops were confined to the Canal Zone, and their presence was declared to be neither an occupation nor an infringement of Egyptian sovereignty. To the Egyptians, however, British soldiers on their soil continued to represent a violation of Egyptian independence, pride, and dignity.

World War II intensified Egyptian nationalism and heightened the demand for a withdrawal of British forces from Egyptian soil. But negotiations on this question broke down, while other postwar events further increased Egypt's anti-British sentiment. The Egyptians resented the Palestine partition plan, for which they blamed Britain as well as the United States. In late 1951, the Egyptian parliament abrogated the 1936 Anglo-Egyptian treaty, and in July 1952, the new military regime that took over the Egyptian government from King Farouk pressed with renewed vigor for the removal of British troops. The Eisenhower administration supported this Egyptian demand. Faced with this opposition, and aware of its own unpopularity in Egypt, Britain signed a new Anglo-Egyptian treaty in 1954, by which it agreed to withdraw all its troops from Suez over a twenty-month period. British influence over Egyptian politics had come to an end.

Britain now shifted the focus of its power from Egypt to Iraq, a longtime ally. It therefore joined the Baghdad Pact, of which Iraq was already a member, in order to protect its vital strategic and economic interest in the Middle East. But President Gamal Abdel Nasser of Egypt did not regard METO merely as a means of containing the Soviet Union; he saw it as an instrument to preserve Western domination throughout the area, and, since Iraq had always been Egypt's traditional rival for Arab leadership, he considered it a personal challenge as well. Nasser therefore set out to destroy the Baghdad Pact by forming a counteralliance and undermining pro-Western Arab governments. His means of achieving these objectives was to place himself at the head of the Arab struggle against Israel and Britain. Thereby, he would become the foremost exponent of Arab nationalism and win the allegiance of the Arab masses. Once he had gained this loyalty of the people, no Arab government would dare oppose him, for if it did he would call on the people to overthrow that government. "Revolution in the street" was an accepted Arab method of making and unmaking governments.

Moreover, by exerting his influence over the Arab world in this manner, Nasser might gain control over the area's oil resources; this would place him in a position where he could siphon off the oil revenues to help Egypt's economic development. Thus, partly as a reaction to Israel and Britain, but also as a result of his own strong ambitions and the Arab states' domestic condition, Nasser began to promote Pan-Arabism as an instrument of expanding his own and Egyptian influence. By turning to nationalism, and thereby asserting the Arabs' pride, sovereignty, and dignity, by humiliating those who had in the past humiliated and subjected them, he consolidated his leadership at home, gained the admiration and enthusiasm of the long-suffering masses in other Arab countries, and compelled their rulers to follow him if they did not wish to be overthrown by popular revolutions led by pro-Nasser forces.

Nasser's influence grew quickly. The act that endeared him to the Arab masses was his dramatic arms deal with the Soviet Union. This agreement made Nasser the great new hero, the modern Saladin—the staunch opponent of the West and the champion of Arab nationalism. At the same time, the Soviet Union became the Arabs' greatest friend. But this Moscow-Cairo axis frightened not only Israel but also Britain; if the Soviet Union and Egypt gained control over the Middle East, Britain would be cut off from its oil supplies, which for it was a question not just of profit, but of survival. The situation thus became inflammable.

Only an incendiary incident was needed to start a conflagration. The United States provided this when, on July 19, 1956, it informed the Egyptian government that it would not help finance Nasser's Aswan Dam, a high dam on the Upper Nile whose purpose was to raise Egypt's low standard of living by irrigating new land and providing electricity for industrial development. The American retraction of its offer to help build this dam was a heavy blow to Egypt's hopes to raise itself by its own "sandalstraps." For the American loan had been a prerequisite for further aid from the World Bank and Britain; these offers, too, were now withdrawn. The Eisenhower administration's action was occasioned by several considerations: Nasser had attempted to blackmail the administration into providing more money by hinting that the Soviets had offered to finance the entire project; Egypt had moved too close to the Soviet Union and had recognized Communist China; Nasser had also probably mortgaged the funds he was supposed to provide for Egypt's share of the cost of the dam to buy Soviet arms—which, in effect, meant that the entire cost of the dam would fall upon the United States and Britain.

Nasser regarded the American decision as a personal and national humiliation. A few days later, on July 26, he announced that he would nationalize the Suez Canal and use the revenues collected from it to finance the dam. Arab nationalists were ecstatic, and Nasser's stature, already great, reached new heights.

Unlike the crises in Korea and Taiwan, however, the consequences of the United States' act fell not on itself but on its allies—above all, on Britain. And its government reacted sharply to Nasser's seizure of the canal. Prime Minister Anthony Eden did not trust the Egyptian dictator; although Nasser guaranteed that all ships, except Israel's, could still pass through the canal, Eden feared that the Egyptian would use the canal as an instrument of political blackmail. Moreover, if Nasser could face the West with such a major act of defiance and go unpunished, Western influence would be destroyed throughout the Middle East. Other Arab governments would expropriate Western oil interests, and all opponents of Nasser would be discouraged and come to terms with him. Western prestige—and especially British prestige, since south of America's "northern tier" Britain was the leading Western power in the Middle East—had to be upheld. If it were not, the Cairo-Moscow axis would dominate the entire area and be in a position to strangle Europe. The British were therefore determined to stand up to Nasser, and they insisted upon some form of international control for the canal. But the Egyptians rejected all proposals to wrest their newly won control out of their hands and denounced them as "collective colonialism." All attempts to bridge this gap were therefore doomed to fail.

It was in these circumstances that war broke out. The United States was busily engaged in the last days of its presidential election campaign, and the Soviet Union was concentrating on crushing the Hungarian uprising. On October 29, only four days after Jordan's chief of staff announced that the time had come to launch the Arab assault on Israel, the Israeli army marched into

Egypt. The Israelis quickly defeated the Egyptian forces in the Sinai peninsula. The British and the French (who sought Nasser's downfall because of his aid to the Algerian rebels, who wanted to free Algeria from French control) intervened twenty-four hours later. At this point, the United States saved Nasser. Although the administration had pressured Britain to sign the Anglo-Egyptian treaty by which all British troops had been removed from Suez and had withdrawn the Aswan Dam offer, thus precipitating Nasser's seizure of the canal and the British attack, it now opposed the use of force to settle this issue.

The reason was that despite the administration's disapproval of Nasser's action and the pro-Soviet direction in which he was leading Egypt, it saw his foreign policy as a reaction against Israel and Western colonialism. If Israel had not existed, and if Egypt and the Arab states had not long been subjected and exploited by the Western powers (especially Britain), Arab nationalism would not be anti-Western and pro-Soviet. The administration therefore saw the invasion of Egypt as a golden opportunity to win Egyptian and Arab friendship. When the Jews had originally proclaimed the state of Israel, the United States had, because of domestic political considerations, recognized the new state within eleven minutes. Here was a chance to show the Arabs that the United States was not as pro-Jewish as they thought it to be, and that the country could even be pro-Arab. Since Egypt's actions were also the product of its anti-British resentment, it would be beneficial to oppose the British attempt to reassert control over the Suez Canal. By saving Nasser, the United States could align itself with Arab nationalism; supporting Britain, France, and Israel would have left the Soviet Union as the sole champion of Arab aspirations. American opposition to the invasion would, in short, identify the United States with the anti-colonialism of the entire underdeveloped world, and particularly with the anti-Israeli and nationalistic sentiments of the Arab world. Since continued evidence of British power in the Middle East only antagonized the Arabs, the destruction of this power and its replacement by American influence would be in the interest not only of the United States but of all the Western powers. In this way, the West's strategic and economic interests could be more adequately safeguarded.

America's opposition to the Suez invasion was the decisive factor in stopping the fighting. Egypt had already blocked the canal, and the Syrians had cut the pipelines running across their country from Iraq. Britain was therefore dependent upon American oil to replace its losses from the Middle East; and the administration threatened to use this economic sanction if Britain did not cease the attack. Faced with this dire prospect—plus opposition to the invasion within Britain, the Commonwealth (Canada, India, and Pakistan), and the United Nations—the British government accepted a cease-fire and later withdrew its forces; France and Israel had little choice but to follow suit.

It is ironic, however, in view of America's leading role in halting the attack on Egypt, that it should have been the Soviet Union—and not the United States—that was to reap the benefits from America's opposition. After it had become clear that the United States would not support the British and French invasion, the Soviet Union threatened "to crush the aggressor"; it sent notes to the British and French governments warning of possible rocket attacks on their countries, and it bluntly told Israel that its very existence was at stake. It even asked the United States to join forces with it to stop the war. And after the cease-fire, the Soviet Union and Communist China threatened to send "volunteer soldiers." In short, the Soviet Union risked nothing to deliver these threats, but it was the country that received most of the credit from the Arabs for saving Nasser by its threats to exterminate Israel and attack Britain and France. Suez thus resulted in the collapse of British power in the Middle East, the strengthening of Arab nationalism, and the consolidation of Egyptian-Soviet links.

Nasser's great political victory—despite a humiliating military defeat at the hands of Israel—increased his self-confidence. Supported by the Soviet Union, whose aim it was to weaken if not to eliminate all Western power in the Middle East, Nasser continued his expansionist drive. Jordan abrogated the Anglo-Jordan Treaty by which Jordan had received an annual subsidy to maintain its economy; Egypt, Saudi Arabia, and Syria promised to replace the British funds, and Jordan announced that it would seek to establish a federal union with Egypt and Syria. The last two states did, in fact, join together into a union, the United Arab Republic, in early 1958. Attempts to undermine the Iraqi government continued throughout 1956, and in the spring of 1957, the Egyptians organized riots against the government in Lebanon.

The first step taken by the Eisenhower administration after the Suez crisis was the formulation of the Eisenhower Doctrine. This joint resolution of Congress in the spring of 1957 declared that the United States considered the preservation of the independence and integrity of the Middle Eastern nations vital to American security, and that it was prepared to use armed force to assist any nation or nations "*requesting* assistance against *armed* aggression from any country controlled by international Communism [italics added]." It was difficult to understand what this doctrine meant. The Soviet Union did not border on any Arab state. Iraq, to the south, was already protected by the Baghdad Pact and, through its association with Britain and Turkey, by NATO; so the doctrine could not be directed against the Soviet Union. Moreover, the Soviet Union had already leapfrogged the "northern tier" by establishing close relations with Egypt and Syria. And Suez had demonstrated that the United States did not regard such association as turning a country into a Communist-controlled vassal; if it had, it would surely have supported the invasion of Egypt.

But the administration, viewing Nasser's continued attempts to undermine Western power in the Middle East, his vicious attacks upon all the Western nations, including the United States, and his continued flirtation with the Soviet Union, soon reconsidered its views of Nasser. At Suez, it had thought that by demonstrating its friendship, the United States could win his trust. Post-Suez events proved this expectation to have been ill-founded. A reversal of policy was thus in order, and this required a reinterpretation of the Eisenhower

Doctrine. First, the term "armed aggression" was no longer to refer only to the direct attack of one nation upon another but also to attempts to overthrow pro-Western governments through internal revolt aided from the outside; and second, "any country controlled by international Communism" was now meant to include nations with close bonds to the Soviet Union.

The doctrine was first applied in Jordan, where King Hussein's dismissal of the pro-Nasser and pro-Communist government led to a general strike, massive street demonstrations, and riots. Jordan's days as an independent state appeared to be numbered. In this crisis, Hussein charged in April 1957 that international Communism was responsible for the efforts to overthrow him. On the same day, the United States announced that it regarded "the independence and integrity of Jordan as vital." And to prove that it meant what it said, the administration dispatched the United States Sixth Fleet to the eastern Mediterranean and extended Jordan $10 million for the support of its army and economy. The Hussein government survived.

In the summer of 1958, an even more serious crisis arose when a group of nationalist officers led by General Abdul Karim Kassem overthrew the pro-Western government of Iraq. Although the new regime did not withdraw from the Baghdad Pact until some months later, this revolt, in effect, eliminated Iraq, the pivot on which the alliance had been centered. The United Arab Republic immediately hailed the revolution and recognized the new government, and the two countries quickly signed an alliance. There was little the United States could do but recognize the Kassem government. Arab nationalism seemed to be sweeping everything in front of it. Only Lebanon, Jordan, and Saudi Arabia were still outside the Nasser camp, and the first two were teetering on the verge of revolution. The whole Western position in the Middle East seemed to be on the brink of disintegration.

The Eisenhower administration now resorted to force. Lebanon had been plagued for some time with civil war between Muslims and Christians. The Muslims wanted close relations, if not union, with the United Arab Republic, and the Christians favored a pro-Western policy and the continued independence of Lebanon. With the Iraqi revolution, men and arms for the pro-Nasser elements began to be smuggled in over Lebanon's Syrian border. In Jordan, too, the situation took a turn for the worse; the Iraqi example was hardly a happy one for King Hussein, who also had his pro-Nasser masses and army officers. Both countries now invoked the Eisenhower Doctrine and asked for military support. The British sent paratroopers into Jordan, and the United States sent 14,000 men into Lebanon. The large size of the American contingent seems to have been deliberate. Apparently, it was meant to warn the new Iraqi government against nationalizing Western oil resources. Kassem quickly gave the assurance that he had no such intention, and possible American intervention in Iraq was thereby forestalled. Loud Soviet hints of intervention also turned out to be hollow when countered by resolute American action. Both Britain and the United States withdrew their troops in late October.

The Anglo-American action had saved, at least temporarily, Lebanon and

Jordan. But it was also intended to have another important effect: to show Nasser and the Arabs that there were limits to Soviet willingness to come to their aid. Nasser's personal ambitions were, by themselves, relatively unimportant; the decisive factor that had reaped success for Egypt's Pan-Arab policy was Soviet power. The Western powers, in thinking of counteraction against Egypt, could never eliminate the possibility of Soviet intervention. This, in turn, further encouraged Nasser's expansionist drive. The Anglo-American action in Lebanon and Jordan disabused the Arabs of this notion. Prior to the intervention, the Soviets had again threatened to send "volunteers" to oppose the Western "imperialists" and had carried out conspicuous military maneuvers in Soviet Central Asia and Transcaucasia. The firmness of the American position, and the failure of the Soviet Union in the face of Eisenhower's determination to do more than to denounce the intervention and call for a diplomatic settlement, made it very clear that there were limits to Soviet willingness to bail out the Arabs. This had a dampening effect on Nasser's anti-Western drive.

Another unexpected turn of events influenced this situation. The new regime in Iraq, instead of turning out to be pro-Nasser—as almost everyone, including Nasser, had expected—took an anti-Nasser position. It was not long before it began to challenge the Egyptian ruler's leadership of Arab nationalism. Nasser quickly recognized this threat of Egypt's traditional rival and attempted to overthrow the Kassem government. But the revolt by a group of pro-Nasser officers was quickly squashed. At the same time, the Soviet Union gave economic and military support to the Kassem government. Nasser was becoming increasingly isolated in the Arab world: Jordan, Lebanon, and Saudi Arabia had remained independent; Libya and the Sudan had resisted his attempts to subvert them; Syria was restless in the United Arab Republic; and Iraq had become a rival for Arab leadership. Nor was this situation materially changed by the events of the early 1960s: Kassem was overthrown and Syria revolted to quit the United Arab Republic. Despite the common Pan-Arab aspirations of Egypt, Syria, and Iraq, a real Arab union remained as elusive as ever. Syria and Iraq were unwilling to permit Nasser to dominate them; and Nasser was unwilling to form a union he could not control. The Egyptian leader's new emphasis on domestic reform—or what he called "Arab Socialism"—therefore became crucial to his fight for Arab leadership, even though he continued his attempts to overthrow traditional pro-Western regimes and remained generally anti-Western in his policy positions.

Meanwhile, the United States had almost become a full-fledged member of the Baghdad Pact (now renamed the Central Treaty Organization) by joining its economic, military, and countersubversion committees; it was also bound to each of the three Muslim states individually by bilateral defense agreements. But behind these developments remained all the essential problems that had given rise to the turmoil after 1955: the conflicts among the Arab states, the Arab-Israeli quarrel, the overshadowing competition between the United States and the Soviet Union, and, above all, Arab nationalism with its frequent xenophobic overtones. Despite the vast oil wealth, the Arab masses remained very poor and suffered from illiteracy, malnutrition, and disease. Social discontent and political instability were the result. While the area settled down to relative quiescence, the American attempt to fill the vacuum left by the reduction of British power and draw another "frontier" was unsuccessful. Ironically, it was the attempt to do this that drew the Soviet Union and Egypt together to destroy the "northern tier," permitting the former to jump over the line that was supposed to contain it.

WESTERN EUROPEAN UNION
AND THE COMMON MARKET

In Europe, the defense line had already been drawn by NATO. But the strength of this line on the ground depended upon supplementing NATO forces with West German troops. The European Defense Community was the means the Allies had chosen to achieve this goal. But in August 1954, the French National Assembly rejected EDC by a decisive majority. Fear of Germany remained too great, and French nationalists wished to maintain France's identity and honor. This was a real blow to the efforts toward creating a situation of strength in Europe. The whole basis of NATO strategy and European integration was suddenly imperiled.

The response of the Eisenhower administration was a self-righteous one. Instead of taking the lead in finding a way out of this impasse, it simply withdrew from the problem and waited for the European powers to resolve it. Secretary Dulles only repeated his threat that the United States would make an "agonizing reappraisal" of its NATO commitments if the deadlock were not broken. It was Britain's Prime Minister Eden who initiated averting such a reappraisal by seeking a way of rearming West Germany with French approval. He found it in the forgotten Brussels Treaty.

This organization was now to be revised by the inclusion of Germany and Italy. The new alliance, which pledged all its members to come to one another's aid if attacked, would be known as the Western European Union (WEU). Yet WEU was not really an alliance, no forces were assigned to it, and it had no responsibility for formulating a strategy to defend its members. These remained within the functions of NATO. WEU's role was to channel West German troops into NATO, while at the same time maintaining a set of controls over West Germany similar to those included in EDC. Furthermore, Britain agreed to keep a minimum number of troops on the Continent. Britain's pledge was a formalization of its responsibilities under the Dunkirk, Brussels, and NATO treaties. But to the French it seemed an important new commitment; they now felt assured that they would not someday be left to face German troops alone.

These commitments, embodied in the Paris Pact, came into force in May

1955. Thus, ten years after Germany's defeat, the occupation came to an end, and the Federal Republic regained its sovereignty and entered NATO via WEU. West Germany's military power could now be added to Western strength. Two important declarations were appended to these Paris agreements. In the first, the West German government subscribed to the principles of the United Nations, undertook "never to have recourse to force to achieve the reunification of Germany or the modification of the present boundaries of the German Federal Republic," and to resolve all disputes between itself and other states by peaceful means. In the second, however, the United States, Britain, and France declared that they recognized the Federal Republic as the only freely and legitimately constituted government entitled to speak for all of Germany—which indicated a policy of nonrecognition of the East German government. In addition, the Allies would pursue German reunification by peaceful means—which meant that the alliance with West Germany, while revisionist in its political objective, was conceived of as being defensive in nature. Finally, the Western powers stated that they would continue to exercise their responsibilities with regard to the security of West Germany and West Berlin.

With Germany safely enrolled as a member of NATO, the WEU members now took a momentous step toward further economic and political integration. The six states that composed this Little Europe had gained increasing benefits from this movement. On June 1, 1958, they established the European Economic Community (EEC), usually referred to as the Common Market, whose objective was to join them together into an economic union. Their plan was to achieve this in a twelve- to fifteen-year period. During this time, all six states would completely eliminate the tariffs and quota systems still hampering trade among them (agriculture was to be the exception—the Common Market expected to develop a common policy of subsidies and price supports, and eliminate discriminations among farmers within the community); they would also abolish restrictions on the movement of labor, capital, and services among them, although this commitment was qualified. But these moves, the "Six" realized, would not suffice. A government might abolish a tariff, but it could compensate its producers through subsidies or impose internal taxes that would discriminate against foreign products. Production costs also reflected national regulations on wages, hours, working conditions, and social welfare programs; producers in nations with lower standards would have an obvious advantage against foreign competition. Thus, to ensure maximum free competition in the Common Market, subsidies were forbidden (except for use in developing backward areas); discriminatory taxes, price-fixing, and division of markets by cartel arrangements were not permitted; and the need to equalize hours, wages, and working conditions was recognized as urgent.

What were the chances for the development of this Common Market? The economic benefits suggested that they were excellent. As trade barriers were lowered and then disappeared, the increasing competition would result in the growth of efficient companies and the elimination of the less efficient ones unless they modernized or converted to new lines of production. All members would also gain from the capital funds. Italy would receive capital for the development of its southern area; France and its overseas territories would also receive development capital. While Germany would contribute a large share of these funds that would benefit its partners, it would in return receive access to their European and African markets—and Germany was in the strongest competitive position of the Six. A final factor was that the community expected to receive advantages against third parties. It would be in a strong bargaining position to demand reciprocal lowering of tariffs. All these advantages outweighed the burdens each nation would suffer as a result of economic dislocation and hardships, which would, in fact, be minimized by being extended over a twelve- to fifteen-year period (the plan's initial successes were to cut this period down by several years) and by being shared among all members.

Above all, the principal advantage of the Common Market would be political. For a common market needs common policies; only one set of rules—not six—can govern its competitive behavior. One nation cannot be allowed to pay its workers considerably lower wages than its neighbor in order to achieve a competitive advantage. There would therefore have to be some standardization of wages, as well as of such related items as overtime, hours worked per week, and various welfare benefits. In the long run, if the Common Market developed successfully, it would therefore also undoubtedly lead to the adoption of common fiscal policies to control the ups and downs of the business cycle, a common currency, and a central bank. Thus the economic "spillover"—from a common market in coal and steel into a common market for all sectors of the economy—was expected by the Common Market's founding fathers to stimulate political unification as economic integration compelled the Inner Six members to harmonize their social and economic policies. Economic union was expected to encourage increasing political integration. It was precisely this objective to form a political union that had originally inspired the European Coal and Steel Community (ECSC).

The European Economic Community was the culminating act of the movement, initiated by France and strongly supported by Chancellor Konrad Adenauer, to tie Germany so closely to a European community that it would never again be able to use its power for purely national ends. The formation of the Inner Six was nothing less than the last link subjecting Germany to European restraints and responsibilities. Its success would make it impossible thereafter for Germany ever again to pursue a unilateral course. The Common Market was also the end product of France's desire to supplement its own strength with that of a united Europe, so that it would gain an equal voice with Britain in the Atlantic Alliance and not always remain subservient to the United States. France did not want to pursue a NATO policy dictated largely by Anglo-American interests; it wanted the alliance to take its interests into account as well.

It was hardly surprising that the Soviet Union reacted quickly against the Common Market and attempted to break up this potential united states of

Europe. A strong and united Europe, economically prosperous and politically stable, would not only prove to be a powerful barrier to Soviet expansionist ambitions, but it might well threaten the Soviet *status quo* in Eastern Europe. The existence of a free Germany had already had an unsettling effect upon the whole satellite system.

West Berlin, especially, had had a tremendous impact in this respect. The existence of this city, alongside Communist East Berlin, had hampered Soviet control of East Germany. Through West Berlin escaped many young, skilled, and professional men and women of East Germany; it was an escape hatch that was depopulating East Germany of the very people it needed to run its society. In West Berlin, the United States, Britain, and France had, moreover, established agencies to gather intelligence about Eastern Europe. There was a constant flow of information about the West from West Berlin into the Soviet-controlled satellites; this defeated one of the major purposes of the iron curtain, which was to stop incoming information that might lead to comparisons of the Communist and free systems. West Berlin, in short, affected the political stability of all of Eastern Europe. If the existence of West Berlin and West Germany made the Communist *status quo* insecure, how much greater the Soviet apprehensions of a united Europe must have been.

The stability of the Soviet position in Eastern and Central Europe, as apparently seen by Moscow, depended upon two factors: one, gaining Western recognition of the East German "Democratic" Republic; and two, destroying the freedom of West Berlin. To achieve these objectives, the Soviet Union announced in November 1958 that at the end of six months it intended to end the four-power occupation and would hand control of East Berlin and the routes leading into West Berlin over to the East Germans. The clear implication was that in the future free access to Berlin would require that the Western powers deal directly and officially with the East German government. The Soviets also repeated their former proposal for the unification of Germany: that East and West Germany should join in a confederation. This, too, was a tactical device to gain the Federal Republic's recognition of East Germany. The Soviets obviously wanted to entice the West Germans to start negotiating with the East Germans on the issue of unification; at the same time, it was also clear that the Soviets were not in the least interested in any form of unification.

The Soviet proposal was, in fact, so constituted that it precluded Western acceptance. A confederation half democratic and half dictatorship was a contradiction in terms and was totally unfeasible. Most industry in East Germany was owned by the government; West Germany was a booming private-enterprise state. To ensure the rejection of their terms, the Soviets also demanded that East Germany, with a population of a little more than 17 million, and West Germany, with a population of more than 53 million, should be equally represented in the confederated government. The Soviet Union naturally did not want the East Germans to be outvoted—with the possible result that East Germany would be voted out of existence—but Khrushchev could hardly have expected the Western powers or the Adenauer government to accept such equality.

If the Soviet proposals, then, were meant to elicit Western recognition of East Germany, this goal still remained subsidiary to the primary aim of strangling West Berlin. What the Soviets were actually calling for when they declared the end of the four-power occupation was an Allied withdrawal from West Berlin, turning it into a "free city." This was, in effect, a demand for the incorporation of West Berlin into East Germany. Once Western troops had left the city, the West Berliners would feel isolated and unprotected, abandoned and completely helpless. They would be surrounded by the Soviet army and the East German army and police. In these circumstances, the defenseless West Berliners would have to come to terms with the East German regime. On the other hand, if the West would not sign a treaty turning Berlin into a "free city," the Soviet Union would then sign a separate peace treaty with East Germany, thus automatically abrogating the West's right to be in Berlin and making any further Western stay dependent upon the terms that could be negotiated with the now "sovereign" German Democratic Republic. This would mean that the West would remain in Berlin by the consent of East Germany, which would then gradually intensify its pressure and gradually undermine the West's position until it became untenable.

At this point, one way or the other, the Soviets would have eliminated a very troublesome thorn in their side. They would then be in a far better position to stabilize the *status quo*. But the destruction of West Berlin would not only have accomplished the Soviet Union's defensive aims; it would simultaneously have attained the Soviet Union's long-standing offensive purpose of weakening its opponents, perhaps fatally. If the Soviets could drive the Western powers, especially the United States, out of Berlin, they would also be able, first, to cut off the development of the Common Market before it gathered too much momentum, and second, to shatter the NATO alliance. It was, above all, American power that guaranteed the freedom of the 2 million Germans living in West Berlin. If the United States abandoned these people under pressure, faith in America's protective power and willingness to live up to its commitments would collapse in Europe. The Germans would be the first to read the lesson: since America could not guarantee their security, they must approach the Soviets independently.

Whatever the nature of the terms the Soviets would offer them, they would certainly include clauses demanding the abandonment of all Germany's political, economic, or military ties to the West. But without Germany, there could be no Common Market, since Germany's partners were dependent upon it for much of the capital required for their economic development. And if Germany pulled out of the Atlantic Alliance, American troops would have to be withdrawn back to the United States, since it would be politically and strategically impossible to station them in France. Yet, these troops were a symbol of the American commitment to defend Europe; they were psychologically and politically indispensable. No written guarantees could be substituted for this living embodiment of America's stake in Europe.

Was America, therefore, willing to defend Europe now that the United States was itself becoming increasingly vulnerable to a Soviet nuclear attack? This was, in the final analysis, the fundamental question posed by the Berlin crisis. The Soviet proposals had included the ultimatum that if West Berlin's status had not been "renegotiated" within six months, the Soviets would place the East Germans in control of the railroads and highways leading into West Berlin. If the East Germans then interfered with Western traffic, the West would have to employ force to break any blockade; and Khrushchev stated that any such Western attempts would meet Soviet resistance. The defense of West Berlin therefore raised the possibility of war. The Soviet challenge was a clever one: It presented the United States with a limited challenge and offered it the choice of surrendering West Berlin or fighting a total war for its preservation. It was America's will that was thus really at stake in Berlin.

Berlin was thus a major test of postwar American policy. Nor was it a repeat of the 1948 situation. At that time, Stalin had acted upon two assumptions: first, that the far larger Red Army contingents would deter an Allied attempt to break through on the ground; and second, that the United States and Britain could not keep West Berlin alive. The first assumption proved to be correct, but the second was mistaken. When Stalin realized this, he had either to call off the blockade or shoot down Allied planes and risk a war. America's atomic monopoly favored the first solution. In 1957, however, the Soviet Union had tested the world's first Intercontinental Ballistic Missile (ICBM). American brinkmanship would now be risky. This test, moreover, had followed a series of spectacular Soviet space shots. These Sputniks, or satellites, which flew around the world every 90 minutes plus the ICBM test, were impressive symbols of Soviet technological progress and raised serious questions in the United States about its historic technological leadership and the future of the balance of power. For Khrushchev immediately began to talk of mass-producing ICBMs and asserted that the balance of nuclear or strategic power was shifting toward the Soviet Union. There was widespread public concern and anxiety about a future "missile gap," which, given that ICBMs were faster than bombers, meant that U.S. deterrent forces would become vulnerable to a surprise attack— and might, therefore, no longer deter. American brinkmanship in this circumstance would be very risky. Yet, given the limited nature of the Soviet challenge and the nature of all-or-nothing massive retaliations, how could the United States prevent the Soviet Union from slowly strangling West Berlin to death?

Berlin was thus a crisis of massive retaliation; for the Soviet action put into question the very feasibility of basic American strategy. Could strategic air power, upon which the Eisenhower administration depended almost exclusively to preserve the line around the Sino-Soviet periphery, fulfill this task in an age of nuclear plenty, when World War III was becoming a pseudonym for suicide? The answer seemed to be that too great a reliance upon SAC was gravely weakening the American ability to preserve this line. Nuclear bombs were just *too* powerful; they were *too* enormously destructive to be used in any situation but the ultimate one. U.S. strategic power was—ironically—*so* great that it tended to paralyze the will to use it; it therefore paralyzed diplomacy as well.

The Berlin crisis, a limited Soviet challenge but one that had enormous stakes for the United States, was the most serious challenge Washington had confronted since 1948–1949. The Truman Doctrine, Marshall Plan, Berlin airlift, and NATO had made it very plain to Moscow that Western Europe was an area of vital American interest. Soviet domination over this Western rimland of the Eurasian continent was no more tolerable to the United States than German control. Presumably this knowledge had deterred the Soviets in the late 1940s, and it was this fear of war that had led them to redirect their challenges to Third World areas.

Now, however, ten years after the first Berlin crisis, the Soviets had once more challenged the West in Europe. Indeed, the reopening of the Berlin issue—and especially that for the first time in the postwar era the Soviets were publicly demanding that the Western powers abandon territory they controlled and were threatening them with an ultimatum—suggested a new Soviet confidence in the ability of their power to achieve their stated political aim of converting the Western half of Germany's former capital into a "free city." Not only did the West not have a capacity for a limited response to a limited challenge but, worse, the strategic balance appeared to be changing. The Soviets were claiming that they were mass-producing their new ICBM. America's deterrent bomber force, they said, was now vulnerable and its deterrent capacity declining. The Central Intelligence Agency seemed to agree by forecasting a missile gap as the United States entered the 1960s, and many Americans, both in and out of government, became concerned that Khrushchev might be right. Clearly, he was attempting to cash in on what the Soviet leader already asserted was a changing distribution of power that had become favorable to the Soviet Union.

Chapter 6

BERLIN, CUBA, AND THE CRISIS OF MASSIVE RETALIATION

DETERRENCE AND THE LIMITED CHALLENGE

American policy has traditionally thought of the world in terms of mutually exclusive conditions: war or peace, force or diplomacy, aggressors or peace-loving states. Peace was normal; war was abnormal. Force was unnecessary in the absence of conflict and hostilities; it was to be used only in wartime to destroy the source of war itself. Massive retaliation fitted this American approach completely. It was an all-or-nothing strategy. On the one hand, short of a Soviet attack on the United States or invasion of Western Europe, it could not be used. Preventive war was consistently rejected by American administrations, both at the time of the nation's atomic monopoly and later, in the 1950s and 1960s, during the period of gradually declining strategic superiority. Deterrence was the American goal, and the nuclear strategy was therefore one of only retaliating after the opponent had struck first. On the other hand, once the enemy had attacked, massive retaliation would, as in World Wars I and II, punish him totally and destroy him utterly in ways not conceivable until 1945. Massive retaliation, by reducing the enemy's population and industrial centers to a mass of rubble and radioactive dust, carried the American approach to war to its ultimate but logical conclusion.

In one sense, atomic and then the even more destructive nuclear weapons made it possible to pursue an old American dream in a rather new and gruesome manner. By making nuclear war too destructive to fight, by increasingly making the distinction between victor and loser in such a conflict meaningless, the deterrent strategy aimed at eliminating war itself. This old goal, previously sought through the crusade or "war to end all wars," or through international organization and cooperation, or free trade and economic interdependence among nations, was now realizable because war had, in the popular phrase, become "unthinkable."

Yet unfortunately, precisely because it was an all-or-nothing strategy, massive retaliation could not ward off limited challenges. Even in the immediate postwar period in which America had possessed an atomic monopoly, the Soviet Union was not deterred from consolidating its grip on Eastern Europe, attempting to seize a northern province of Iran, exerting great pressure on Turkey, permitting Yugoslavia and Bulgaria to intervene in the Greek civil war, or urging the French Communist Party to try to exploit France's postwar economic misery after 1947. It had not even prevented the North Korean attack upon South Korea. Nor had the threat of massive retaliation stopped either the Chinese Communists from helping the Vietminh or prevented the latter from defeating the French in Indochina in 1954. The only thing the Soviets had to avoid was an attack upon the United States itself or upon those areas the United States had designated as of vital interest to its security; short of that ultimate provocation, the Soviet Union, the strategically weaker party during the first decade of the cold war, could raise tensions and challenge the United States.

If this was the pattern during the period of America's atomic monopoly and superior strategic power even after the Soviet Union had acquired its own atomic bomb, the possibility of challenges in areas vital to the United States— such as Europe—increased as the Soviet Union's nuclear stockpile and capacity to hit the United States increased during the late 1950s. As massive retaliation became more of a two-way street, the Soviet Union's growing ability to inflict catastrophic destruction upon America meant that the two nuclear states would increasingly stalemate one another's strategic striking power. Mutual deterrence, or the "balance of terror," as Winston Churchill called it, would ensure the peace; indeed, in President Dwight Eisenhower's words, "there is no alternative to peace." His participation at the 1955 summit conference in Geneva with Soviet Premier Nikolai Bulganin (Nikita Khrushchev was at that time not yet premier but first secretary of the Communist Party of the Soviet Union) was generally recognized as testimony to this fact. War was no longer a rational instrument of national power; by simply meeting, the leaders of the two most powerful countries of the world were said to have "signed" a tacit nonaggression pact.

Actually, American policy handed the Soviet Union the opportunity to break this stalemate. For the age of atomic plenty has increased America's strategic dilemma. The Eisenhower all-or-nothing strategy meant that each limited Soviet challenge confronted Washington with the question of whether the defense of American interests was worth the destruction of most of America's cities and their inhabitants. Faced with this prospect if it responded to the less than total Soviet challenges, the American government had a strong incentive to do nothing. This meant that Moscow could gradually turn the nuclear balance of power in its favor by imposing a series of piecemeal defeats upon the West. It could erode the *status quo* by nibbling away at it bit by bit, without ever once facing the United States with the one kind of challenge for which it was prepared. According to Henry Kissinger in 1957:

> It can be argued that the fear of all-out war is bound to be mutual, that the Soviet leaders will, therefore, share our reluctance to engage in any adventures which may involve this risk. But because each side may be equally deterred from engaging in all-out war, it makes all the difference which side can extricate itself from its dilemma *only* by initiating such a struggle. If the Soviet bloc can present its challenges in less than all-out form it may gain a crucial advantage. Every move on its part will then pose the appalling dilemma of whether we are willing to commit suicide to prevent encroachments, which do not, each in itself, seem to threaten our existence directly but which may be steps on the road to our ultimate destruction.
>
> To be sure, we shall continue to insist that we reject the notion of "peace at any price." The price of peace, however, cannot be determined in the abstract. The growth of the Soviet nuclear stockpile is certain to widen the line between what is considered "vital" and what is "peripheral" if we must weigh each objective against the destruction of New York or Detroit, of Los Angeles or Chicago.

Was Berlin still a "vital" interest? Or was Berlin now a "peripheral" interest? These were the stark questions that confronted the United States in the late 1950s.

MASSIVE RETALIATION AND NATO

The questions raised by the Soviet challenge were further underlined by the lack of sizable shield forces on the Continent. The original tasks assigned to these troops were twofold: first, to strengthen deterrence by assuring the Soviets that an attack upon Europe would break the tripwire and unleash the Strategic Air Command (SAC) and second, in case deterrence failed, to implement the "forward strategy" and hold the Red Army at the Elbe while SAC was laying the Soviet Union waste. The success of the deterrence of total war, however, dictated yet a third operational assignment for North Atlantic Treaty Organization (NATO) forces: to conduct limited operations and thereby deter less than total challenges. It was preposterous to assume that the United States would continue to risk suicide no matter what the level of Soviet provocation. Would it really be willing to initiate an all-out nuclear war if the Soviets seized a small portion of Turkey? Would it really precipitate a total nuclear exchange if the Red Army or satellite East German troops seized all or part of West Berlin or a small enclave of West Germany? Would suicide in these instances be preferable to accepting limited losses? Only a capacity for limited war would allow the United States and its allies to escape this dilemma.

But it was exactly this capacity to respond to limited challenges that was missing in Europe. In a large measure, this was a result of the Eisenhower administration's determination to "maximize air power and minimize the foot soldier." By January 1960, NATO had only seventeen or eighteen ready divisions. Apart from the numerical deficiency of NATO ground forces, their equipment with tactical nuclear weapons raised the same question as did SAC: Would they be used? Would NATO not grow increasingly reluctant to rely on these forces to respond to Soviet moves? When the original decision to equip Allied forces with nuclear battlefield weapons was taken, it was believed that the Soviet Union would have few, if any, tactical nuclear weapons in the near future. Thus, the damage caused by these weapons could be absorbed—particularly since East Germany and Poland would have to absorb most of it, and Soviet and satellite troops would have to suffer the nuclear blows. The picture changed, however, when the Soviets, too, acquired these weapons and thereby ensured that their use would be reciprocal. In these circumstances, the advantages that tactical nuclear arms were supposed to confer upon the West began to diminish, if not to disappear.

These weapons would not protect Europe; they would devastate it. Europe is densely populated; its cities are too close to one another; civil, military, tactical, and strategic targets are all intertwined. A nuclear ground war would be a catastrophe for Europe, probably spelling the end of European civilization. The distinction between a limited and total nuclear war was meaningless for Europeans. NATO's capacity to fight a limited tactical nuclear war would therefore not allow the West to escape the dilemma of suicide or appeasement. A limited war in Europe was meaningless unless it also limited the devastation. But the concentration on massive retaliation—on NATO's sword—had reduced the apparent necessity of raising sufficient ground forces and strengthening the NATO shield. This, in turn, reinforced the need to stake Western survival on each issue, no matter what the level of provocation, since America was left with no weapon but strategic air power with which to respond to the Soviet challenge in the heart of Europe.

THE BERLIN RETREAT

It was this reliance upon SAC that made it very difficult for the Western powers, especially the United States, to impress the Soviet Union with NATO's unity and resoluteness. On the one hand, the United States was determined to stay in Berlin; on the other hand, having stated that it would defend Berlin by massive retaliation, it simultaneously sought to escape the consequences of its own military strategy. This it could do only by granting concessions. Shortly after the presentation of the Soviet ultimatum, Secretary of State John Foster Dulles talked of accepting the East Germans as "Russian agents" at the checkpoints on the route leading into Berlin. The secretary also declared that the reunification of Germany could be brought about by means other than free elections. Both statements threatened a complete abandonment of the previous and long-held American positions of nonrecognition of the East German regime and Germany's right of self-determination. The administration, already pressured by the British, also accepted the standing Soviet call for a summit conference. But it insisted on the prior fulfillment of two conditions: withdrawal of the Soviet six-month ultimatum and a foreign ministers' conference to lay the basis for a settlement of the Berlin and the general German issues. The purpose of a "meeting at the top" was, in the administration's opinion, essentially to ratify decisions already reached at a lower level; Eisenhower definitely rejected a meeting that would settle nothing and end in a fruitless propaganda debate.

The Soviets reluctantly accepted the precondition of a foreign ministers' conference and at the same time denied that the six-month ultimatum was an ultimatum. But they refused to budge from their position at the foreign ministers' marathon held in Geneva in the spring and summer of 1959. It was the West that offered the concessions. In the first place, the United States allowed an East German delegation to sit in on the deliberations and thereby took a step toward *de facto* recognition of the Soviet-installed regime. The Soviet Union had threatened not to negotiate at all if the East Germans were not permitted to attend. Second, the West abandoned its plan for the reunification of Germany at the first sign of Soviet opposition. Third, the foreign ministers then took up the problem of an interim settlement for Berlin. In short, after years of stating that it was the Soviet division of Germany that was the cause of European instability, the United States and Britain accepted the Soviet definition of what constituted the principal source of European tension. They offered several concessions as well.

The Soviets simply refused to renew their endorsement of Allied rights in Berlin and reasserted that they would end the occupation regime. The Allies thus failed to obtain the Soviet guarantee they sought, but the fact that they had attempted to arrive at an interim arrangement for Berlin at all, and had been willing to grant concessions to obtain it, is eloquent testimony to the dilemma in which American strategy had placed them. For, in effect, the Western powers—in this case, America and Britain—were willing to transform the Western position in Berlin merely in return for the withdrawal of the Soviet threat to the city. In an attempt to extricate themselves from the dilemma of suicide or surrender, the two countries were placing themselves in the humiliating position of calling into question their well-established rights in Berlin. No wonder Khrushchev felt that all he had to do was maintain a high level of tension.

Khrushchev's bellicosity and rigidity were thus paying handsome dividends. The more menacing he sounded and the more inflexibly he stood, the greater the number of voices in the West that called for more Western "flexibility" and "new approaches" to the Soviet Union on the whole problem of Germany. Policies that had almost become "untouchable" over the years were suddenly placed in flux and condemned as dangerous. The West was torn apart by precisely this kind of controversy. The British denounced Chancellor Konrad Adenauer's "rigidity"; the Germans, in turn, accused the British of "appeasement." Franco-British relations cooled considerably. And both Adenauer and Charles de Gaulle demonstrated increasing suspicions of United States intentions and resolution. America's apparent willingness to discuss Berlin with the Soviets seemed to the French and German leaders to show little American conviction or courage to uphold a previous position; to them, Eisenhower was showing far too much flexibility.

As if to prove Khrushchev's theory that his threats of war against the West would have rewarding consequences, and to confirm De Gaulle's and Adenauer's apprehensions, President Eisenhower issued an invitation to Khrushchev to visit the United States in September 1959. This invitation represented a major Soviet tactical victory. Such a summit *à deux* would show Khrushchev's equality with the American president and convincingly demonstrate to the world the Soviet Union's status with the United States as one of the two great superpowers. And, as Khrushchev knew, it would deepen the divisions within Western ranks by increasing the Allies' apprehension of a separate United States-Soviet agreement at their expense, and conversely, would persuade President Eisenhower that the crisis was caused by the rigidity of certain Allied leaders who were opposed to the "normalization" of relations.

The Eisenhower-Khrushchev meeting did, however, have one positive result: The Soviet Union withdrew its threat to take unilateral action in Berlin in return for American willingness to negotiate on the problems of Berlin and Germany at a four-power summit meeting. For American policymakers, this meant another postponement of the day on which they would have to decide the painful question of whether Berlin was worth the cost of a total war. But if the administration believed that the crisis had been ended, that from then on it could leisurely negotiate on these issues and, if the Soviets did not accept its terms, preserve the *status quo*, it was soon disabused of this notion. Khrushchev was soon reiterating his threat to sign a separate peace with East Germany.

Shortly before the scheduled Paris summit conference in May 1960, an event took place that was to shatter the summit conference after only one session and further postpone negotiations on Berlin. On May Day, 1300 miles within Soviet territory, the Soviets downed an American U-2 "spy plane" that was loaded with photographic equipment for the gathering of intelligence data. The Eisenhower administration reacted to this unexpected and unhappy turn of events with considerable diplomatic ineptitude. When Khrushchev initially announced only the shooting down of the U-2, the U.S. government responded that the plane had been engaged solely in meteorological observation and speculated that the pilot must have flown off his course. When the Soviet premier then revealed the real mission of the flight and produced an alleged confession by the pilot, the administration reversed itself. In a move unprecedented in diplomatic history, it admitted that the U-2 pilot had been taking aerial photographs of the Soviet Union and that it had lied in its previous announcement. Nor did the administration stop there. It claimed that similar flights had been sent into Soviet skies for several years and strongly intimated that such flights would continue. The reason advanced was that Soviet secrecy made it necessary to gather information by this means in order to prevent a surprise attack. But it is one thing to be caught red-handed in spying and to admit it; it is quite another thing to assert that you will continue to do so in the future. In effect, the United States claimed the *right* to fly over Soviet territory (one need only imagine the uproar in the United States if the Soviets were to announce calmly that they had the right to fly over American soil and take photographs of military installations).

Such a challenge could hardly have been left unmet. For the Soviet premier to have bypassed this claim would have been equivalent to acknowledging to the world, to his people, to his domestic enemies, and to his allies that he had surrendered to the United States the right to violate Soviet territory. Khrushchev could not have survived such an admission. The alternative course he took was to strike a belligerent pose in Paris. He launched a blistering personal attack upon President Eisenhower, demanding from him personal apology for past U-2 flights, a promise that no such flights would be undertaken in the future, and punishment of those responsible for the spying operation. Eisenhower's promise that no more reconnaissance missions would be undertaken during his term of office did not satisfy Khrushchev; he apparently considered this to mean merely a temporary suspension. The other conditions demanded by the Soviet premier were rejected outright by Eisenhower. Khrushchev thereupon suggested that the summit conference be postponed for a period of six to eight months, and he bluntly told Eisenhower that he would not be welcome if he came to the Soviet Union in June to return the premier's visit to the United States. In short, Khrushchev said that he wanted nothing more to do with Eisenhower and that he would wait to negotiate the Berlin problem with the next administration. A new crisis had been put off for a little while longer.

It was inevitable, therefore, that the Berlin problem would be raised again by the Soviets once the new administration had established itself in power. Khrushchev was still convinced that the global balance was shifting in his favor, and he remained confident that he was strong enough to acquire West Berlin. President John Kennedy, fearing that Khrushchev might miscalculate, therefore journeyed to Vienna to emphasize America's determination to defend West Berlin; the United States would stand firm and protect the free half of the city. Khrushchev, however, took these warnings lightly. His response was characteristic: to test the president's resolution by reviving the original threat that the Berlin situation would have to be resolved within six months—that is, before the end of 1961. The fruits of the Vienna summit meeting were thus precisely the opposite of what was intended: It resulted in the very type of Soviet brinkmanship against which Kennedy had sought to caution the Soviet leader.

Kennedy was thus confronted with a crisis. On the one hand, he fully realized the significance of Berlin. While he declared his willingness to negotiate, he also stated that he did not expect the Soviets to confront him with the accomplished fact of a treaty with East Germany. The United States was not willing to discuss merely how the West would withdraw from the beleaguered city, thereby leaving it for the Communists to swallow. The West's right to be in the city stemmed from its victory over Nazi Germany. Western presence and access to the city, and the freedom of West Berlin, therefore were not negotiable. In the president's words: "We cannot negotiate with those who say: 'What's mine is mine, and what's yours is negotiable.'" More specifically, he asked, if the West refused to meet its clear-cut commitments in Berlin, where would it meet them? Yet it was also clear on August 13, 1961, when the Communists built a wall dividing the city, that they had eliminated the escape hatch for East Germans, ended West Berlin's usefulness as a "showplace for Western capitalism," and violated the quadripartite status of Berlin. But the West did not react by resisting the erection of the wall with bulldozers and tanks for fear of military conflict with Communist—especially Soviet—forces. This passivity intensified Khrushchev's conviction that the United States would not fight and that he could, slowly but surely, increase the pressure on NATO and drive the West out of Berlin.

It was this possibility, and the American fear that the Soviet leader might miscalculate Western resolve and thereby accidentally trigger a war, that accounted largely for the difference between Kennedy's and his predecessor's reactions to the Berlin crisis. Unlike Eisenhower, Kennedy used the tensions over Berlin to further the build-up of American military power; the new president was determined to show Khrushchev that the United States was not bluffing when it declared its intentions to defend West Berlin. Kennedy moved in two directions; indeed, he had begun to do so almost immediately after assuming office. One was toward "flexible response." The United States had to have more options than suicide or surrender. This increased flexibility was to be achieved by building larger conventional forces. In Europe this meant that NATO would have a credible defense, one that would not have to resort immediately to destructive tactical nuclear weapons; outside Europe, the United States would be provided with a capability to respond to limited challenges.

The other critical aim of the Kennedy administration was to reduce SAC's vulnerability during the changeover from bombers to missiles that had begun in the late 1950s. Bombers located at known sites were highly vulnerable to surprise attack. Thus, even in a situation of mutual deterrence, the possibility that many or most of the enemy's bombers might be surprised and destroyed on the ground remained an incentive to attack. If they could be destroyed, the retaliatory attack by a small remnant force might not be fatal to the attacking nation. In a crisis situation, this possibility could tempt either side to launch a preemptive strike in order to forestall a possible blow by the other side—even if the other side actually had no intention of striking. But solid-fuel missiles, like the air force's Minuteman, could be widely dispersed and protected, or "hardened," in underground silos instead of being concentrated on a few above-ground bases, as bombers were; missiles were not yet accurate enough to hit such silos. And the navy's Polaris missiles would be moved underwater so that the enemy would at no time know where to strike them.

The importance of the dispersion, the "hardening," and especially the underwater mobility of missiles lay in the fact that it deprived a surprise attack of its rationale. Obliterating the enemy's cities would benefit the aggressor very little if the enemy still retained his retaliatory capacity. Surprise, therefore, no longer conferred any significant advantage to the side that struck first. Indeed, there was no need any longer to hit preemptively, since enough of the missiles would survive an initial strike and still be able to retaliate fully against the aggressor in a second strike. A first strike in these circumstances—which American policymakers generally conceded to the Soviets—would be completely irrational.

Yet these changes were long-range. Kennedy, as cautious as his predecessor, therefore vacillated between his determination to stay in West Berlin and his equally strong determination to avoid conflict. Thus, like Eisenhower, he was willing to offer concessions and negotiate with the Soviets alone if West Germany and France remained "inflexible." The meager results of these bilateral American-Soviet negotiations were primarily due to Soviet unwillingness to concede the right to any Western presence in Berlin, which, in turn, was in all probability due to Khrushchev's conviction that he need only maintain Soviet pressure finally to evict the Western powers from the Communist-surrounded and divided city. If during this early period of the Kennedy administration, as during the late years of the Eisenhower era, the Soviets were unwilling to risk the final test, they had shown they were not hesitant to push the issue to a point of high tension. And while the United States had upheld the *status quo*, the manner in which it questioned its own position in Berlin and the concessions it offered in the name of flexibility demonstrated a lack of will and sense of purpose. This augured ill for the future, if: (1) the Soviet leaders could keep their challenges below the level of provocation that might arouse an American nuclear response (while the exact level of tension could not be known to them, they did keep well below it); and (2) the Soviets confined their challenges to the periphery of Western power, and especially such an isolated outpost as West Berlin. As long as they followed these two fundamental precepts, they could continue to try and exploit the dilemmas of American strategy.

It was the second rule that the Soviets failed to follow when they shifted the challenge to ninety miles from the American mainland—to Cuba—where the United States had no choice but to respond in defense of what Washington conceived to be its vital interests.

CASTRO AND THE MISSILE CRISIS

Cuba's revolutionary government had been established on January 1, 1959, after its leaders had overthrown the tyrannical dictatorship of Fulgencio Batista. During his struggle against Batista, Fidel Castro had identified himself with both democratic government and social and economic justice and had gained widespread popularity among the Cuban people. This public support ensured the victory of his guerrilla army against the larger government forces. The Castro revolution was essentially a social revolution. In the opening months of its rule, the new government moved to remedy the conditions of the people by instituting land reforms and by building low-cost housing, schools, and clinics. But some features of this social revolution were bound to clash with the interests of the United States. Castro was highly nationalistic, and therefore anti-American because of past American domination of Cuba.

Although the United States had been instrumental in freeing Cuba from Spain, it had subsequently passed the Platt Amendment, which granted the Americans the right to intervene at any time in Cuba for the preservation of Cuban independence, for the protection of life, property, and individual liberty, and for the discharge of Cuba's treaty obligations. By 1934, when the amendment was repealed, the United States had intervened militarily three times; it also had established a naval base at Guantánamo Bay. American capital was even more effective in controlling Cuba. By 1956, the United States controlled 80 percent of Cuba's utilities, 90 percent of its mines and cattle ranches, nearly all its oil, and 40 percent of its sugar. It was thus not surprising that the Cuban revolution should in large part direct its long-pent-up nationalism and social resentment against "Yankee imperialism." America's support of the Batista dictatorship until the moment of its collapse only intensified this anti-American sentiment. "Cuba, si! Yanqui, no!" became the Castro regime's rallying cry, the ceremonial burning of the American flag its ritual, and the confiscation of American property its reward (although Cuban industry and land were also nationalized).

This anti-American nationalistic feeling, deliberately fostered by Castro to increase the popularity of his regime, led to an increasing identification of Castro's government with Communism. Before long, the regime betrayed its original democratic promises and became a dictatorship with centralized control over all phases of Cuba's life. All parties were abolished except for one— the Communist Party, upon whose organizational strength Castro had become increasingly dependent. Castro also linked Cuba closely to the Communist bloc. The Soviet Union supplied Cuba with vast amounts of arms and accompanying military advisors. Cuban airmen were sent to Czechoslovakia to learn how to fly Soviet fighters, and a large number of Cuban technicians were trained in Communist countries. Cuba's armed services soon ranked second only to America's as the largest in the hemisphere. Diplomatic relations were established with all Communist countries except East Germany, and economic agreements were signed with many of the same countries, including East Germany. Cuba's economy became integrated into that of the Communist bloc; 75 percent of the island's trade was with countries behind the iron curtain. In January 1961, the United States cut off diplomatic relations with Cuba. If Castro had at that point attempted to seize the Guantánamo base, there would have been an excuse for open American intervention.

Castro was much too shrewd to do so. Consequently, in April 1961, the

United States supported an attempt by a small force of Cuban exiles—many of them former Castro associates who had become disillusioned by the premier's tyranny and his Communist sympathies—to land in Cuba and attempt to overthrow Castro. Plans for this operation had been begun during the Eisenhower administration, and Kennedy decided to support them, when he came into office. The U.S. intelligence community believed that, once the exiles had gained a beachhead in the Bay of Pigs, some units of Castro's army and Cuba's population would welcome the invaders as liberators. But when the American-organized and -financed operation was launched, it turned out to be a dramatic and appalling failure. America had bungled because it launched a major foreign policy move involving American prestige on the glib assumption that a feeble beachhead operation would result in a mass uprising of Cubans against their government. The rumors and press reports, which conveyed the impression of a major invasion, only made the failure appear to be even greater.

If nothing succeeds like success, it can also be said that nothing fails like failure. American prestige, already lowered by the Soviet Union's man-in-space achievement, sank to a new low. In Cyrus Sulzberger's succinct sentence, "We looked like fools to our friends, rascals to our enemies, and incompetents to the rest." The administration had fallen victim to its own half-heartedness. The results of an unsuccessful invasion could have been predicted: an increase in Castro's domestic support, a revival of Latin American fears of "Yankee imperialism," a blunting of Kennedy's initially successful attempts to identify the United States with anticolonialism, and a loss of confidence in America's leadership by its allies.

Thus, Cuba survived as a Communist base from which the Soviet Union could threaten the United States itself and subvert the security of the other nations in the Western hemisphere. The importance of this cannot be underestimated. The American position in this hemisphere had been preeminent. The Monroe Doctrine had announced to the world that Latin America fell within the American sphere of influence and that Europe's great powers were to keep their hands off. In subsequent decades the United States had intervened repeatedly, especially in the Caribbean-Central America area. While the motives for intervention varied, principal among them was the fear that one of Europe's great powers might establish its influence in an area that might be called America's "strategic rear," or to use a Churchillian phrase, its "soft underbelly." During the early 1940s the concern was with German power; after that, with Soviet power. In 1954 a Marxist government had come to power in Guatamala; when it received arms from Czechoslovakia, the Eisenhower administration had intervened covertly and overthrown it, thereby setting a precedent for the Bay of Pigs. In short, the United States has never tolerated Latin American governments that were seen to be leaning toward Germany or the Soviet Union, at least not the smaller countries so close to the Rio Grande and Florida.

Castro's survival after the Bay of Pigs was a significant exception and to become an increasingly sore point, especially in the 1970s and 1980s. It was the result of the failure of covert intervention and the unwillingness to resort to overt intervention that might alienate the rising Latin American middle class whose support, it was thought, the United States needed. This country wished to remain a "good neighbor."

Thus a self-proclaimed Communist regime in Cuba was tolerated; the line was now drawn at a Soviet attempt to establish a missile base there. It was believed that the Soviet Union would not dare to do so in America's sphere of influence. Thus there was a shock when in the fall of 1962 U.S. intelligence suddenly discovered, to its great surprise and consternation, that the Soviets were building launching sites for approximately seventy medium- and intermediate-range ballistic missiles. The very fact that Khrushchev had dared to move his missiles so near the United States, and apparently expected no counteraction beyond ineffective diplomatic protests, was a dangerous sign. The great danger of all-out war is war by miscalculation; to prevent such a miscalculation is therefore an absolute necessity. But American actions had seemingly convinced the Soviet premier, the apostle of "peaceful coexistence," that the United States would not fight to protect its vital interests. He recalled recent events: the desire of Kennedy to eliminate Castro but his unwillingness at the moment of truth to send in American forces to eliminate a pro-Soviet regime from America's sphere of influence, and, in Berlin, his paralysis when the Soviets built the wall. In each instance, Khrushchev had seen the fear of conflict deter the United States. Thus, he apparently came to believe that he could install his missiles in Cuba with impunity; the United States would rather accept this result than risk the use of force. Kennedy, Khrushchev told an American visitor, was "too liberal to fight."

For Khrushchev, the stakes were high. American failure to respond to his move would have proved to its NATO allies what they feared already—namely, that the United States, having itself become highly vulnerable to attack, could no longer be relied upon for the protection of its vital interests in Europe. Inaction in the face of Soviet missiles installed only ninety miles away from the American coast would have emphasized dramatically this consequence of the nuclear balance. And the promised renewal of Soviet pressure on Berlin after the midterm U.S. congressional elections, together with the likelihood of an even more cautious American reaction than before, would only have reinforced this impression. This time, the Soviets would have issued an ultimatum to get out or else—and the "else" was the fact that the Soviets could for the first time cover a large part of the North American continent with their missiles, which would come flying in over areas where there was no adequate protection against them. The early warning systems against bombers and missiles were in the north, since a Soviet attack had always been expected to come in over the Arctic. American vulnerability to attack had therefore risen. Furthermore, the U.S. position in the Western Hemisphere would have been undermined as well. The sudden and unchallenged appearance of another great power in the area where the United States had long been paramount would have eroded

America's's authority and status and encouraged the spread of Castroism throughout Latin America. All anti-Castro forces, including the indispensable and all too few genuinely democratic reformers, would have been demoralized and perhaps paralyzed by Washington's inaction.

The political and psychological implications of Khrushchev's limited challenge were thus enormous, for the global distribution of power could well be affected. But Khrushchev had for once overplayed his hand. He had raised the pressure on the United States too quickly and too near the United States itself for Washington to be able to avoid the test. If the political benefits to the Soviet Union of placing missiles in Cuba were potentially great, the American stakes were even greater. Khrushchev might have wanted to "win" this one, but Kennedy felt he could under no circumstances afford to lose it. Indeed, he had warned the Soviet leader against placing offensive missiles in Cuba; therefore, if he did not compel their withdrawal, his and American credibility would be worthless. If previous American actions and inactions had convinced the Soviet leader that he could "get away with it," it was imperative to set him straight about this issue. Such confidence on Khrushchev's part could only be the result of a conviction that the United States no longer possessed the will to defend its interests. Such a notion was dangerous for, if it remained uncorrected, it would lead to an even greater challenge in Berlin—as Khrushchev had already announced. If the United States then declared it would stand firm there but the Soviet leader did not believe it because of American inaction in Cuba, a violent clash, possibly a nuclear war, would be the result. Characteristically, the Soviets had not committed themselves irrevocably in Cuba. They were willing to gamble for a big payoff, but they were also willing to suffer a serious loss of face in order to avoid a catastrophic clash.

American firmness and determination left Moscow little choice. For once, therefore, it was the Soviets who had to decide whether to fire the first shot—to break the American blockade of their missile-carrying ships—and thus risk a possible escalation of the conflict. The Kremlin backed down. The level of tension having been raised, it also was rapidly lowered once American determination and the willingness to use American power became clear. In Secretary of State Dean Rusk's picturesque phrase, "We were eyeball to eyeball, and the other fellow just blinked." Interestingly enough, particularly in view of Kennedy's critics who felt a Soviet humiliation in Cuba would compel the Soviet leader to recoup his lost prestige by forcing the West out of Berlin (with the clear implication that the United States should let him do so or desist in Cuba), Khrushchev called off *both* challenges. America's superior power, as demonstrated in the Caribbean, could also be marshaled in Berlin, and it therefore seemed advisable to terminate the tension over the Western half of the former German capital city as well. But it ought to be noted that while the Soviet Union withdrew its missiles, the United States publicly declared that it would not invade Cuba. Thus Castro survived.

AMERICAN STRATEGY AND FRONTIER DEFENSES

The recurrent crisis over West Berlin from 1958 to 1962, plus the Cuban missile crisis, held several lessons for the United States if it wished to preserve the frontier line around what was then still considered a cohesive Communist world. First, despite U.S. retaliatory power, the Soviet leadership, when it thought circumstances propitious, did not hesitate to raise international tensions with limited political challenges in order to compel the United States to make unilateral concessions. While Moscow was fully aware of the dangers of nuclear war and the consequent need for the avoidance of acts that would expose the Soviet Union to nuclear conflagration, it had not allowed this recognition to deter it from seeking to exploit the West's fear of nuclear war to transform the *status quo* in its favor. The Soviet leadership had felt confident that it could raise tensions *without* provoking the United States; as long as this tension was not raised too high, it could control the risk of war.

To ensure that tensions would not escalate beyond control, the Soviets either left themselves a diplomatic escape hatch or were willing to make timely withdrawals in case they underestimated the American reaction. When met by a determined countermove, a Soviet-initiated rise in tension did not, therefore, cause this tension to spiral further upward; Soviet concern to preserve a ceiling on this tension, lest it precipitate an American nuclear response, tended to lower tension and possibly end the specific crisis. The Cuban missile crisis in 1962 was testimony to the Soviets' confidence that, short of a major provocation, which they were not willing to offer, they could challenge the United States without fearing a nuclear response; their rapid retreat was even stronger testimony to their intense concern to avoid a further upward spiral of tension that might possibly reach the ceiling level.

Second, mutual deterrence was clearly not automatic, needing little attention to maintain it. For technology particularly can upset the stability of the deterrent balance. Simply possessing the bomb was insufficient. The key to a *stable* deterrent balance is an invulnerable retaliatory force; if one's force is vulnerable to attack, it may tempt its possessor to strike preemptively lest his forces be caught on the ground, or lead the adversary to strike first since he fears such a preemptive strike if he does not himself preempt. In the late 1950s and early 1960s, the Soviets were claiming that they were mass-producing missiles that made American bombers vulnerable. If this were true, it meant that the deterrent capacity of the United States was declining. This was bound to affect policymakers in Moscow and Washington, emboldening the former and making the latter more cautious. The Soviet Union's willingness to challenge the United States in Europe again after a period of ten years and the manner in which America reacted were symptomatic of this perceived change in the balance by the superpowers. Only in Cuba in 1962, after it had become clear that Khrushchev had been bluffing—that he was not mass-producing

ICBMs, that the United States was now ahead in armaments because, in reaction to Khrushchev's claim, Kennedy had started a massive missile build-up on land and sea—did Washington once more regain its confidence and, given the immensity of the stakes, react vigorously. Preserving stable deterrence is thus a continuing, never-ending task.

Third, even before the stabilization of the "balance of terror," the United States refused to invoke its great strategic forces to respond to limited challenges; hence the need for limited-war forces. An all-or-nothing option was no option at all. Theoretically, a series of piecemeal defeats could turn the balance of power against America. At some point, the United States would be compelled to take a stand to prevent further deterioration of its position. But the Soviets were not likely to believe in the firmness of this commitment, massive retaliation and the threat of suicide being less and less credible. If, however, America were willing to accept that risk, the Soviet challenge would precipitate a war by miscalculation. Thus by its reliance on massive retaliation the United States could in fact bring about the very war massive retaliation was ostensibly supposed to deter.

Fourth, massive retaliation foreshadowed the gradual weakening of the bonds of America's foremost alliance, NATO. Its European allies had joined NATO to gain the protection of U.S. power, particularly SAC. But in an era in which the United States no longer held a nuclear monopoly, what ally could truly be expected to put its very survival behind the defense of its allies' interests? Baldly stated, what would be the U.S. response to limited Soviet demands in Europe? If America did react all out, Europe would be "saved from Communism" by being reduced to rubble. On the other hand—and this seemed more likely—if America was unwilling to risk its existence for specific issues the Europeans deemed vital, then the alliance would become increasingly meaningless.

Finally, as Berlin and Cuba again demonstrated, the chief function of a military power was to draw and protect "frontiers." These frontiers had been clearly drawn: along the Elbe and through the middle of Berlin; at the thirty-eighth parallel in Korea and the seventeenth parallel in Vietnam; along the coast of China at Quemoy and Matsu; and, more tenuously, at the "northern tier" from Turkey to Pakistan. Any attempt to cross these frontiers, openly by direct attack or covertly by guerrilla warfare, would risk hostilities. Admittedly, the lines drawn outside of Europe were extremely tenuous. The Middle East Treaty Organization (METO) and the Southeast Asia Treaty Organization (SEATO) were alliances in areas where nationalist forces opposed the Western-formed and -led alliances. These therefore had little popular support, even in those states that were members. One result was that the Soviets might leapfrog the line, as in METO; another result could be that the governments seeking to maintain this line would be unable, despite American help, to mobilize the requisite indigenous morale and support, as was to become evident in Vietnam during the 1960s.

Indeed, it might well be that the United States would have been better off had it not created what turned out to be poor replicas of NATO. That organization had been formed in an area in which nationalism supported containment against a clearly perceived potential external aggression; the METO and SEATO alliances were organized in non-Western areas where containment was widely perceived as an attempt to preserve Western influence and reactionary regimes. Nevertheless, because the lines drawn in Europe created a great danger of conflict, particularly of an American-Soviet clash, this process of delineation had in the 1950s shifted the attention of the superpowers increasingly toward the Third World as an area where they believed that they could more safely transform the bipolar balance in their favor.

Chapter 7

THE THIRD WORLD
DURING THE
COLD WAR YEARS

THE REVOLUTION OF RISING EXPECTATIONS

"Four areas in the world," Guy J. Pauker wrote at the height of the cold war, "are at present or potentially major power centers: the United States, the Soviet Union, Western Europe, and Communist China. In all four, productivity is on the increase, and the political system performs relatively well its integrating and decision-making functions. Despite major differences among them . . . these four areas are likely to be in a position to play major roles in political, economic, and cultural international affairs in the coming decade. In contrast, the Middle East, Southeast Asia, tropical Africa, and Latin America are apt to remain power vacuums during this period, owing to their lack of unity, political instability, economic stagnation, and cultural heterogeneity. It seems highly improbable that ten years from now any of the areas mentioned above will cease to be, respectively, a power center or a power vacuum."

During the 1950s and 1960s such possible vacuums in the Third World, composed largely of ex-colonial, economically less-developed countries, were viewed in Washington as dangerous. For in a bipolar world, the two superpowers felt compelled to compete for the support, if not the allegiance, of the new emerging states who were not politically and militarily aligned with either one. Moscow perceived the anticolonial revolt against the West as part of the disintegration of the international capitalist order and an opportunity for attracting the less-developed countries into partnership with the Soviet Union in the building of a new Soviet-led Communist international order. The challenge of Soviet Communism and Chinese Communism in the Third World was, therefore, seen in Washington as stemming not so much from some conspiracy or military takeover as from the totalitarian model for modernization that Commu-

112

nism offered the less-developed countries. The majority of the world's population lived in those countries. If those people in their search for the freedom President Franklin Roosevelt had once called "freedom from want" turned to dictatorial means, it would profoundly affect whether the democratic or the totalitarian way of life would flourish throughout the world. Their choice was therefore seen as critical to American security and, more broadly, an international environment in which open societies and democratic values would be safe. Thus it was vital to help the new countries develop; it was a matter of basic self-interest rather than humanitarian concern for the poor. Said a leading scholar: "Whether most of these countries take a democratic or Communist or other totalitarian path in their development is likely to determine the course of civilization on our planet."

It was a paradox that the disintegration of Western colonialism after World War II afforded the most eloquent testimony to its success. For the Western powers, including America in the Philippines, had justified their imperial domination in terms of bringing the backward peoples of the earth the benefits of Western democracy, medical science, and technology. It was the "white man's burden," or duty, to educate the people so that one day they could govern themselves. The colonial powers had clearly taught their lesson well. They had ruled their colonies autocratically, while simultaneously propagating the virtues of democracy. It was in the name of these ideals that the Western powers had come as colonizers; it was in their name, too, that the nationalist movements challenged their rulers and asked them to practice what they preached. The leaders of these nationalist movements had invariably been educated in Europe or America, or in a Western school in their own country. They fought the European powers in terms of the principles of democracy and national freedom that they had learned in the West. They saw that these principles were incompatible with imperialism.

Once these countries became independent, however, they were left with a legacy of poverty, illiteracy, and disease. Rarely in these nations did the annual per capita income reach $100. Because this condition of economic underdevelopment, compared with that of the economically developed nations (indeed, we generally refer to this division as one between the poor and rich nations) was so startling, economic development—often equated with industrialization—was the generally recommended remedy. Industrialization modernized—that is, transformed—a backward, traditional, agrarian society into a twentieth-century industrial urban community. More specifically, industrialization would help consolidate the rather tenuous bonds holding the infant nation together as a political entity. For industrialization requires a high degree of specialization. The resulting division of labor between the various sectors of the economy located throughout all regions of the country and the need for all these branches of industry to cooperate would forge new cohesive links and place the still fragile political union upon the base of an interdependent economic union. Industrialization was also expected to improve the welfare of all the nation's new citizens. This, too, would be of great political significance. The people in the less-developed countries were familiar only with their immediate surrounding area, and they were loyal to this region; national loyalty was unknown. Consequently, the newly formed nation must prove to them that it could offer them something they could not otherwise attain. This "something" would be an improvement in their standard of living. By achieving this, the nation would demonstrate its utility and, in turn, would be expected to receive from its people the popular support and allegiance it needed to survive and grow.

Yet the question confronting the new countries in the 1950s—as today—is whether they can develop themselves economically. The answer will to a large extent depend upon whether their economic progress will be faster than their population growth, or whether their "population explosion" will eat up any increase in national income. The world population by the mid–1980s is 4.7 billion. In 1830, it had been 1 billion; by 1930, it had doubled. Thus, while the first doubling took 100 years, it took only 40 years more to add another 1.5 billion. Experts predict 6.5 billion by the year 2000. In 1900, there was one European for every two Asians; in 2000, the ratio will probably be one to four. In the Western Hemisphere, there will, perhaps, be two Latin Americans for each North American. Despite later reports in 1978 that population growth was slowing down somewhat, these countries may still come face to face with the Malthusian problem; the constant hunger and grinding poverty that result when the population grows faster than do the means of subsistence. More than 150 years ago, the Reverend Thomas Malthus, who was also an economist, predicted this fate for the Western world—unless the population growth were limited by either "positive checks" such as wars or epidemics, which result in a high death rate, or by "preventive checks," which result in a low birth rate. Yet, despite the huge population increase since 1800, the West made great economic progress: Agricultural production provided a plentiful supply of food, and industrial production raised the standard of living to heights never before attained. The West's recent history would thus appear to refute Malthus's gloomy prediction.

Unfortunately, the conditions that faced the less-developed nations were quite dissimilar from those experienced by the West. One of the chief differences is that the Western countries had far smaller populations when they began industrializing, and their population increase did not outdistance the economic improvement. But India set out on its modernization with a population of more than 400 million, which is expected to reach 1 billion people by the year 2000. China was expected to reach this staggering total much earlier (in 1979, the Central Intelligence Agency [CIA] predicted that China's population would approach 1.5 billion by the end of the century). If the United States after the War of Independence had had a population density equivalent to that of Egypt, it would have today a population exceeding 2 billion people instead of one over 200 million. Under these circumstances, it would hardly have become a "developed" nation.

The European nations were also aided by the New World and by their colonial empires, which provided them with outlets to relieve their population pressures. About 60 million Europeans emigrated during the nineteenth and early twentieth centuries. The United States and Canada, rich in resources and fertile land, easily absorbed millions of immigrants and still increased their living standards; Australia, New Zealand, and South Africa experienced similar population and economic expansions, although on a smaller scale. From 1650 to 1950, the European population (excluding Russia) increased by approximately 300 million. By the 1950s there were about 400 million people of European descent living outside Europe. The colonies thus served Europe as a frontier similar to that of the American West, which absorbed population that might otherwise have overcrowded the Eastern seaboard and thus added materially to the nation's wealth. But the less-developed countries can generally find no such relatively empty and rich spaces to absorb their surplus populations (although Mexico exports some of its unemployed to the United States and economically backward countries such as Greece, Yugoslavia, Turkey, and Spain export workers to the Common Market countries).

In the West, moreover, the Industrial Revolution made possible the use of machinery in agriculture. This permitted a great increase in the food supply; efficient agriculture also meant that food could be produced by a smaller farm population. Excess labor from the land was thereby forced to go to the city, where it was used in the factories; this in turn accelerated the industrialization process. Quite apart from modern technology, however, Europe was blessed with sufficient sunshine and rain. Temperate lands are more favorable to food production than tropical and monsoon areas, where many of the less-developed countries are found. Europe could thus grow sufficient food for its multiplying population; what it could not produce, it imported from the colonies and the New World in exchange for industrial products. This enabled some European countries to support larger populations than their domestic food resources would otherwise have permitted. By contrast, in the nonindustrialized nations, the majority of the population is still engaged in a primitive agriculture. Many of the new countries' governments equate development with industrialization and therefore have neglected agriculture, which to its leaders often remains the symbol of their former colonial status as agrarian, raw-material-producing nations—which they are trying to get away from in their quest to be modern. In some countries more-intensive farming of land already under cultivation—that is, using better seed, more chemical fertilizers, and insecticides—may yield enough food to keep pace with the population growth. But many countries cannot feed themselves sufficiently for yet another reason. "If our population continues to increase as rapidly as it is doing," a former president of Pakistan said, "we will soon have nothing to eat and will all become cannibals."

If this statement appears exaggerated, it nevertheless dramatizes the less-developed countries' problem of overpopulation. There are simply too many poor people. This might have been all right if the sleeping masses had not awakened—if they had continued to accept their miserable lot as natural and not suddenly become conscious that it was not a fate ordained by God but a man-made one, if they had not made this discovery and therefore demanded to eat more and live better. It is this "revolution of rising expectations" that creates the problem, for it will be impossible to fulfill these expectations unless there is a reduction in birth rates. The population pressure keeps the masses living close to subsistence; and such widespread poverty makes it very difficult to accumulate enough capital to stoke industrial growth.

In the West, the birth rate declined after 1850; with industrialization and the growth of cities came the spread of literacy and knowledge of artificial birth-control techniques. Malthus was thus right even for the West, because preventive checks were adopted. But the Third World has not yet reached a similar level of economic development, and knowledge of birth-control methods has spread only very slowly.

It remained questionable, therefore, whether the birth rate would decline significantly in the near future. This meant that the pace of economic development had to surpass the fast-rising rate of population growth. But these countries simply did not have enough capital. Internal savings in sufficient amounts could not be squeezed out of peoples living at subsistence level—at least, not without totalitarian controls. An alternative means of obtaining capital was to earn it by trade. The less-developed areas are exporters of primary products or raw materials, such as coffee, tea, rubber, and tin. But it was precisely this fact that in the past had limited the earning capacity of many of them; for these exports rose or declined with every fluctuation in Western prosperity. A major Western recession lowered the demand and price levels of natural resources; the resulting losses of income tended to exceed the Western aid extended during the same period. Furthermore, markets may become glutted with certain items because of overproduction or substitution. A nation may have sought to raise its income by increasing production, but the fact that its competitors have done the same only lowers world prices further; or the Western industrial nations, whose ever-increasing demand for raw materials was supposed to furnish the capital for economic development, may no longer have needed them because of the development of synthetics. The lack of stabilized international commodity prices, similar to the parity prices paid to American farmers, plus the inventiveness of modern technology (which may in the 1980s start extracting resources from the ocean's seabeds) thus hampered the prospects of financing industrialization via trade.

Foreign investment was the third source of capital for economic development. Private capital has, however, been in short supply for the kind of long-range development that the less-developed nations need. Most private American investments outside the United States have been made by a small group of oil companies to build refineries and to discover and pump out oil fields in Latin America and the Middle East. The reasons for this lack of private Western—and especially American—capital for foreign investment were not hard to find. The American economy experienced a boom for most of the cold war period. Investment capital stayed mainly at home. This was true for Europe as well. European capital concentrated on rebuilding, modernization, and expansion of its own capital plant. American capital that did go abroad often went to the Common Market. Private capital is drawn to investments that will return sizable and relatively speedy profits.

But perhaps the basic reason that private funds were so small for the new nations was that public funds were so small. Businessmen could not be expected to invest in hospitals, ports, schools, and roads. The returns from such projects were insufficient; and even if there were any profits, it would take too long to reap them. Optimists who felt that this first stage of economic development could be undertaken by private funds forgot that in the West the speedy economic growth of the nineteenth century, financed largely by private enterprise, rested upon an economic base developed by the mercantilist state; in brief, it was political authority, the state, that had initiated the process that transformed the underdeveloped Western economies into the highly modern, industrialized economies we know today.

Modernization, then, was the new nations' principal task. But this became increasingly seen as *not* essentially an economic undertaking. More and more, modernization, of which economic development is a major ingredient, was viewed as a political, social, and intellectual task. Moreover, it was a revolutionary process frequently marked by political instability and violence rather than evolutionary peaceful change. One reason for this, in addition to their low level of economic existence, was that most of the nations that so recently gained their independence lacked administrative and political cohesiveness. Generally, the peoples had no single common culture or language; tribes were opposed to one another; different areas were in conflict with one another. There was no natural loyalty to the state, no tradition of cooperation except, of course, on the one overriding issue of eliminating the colonial ruler. But once that struggle for independence ended, power tended to fragment. Thus, colonial India disintegrated violently into Hindu India and Muslim Pakistan following independence, and the latter dissolved further into Pakistan and Bangladesh— with the help of India, which may itself fragment further; the Congo (now renamed Zaire) fell apart when the Belgians withdrew; Cyprus divided into Turkish and Greek factions; and Biafra split from Nigeria, only to lose the subsequent civil war. Even where actual disintegration has not occurred, religious, linguistic, and racial differences and antagonisms tend to tear apart the fabric of these states that lack any history of nationhood. In Burundi in 1972, for example, Tutsi tribesmen reportedly slaughtered 120,000 Hutus. Nation building thus becomes the first task.

The absence of a strong sense of national consciousness was soon reflected in the manner in which many of the leaders of the new countries built themselves up as symbols of nationhood. It was not too difficult for them to do this, since their prestige was usually high as a result of the roles they had played in leading the nationalist movements for independence. But the task was an essential one. With Louis XIV, they said, *"L'état, c'est moi."* For they *were* the state; without their presence as its symbol, the nation would not hold together as a unit. One-party rule or military governments exist almost everywhere in the Third World. In Africa, for example, the world's last continent to be freed from colonialism, three-fourths of its 345 million people by the late 1960s already lived under single-party and military rule ten years after these nations had become independent.

Such policies might seem undemocratic, but they were widely perceived to be necessary. Loyalties in the new nations were less to the state than to ancestors, family, village, or tribe. Wherever the opposition represented these centrifugal forces, an American-style democracy would lead not just to a change of government but to the disintegration of the state. The alternatives facing the leaders of these countries have often been not democracy or dictatorship but statehood or disintegration.

Another reason that modernization was increasingly seen in an essentially political and revolutionary context is that the nationalist revolutions direct their opposition not only against the dominating foreign ruler but also against the domestic ruling elite. Many less-developed countries were split into two main groups when they gained independence. The first was the ruling minority, usually composed of the landlords, tribal chiefs, priests, and great merchants, sometimes fronted by an old-regime king. The second group, which still constitutes about 80 percent in most less-developed nations, encompassed the peasants, villagers, small artisans, and shopkeepers—those whose efforts have been concentrated largely on the sheer struggle for day-to-day survival. It is this group, which has for centuries borne its hardships silently, that has awakened and is now demanding a better life. It is the urban intelligentsia, educated in Western ideas and committed to modernization, that voices these resentments against the old way of life and proclaims the new aspirations most articulately and loudly. Change and more change is the demand of the day.

Without such social change—that is, the overthrow of the old ruling elite that is often identified with foreign influence and control, if not imperialism—modernization will be inhibited. This is not a matter of "reform" but of revolution because the crucial issue relates to power: Who controls the nation—the old ruling elite, committed to the preservation of the traditional, religiously oriented, preindustrial society, or those who seek to secularize, modernize, and industrialize the nation? Only one thing was certain: Few who rule yield their dominant political, social, and economic position without a struggle.

Instability is promoted even where economic development occurs, where national bonds do not disintegrate, and where a secular modernizing elite is in control. The cause of this is that the slowly rising standard of living does not normally create an increasingly satisfied—and therefore happy and peaceful—population. Capital for investment can only be saved from money not paid to the workers; low wages militate against mass consumption and allow the reinvestment of the capital saved into further economic expansion. While there may be some improvement in living conditions, it will probably not suffice to satisfy the "revolution of rising expectations." Dissatisfaction will result from the fact that the population, knowing that it no longer has to live in the poverty and filth of the past, that man can create a better life for himself here on earth through his own efforts, will be frustrated by the continuous gap between achievement and expectation, which becomes particularly aggravating when the modernizers live well, even ostentatiously, while the rest of the population still lives in poverty. When this comes on top of the resentment produced by the uprooting of a large number of people as they shift from the countryside to the city, whose factories need manpower, the bewilderment resulting from the anonymity of the city, and anger caused by a miserable existence in the slums, social discontent and an increasingly sullen, hostile, and more radical mood are bound to rise.

The resulting growth of social instability and turmoil is further enhanced by the intellectual and cultural changes that accompany the transformation of a traditional, static, rural society into a modern, dynamic, urban-industrial state. Many of the old customary and religious values that helped man to accept his place in society and conduct himself throughout life simply collapse and the individual becomes disoriented, torn from his age-old moorings for which he has not yet found a substitute. Robbed of the status and function of his ancestors, he is left as an isolated and insecure atom in a rapidly changing environment that he neither made nor comprehends. Secular values, emphasizing material values and progress, replace religious values denying the importance of earthly existence and material possessions. A society in which individual effort is rewarded and a man can rise socially into a higher class replaces a society with a rigid social structure in which birth determined his place and religion his code of conduct. Nationalism replaces local loyalty, and modern means of transportation and communication bring the individual to an awareness of the larger society in which he must now live and work. Impersonal ties to people far away in "his" country replace former face-to-face relations with neighbors, and he must learn new skills and ways of thought. In short, he must forget many of his old ways and cut long-time ties and adjust, readjust, and adjust once more. In the best of circumstances, this is a difficult and agonizing process even if it does not arouse effective opposition from the traditional elite (as, for example, in Iran in late 1978 and early 1979, when the religious leaders led a powerful opposition movement to the Shah and his modernization so that they could establish an Islamic Republic).

DOMESTIC INSTABILITY AND INTERNATIONAL TENSIONS

It is hardly surprising in these circumstances that the domestic transformation of the less-developed nations had international repercussions that tended to destabilize an international system largely defined by the frontiers drawn between the two superpowers and by the nuclear stalemate. For when the internal difficulties of the countries of the Third World spilled over into the external arena of international politics, they attracted the Soviet Union and the United States, thus leading to possible confrontation with the attendant danger of military conflict. The reason these difficulties have attracted the two superpowers is that they could bring to power a group one superpower likes and the other dislikes or result in regional expansion and influence that could be perceived as benefiting one and hurting the other. If one of the two superpowers is unwilling to tolerate what it may, in terms of the global balance of power, consider a local or regional setback, it will intervene; or, if it fears that if it does not intervene its opponent might, the result may be a preventive intervention. In both cases, it risks counterintervention.

If a new nation disintegrates into two or more parts, those who seek to reunify their land or establish their new splinter states may appeal for help to sympathetic states that, for reasons of their own, may wish to see either a nation preserve its unity or a splinter state its independence in order to support a favorable faction in power. Such appeals were—and continue to be— addressed especially to the Soviet Union or America. One of the more dramatic examples of the manner in which the survival of the new states as national entities involved the superpowers was given when, in 1960, the Belgian Congo became independent and Patrice Lumumba, leader of the nationalist party, became the country's new premier and Joseph Kasavubu its first president. Almost immediately, the Congo began to disintegrate into disorder. First, the rich mining province of Katanga, upon whose copper and cobalt exports the Congo was largely dependent as a major source of revenue, split off into a separate state. In this venture, Katanga's president, Moise Tshombe, had the support of the powerful Belgian mining interests, anxious to protect their investments. Then the army began to revolt because it resented the continued presence of its Belgian officers and wanted them replaced with native leadership. In a wild spree, the soldiers began to attack white women (including nuns) and children. The Belgian settlers' reaction was to flee. Among their numbers were the experts the Belgians had expected to leave behind in order to help the Congolese in their early period of self-government. All public services now collapsed because the Congo lacked an educated native elite. The Belgians had never trained one.

In the midst of this situation, the Belgians flew in paratroopers to protect their nationals. Lumumba, however, saw this move as a Belgian attempt to restore colonial rule, and he appealed to the United Nations to send forces to help him against the Belgians. It was at this point that the cold war was injected into the Congo. For the United Nations troops, whose composition did not include any forces from the Great Powers, did not compel the Belgians to evacuate their paratroopers or agree to Lumumba's demand that they help him reestablish control over Katanga Province. Secretary-General Dag Hammarskjöld ordered that the international organization's forces were not to be involved in the internal squabbles of the Congo or employed by the different contending political factions for the purpose of gaining power over their rivals. This, however, had the effect of underwriting the divisions of the Congo, and the country could not survive without Katanga. Since no leader likes to preside over the disintegration of his nation—particularly when that disintegration is being encouraged by the former colonial power seeking to preserve a base of control—Lumumba turned against the United Nations, bitterly attacked the secretary-general, and accused Belgium and the Western powers, especially the United States, of conspiring against him; in these attacks, Lumumba resorted increasingly to antiwhite racial appeals and finally asked the Soviet Union for help to prevent the disintegration of the Congo. He received Soviet diplomatic backing, military supplies, and offers of troops or "volunteers"; several neutrals, especially the United Arab Republic, Guinea, and Ghana, also extended their sympathy and support.

The United States now supported President Kasavubu (who dismissed Lumumba) and his army commander, Colonel Sese Seko Mobutu, who established a caretaker government composed of the Congo's only fifteen university graduates. Mobutu also infuriated the Soviet Union by driving out all Communist-bloc personnel, who had been aiding Lumumba. The Soviets insisted that Lumumba was still the Congo's legitimate ruler and demanded his restoration; so did the neutrals, who supported this demand by threatening to remove their contingents from the U.N. army. This would have left the Congo in utter chaos. The United States, however, refused to budge and continued to give its support to Colonel Mobutu, in whom it saw the best means of eliminating Soviet influence in the Congo and possible Communist penetration into the heart of Africa.

Soviet-American differences now became extremely bitter. The Soviets, thwarted in the Congo for the time being, made two demands: the resignation of Dag Hammarskjöld and a veto over the secretary-general's activities. These demands were rejected. But by early 1962, after all efforts to unify the Congo had failed, the international organization reversed its original stand. It finally adopted the policy of forcefully squashing the opposition. Although it was still to be many months before the country was "unified" through the deposition of Tshombe and his Belgian advisers and foreign mercenaries, this task was eventually accomplished, although not without bloodshed. Ironically, this restoration of national order, accomplished with U.N. support, proved to be a posthumous victory for Lumumba, who had in the meantime been assassinated. (The Central Intelligence Agency [CIA] reportedly had assassination plans for Lumumba too but was beaten to it.) If the central government had not received American and U.N. support and had been unable to reunite the Congo, it, like Lumumba, would have been compelled to turn toward the Soviet Union. National unity was clearly dangerous because it attracted superpower interference, which attempted to impose on the country those factions it favored; moreover, a military clash was possible.

Even if a new nation with tenuous bonds does not disintegrate, the political leaders may well invoke the only emotion the people ever shared in order to hold the nation together. This emotion is, of course, the nationalism born of the hatred of the former colonial power and directed against both that country and, more broadly, "Western imperialism." The granting of independence has not meant that colonialism was no longer an issue; rather, to preserve national unity the fight against colonialism and imperialism had to continue. The same technique may be invoked by a country with the even more common condition of a stagnant economy in which the "revolution of rising expectations" is turning into a "revolution of rising frustration." The political leadership will then be tempted to preserve its power by externalizing domestic dissatisfaction; foreign scapegoats will be needed to relieve internal stresses and strains. It is simply easier and therefore more attractive for leaders to play a prominent and highly visible role on the international stage before their countrymen than to undertake the hard and difficult work of modernizing their nations. The people can take pride in their leader's—and hence, their nation's—new status and identity in an international society that, under colonialism, had been denied importance and dignity as a nation and a people. Kwame Nkrumah of Ghana, Achmed Sukarno of Indonesia, Muhammad Ben Bella of Algeria (until their deposal by military regimes), and Gamal Abdel Nasser of Egypt were among the most prominent and skillful practitioners of the art of channelling domestic grievances into international strutting and adventures during the 1950s and 1960s.

The most dramatic example of the dangers this can hold for the peace of the world was given by Nasser, who, as in 1956, provoked a war with Israel in 1967 when he confronted increasing economic hardship at home and a militant anti-Israeli Arab nationalism in Syria, a notoriously politically unstable and stagnating country. Nasser, increasingly compelled after 1958 to turn his attention and energies inward to "Arab socialism" in his fight for Arab leadership, had after more than a decade of rule still not managed to launch Egypt on a path of self-sustaining economic growth. Egypt was desperately short of funds to finance its development, buy food, support its sizable army, and provide enough jobs for its unemployed and underemployed population. The national debt in 1966 was estimated at $2 billion; more than $100 million was overdue to Western states; foreign credit was very tight, and the balance of trade was declining. The second Five-Year Plan, already extended to seven years, was shelved. An estimated 30–50 percent of the productive capacity of the government-owned industry was idle because of a lack of money to buy parts. The growth rate, which in the early 1960s was 6–7 percent, had fallen to an annual 2–4 percent, hardly sufficient to keep up with the population growth. The birth-control program had failed to have any significant impact; the birth rate added 800,000 people annually to a population of over 30 million. The pace of inflation was approximately 15 percent a year. Nasser's program of nationalization and expropriation had brought domestic investment to a near halt and discouraged foreign investment. And his virulent anti-American attitude resulted in a cut-off of the American surplus food shipments. So he had to buy his food elsewhere and use up funds that might have been invested in the economic development of Egypt. The heavy expenditures on military equipment, probably amounting to one-third of Egypt's annual budget, also diverted funds from development.

Arab socialism, having lost its glamour and thereby weakened Nasser's claim to Arab leadership, left him only the arena of foreign policy in which to recoup his prestige and hold on to the Arab masses. But here, too, his stature had declined. He had reached the height of his self-proclaimed leadership of Arab nationalism at the time of the seizure of the Suez Canal a decade earlier. Nationalism had also affected Nasser's neighbors. Iraq refused to subordinate itself to his direction, and Syria quit its short-lived union with Egypt in 1961. Nasser then resumed his verbal attacks on the traditional monarchies of Jordan and Saudi Arabia; Egyptian forces also helped the revolutionary forces who had overthrown the Yemenite monarchy supported by Saudi Arabia. He was clearly seeking to extend his influence southward into the sheikdoms and sultanates of South Arabia, a British protectorate scheduled to become independent in early 1968. This would give him control over the Red Sea entrance to the Suez Canal. But the Egyptian army was unsuccessful in destroying the royalist supporters. In 1967, intra-Arab rivalries thus combined with economic failure to pressure Nasser to reassert his leadership of Arab nationalism.

First, he had to act if he was to be successful in establishing his influence in the former British protectorate of Aden upon its independence. Second, the Jordanians, in response to Nasser's hostility, taunted Nasser with hiding behind the U.N. forces stationed between the Israeli and Egyptian forces at the close of the Suez War. Third, the Syrians, trying to displace Nasser as the leader of Pan-Arabism, openly and repeatedly called for Israel's destruction and stepped up their terrorist raids into Israel. After a retaliatory Israeli raid, the Syrians even claimed in May 1967 that the Israelis were assembling their forces for an invasion of Syria. This rumor, reportedly also brought to Nasser's attention by the Soviet Union, which was seeking to exploit the Arab-Israeli-Western quarrel for its own purposes, was found to be untrue by U.N. observers. But Nasser, the great hero of the Arab peoples, either felt compelled to act or saw in the invasion rumor his opportunity to restore his leadership of Arab nationalism. Since Arab nationalism fostered competition regarding who was the most anti-Israeli—Israel being alleged the extension of Western "imperialism" into the Arab world—there was bound to be trouble. This was particularly true because, after eleven years of receiving Soviet training and arms, Nasser seemed very confident that his forces could beat Israel, which this time would be fighting by itself, without the aid of France and Britain.

The Egyptian leader therefore made several moves. He moved reinforcements into the Sinai Desert. Next, he demanded and obtained the withdrawal of the U.N. peace-keeping forces; Egyptian and Israeli forces thus confronted each other for the first time since 1956. In addition, he proclaimed the blockade of the Gulf of Aqaba, through which Israel received its oil and other goods.

Israel had long declared this to be a vital lifeline, since Nasser barred its shipping from the Suez Canal, and he knew Israel had stated that it would consider a blockade intolerable and an act of war. In short, Nasser was deliberately provoking a military conflict. Finally, he signed a pact of alliance with Jordan. This meant that Arab armies were surrounding Israel: Syria in the north, Jordan with its highly regarded army directed to cut Israel in two at its narrow waist, and Egypt in the south. All these moves were accompanied by increasingly shrill calls for a holy "war of liberation" and the extermination of all of Israel's inhabitants—in brief, genocide.

In these circumstances, war was inevitable, unless Israel was willing to accept a major political defeat, an unlikely prospect. Whether peace could be preserved, primarily by Nasser's "unblockading" the Gulf of Aqaba, depended now on the United States and the Soviet Union. Washington was, however, caught in a dilemma. On the one hand, it had recognized Israel's right to send its ships through the gulf after compelling it to withdraw in the wake of its 1956 victory. But it also recognized that if Nasser did not relent, a forceful test might be necessary; seeking support from other maritime powers, it found the major nations were reluctant to use force. On the other hand, it was deeply involved in Vietnam and therefore reluctant to become engaged in a second conflict with Egypt. Furthermore, a key question for American policymakers was whether such a test would precipitate a clash with the Soviet Union, which had with great fanfare sent warships into the eastern Mediterranean, fully supported the Arabs in their aims, continuously denounced Israel as an aggressive tool of American imperialism, and perhaps even spurred Nasser on with the false story of an imminent Israeli invasion of Syria.

For Moscow, the Arab-Israeli conflict had, as earlier, not merely regional but global implications. If Western influence could be expelled from the Middle East and if the Soviet Union could establish itself as the dominant power over this oil-rich region, Europe might possibly be weakened and perhaps even neutralized. Soviet political support and the naval show of force undoubtedly contributed to Nasser's intransigence. Certainly it helped restore his reputation in the Arab world, and, had the blockade been successful, the Soviet Union would have earned the Arabs' everlasting gratitude, since it would have been chiefly responsible for Egypt's political victory, having demonstrated its ability to inhibit the American navy and having eroded American commitments to Israel. Thus Moscow was unwilling to restrain Damascus or Cairo.

Since Washington was unable to arrange a diplomatic solution, the Israelis, tired of waiting for one, attacked. Routing the air forces of their Arab opponents in a brilliantly coordinated set of air strikes in the first hours of hostilities, they defeated the Egyptian army in short shrift and reached the Suez Canal in three days—two days ahead of their 1956 record! They then routed the Jordanian army and captured half of Jerusalem and the western bank of the River Jordan. Finally, they turned on the Syrian army and eliminated the bases from which Syria launched the terrorist raids and shelled Israeli settlements. Nasser's dreams of an Arab empire were shattered, despite his efforts to salvage his reputation by blaming his defeat on alleged American and British air intervention on behalf of Israel. Arab nationalism and intra-Arab quarrels had once again intensified the Arab-Israeli conflict and precipitated war; and the bipolar competition for influence in the Middle East had once more exploited its problems, turning it into a "Balkans of the twentieth century," an inflammable area of political instability, regional rivalry, and Great Power conflict likely to explode at any moment and spread the resulting war far beyond its immediate scope. Domestic Arab problems only aggravated the tendency of leaders to engage in adventurism, export internal dissatisfaction and grievances, strike tough and inflexible poses, and expose the world to the dangers of a superpower clash.

Even more broadly, Washington defined the greatest danger to American security as stemming from the new states' functional—not ideological—attraction to Communism. Confronting an amalgam of political, social, and cultural changes (not just an economic transition), experiencing revolutionary transformations (not just evolutionary progress), the non-Western nations have no guarantee that they will successfully climb what Robert Heilbroner has termed the Great Ascent; even the attempt may well call for some sort of left-wing authoritarian rule. In this context, the Soviet Union represented itself as a model of development. The Soviets could point to the Soviet experience and say: "In 1917, Russia was also underdeveloped but now, within the space of one generation, it has become militarily one of the two superpowers, the second largest industrial country in the world. You, too, can be industrialized quickly and live a better life." To people who already suffered from chronic hunger and poverty, it presumably would not matter greatly that the Soviet Union achieved industrialization by means of totalitarian governments that brutally squeezed the necessary sacrifices out of the people; the loss of liberty would not mean much to people who had never known it anyway, who had lived for centuries under authoritarian governments, whether domestic or foreign. Soviet totalitarianism would provide the organization and efficiency to extract the sacrifices from the masses, the discipline to hold the nation together, to speed up the pace of the cultural revolution while controlling the social tensions produced by the early stages of development, and, where necessary, ruthlessly to depose the traditional ruling class blocking the path to modernization. In short, just as capitalism was the chief means of modernization in the nineteenth century, Washington feared that Soviet Communism would be able to present itself as a successful model for modernization for the new nations seeking to enter the twentieth century. (After the Sino-Soviet schism, China too promoted itself as a model for modernization, one superior to its European rival.)

Thus, Communism was seen not just as a military threat. In the newly politically aware and poorer areas of the Third World, Communism was viewed as attractive because it appeared to promise a fairly rapid and disciplined way of bringing about political, social, economic, and cultural changes. The competition with the Soviet Union was in terms of improving the conditions that allegedly breed Communism. Poverty, ignorance, hunger, and social injustice lead to the growth of Communism; curing these conditions and giving people hope for a better life was the means, then, of defeating Communism. This would be achieved once the new nations' development had gained a self-sustaining momentum. Communism, therefore, had only a short time during the initial phase of modernization to enhance its appeal; during this period, Communists would act as "the scavengers of the modernization process." But with Western help, it was optimistically believed, more modern, urbanized, and industrial societies that would look Westward could be created.

GLOBAL INEQUALITY, FOREIGN AID, AND SOCIAL POLITICS

It was in terms of this competition of models that the United States and other Western states first offered economic aid and technical assistance. For, in the final analysis, the fundamental problem was perceived to be the growing division of the world between the rich and poor nations. Western aid was intended to close this gap, modernize the new nations without compelling them to resort to totalitarian methods, satisfy the revolution of rising expectations and thereby create politically and socially stable societies—and possibly lay the basis for democracy—which, in turn, was expected to create a more peaceful world by giving these developing societies a vested interest in the international order and Western values. Thus, in the rationales for sympathy and material and political support for the countries of the Third World, it was clear that besides simple humanitarian sentiments for peoples living in such abject poverty, squalor, disease, and ignorance, security considerations were uppermost. A world divided into rich and poor nations was said to be an explosive one, for it set the majority of the poor against the privileged minority. Such a gap was no more acceptable internationally than it had been within each of the Western nations 100 years ago.

The two situations were believed to be so similar that the "lessons" of the previous experience were applied to the international division of wealth. As the Industrial Revolution gathered momentum in each of the European countries and America, it created a privileged minority that owned most of the wealth. The distribution of income was, to say the least, unequal. Laborers, including many children and women, worked fourteen to sixteen hours per day, six or seven days a week, earned little beyond what was considered a living or subsistence wage (and sometimes less), and lived in overcrowded slums. The rich got richer and the poor got poorer. This trend was so obvious that Benjamin Disraeli talked of England not as one nation but as two.

But the prevailing *laissez-faire* philosophy argued that nothing could be done to alleviate this situation. Government intervention, whether to end the grosser forms of exploitation such as child labor or to redistribute the income to help the poor lead a decent and dignified life, was rejected as contrary to the "iron laws of economics." Any outside interference with the workings of the market would stifle the private incentive and initiative that stoked the competitive capitalistic system. These "laws," which condemned a large section of the population to a hopeless and miserable existence, received even further support from Charles Darwin's theory of evolution, with its emphasis on the "struggle for survival" and the "survival of the fittest." This philosophy, called social Darwinism, argued very simply that the rich were wealthy because their success in the competitive struggle had demonstrated that they were the most fit; conversely, the poor were destitute because they were unfit. It never occurred to social Darwinists to ask themselves whether everybody had had an equal start or opportunity in this struggle.

These philosophical justifications for leaving the poor very poor were ultimately rejected in all Western societies. The long working hours, the unsanitary and unsafe working conditions, the teeming slums were a blot on the West's conscience. They were also politically shortsighted and economically foolish. Politically, the division of people into "haves" and "have-nots" could only end in revolution, with the bourgeoisie being overthrown by the working class, or proletariat; or, if it surrendered its democratic beliefs and values, the bourgeoisie could perhaps retain its power by establishing an authoritarian government and crushing any proletarian protests and uprisings. Neither of these alternatives was a very happy one for the ruling middle classes. Nor did this policy of squeezing the workers for maximum profit make sense economically, since the less money people have, the fewer things they can buy. Thus, social justice made sense—morally, politically, and economically.

In every Western society, government in the late nineteenth century began to intervene increasingly in the economy. Growing public awareness of social problems and ills eventually led to the regulation of business; the passage of minimum-wage and maximum-hours legislation and the abolition of child labor and "sweatshop" working conditions; the organization of trade unions, thus enabling workers to bargain collectively with their employers for better wages and terms of employment; measures to counteract the swings of the business cycle; the implementation of the progressive income tax; and the initiation, during depressions, of unemployment insurance, public-works programs, and other "pump-priming" projects to increase the purchasing power of the people, thereby stimulating renewed demand and production. These measures, especially in the United States, widened and raised the base of wealth, giving rise to the twentieth-century mass market. They also led to a discovery so simple and yet so hard to understand that Europe, particularly continental Europe, learned it only after 1945: namely, that a worker is also a consumer. If he is paid a good wage, he will also buy the goods he produces. This is profitable all around: The worker is economically satisfied and therefore gains a vested interest, politically, in the social and economic order; capitalists earn handsome profits by selling volume at reasonable prices, and they retain their social status and political influence.

It was this same problem of an inequitable distribution of income that was seen as once again plaguing the world. Only this time the problem did not exist within nations, but *between* nations. The rich countries were becoming wealthier, the poor ones more poverty-stricken. The iron laws of economics seem to hold the same fate in store for them that they once did for the Western working classes. Had the Marxist prophecy that the exploited proletariat would overthrow the bourgeoisie been defeated domestically only to reappear internationally and defeat the West on the global plane? Would the poverty-stricken nations of the world, the international proletariat, rise up in revolution against the privileged and wealthy Western countries, the international bourgeoisie? Modernization was expected to give the new states a stake in the international system and help create a world in which Western values would be more secure.

Although the nature of the problem seemed clear to many policymakers, the rationale for economic aid to assist the new nations develop never attracted the degree of public support that the more easily understandable military preparations against the Soviets did. What was probably required, as Barbara Ward (among many) had suggested, was a progressive international income tax by which all the advanced Western nations would contribute 1–2 percent of their annual national income for this development process. The World Bank's Pearson Commission in 1969 endorsed the 1 percent figure. But no Western country was giving sums amounting to that percentage by that time. Despite the rapid economic growth of the industrial states during the 1960s, their foreign aid spending had declined. This was particularly true for American aid. At the time of the Marshall Plan to Europe, the figure had been 2.75 percent of the gross national product (GNP); for the less-developed countries, this figure was always less than 1 percent. In short, at a time when the American GNP had risen by hundreds of millions of dollars, the national effort was puny compared with its increasing capacity to pay and to the growing gap between the rich and poor nations.

Indeed, the term "economic aid" was itself something of a misnomer. After 1950 and the eruption of the Korean War, most economic aid was, in fact, military aid. Moreover, since Western Europe's recovery, most of this aid was channeled to allied countries: Turkey, Pakistan, South Vietnam, South Korea, Jordan, and Nationalist China. Even of the sum designated for economic assistance, a good part was "defense support"; this provided money to sustain the economies of allies such as South Korea or South Vietnam, which, in the absence of this support, could not maintain their standing armies. And the final sum actually allocated to economic development was also concentrated in relatively few countries. Most less-developed nations got next to nothing.

Apart from the lack of public support for foreign aid, the existing aid programs suffered from three other liabilities. One was that American dollars were all too often offered with the explicit or implicit assumption that the recipients should associate themselves with U.S. cold war policies; that even if they do not formally ally themselves with the United States, they should often thank it for its generosity, praise it for the morality of its anti-Communist stand, and certainly refrain from criticizing it. The United States has been reluctant to give dollars to nations that would not join its side. After all, could any nation really be neutral in a struggle between right and wrong? Was not democracy good and Communism evil? If countries wanted U.S. money, surely the least they could do was "to stand up and be counted." But their basic aspiration was to concentrate their attention and energy on internal matters, to raise their standard of living and strengthen their independence, and to minimize their involvement in the cold war. Most therefore preferred to remain nonaligned in the struggle between the West and the Communists, avoiding all "entangling alliances." Attempts to use economic aid as a means of forcing them into an American alliance system only failed.

In preferring a generally nonaligned position, the less-developed nations in the 1950s were following America's own earlier experience. After it had gained its independence, it, too, had abstained from all entangling alliances and preoccupied itself with internal developments; as a less-developed country itself, it was very much aware that its newly realized independence meant very little until it had gained economic and political strength. Moreover, having just thrown off the shackles of colonialism, the Americans had no desire to be once more tied to the European powers.

Second, the American position was severely handicapped by the continued discrimination that prevented blacks from realizing their full measure of civil rights and equal opportunities in American society. To a world in which the vast majority of the population is nonwhite, the persisting segregationist practices and exploitation of blacks in both the South and the North were flagrant violations of the democratic principles of freedom and human dignity so often proclaimed by the United States. The peoples of the less-developed areas not only claimed equal status as nations but also sought equality as human beings; when they heard about segregation in America, they could only be reminded of the old days when the white man had treated them as inferiors simply because of the color of their skins. This situation began to change during the Kennedy and Johnson administrations, as blacks listened to Martin Luther King articulate their aspirations for a life of more dignity and full participation in American life, as the ghettos exploded, and as the government itself began to act by removing certain discriminatory practices against blacks, as well as providing greater opportunities in such areas as jobs and housing.

However, racial problems continued to haunt the United States on the foreign front. In Rhodesia and South Africa, minority white-controlled governments determined to stay in power used abhorrent methods such as apartheid and the strictest police surveillance. The United States, despite its often expressed disapproval of these policies, did not follow through in its actions. It imported Rhodesian chrome for years despite a U.N. embargo, and in South Africa American companies, although often providing their black workers with better working conditions and pay than local companies, continued to invest. America, the world's first state to insist that all men were created equal, seemed all too often to say to the world that there was a qualifying phrase "except black men."

Third, United States relations with the developing states was hampered by the American lack of understanding of class struggle and social politics. America, "born free" as a bourgeois democratic society, had managed to avoid the kind of domestic conflicts over basic values that the countries of Europe experienced and that now plague many of the less-developed nations.* Not having experienced a genuine social revolution at its own birth—only a War of Independence and a set of institutions that were "given" to it by the Founding Fathers and that have been remarkably adaptable to the changing needs of the American people as the United States grew from a small rural to a continental urban-industrial society—America was not particularly sympathetic to revolutions and tended to identify revolutionaries with radicalism. Deviations from what were generally considered to be middle-class American values were likely to be condemned as "un-American" and sinful, to be rooted out so that the "American way of life" would remain pure and unadulterated.

The principal challenges to these values have indeed come not from within the system but from outside the U.S. borders, and the United States has reacted to foreign threats—German, Japanese, Communist—in two ways: internally, by hunting for "subversives," a procedure that inevitably has infringed upon civil liberties and endangered the security of traditional freedoms; and externally, before the atomic bomb, by the total destruction of the hostile regime so that American principles could continue to live untainted.

Thus, domestically, the Communist threat in the early 1950s led to McCarthyism, a search for heresy in which the goal of eliminating alleged un-American attitudes and behavior justified any means, including disregard for "due process of law," the basic guarantee of all civil liberties. At times, this hunt went to frightening lengths, as when the U.S. Information Agency actually burned "suspect" books—and, even worse, when the careers and lives of people were jeopardized and sometimes ruined. In foreign policy, the reaction to the Communist threat to the American way of life was to support almost any "anti-Communist" regime. Therefore, the United States associated itself with traditional regimes whose days were numbered because they had alienated mass support: Jiang Gaishek in China and Bao Dai in Indochina are two examples.

This attitude was typical of American absolutism and inability to understand the deeper social struggles of Asia and the Middle East in the attempt to contain Communism—that is, to preserve the global *status quo*—the United

*See Chapter 1, p. 6.

States became committed to the domestic, social, and political *status quo* in these countries. Thus America, in seeking stability, was paradoxically trying to preserve freedom by supporting ramshackle autocracies that were unrepresentative of their peoples' aspirations. But this internal contradiction within the U.S. alliance system had eventually to resolve itself. American support for traditional regimes only bottled up the social and political resentment and ferment even more, thereby adding to the explosive forces that someday would burst forth and further upset the global balance of power.

THE EXAMPLE OF LATIN AMERICA

Latin America was a good example of the manner in which U.S. foreign policy, even when realizing the need for development aid, became a prisoner of its own domestic experience. Much was said in this country in the 1960s about Cuba as a base for the subversion of other Latin nations. If such subversion were successful, this would constitute a great threat to the United States. But the possibilities for success were believed to exist as a result of a number of factors: resentment against a history of past American interventions in the Caribbean and Central America; vast-scale, private American capital investments and economic control of many Latin American economies; frequent American support for the privileged few who, usually closely linked to American capital, sought to preserve their position by ignoring social grievances and establishing right-wing military dictatorships; and finally, the misery, poverty, and mass illiteracy of the vast majority of the people, who, although they lived in the countryside, were landless.

Latin America shared two aspirations that were sweeping through all the less-developed areas: the urge for a better life for the mass of people who, dispossessed and exploited, were filled with deep and bitter social resentment; and the desire of countries to determine their own national destiny. The United States has exercised its hemispheric domination by indirect means, usually an alliance with the wealthy landowning governing class. Americans may believe that they are free of Europe's taint of colonialism, but that is not what Latin Americans think. The Monroe Doctrine turned the southern part of the hemisphere into a U.S. sphere of influence; America did not have to resort to direct colonial rule. Invested American capital spoke louder than guns; and political orders were unnecessary when a nation was a "banana republic" or an economic satellite. The economies of many Latin American nations remained backward, undiversified, and agrarian; they therefore continued to depend for a livelihood on the export of one or two raw materials to the United States, their largest market. In good years, they earned money; in bad years, the normal measure of unemployment, poverty, and hunger increased. Their very lives depended on the fluctuations of the business cycle, as well as, of course, their sensitivity to American interests.

In these conditions, the success of Castroism was thought to depend on two

Latin America

factors. First, it would depend upon the Latin American governments themselves; whether they would undertake large-scale social and economic reforms
or cling to their privileges; whether these privileged few were wise enough to
understand the need for internal changes or whether they would prefer to
commit suicide after fearfully clinging to their fading power for a few more
years. Public pressure for change was rising. The only question was whether
this change would be revolutionary or evolutionary. If the ruling classes remained as hostile to reform and as irresponsible toward public welfare as in the
past, Fidel Castro might be able to export his revolution. For wherever there is
social injustice, destruction of the *ancien régime* will appear as the sole way of
gaining a job, a piece of land, or enough food. Revolution and a "radical solution" will seem the only hope for a better life.

Second, the success of Castroism would depend on the effectiveness of an American policy directed toward alleviating the conditions that fostered popular resentment in Latin America. Whether America would be able to guide this revolution, however, was another matter. For it was a task that would require American support of non-Communist left-wing movements and acquiescence in the expropriation of American property, neither of which would be easy because of the frequent identification of democratic "socialism" with revolutionary Communism. Moreover, the United States was expected to invest billions of dollars in the Latin American economies in order to help them achieve a self-sustaining rate of economic growth, to develop conditions in which private capital would be attracted to projects other than the extraction of raw materials, and to aid in the transformation of backward societies into modern, urbanized, industrial nations. Latin America's projected rapid increase of population only underlined the urgency of this developmental task. In the absence of an adequate effort, the already far too low standard of living would deteriorate even more. This would probably assure the success of future radical revolutions and the alienation of Latin America from the United States.

It was to meet the challenge of the Latin American "revolution of rising expectations" that President John F. Kennedy, soon after assuming office, called for an Alliance for Progress between the United States and the nations of the south. He pledged $20 billion of primarily public capital over the next decade to Latin America and, even more significantly, placed great emphasis upon the need for social politics. In the absence of the necessary reforms, he realized, the possibilities of economic and political development were slight. The alliance, in short, was a post-Castro attempt to abort any future Castros.

Would the ruling oligarchies, however, surrender their power, status, and prestige, or commit themselves to fundamental reforms? In the words of a veteran observer of the Latin American scene at that time, Herbert L. Matthews:

In the whole of Latin America, the rich are getting richer and the poor poorer. This is the worst, the most difficult and the most dangerous feature of the area. The Alliance for Progress was created primarily to tackle this essentially social problem. . . .

The most serious feature of this problem centers around agriculture and land reform. The frantic urge to industrialize that seized Latin America after the Second World War was, in part, satisfied at the expense of the agrarian sector. Yet virtually all the countries are from half to three-quarters agricultural. Latin exports are overwhelmingly agricultural and mineral.

The abnormal and dangerous urbanization, caused by the flight of impoverished peasants from the rural areas to the urban centers, has led to some of the largest cities in the world and some of the worst slums. Countries with plenty of land were, and are, importing food at high cost.

Most landowners are resisting the reforms that their governments and the Alliance for Progress desire. . . . Much will depend on whether the ruling classes see the need to make drastic structural reforms. Much, also, will depend on the state of the world and the world markets for raw materials, not to mention the ability of the United States to invest and to aid. . . .

There are revolutions and revolutions. The fascist-military type in Latin America comes from the right; the socialistic-communistic from the left; and in between is the sort of peaceful, voluntary, gradual but genuine type of revolution which the Alliance for Progress is trying to promote.

Latin America is such a dynamic area of the world that it is bound to have revolutions. The only unknown factor is: what kind?*

The paralysis imposed on the alliance by Castro was abundantly illustrated at the time of the Dominican intervention. The background for this event was the overthrow in 1961 of the cruel thirty-one-year-old Dominican dictatorship of Rafael Trujillo. Following a brief intervening period of political turmoil, Juan Bosch, a man of genuinely democratic convictions, had been elected to the office of president. Seven months later, Bosch was overthrown by a military *coup d'état* whose leaders announced that they would reestablish a "rightist state." In April 1965, the pro-Bosch forces revolted against this right-wing military government. But the leadership of this revolution swung increasingly, according to Washington, in a Communist direction. Communists were thought to be active in the antijunta movement, and Washington feared they would gain control of the pro-Bosch forces and that the result would be a second Cuba in the hemisphere. The rebels claimed that while some Communists might support their movement, their revolution was led by non-Communists who only sought a return to constitutional government. President Lyndon Johnson, however, ordered American armed intervention before the evidence was clear that the revolution was in fact Communist-controlled—even though this action once more raised the old specter of American intervention, so common in the days before Franklin Roosevelt's "Good Neighbor" policy.

The Dominican intervention demonstrated that the Alliance for Progress continued to be haunted by the Cuban leader. Castro was responsible both for the alliance and for its failures. Without him, there would have been no large-scale efforts to seek the democratic development of Latin America. But the American fear that any Latin American revolution might end up being Communist-controlled and that this required preventive action would also not have sprung up without Castro. The overt United States intervention—the first in fifty years in Latin America—therefore helped undermine the Alliance for Progress, which had tried to persuade the region's ruling elites that they ought to reform the *status quo* if they wished to avoid revolutionary violence. Latin America's ruling classes could now relax, for there was an alternative: American intervention would save them from the consequences of their own folly in holding onto an unjust *status quo*. United States policy, south of America's border as in other areas of the world, thus continued into the middle 1960s to be motivated by a bipolar image of the world.

*The New York Times, March 15, 1965.

WAS UNITED STATES' THIRD WORLD POLICY IMPERIALISTIC?*

Especially since the American involvement in the Vietnam War, some radical writers, often referred to as the New Left, have said that American actions such as those in Cuba and the Dominican Republic were hardly accidental; nor was the failure to provide meaningful economic aid for the modernization of the new nations a mere oversight. Indeed, this line of argument maintains that while these nations may have been new in the sense of formal political independence, they were in reality economically controlled by the dominant economy in the "global capitalist system," the United States economy; the so-called new and independent nations thus in fact remained colonies. "Neocolonialism" was the term popularly used to refer to their alleged status. Whereas in European eighteenth- and nineteenth-century colonialism the European state had usually invaded a piece of territory and established direct rule of the newly acquired colony, American imperialism in the contemporary age of nationalism controlled its colonial appendages through less visible but equally binding economic chains: corporate investments, economic aid, and the needs of the Third World countries for advanced technology and for markets in which to sell their raw materials. And, of course, the United States supported reactionary political and social elites who survived only with American backing which, when necessary, was supplemented with American training and arming of local police and military forces, CIA bribes, subsidies for private armies, and all sorts of "dirty tricks," including assassinations and *coups d'état.*

Why all this bother about the poor countries of the world? Because they are, according to this radical critique, enormously profitable. They are sources of cheap raw materials to stoke Western industry; they constitute potentially sizable markets for Western goods; and they provide places for the investment of private capital at large returns. Capitalist economies like that of the United States, the leading Western capitalist state, constantly need profits; without them, unemployment would increase, standards of living decline, and the struggle between capitalists and those who worked for them resume. This struggle is muted in the capitalist country where some of the enormous profits reaped by the capitalists, basically from exploiting the less-developed countries, trickle down to the workers in the form of higher wages and living standards, thereby drawing their revolutionary fangs and winning their support for

---

*This section, while brief, was included because U.S. policy toward the Third World is often described in imperialistic terms. This important alternative explanation deserves brief mention, therefore, as does the critique of it. I relied especially upon Jerome Slater, "Is United States Foreign Policy 'Imperialistic' or 'Imperial'?" *Political Science Quarterly*, Spring 1976, pp. 63–87; Robert W. Tucker, *The Radical Left and American Foreign Policy* (Baltimore: Johns Hopkins University Press, 1971); and Stephen D. Krasner, *Defending the National Interest* (Princeton: Princeton University Press, 1978).

capitalism. Without this trickle, the class struggle would resume. Therefore, even with the best of intentions, America, as a capitalist society and guardian of Western capitalism, could not surrender its "neocolonial control" over the less-developed states. It was structurally necessary; if capitalism was to be preserved and domestic social revolution avoided, the Third World countries had to be maintained as profitable dependencies and suppliers of raw materials. Hence the American pursuit of counterrevolutionary and interventionist policies.

In fact, this economically imperialist interpretation of American foreign policy from 1945 to Vietnam is testimony to the significance of faith and attitudes over facts. Little evidence supported such a purely economic interpretation. The vast bulk of American private investments had been made in the American economy; and of the approximately 5–6 percent of American investment that was made abroad, most, even at the height of the Vietnam War in 1968, went to Western Europe, Canada, and Japan. In short, investment in non-Western economies was hardly significant for the welfare of the American economy. In trade, the pattern was identical. The United States traded primarily with the other industrial countries. They had something to sell to one another. Again, the Third World states were not essential to the well-being of the American economy. It is primarily in the area of natural resources that the dependency argument carries a degree of plausibility, for clearly America, like other Western industries, needed raw materials. But even here, with the possible exception of oil, the case is far from persuasive. Substitutes, alternative raw materials, the domestic availability of a vast array of raw materials, and the discovery of new resources on the world's seabeds in fact made the country less dependent upon the Third World than the imperialist interpretation would suggest. (Admittedly, the cost of materials from domestic sources may be higher than from the less-developed countries, although not necessarily higher than the prices these couuntries hope to get or, in the case of oil, are already receiving. Even in oil, as the price continues to rise, alternative sources of energy or oil from deeper wells become economically more feasible.) The United States, in fact, possesses many of the raw materials it needs, including energy resources, especially coal.

What is equally clear is that the imperialist interpretation that suggests that capitalist countries either exercise control of Third World economies in order to make a profit, or have no control, which leads to a collapse of capitalist economies, could not be more wrong. The Western states that, since 1945, have achieved the highest rates of economic growth are countries such as Japan, West Germany, and those of Scandinavia, states that obviously had no colonies and that exercised no "control" over non-Western countries. They bought what they needed. Imperialist control was completely unnecessary for these states with "capitalist" economies; indeed, such control was inversely related to their prosperity. It was former colonial states such as Great Britain and the last colonial state of all, Portugal, whose economies fared the worst of all Western economies. Thus, domination of the less-developed countries for the purpose of having access to their raw materials is not required. Indeed, and no doubt disillusioning to radical critics who would like the Third World countries to withhold their resources to bring down American capitalism, these nations, radical or not, sell their resources to all Western countries—if the price is right.

But to return to the main point: The picture of the United States controlling Arab oil countries or even Latin American states is ludicrous. As became clear in 1973 with the Oil Producing Exporting Countries' (OPEC) fourfold increase of oil prices, and should have been clear even before that historic date, the Third World, country after country, has been expropriating American investments and property. Nationalization has been the trend in this age of nationalism, and there is little that can be done about it except to acquiesce and officially protest—with anger sometimes, but not too much—and seek some compensation for the expropriated industry. But the United States does not send in marines or overthrow governments to save a corporation's sugar fields or banana crops, not even to lower oil prices. Economic and other pressures, as well as covert operations and overt interventions, have been resorted to only where Washington perceived the stakes to be far broader than simple expropriation—that is, where the stakes were not simply those of corporate property, indeed where the stakes were perceived to be far broader than merely economic ones. In Guatemala in 1954, in Cuba in 1961, in the Dominican Republic in 1965 (and later, as we shall see, in Chile in the early 1970s and El Salvador in the early 1980s), the American government intervened—even if, as in Cuba, unsuccessfully—because it viewed the governments in these countries and their international orientation in the context of cold war bipolarity. All these countries seemed to be slipping into or aligning themselves with the Soviet camp. This appearance, which led to the U.S. interventions, may have been in error, but, it needs to be noted, it is not one that stems from an *a priori* antileft or anti-Socialist animus; the United States has allied itself and cooperated with Democratic Socialist or Labor party governments in many countries, especially in Europe, as well as with nondemocratic Communist regimes in countries such as Yugoslavia and China.

American policy in the Middle East is probably the strongest refutation of the imperialist interpretation. If the corporate capitalists did indeed control Washington, it is impossible to understand why the United States has since 1948 so strongly supported Israel, alienated most Arab states, jeopardized access to the oil needed so badly by Europe and increasingly by America, and risked the nationalization of Western oil companies (almost everywhere now controlled, even if not yet totally owned, by OPEC). In fact, what this policy shows is that economic considerations, if present and important, are not at all necessarily predominant in the making of the nation's foreign policy. If only the United States did control Saudi Arabia, Iran, Kuwait, and Venezuela! American motivations in foreign policy must be sought elsewhere than in the economic realm, primarily in security considerations and the fear of Soviet power and the identification after 1946–1947 of the expansion of Soviet power and influence with the expansion of Communism. In the pre-Vietnam era of two relatively cohesive alliances, the North Atlantic Treaty Organization and the Sino-Soviet alliance, this identification was easy to understand, even if it was not always correct.

Chapter 8

VIETNAM AND THE COLLAPSE OF CONTAINMENT

AMERICA AS "GLOBAL POLICEMAN"

The world that emerged from World War II and dominated most of the twenty years from 1945 to 1965 was bipolar. The United States and the Soviet Union, plus their allies, confronted one another directly and globally. In a series of crises, they drew the "frontiers" between their worlds and extended their competition to the Third World. This bipolar world was very dangerous, because the distribution of power in the state system between two poles is extremely sensitive. Both are constantly alert to the slightest shifts in power lest they upset the equilibrium and give one adversary a superiority of power. Each side perceives a gain of power and security for one as a loss of power and security for the other. Each views the opponent's moves, even if alleged to be defensive, as deliberate and offensive; and moves in areas of secondary importance are ranked as significant and countered because they are seen as symbolically vital.

The first characteristic of the resulting American containment policy was its involvement on all continents of the world, thereby becoming what some of its critics called a "world policeman." Thus, initially in the eastern Mediterranean and Western Europe, then in Asia and the Middle East and, to varying degrees, in Africa and Latin America, Washington sought to contain what it saw as Soviet and/or Chinese attempts to exploit power vacuums, intraregional conflicts, and differences between Western countries and the Third World. As a result, the United States, the formerly isolationist nation that felt that no quarrels anywhere affected its security, developed into the world power that became involved in all regions (except up to then sub-Sahara Africa), drawing "frontiers" around the areas it deemed vital.

The second characteristic of the American role was the continuous vigilance and effort needed to protect these "frontiers." Strategic deterrence was the principal means of preventing a major incursion of Western Europe and subsequent strike against the continental United States. Limited challenges were met by a variety of means: nuclear blackmail by a mixture of military and diplomatic tactics and actual frontier crossings by "frontier wars."

A third feature was that these challenges normally have taken place at the farthest point from the United States. This is, of course, where frontiers meet and where the opponent finds it easiest to cause trouble and the defender is likely to show the least resolution. The frontier is far away and may not seem clearly related to America's security interests of the center; it is also nearer to the opponent and its defense therefore may involve great risks and costs. Indeed, such peripheral involvement may seem like an overextension of the center's power, which, it will be claimed, is not only dangerous but also expensive and unnecessary. Yet these frontiers have been guarded by America's armed forces. When the occasions have arisen in the ex-colonial areas of the world, the two superpowers have agreed to allow U.N. forces, staffed primarily by nonaligned members, to keep the peace in order to avoid a clash between themselves.

A fourth and key characteristic of the American role is the U.S. belief that in a bipolar system, deterrence, total and limited, requires the opponent to believe that this country will honor its commitments. It follows that if commitments to maintain a particular frontier are no longer credible—no matter how distant or unimportant this frontier may seem to some—the adversary may come to believe that other frontiers too may be crossed with impunity. It may be true that one frontier is more vital than another, but how is the opponent to know which one? The failure to honor a commitment in one area may thus be seen by the adversary as an indication that another commitment elsewhere may also not be honored and tempt him to test the defender's will. A commitment, whether eagerly sought or reluctantly accepted, therefore becomes a matter from which it is very difficult to withdraw without dangerous consequences.

This is also because, fifth, America's allies and friends know that their defense depends upon the United States and they are therefore constantly alert to signs of a weakening will. Precisely because they are keenly aware of their geographic location and know that the defense of their security may at times seem either hazardous or unimportant to their protector, they will live in a continuous state of apprehension lest they be left undefended; if they are, they may well consider approaching the opponent and bargaining for the best terms possible. As President John Kennedy said with regard to Soviet policy on Berlin: It was designed to neutralize West Germany as a first step toward the neutralization of Western Europe. If the United States did not meet its commitments in the divided city, it would mean the destruction of the North Atlantic Treaty Organization (NATO) and a resulting dangerous situation for the whole world. All of Europe was at stake in West Berlin.

VIETNAM AS A "FRONTIER WAR"

The United States became involved in the Vietnam War in Southeast Asia because, first of all, it was a frontier war. In the words of Eugene Rostow, formerly of the State Department and later the head of the Arms Control and Disarmament Agency:

> In Indochina the North Vietnamese government has broken the first and most basic rule of Peaceful Coexistence: That the frontiers of the two systems not be altered unilaterally, or by military action. To cite a clear parallel, it has been deemed self-evident in Washington and in Moscow that it would be unthinkably dangerous for either East Germany or West Germany to attack the other, either openly or through infiltration. Yet what North Vietnam . . . is attempting in Indochina—to conquer a country the United States has agreed to protect—is the precise analogue of such a hypothetical German conflict, or of the Korean war of 1950–53, or of the Soviet Union's early postwar probes against Greece, Turkey and Iran.

The Kennedy and Johnson administrations assumed that the Soviet Union and Communist China were behind North Vietnam. Most American policymakers still talked of the Sino-Soviet bloc and perceived the Communist world as monolithic; those who did see the growing Sino-Soviet rift were even more convinced of the need to contain "Chinese-directed Asian Communism" because China was viewed as even more militant and expansionist than the Soviet Union.

Second, it was a war fought at a great distance from the center, in a place where the frontier was very accessible to the enemy. South Vietnam was a badly divided society; refugees (approximately 1 million, about half of them Catholic) against indigenous South Vietnamese; Buddhists against Catholics; lowlanders against *montagnards;* and peasants against urban inhabitants. Loyalties were, as in most new nations, primarily local. Hostility to a central government was deeply ingrained since, as in most less-developed countries, the government historically has been that of the colonial power, as represented by the tax collector and recruiting sergeant. Transportation and communication were primitive and industrial development nonexistent. In addition, this was a new state that had emerged from the 1954 Geneva conference concluding the First Indochina War between France and the Vietminh forces, with no established political institutions and a precarious economy. Not surprisingly, the Vietminh expected South Vietnam to collapse: The Geneva agreement called for a general election to be held in 1956, and it was assumed by Hanoi that a majority of the 12 million South Vietnamese would vote for the man who had led the nationalist struggle against the French, Ho Chi Minh (who obviously could have delivered most of the North's 15 million votes). Thus the country would be reunited under Communist control.

It was for this reason that neither the United States nor the new Diem government in the South favored the election; the former wanted the seventeenth parallel to be accepted as the new frontier, and Ngo Dinh Diem, a fervent Catholic and anti-Communist, was not about to eliminate himself. Their opposition was decisive, irrespective of the issue as to whether the unsigned Geneva declaration about the election was politically binding. Thus Hanoi's chances for a peaceful takeover of the South ended, and so did its stance of reasonableness and restraint. At the time of the Geneva settlement, approximately 5000–6000 local hard-core guerrillas, presumably the Vietminh's political and military elite, went underground and became anonymous peasants. About 90,000 others went north (to be infiltrated into the South again later) while about 1 million northerners, mainly Catholics, went south. In the late 1950s, the guerrillas who had stayed in the South began to murder village chiefs and other government officials. The Second Indochina War had started; the immediate guerrilla objective was to isolate the central government from the majority of its population and substitute Vietcong control over the peasantry by killing the government's local representatives.

This war, in short, started in quite a different manner from the Korean War. Korea had begun with a clear-cut, aggressive attack, which aroused the American public and united the principal Western allies against the common threat. It had also been a conventional war in which regular Communist forces had been checked by regular South Korean, American, and U.N. troops. By contrast, Dienbienphu had been a decisive moment in contemporary history, for, apart from defeating France and throwing off French colonial shackles, the battle demonstrated that *guerrilla warfare* could defeat the larger, stronger, conventionally equipped army of even a major power. It also showed that nuclear weapons would be useless in countering the tactics of such a war. An internal uprising of guerrillas, directed and organized by the North, was therefore a shrewder manner of "crossing" the seventeenth parallel. It would lend the resulting struggle the aura of a civil war, which, if taken at face value by the United States and the West, would paralyze any united response and cause domestic doubt about the morality and wisdom of fighting in such a conflict. Diem's increasingly autocratic rule and his failure to enlist the support of his population, especially the peasantry, through political, social, and economic reforms helped prepare the ground for a successful guerrilla campaign and lent support to the view of the conflict as a civil war.

A third reason for involvement was that the war was seen in Washington as a test of its will, and meeting the test was believed to be necessary to maintain all frontiers. The Asian balance depended upon the United States until the non-Communist states of the area became economically developed and possessed sufficient capabilities of their own. Commitments—and the administrations of Presidents Dwight Eisenhower, John Kennedy and Lyndon Johnson all considered the United States to be committed to the defense of South Vietnam—were interdependent. The United States could not choose to defend West Berlin and Quemoy but not Matsu and South Korea (an American protégé that in 1950 did not even have a formal treaty of defense with the United States).

Washington believed that it could no more forego the defense of the frontier in South Vietnam than in Greece and Turkey, in Western Europe and Berlin, or in Korea and Cuba. If one country fell it would, in its turn, knock down the next one and so on down the line like a row of dominoes; the political and psychological impact of an American pullout would be felt throughout the area, if not in other regions as well. All commitments were viewed as interdependent; being unfaithful to one risked the collapse of all.

THE MISCONDUCT OF COUNTERGUERRILLA CONFLICT

During the Kennedy and Johnson administrations, therefore, justifications for an increasing military commitment to South Vietnam were made in terms of America's global responsibilities for maintaining the general peace and stability of the international system. Despite this, the wisdom of the policy was debatable. During his years as president, Kennedy sent 16,500 military advisors; Johnson, beginning in the spring of 1965, augmented this number to more than 500,000. Particularly significant during the years of piecemeal commitments was that at no point did policymakers in Washington ever sit down, take time, and ask themselves some fundamental questions about Vietnam: Was it vital to American security interests and, if so, how vital? Could the situation in South Vietnam be saved militarily, given the nature of the Saigon government and its seeming lack of popular support? If American forces should be sent, in what numbers? And how could they be effectively used in an unorthodox type of war? What cost, if any, was South Vietnam "worth"? As incremental commitments were made whenever conditions in South Vietnam appeared ominous, these questions continued to be avoided.

During the Kennedy period, military advisors managed to prevent total collapse, but by 1965 his successor—who had spent his time since Kennedy's assassination passing a major domestic reform program and getting reelected—could no longer operate on this basis and avoid the central question of what the United States ought to do. South Vietnam was about to be cut in two, and the Vietcong would then be in a position to mop up first one part, then the other. In the face of this reality, Johnson sent in 200,000 troops that year, extending U.S. involvement and turning an incremental policy into a long-term commitment. After years and years of neglect and procrastination and with the situation growing worse daily, Washington had neither the time nor the inclination to make a carefully calculated basic decision; when the crucial decision was made, it was made by a new president—whose primary interest, experience, and skill were domestic—on the advice of the Kennedy staff and cabinet he had inherited. Long-range policy has thus become the prisoner of a number of prior short-range decisions that had been made to tackle immediately critical problems.

The key to the successful deployment of American arms—the political structure of South Vietnam—was virtually ignored. For years, the United States had supported Diem, whose increasingly authoritarian rule and aloofness from his people had alienated most of them. By the time the military overthrew Diem, with Kennedy's knowledge and tacit blessing, the Vietcong already controlled much of South Vietnam; the social, political, and economic reforms needed to win the war had for too long been disregarded. The very fact that the United States acquiesced in the coup against Diem should have alerted future administrations; that Kennedy had himself said Diem had "gotten out of touch with the people" testified to the political bankruptcy in Saigon, as well as to the questionable wisdom of having begun the military commitments in the first place. Diem's successor governments proved no more able to rally popular support for a vigorous prosecution of the war against the Vietcong. Saigon's succession of corrupt, reactionary, and repressive regimes apparently never reawakened thoughts in the minds of U.S. policymakers of Jiang Gaishek and his Nationalist government in postwar China.

The Truman administration at the time had decided China could not be saved, except perhaps—and it was only *perhaps*—at an enormous military and economic cost. This, it felt, the American public would not be willing to pay; in addition, this would have diverted the nation's resources and efforts from its area of primary interest in Europe where these could be productively used to enhance American security. In Secretary of State Dean Acheson's words at the time: "Nothing that this country did or could have done within the *reasonable* limits of its capabilities" could have changed the result in the conflict between Mao Zedong and Jiang [italics added]. In short, containment could not be achieved through a sieve. By attempting it in South Vietnam, Harry Truman's successors in Democratic administrations were in fact risking major domestic discontent. They were also risking a public questioning of the fundamental assumptions of American postwar foreign policy that had led to the war.

Certainly, the possibility of achieving a quick victory over the Vietcong was remote, for a guerrilla war is anything but the traditional type of Western warfare. Its aim is to capture the power of the government from within, and to do so by eroding the morale of the army and by undermining popular confidence in the government. To achieve this objective, it is necessary neither to inflict a complete defeat on the government's forces nor to compel them to surrender unconditionally. Indeed, until the final stage of the war, guerrillas do not even meet these forces openly, and then they do so only to apply the *coup de grâce*. Guerrilla forces fight a guerrilla war because they are compelled to; in the initial phases, they are the weaker side militarily. Guerrilla war is therefore a protracted conflict in which the guerrillas resort to hit-and-run tactics—here, there, everywhere—and engage only those smaller and weaker government forces they can defeat. In order to cope with such tactics, year in and year out, the government troops must be dispersed to guard every town, every hamlet, and every bridge against possible attack. Unable to come to real grips with the enemy and impose a heavy defeat upon him as in a conventional and set battle, and suffering defeat after defeat, however small, the army is subject to great loss of morale and its mood becomes defensive.

Although such tactics gradually weaken the military strength of the army, the guerrillas' main effort remains directed at the civilian population. As they are the weaker side, the guerrillas' principal aim becomes one of wresting the allegiance of the population from the government. Without popular support, the government will simply collapse. The guerrillas proceed to do this in two ways. First, by their increasing control of the countryside, where the vast majority of the population live, and by their defeats of government forces, they demonstrate to the peasants that the government cannot protect them. The execution of the village headmen, who are generally government representatives, and of any persons who may have helped the government forces proves this most vividly. Second, and even more important, the guerrillas exploit any existing popular grievances. Communist guerrillas do not pose as Communists, and they do not usually receive support because they are Communists. The populace will support them because it believes the guerrillas will oust the government with which it is dissatisfied and that a new government will meet its aspirations. Mao Zedong said that guerrillas need the people as fish need water; without popular support, the guerrillas would not receive recruits, food, shelter, and above all, information on the government forces' disposition. Thus, in contrast to conventional warfare, in which each army seeks the destruction of the other's military forces, in guerrilla warfare the guerrillas seek to win the support of the people. A government that has the allegiance of its population does not provide fertile soil for guerrillas; where social dissatisfaction exists, however, the ground is fertile for what is the essence of the guerrilla recipe for victory—a *social strategy*. The guerrillas gain the support of the peasantry because they successfully represent themselves as the liberators from colonialism or foreign rule, native despotic governments, economic deprivation, or social injustice.

Counterguerrilla war is therefore not a purely military war but a political war as well. While the defeat of guerrillas in the field must be vigorously pursued, the principal task is to tackle the political, social, and economic conditions that bred the support for the guerrillas. Fundamentally, counterguerrilla warfare is therefore an extremely difficult and sophisticated form of war to wage—far more so than the traditional clash of armies—because the war cannot be won without thoroughgoing reforms. Yet these have to be carried out in the midst of battle. Such a war is also likely to take years; five to ten years is not at all out of the ordinary. And finally, it takes approximately fifteen counterguerrilla fighters to one guerrilla—in short, a sizable army, and one trained not in conventional fighting but in counterguerrilla tactics. What all this meant was that the United States would find such a war extremely difficult to fight. America likes its wars "strictly military." A war that is concerned primarily with social and political reforms—and thus opens itself up to all the usual domestic criticisms of "socialistic," "pro-Communist," and "do-gooder" reforms—runs completely counter to the American approach. The war's length would also cause great frustration, because the United States likes to get its "boys home by Christmas"; not a lengthy, drawn-out affair, but a quick and happy ending à la Hollywood is the American way of fighting. If this new kind of warfare did not yield swift and successful results, the American temptation would be either to pull out or to seek a short-cut to victory by purely military action.

American policymakers, however, misplaced their confidence in the nation's military prowess and its ability to change the guerrillas' "rules of the game." In 1965, the illusion of American omnipotence had not yet died. Had not the United States successfully confronted the Soviet Union in Cuba and compelled it to back down? Could there really be much doubt that its well-trained generals in command of armies equipped with the newest and latest weapons from America's industry and under the leadership of that most efficient Pentagon manager, Secretary of Defense Robert McNamara, could beat a few thousand "peasants in black pajamas"? With its sizable forces and its superior mobility and firepower, could not America find the enemy's troops and destroy them, compelling that enemy to desist from taking over South Vietnam? Characteristically, then, the principal emphasis was strictly military.

In a war that required forces to secure villages and to stay there in order to root out the Vietcong cells and possibly give Saigon the opportunity to prove to the villagers that "their" government did care for them, the military carried out massive search-and-destroy operations. The guerrillas, even when defeated (as they usually were when they were found), returned after the helicopters had left and continued to control the countryside. Since such large-scale operations could hardly be launched without preparation at the base camp and were usually preceded by airstrikes and artillery bombardments of the area in which the troops would land, the Vietcong often disappeared and the whole operation ended in frustration.

The American military clearly did not understand the political nature of counterguerrilla war. They had been trained for conventional battle and their strategy was to bring maximum firepower to bear, even when, for example, by destroying a village from which a few shots had apparently been fired, they alienated the villagers without whose support the war could not be won. The government, too, tended to become increasingly enamored of the military approach—probably because the political nature of the war remained so elusive and difficult to grasp. The military "kill" thus became the prime aim, because that seemed tangible and attainable. The war was also extended by air to the North. The purpose of the beginning was clearly not primarily military. Guerrillas can live off the land and capture many of their weapons from their enemies; and, in any case, the sustained American attacks on Chinese supply lines in North Korea during the Korean War had shown that air power alone was unable to stop the flow of supplies to the fighting zone. The aim of the attacks was political—to persuade North Vietnam to call a halt to the war. The gradual extension of these attacks was intended to stress the fact that the United States meant to protect South Vietnam and would not withdraw; that the price Hanoi might have to pay for victory would be disproportionally costly, and therefore that it had better desist. But the bombing did not weaken Hanoi's will to prosecute the war, cut the supplies sufficiently to hamper the fighting in the South, or greatly reduce troop infiltration. This, in turn, led to increased military and political calls for *more* air strikes and against new targets. These calls did not acknowledge that air power could not by itself win the war; rather, they insisted that it could win the war if it were used with maximum efficiency. Air power, in short, came to be seen by some as an immaculate way of fighting the enemy, of efficiently inflicting great destruction on him, throttling his supply lines, breaking his morale, and finally compelling him to seek an end to the conflict.

This objective, however, remained unattainable. Even the more stable Thieu-Ky military regime, which sought to legitimate itself in the election of 1967, failed to implement a program of social and economic reform; it was particularly remiss in not carrying out a necessary redistribution of land from the usually absentee landlord to the peasant. Without such reforms, the ground could not be cut out from under the Vietcong. Militarily, every increase of American forces was met by increased infiltration of both guerrillas and conventional troops from the North to the South. Nevertheless, optimistic battle reports and forecasts of victory were frequent. It was the 1968 Tet (or Vietnamese New Year) offensive that was to be the Johnson administration's Dienbienphu. Tet showed once and for all—and Americans could see it nightly on their television sets—that, despite the repeated optimistic predictions of the past, the enemy had again been badly underestimated. He had launched a major countrywide offensive and penetrated Saigon, Hué, and every other provincial capital; a Vietcong squad had even penetrated the American Embassy compound, thereby scoring a significant symbolic victory. Above all, the Vietcong had clearly demonstrated that neither an American army of a half-million men nor Saigon with its vastly larger army could give the people living in the urban areas security—and the Communists already controlled much of the countryside.

American power and its effectiveness in unorthodox warfare were revealed as greatly exaggerated. Tactically, American forces had seized and retained the offensive, claiming the destruction of large numbers of enemy soldiers, but strategically the Vietcong had maintained the upper hand. The Americans were still very much on the defensive and, by using about 80 percent of their forces to find and destroy North Vietnamese troops in the relatively unpopulated central highlands and frontier regions, they were unable to secure *and* protect the 90 percent of the population living in the Mekong Delta and coastal plains. The pursuit of victory through physical attrition clearly could not be transformed into military and, especially, political advantages. Indeed, in question was not just America's protective capacity but also its wisdom. Having left the cities unprotected, except for elements of the South Vietnamese army (Tet revealed Saigon's impotence dramatically), allied forces then had to fight their way back into the hearts of the various cities and towns the Vietcong had infil-trated. If, after almost three years of American help, South Vietnam was still that insecure and the enemy that strong, the wisdom of continuing the war, let alone sending further American reinforcements, was bound to be intensely debated.

This was particularly so because many Americans increasingly perceived the war to be morally ambiguous, if not downright immoral. There had never been a clear-cut crossing of the seventeenth parallel dividing North and South Viet-nam; this made the accusation against Hanoi as an aggressor less believable. The undemocratic nature of Saigon's government and its apparent lack of popu-larity gave credence to the view of the war as a rebellion or civil war against Saigon's repression. (Interestingly, in 1950, the South Korean government had a similar autocratic reputation, but the attack across the thirty-eighth parallel focused attention on North Korean ambitions and justified the American inter-vention. No one in the United States raised questions about defending a "cor-rupt dictatorship.") The massive and often indiscriminate use of American fire-power leading to widespread destruction of civilian life and property, the creation of thousands of refugees, and, allegedly, the hostility of the very peo-ple upon whose support military success depended had already pricked the conscience of many Americans concerned with their nation's historic image as a compassionate and humane country. The tanks rumbling into cities after Tet, the dive-bombing of apartment houses, the civilian suffering and personal trag-edies left many a television viewer asking himself whether there was any point in "destroying a country in order to defend it."

Within the United States, Tet coalesced the opposition that had been grow-ing throughout 1967 as the war had continued, seemingly without end, and President Johnson's initial support eroded on both right and left—the former demanding an end to the war through escalation and the latter through dees-calation, if not outright withdrawal. (Sometimes, in fact, the same people held both views.) The articulate opposition to the conflict by a number of liberal and moderate Republican and Democratic senators, especially the chairman of the Senate Foreign Relations Committee, J. William Fulbright, made the opposi-tion of many politicians, professors, students, journalists, and editorial writers and television commentators respectable instead of "un-American." Indeed, after Tet, Fulbright and his committee became an alternative source of inter-pretation and policy recommendations to the president. Thus, despite the fact that the Vietcong were almost destroyed during the Tet fighting (after Tet, the North Vietnamese army took over almost completely), politically the United States suffered a defeat. Despite the American military success, Tet demon-strated that the real domino that had collapsed was American public opinion. The guerrilla strategy of *psychologically exhausting* the opponent—as the mili-tarily weaker side, unable to defeat the adversary on the battlefield, that was the only available strategy—had been successful. The American strategy of *physical attrition* was the wrong strategy. The military won almost all the bat-tles but "lost" the war as the public grew tired of it.

This led two senators from the president's own party, **Eugene McCarthy** and Robert Kennedy, to contest Johnson's renomination as the Democratic stand-ard-bearer. Running as "peace candidates," they provided a rallying point for the ever larger numbers of Americans disenchanted with the war. Then, in March 1968, at the end of the speech that laid the basis for the Paris peace talks, the president announced that he would not run for a second term. In the words of the political commentator Tom Wicker of the *New York Times*, Lyndon Johnson's tragedy was that he "came into office seeking a great society in America and found instead an ugly little war that consumed him." The changing American mood was evident in the 1968 election campaign. Vice-President Hubert Humphrey, nominated in Chicago after bloody clashes between police and antiwar students (many of them McCarthy supporters) and bitter disagreement among the delegates over the Vietnam platform, was mercilessly heckled during most of the campaign. As a member of the administration, he found it difficult to disavow the war; when he did take his own "risk of peace," it was very late in the campaign. In these circumstances of Democratic disunity, former Vice-President Richard Nixon, a long-time hawk, found it inexpedient to charge the Democrats with a "no-win" policy; instead he softened his views on the war. Indeed, in his speeches the menace abroad suddenly ran a poor second to the "moral decay" at home. Generally, both candidates fell over themselves in their eagerness to abandon both anti-Communist slogans and the war, offering instead hopes for an "honorable" peace in Vietnam and for "law and order" at home. Halting Communist aggression was abandoned as an issue; stopping further costly foreign adventure—"No more Vietnams"—became the issue.

A NEW MOOD

America's mood reflected weariness, disillusionment, and retreat from global commitments and involvements. One feature of this mood was the attempt to curb presidential power in foreign policy, especially the power as commander-in-chief to commit American forces to battle. Under the Constitution, the president is chiefly responsible for the conduct of foreign policy; it is not surprising that those opposed to these policies focus their attention on him. Just as conservatives during the 1950s wished to limit presidential authority because the president was, in their minds, not anti-Communist enough and might, therefore, upon the advice of the "pro-Communists" in the State Department, sell the country down the river (as the State Department had already "sold" Eastern Europe and Nationalist China), so liberals started in the late 1960s to seek to restrain the president's authority because in their opinion, he, the military industrial complex, and the Central Intelligence Agency (CIA) supporting him were too anti-Communist, intent on involving the country in too many places, in too many costly adventures abroad.

Conservative or liberal, the remedy for the "imperial presidency's" alleged abuse of its authority and its virtually solo determination of foreign policy was identical: to reassert the control of Congress in the formulation of external policy and to restore the constitutional balance that had purportedly been upset. Thus, the president would presumably be restrained so that he would no longer be, for conservatives, able to "appease" America's enemies or, for liberals, able to act in an interventionist and warlike manner. The abuse of power by Richard Nixon, a conservative president, reinforced the liberal sentiment to curb his powers and compel him to conduct a more restrained and moderate policy.

A second symptom of the new mood was that priority should be paid to the nation's domestic problems. These became very clear as the affluent society began to reveal its seamier and more violent sides in the 1960s, such as urban slums, air and water pollution, and the dissatisfaction of the poor, who were composed primarily of those discriminated against by society—blacks, Puerto Ricans, Indians, Chicanos, and Orientals. It was on such problems that critics of the war wanted to spend money to improve the quality of American life for all citizens and prevent the fabric of their society from being torn apart. Instead of crusading for democracy abroad, they argued, the United States should start crusading to make *America* safe for democracy. Liberal critics of the war in Vietnam quoted Edmund Burke to the effect that "example is the school of mankind, and they will learn at no other." The example should be one of a free society enjoying its freedom fully.

Yet these blessings could not be fully realized in a nation whose excessive preoccupation with foreign affairs drained its powers and resources, both human and material. A "strong" foreign policy was unlikely to bring with it any lasting greatness, prestige, and security; rather, the constant expenditure of energy in foreign adventures would ruin the domestic base. The cold war preoccupation was corrupting the very nature of American society. Institutional imbalance was eroding constitutional processes, particularly when powerful and energetic presidents in the name of national security not only committed the nation to war but also appeared to sanction plots to assassinate foreign leaders such as Fidel Castro (with Mafia help), lied to the American people and Congress about what they were doing or why they were doing it, acted secretly (even bombing Cambodia secretly for years), and in various ways violated the constitutional rights of some American citizens. And the large-scale devotion of the country's financial and intellectual resources to its external commitments meant a corresponding neglect of domestic issues. Foreign policy, in short, was tainting the American promise and vision; the priority of foreign policy, therefore, had to be ended. This had always been the heart of the old isolationism: America could only take care of its own needs, serve as an example for mankind, and remain pure in a morally wicked world if it stayed out of or minimized its political involvement in it. The domestic consequence of playing an extensive role internationally was to endanger the very democracy such a role was intended to protect.

Perhaps the most revealing symptom of America's reaction to Vietnam was the reassertion of the deep-seated attitude toward the exercise of power internationally as immoral and corrupting. Once power politics could no longer be moralized in the context of the democracy-dictatorship dichotomy, the sense of guilt awakened by its employment returned. Vietnam seemed to prove again that in the exercise of power the nation had forsaken its moral traditions and violated its own democratic and liberal professions. Not surprisingly, sensitive men deeply committed to humane values—and daily watching the exercise of power in the form of violence in history's first televised war—repented their former support of containment-through-power as if in giving that support they had been unknowing sinners. Thus the chairman of the Senate Foreign Relations Committee, Senator Fulbright, who had been a leading advocate of postwar foreign policy while it could be disguised as a moral conflict, now attacked America's global role as evidence of an "arrogance of power." He did not merely assert that the United States had overextended itself and that its commitments needed to be cut down to its capacities. Nor did he say that Vietnam had been an unwise commitment although the basic policy of containment had been a correct one. He stated something far more fundamental: that all Great Powers seem to have a need to demonstrate that they are bigger, better, and stronger than other nations and that it was this "arrogance of power," from which the United States now suffered, which was the real cause of international conflict and war.

In brief, it was the exercise of power *per se* that, regardless of a nation's intentions, made it arrogant. Power itself is a corrupting factor; even if justified in moral terms, its use is immoral except in clear unambiguous cases of self-defense. No title for a book could have been more characteristically American. Power is evil and its exercise is tantamount to the abuse of power; abstention from power politics, providing an example to the world of a truly just and democratic society, is a more moral policy. America should be loved for its principles and for practicing what it professes, rather than feared for its might. Democracy and "power politics" were simply incompatible.

But if Vietnam and the consequent mood had not led to a reappraisal of America's foreign policy role and objectives, the changes in the international system would have. Vietnam perhaps speeded up this process of reappraisal, but it was in fact already going on at the time of the military intervention. Two changes were particularly significant and were to have a profound impact upon American-Soviet relations: the erosion of NATO's once cohesive bonds and the disintegration of the alliance between the Soviet Union and China, as the former "Sino-Soviet bloc" or "Communist world," including Eastern Europe, became increasingly polycentric.

THE EROSION OF NATO

Having committed their wealth and manpower to the defense of Europe, Americans deemed the states of Europe, particularly the continental states, ungrateful, for during the 1960s they increasingly questioned America's authority to speak for the alliance. But the NATO partners had good reason for doing so. First, the European nations had recovered their economic health and sense of confidence; and their continuing economic integration still held out the possibility that someday Europe would emerge as another superpower. To be sure, this union might not turn out to be the federation envisaged by the functional advocates; for the establishment of a European supranational authority could not, as expected, be an automatic result of the spillover process. The spillover could work "automatically" only if all the member states agreed to form a federal union. During the 1960s, however, President Charles de Gaulle opposed a union in which the Six would lose their individual identities. He therefore sought a "Europe of Fatherlands" in which power would remain in Paris, Bonn, Rome, the Hague, Brussels, and Luxembourg; the Six were, however, to coordinate their political policies through regular meetings of the chief executives, foreign ministers, defense ministers, and other ministers. But whatever Europe's future as a confederation or federation—and a confederation could, as in the case of the American Confederation, be only a stepping stone toward federation—Europe was no longer the weak, divided, and demoralized continent of 1945.

When NATO was formed, Europe had been almost powerless. The imbalance of power within the alliance resulting from Europe's virtually exclusive reliance upon the United States for its defense had placed Washington in a primary and Europe in a subordinate status. Washington's voice had been the voice of the alliance. If France objected to West German rearmament, Paris could delay but not prevent it. If France and Britain acted to defend what they deemed their vital interests, as at Suez, and the United States disagreed and opposed them, they had to withdraw in humiliation. The final decisions were made in Washington in terms of what the United States defined as the West's vital interests. But once Europe had recovered, and even surpassed, its prewar economic vitality, it demanded recognition as America's partner plus a greater share in the determination of NATO's political policies and strategic decisions.

This desire for equality with Washington—and with London, as head of the British Commonwealth—had, of course, been one of the original motives behind the French proposals for European integration. Not surprisingly, therefore, once a more equitable distribution of power had been restored within NATO, the French insisted that the political relationship between the United States and its allies had to be changed, too; and they claimed to speak for continental Europe. The subsequent Franco-American differences may well be ascribed to de Gaulle; but Gaullism was paradoxically both the product of America's postwar policy of rebuilding Europe and proof of its success. Just as the once youthful American republic strengthened its unity by rejecting Europe, so the embryonic Europe of the Six consolidated its bonds by opposition to its "outside" ally, America; this opposition was consistent with the changing distribution of power within the Atlantic community. It would have been unnatural for the Six not to rebel against their subordinate, or "satellite," status in an alliance controlled by Washington with its junior partner in London.

Besides equality, however, the Europeans also sought a greater voice in alliance policy formulation because of fear. As the United States became more vulnerable, they had to ask themselves whether they could continue to rely in the indefinite future upon American protection against the Soviet Union. Without sufficiently large and credible national nuclear forces of their own, they would continue to be dependent upon American power for their national security. But, as Soviet power grew, what would happen if the Soviets ever made demands considered vital by the Europeans but not by Washington? Could the small British or French strategic force be relied upon to deter the Soviet behemoth?

The loosening Western alliance also reflected to some degree the different geographic position of the partners and to the diverse historical roles played by the United States and Europe in the postwar period. Both factors contributed to, and underlined, all of the other differences within the Atlantic Community. From 1945 onward, each of the major European countries, including Great Britain, had relinquished or been divested of its colonies until, by 1960—with but a few relatively minor exceptions—their extra-European role had come to an end. By contrast, during this same period the United States had become a global power. Hence, at a time when its allies were essentially looking inward, seeking a new role, modernizing themselves, and groping toward a larger political organization and identity, the United States found itself having to become concerned with those areas of the world previously under the controlling hand of Europe. Undoubtedly, the European powers resented their reduced role. Tensions were inevitable.

Perhaps more important, the nations of Europe were deeply concerned over any major diversion of American resources and attention away from Europe and to such less-developed areas as Korea and Vietnam. They were equally concerned over the possibility that the United States, in its new global role, might involve them in an all-out war resulting from a head-on confrontation (as had seemed possible in Cuba) or from the escalation of an ongoing limited conflict (such as the Vietnam war). Conversely, U.S. resentment over their lack of sympathy and support for its extra-European ventures merely deepened the already existing American disappointment over the failure of the Europeans to take on a far greater share of their own defense.

The resulting European "revolt" against American hegemony largely revolved around the issue of nuclear weapons, since these have played a triple role within NATO: as the symbol of Great-Power status, as a means of influencing Washington's policy (for contributing to American strategy, which has relied so heavily on nuclear weaponry), and as a means of defense. But it was in the nuclear field that the United States was not willing to surrender its primacy and the accompanying political dominance that the virtually exclusive possession of nuclear weapons gave it. Partly, Washington had become too used to wielding the determining voice in the alliance; partly, too, Washington feared the diffusion of nuclear weapons, which would increase the opportunities for accidents and miscalculations that might trigger nuclear war. For almost two decades the United States had possessed the power to determine an issue on which Europeans might have to die; but now that France, for example, could decide for which issues Americans might die, the United States balked.

What this meant was that the issue of more than "one finger on the trigger" tended to rupture the American-European partnership. The bonds of internal cohesion of the "entangling alliance," and therefore the external security the alliance provided for its members, were thus weakening under the pressure of this ominous question: How does an alliance preserve its unity in the nuclear age when each major crisis poses the risk that actions by one member may precipitate a nuclear holocaust for an issue that the other members may not consider worth so high a price? Washington, particularly during the Kennedy years, had therefore been insistent on maintaining its nuclear monopoly and political supremacy within the alliance.

One of the principal ways it sought to do so was by supporting Britain's bid to join the new Europe. British membership, it was hoped, would mean that one of the leaders of the resurgent Europe would be a close friend who would act as the spokesperson for the American point of view. This would result in a more harmonious American-European relationship. Britain had already achieved its national deterrent and, unlike France, whose atomic development was vigorously opposed by the United States, had received extensive U.S. help. Britain's reasons for developing a deterrent were exactly the same as those stated by France in its quest for nuclear arms—namely, to gain prestige, security, and particularly a voice in Washington. Indeed, it was the "special relationship" between nuclear Washington and nuclear London that had been the incentive for France to follow Britain's lead.

But continental Europe no longer recognized Britain's leadership. Even throughout the 1950s—before de Gaulle—it had been somewhat suspicious on the intentions of America's junior partner. Since the end of World War II, Britain had stayed out of all European integration schemes for two main reasons: first, because it considered its close ties with the Commonwealth and, more generally, its global interests to be incompatible with integration into Europe; and second, to preserve its special position as America's closest ally. The only European organizations Britain had joined were those that committed America to Europe.

Britain's position, however, continued to deteriorate. The Commonwealth, traditionally an outlet for British goods and in this respect Britain's own common market, was buying fewer and fewer British industrial and consumer goods, either manufacturing these themselves or receiving them more cheaply from the United States or Common Market countries. Also, by the early 1960s, after the searing experience in Suez in which London had been forced to desist from its course of action by American pressure, Britain had begun to realize the advantages of a European political union. Increasingly, in the scale of world powers, London's voice would be heard less and less in comparison to those of Washington, Moscow, Brussels (the new Europe's capital), and Peking; nations would pay principal attention to these centers of power, not to a comparatively feeble London. Britain therefore sought entry into Europe. But de Gaulle and Adenauer were suspicious of Britain's bid. What they feared was that if Britain maintained its special relationship with the United States, continental Europe would remain in its subordinate status in what they felt was an Anglo-American dominated alliance.

The crucial task for Britain was therefore to prove its loyalty to the Europe it had shunned at the founding of the European Coal and Steel Community (ECSC), European Defense Community (EDC), and European Economic Community (EEC). This is exactly what it failed to do. Entry into Europe meant accepting the Six's common external tariff, which would, in effect, have ended the preferential tariff relationship Britain enjoyed with the Common-wealth countries. Yet, month in and month out, Britain sought special arrange-ments, arousing the suspicion that all it wanted from the Six was the Common Market's economic benefits. Confronted by a choice between the Common-wealth and Europe, Britain hesitated, implying all too strongly a choice for the Commonwealth.

London's stand on the nuclear issue reinforced this anti-European impres-sion. Since it was economically weak, Britain's only real bargaining point with the Six was, in fact, its nuclear force. If Europe was in the long run to have an economic and political identity, it also needed a nuclear one. As a potential Great Power, this was fitting; for bargaining, this was essential; for defense, in case of American nonprotection, this was vital. For France, still developing its nuclear deterrent, Britain's help in this area, plus its bombers, would have been very important. By breaking its special nuclear relationship with Wash-ington and offering its nuclear knowledge and deterrent to the new Europe, Britain would have demonstrated that it was sincere in its application and that it wished to help build this greater Europe politically, economically, and mili-tarily.

But, in late 1962 at Nassau, Britain made its choice between Brussels and Washington in forty-eight hours and chose the latter. To maintain its "inde-pendent" national nuclear force, Britain became absolutely dependent upon the United States, which promised to supply Britain with the Polaris missile, for which Britain would build its own submarines and warheads. London's decision ended the negotiations and Britain's bid for entry into the Common Market. Just as it had chosen the Commonwealth as between the Common-wealth and Europe, it had now made its choice between the United States and

Europe. The logical conclusion of Britain's continuing "special relationship" was de Gaulle's veto of Britain's entry in January 1963.

Thus, by the middle 1960s, the members of NATO had arrived at a critical point in their relationship. On the one hand, it was quite clear that the United States retained its predominant position in the alliance. It possessed overwhelming nuclear superiority, and this was reinforced, starting in the 1960s, by American business which, with its immense amounts of capital and technical and marketing skills, wished to profit from the Common Market by establishing industries behind its tariff barrier. America, because of its world power and the huge sums of money spent on research and development, had a lead in computers, electronics, space, and rocketry. Although the subsequent American-owned industries in Europe were not to account for more than 5 percent of the total business activity in any one country, they were concentrated in a few highly technological sectors that not only shaped the contemporary economy—such as chemicals and oil—but also tended to reshape the environment of the future: U.S. companies at that time manufactured 75 percent of all computers in Europe, 33 percent of all cars, 35 percent of Britain's tires, 40 percent of France's farm machinery, 70 percent of its sewing machines, 75 percent of its electrical and statistical machines, and 90 percent of its synthetic rubber. There were, of course, many reasons for Europe's technological lag—for example, national markets and industries had been too small in the past; not enough money had been spent on research and development, even by private enterprise; managerial training and skills had been inadequate, as were the general and higher educational system. Moreover, beyond this technological gap was a psychological, political, economic, and social gap.

On the other hand, the Europeans were in revolt against America's political primacy. Even Britain, which reapplied for Common Market membership in 1967, only to be turned down again by de Gaulle, had become more "European." And although a majority of British public opinion remained opposed to going into Europe, Britain's government, led by Conservative Prime Minister Edward Heath, who had conducted the Common Market negotiations from 1961 to 1963, finally took the island-nation into the Europe whose divisions it had historically exploited in order to assure its own security. Together with Ireland and Denmark (Norway voted to stay out), Britain's 1973 entry substituted the Europe of Nine for the Europe of Six. Whether this enlarged Europe would once more give impetus to the movement for a political union remained to be seen; so did the answer to the question of whether this would lead to closer relations with the United States once more or to more intense political competition and major economic and financial rivalry. A confederation could not balance American power in NATO. Only a Europe with economic vitality and a government politically able to establish a European foreign policy and the military strength to support it could in the long run define and support its interests and once more play a major role in the world.

As the 1960s ended, Europe had, however, shown no sign that it even wished to play such a role again. Its growing economic and financial strength, like Japan's, had not yet been translated into political and military terms that looked much beyond Europe. Political unification, even cooperation on forming a joint European foreign policy, still seemed far off. French-British nuclear cooperation for the establishment of a possible European deterrent had not started; and the role of West Germany in such a venture—a Germany that if left out would feel discriminated against and resentful, but if involved might scare many of its partners away and arouse intense Soviet opposition—had scarcely been given any thought. The European countries remained preoccupied with their individual affairs.

THE SINO-SOVIET CONFLICT

The disputes between the Soviet Union and China, paralleling those among the Atlantic alliance, stemmed from the tendency of China, first, to assert its equality with the Soviet Union, and second, to take independent actions in foreign policy. Peking's first major opportunity for the former came during the East European crisis in late 1956. The Hungarian revolt had overthrown the Communist regime, and only intervention by the Red Army had kept Hungary within the Communist bloc; and Poland had also struck for a measure of independence from the Soviet Union under the leadership of a man whom Nikita Khrushchev had personally attempted to keep out of power. For a while, it looked as though the Soviet Union's power in Eastern Europe might collapse. At this point, the Chinese came to the Soviet Union's rescue. They did so by issuing a statement approving of Soviet suppression of the Hungarian "counterrevolution" and by sending Zhou Enlai (Chou En-lai) to Europe to reconcile Moscow and Warsaw. In Joseph Stalin's time, such Chinese intervention in Europe would have been inconceivable; now the Chinese were actually helping the Soviet Union stabilize its position in its own satellite sphere. They achieved this by stressing the unity of the Communist bloc under the leadership of the Soviet Union and at the same time supporting the aspirations of the East European states for greater control over their domestic affairs. This position was not as incompatible as it might seem. The Chinese argued that the Communist states must stand together against the capitalists, and since the Soviet Union was the strongest Communist nation, it was the obvious leader. But the Soviet Union's primacy did not mean that the other Communist states (including China) could not take "different roads to socialism."

The idea that this assertion of China's independence might lead to a break with the Soviet Union gained support as China began to take a different stand on international issues with increasing frequency. For instance, in late 1959 and 1960, the Chinese took actions in opposition to Soviet wishes. First, they crushed a revolt against their rule in Tibet; perhaps remembering Hungary, the Soviets did not criticize this Chinese act. But they openly criticized China's dispute with India. The quarrel with India, which involved minor military skirmishes, was over the precise location of the Sino-Indian frontier in the Himalayan mountains. This was a clear test of strength, and the Chinese were apparently determined to press their point of view in an attempt to inflict serious damage on the prestige of their main Asian rival for power. China's aggressiveness was a shock to Asia. This hurt the Communist cause in Asia and no one realized it more keenly than Khrushchev. He made no attempt to hide his annoyance. Few things could have mattered less to him than a few square miles this way or that on the Indian-Chinese frontier. Compared with the need to make a favorable impression on the less-developed countries, this matter was picayune; for the issue at stake was a triumph of Communism throughout the formerly colonial world and a shift away from the West in the global balance of power.

The Chinese did not really disagree. They merely believed that the Communist victory must be won in a different way. It was on this central issue of the proper strategy with which to win the global victory that the Soviet Union and China differed in increasing vehemence; and their "debate" focused on the two interrelated issues of war and peace, and policy toward the leaders—the so-called national bourgeoisie—of the less-developed countries. The Soviet position was that in a nuclear war the Soviet Union would not only destroy its enemies, but be destroyed itself; therefore, unnecessary risks were to be avoided and the two nuclear superpowers even had to cooperate on some arms-control agreement to avoid nuclear accidents and miscalculations. Consequently, the main line of the Soviet attack upon the West's position had shifted to Asia, the Middle East, Africa, and Latin America; great energy had been devoted to the encouragement of the revolutions raging throughout the less-developed areas.

The aim has been obvious: the establishment of friendly political relations with the nationalist regimes, whose emotional dispositions were generally anti-Western. The Soviet Union tended to encourage their nonalignment (often a pro-Soviet nonalignment in fact, as, for example, Gamal Abdel Nasser's Egypt) in the cold war. This was clearly a tactical device. If the Soviet Union opposed their wish to remain disassociated from the cold war the new nations might become alienated. An attitude of "if you're not with us, then you must be against us," an attitude Stalin and Secretary John Foster Dulles had both frequently expressed, might drive these states back into the capitalist camp. If their neutrality were supported, however, their separation from the West would be widened and world capitalism would be further weakened.

The Chinese Communists had a somewhat different point of view. They seemed more willing to risk war. It was often said that this attitude was probably shaped by China's gigantic population. It could afford to lose 400 to 500 million people, in which case it would still have a population of 200 million or more. No other country in the world could survive such mammoth losses. "On the debris of a dead imperialism," Peking had itself pronounced, "the victorious people would create very swiftly a civilization thousands of times higher than the capitalist system and a truly beautiful future for themselves." Nor did China yet possess a large industrial establishment, as did the Soviet Union, whose destruction its leaders would be unwilling to risk in a total war.

Simultaneously, the Chinese had grown increasingly skeptical of aiding nationalist governments. Though often anti-Western, these governments were also bourgeois and, thus by nature, anti-Communist. Economic aid and technical assistance therefore only built up nations whose true colors would sooner or later come to the fore. Consequently, the Chinese preferred to encourage local Communist parties to seize power. In any case, they held that the Soviet Union should channel its aid exclusively or primarily to Communist countries, especially to China.

These Sino-Soviet disagreements over tactics, however, exaggerated the differences between the two Communist powers. Peking might well talk of several hundred million Chinese surviving a nuclear attack, but it was also aware that such a war would endanger Communist control of the country. The Chinese might talk of constructing a superior postnuclear civilization, but they had also been anxious to avoid any major clash with the United States. In Korea, they warned the United States several times not to advance to their frontier and they finally intervened only for defensive reasons. In the Taiwan Straits, they had not even invaded the offshore islands when the United States openly supported the Nationalist troops on these islands. For all the Chinese leaders' militant talk, they had acted with great caution. And for all his talk of peaceful coexistence, it was Khrushchev who had threatened to attack London and Paris during Suez, who had precipitated the Berlin crisis, who had broken the test-ban moratorium, and who had sought to install missiles in Cuba.

The real difference between the Soviets and the Chinese had not been that one favored peace and the other desired war. Rather, the key issue that divided them had been how much pressure should be exerted against the United States, how far Washington could be pushed before it would react. This was the vital question. For the answer determined both the opportunities that could be exploited and the consequences that might have to be suffered. If not much pressure were applied because of the high risks, then the gains would be small, if any; this is why the Chinese charge the Soviets with betraying the cause through a cowardice that led them to "kowtow" to the United States. If a great deal of pressure were exerted, the "profit" might also be far higher, but so were the risks; this was why the Soviets accused the Chinese of a recklessness that could end in suicide by provoking the United States. Wisdom in these circumstances counseled caution.

The issue of strategy toward the West and the less-developed nations was, furthermore, closely related to the issue of leadership of the Communist bloc. The Soviets had long dominated the Communist world. As the capital of the first Communist-controlled nation, Moscow had since the early 1920s controlled the international Communist movement; and it had been Moscow that had formulated the movement's policies. After World War II, it established control over the states of Eastern Europe, which were unable at that time to pursue an independent policy. Only Yugoslavia had not been controlled by Moscow, and when it did oppose Stalin's efforts to control it, Tito was read out of Stalin's empire. Communist China's birth—another state controlled by the indigenous Party—had thus presented a real problem for the Soviets. Potentially far more powerful than Yugoslavia, China was determined to be the Soviet Union's equal, not its subordinate, in the Communist bloc.

Peking had therefore sought to share Moscow's authority to formulate bloc policies. But Khrushchev would have none of this. Moscow, like Washington, had too long defined the policies for its followers and thus become a poor alliance manager. Instead of sharing authority with Peking, Khrushchev acted as Stalin had—and ironically, he did so first on the issue of de-Stalinization! He had decided to de-Stalinize at home and within the bloc; China was expected to adopt the same policy. It was not that the Chinese had been particularly fond of Stalin, for they had not. Nor was it that the Chinese did not recognize the need for de-Stalinization, particularly some relaxation of the Soviet grip on the satellites and permission for each to travel its own "road to socialism"; they did recognize this need. What offended the Chinese, and therefore initiated the Sino-Soviet dispute, was that Khrushchev pronounced policy for the entire Communist bloc without even bothering to consult them.

This debate over authority, then, was a key issue of the Sino-Soviet conflict. If to this extent it was comparable to the Franco-American conflict, it has also proved to be totally different in one respect: Unlike the French and Americans, the Chinese and Soviets conducted their struggle in ideological terms. And because of this, the struggle held more ominous implications for the Communist bloc. Paradoxically, the very ideology that bound them together also tended to divide them. On the one hand, Moscow and Peking interpreted the world through the same ideological framework; Communism provided both of them with a *Weltanschauung*. Both held the same view of man, society, and history. They both saw world conflict in terms of class struggle and the final triumph of Communism, and they both defined capitalism as their common enemy.

On the other hand, precisely because of the intimate relationship between ideology and action—ideology providing the framework through which events in the world are analyzed and defining the general purposes of the movement—ideology became a divisive factor. Moscow had long been the Communist Rome, and the ruler in Moscow therefore became the Communist pope when he assumed power. If an ideology claimed to represent the truth, there could only be one correct interpretation of that truth. Thus there could be only one correct interpretation and application of the doctrine. No ideological-theological movement can tolerate two Romes and two popes. A schism—and a fight for the leadership of the movement—had therefore to develop, since one of the Romes and one of the popes must per se be heretical. Hence Moscow denounced Mao for having deserted Marxism-Leninism and, by fragmenting what had been a united Communist front against the United States, for having aided the devil's cause, imperialism. Denouncing the actions of the Soviet Communist Party as "Khrushchevism without Khrushchev" after his overthrow, the Chinese charged that it had been seized from within by "revisionists" who were in fact capitalists, cooperating with Washington in order to contain China! Peking called for the overthrow of the Soviet leaders.

Since Mao attributed the caution of the Soviets toward the United States as well as their hostility toward China to the *embourgeoisement* of the Soviet leadership, he launched his Cultural Revolution after 1965 in order to purify his nation and keep it loyal to the true Marxist-Leninist faith. All persons, no matter what their positions and functions, were to be rooted out if they were suspected of "taking the road back to capitalism." Purges—especially by mobs of youth called Red Guards—were conducted in the army, government, industry, agriculture, even the Party itself. The president of China and the general secretary of the Party were among those deposed as the conflict between Mao and his followers on the one hand and his opponents on the other raged on for several months. Central authority seemed to have broken down. In these circumstances, the army increasingly came to the fore, restoring national unity and central control.

The Sino-Soviet schism was, by the late 1960s, dramatically clear. The epithets hurled between Peking and Moscow reached a ferocity unknown since the early days of the American-Soviet cold war. Thus, the Soviets called Mao Hitler and compared the Chinese with the Mongol hordes who overran Russia a millennium ago; and the Chinese talked about the "Soviet revisionist clique" as a "dictatorship of the German fascist type," and quoted Karl Marx as saying already in the middle of the last century that Russia's aim had been, and always would be, world hegemony. For Mao and his followers, the struggle against the Soviet Union became increasingly primary. The infidel had to be eliminated first before resuming the conflict against the evils of imperialism; internal betrayal within the Communist movement had to be rooted out lest those who had strayed from the true faith corrupt and weaken the movement beyond repair for the ultimate struggle. Thus, avoiding conflict with the United States became important. During Vietnam, for example, China continuously counseled Hanoi that revolutions had to be self-sufficient and repeatedly stated that only an American attack on China itself would precipitate Peking's intervention. In brief, North Vietnam should not and could not count on active Chinese help to help defeat American forces in South Vietnam. Mao's policy was therefore militantly anti-American rhetorically, but restrained in its behavior.

Even after Mao's death a complete Sino-Soviet reconciliation was impossible for, quite apart from any ideological issue, these two powers remained divided by the same issues that divided NATO: differences of power and of geographic position; different evaluations of international problems; and the obvious conflict between a power with global interests and an ally whose capabilities were essentially regional. The Soviet Union and China also had a long history of conflict that antedated their becoming Communist states and still affected the intensity of their antagonism. Peking was bitter about Russian retention of lands seized by the tsars when China had been a weak state exploited by all the major Western powers, especially by Russia. But Moscow considered these lands Soviet, regardless of how they were acquired. The two large Communist states also had a number of clashes along their 4500-mile border, the longest in the world. Both had heavily reinforced their troop strengths; the Soviet Army, larger than the one in Eastern Europe, reportedly possessed large quantities of tactical nuclear weapons.

The Soviets even had to bargain with the East European "people's democracies" because, as a result of the Sino-Soviet conflict, these increasingly nationalistic states gained a degree of independence from Moscow in return for their support of Moscow against Peking. Indeed, it is doubtful that most can any longer be called satellites. Their conflict with the Soviet Union, moreover, has taken on a dynamic of its own. Romania is the most defiant of the people's democracies; in 1968, Czechoslovakia was also moving rapidly toward greater independence when Soviet fears that Prague's reforms would jeopardize the survival of Communism in a country bordering on West Germany (Romania, which does not share a frontier with the Federal Republic, is also, internally, a quite orthodox Communist regime) led to the Red Army's intervention. Yet, even while this intervention reminded the East European nations of the limits of Soviet tolerance, none of them was as completely subservient as during Stalin's reign. Indeed, they increasingly looked westward for economic-technological assistance. Concomitantly, they needed a relaxation of international tensions; a return of the cold war would reduce their links to the West and bring back greater Soviet control and intervention in their affairs. On the whole, therefore, they approved of the changing nature of American-Soviet relations "from confrontation to negotiation," which had been going on throughout the last half of the 1960s and which was to become dramatically visible with the advent of the Nixon administration.

A BACKWARD GLANCE

Twenty years after World War I, a new world war had already started. Twenty-four years after the war, in 1969, the two superpowers, while they remained in conflict, were keenly aware of their stake in preserving the peace. Even before the Nixon administration, the "hot line" between the White House and the Kremlin for use in case of crises and emergencies, the limited test ban, the agreement to outlaw nuclear weapons in space, the nuclear nonproliferation treaty, and the outlawing of biological weapons had been among the fruits of this awareness. But there was additional evidence, especially the changeover from "soft" to "hard" strategic weapons which had enhanced American and Soviet national security during the 1960s by stabilizing the bipolar strategic equation. The Soviet-American Strategic Arms Limitation Talks (SALT) of the 1970s were to be particularly significant and symbolic of the new "adversary partnership" emerging between the two nations.

These "arms-control" measures—safer weapons systems and strategies—were supplemented by other actions. The United States restrained Jiang Gaishek from attacking mainland China; it did not intervene on behalf of the Hungarian rebels in the Soviet Union's East European security belt; it compelled its two closest allies, Britain and France, to desist from their attack upon Egypt because it was in America's interest to keep Nasser from being overthrown, an act that might have compelled the Soviets to intervene and would have tainted the Western anticolonial stance, it negotiated with Moscow bilaterally on Berlin when its allies opposed such negotiations for fear of an agreement at their expense. In its turn, the Soviet Union tacitly cooperated with the United States in the United Nations in the establishment of a peace-keeping force to be stationed between Egyptian and Israeli forces in 1956, and did not intervene when Israel defeated the Arabs in 1967; similarly, despite harsh verbal attacks on the United States and on the U.N. secretary-general, the Soviet Union acquiesced in the dispatch of U.N. forces to the Congo a few years later; it did not support Chinese Communist attempts to capture Taiwan; it signed the limited test-ban treaty despite Chinese Communist opposition (just as the United States signed despite French objections); it supported India when China attacked it and constantly denounced Chinese militancy; and during Vietnam, it negotiated with the United States on such key items as the nuclear nonproliferation treaty.

In retrospect, then, could it not be said that this period, despite all the crises, was remarkably stable and "peaceful" in the sense that conflicts in the international system were resolved and adjusted without triggering a world war? And was it, in fact, not the simple and direct confrontation of the two great nuclear powers that accounted for these conditions? When one nation pushed, the other had to push back; and this occurred no matter how distant the arena from Moscow or Washington. The two superpowers, precisely because their attention was riveted on each other, were constantly on guard against any disturbances of the balance between them. The recurrent confrontations in the postwar period, as Kenneth Waltz had pointed out, were in this context an essentially healthy sign, since they meant that attempts at expansion were being met with counteraction. "Rather a large crisis now than a small war later is the axiom that should precede the statement, often made, that to fight small wars in the present may be the means of avoiding large wars later." Furthermore, the general caution and responsibility in handling crises was reinforced by each power's knowledge that if it miscalculated, it might be risking suicide; whereas in an earlier age, a nation in its power calculations could easily overestimate its own strength and underestimate that of its opponent, nuclear arms have compelled policymakers not to commit such errors, and this has had a restraining effect. A *Pax Atomici* it was, but it was precisely this *pax* that constituted the principal restraint upon the superpowers and transformed their relationship to one of a more "limited adversary" nature, which stressed not only their continued competition for influence in the world but their cooperation if that world were to survive and each of the powers' interests were to be relatively satisfied.

Chapter 9

FROM COLD WAR
TO *DÉTENTE*

FROM *IDEALPOLITIK* TO *REALPOLITIK*

Vietnam had left the nation disillusioned with anti-Communism as a rationale for American global involvement. The war having been justified in its name, the reaction was that the price was too high. Before Vietnam, the nation could be mobilized to stop Communist aggression; after Vietnam, the concern became avoiding engagement in further adventures overseas. Even more basically, anti-Communism had been weakened by the increasing pluralism of the formerly cohesive Sino-Soviet bloc.

In the bipolar world, it had been relatively easy to moralize about power politics precisely because the bipolarity had been one of power *and* values. Globalism, which had made sense as long as any Communist expansion meant an addition to Soviet strength, could thus be explained in terms very understandable to Americans, that is, democracy versus dictatorship. But it was one thing to "fight Communism" as long as there was only one Communism to fight; once Communism became a many-splintered thing, which Communism were they to "fight"? Were all Communist states, because they were Communist, enemies of the United States? Or did the United States now have to distinguish among them, determining which was hostile, which friendly, which neutral— in short, which posed a threat to American interests? More specifically, in these new circumstances, what changes in the distribution of power could America safely allow, and where, if anywhere, and against whom did it still have to draw "frontiers"? These questions were more difficult to answer than during the simple days of bipolarity because each situation would now confront policymakers with alternative policies, thereby arousing great debates and possibly intense controversy. Anti-Communism also would no longer be very useful as a means of eliciting popular support, since the United States might well be supporting one Communist state against another.

One crucial question this posed for the future conduct of American foreign policy, therefore, was whether, in the absence of anti-Communism, the United States would "dirty" its hands by playing straight and unadorned power politics. When *Realpolitik* was synonymous with *Idealpolitik,* it had been easy to be a leader and organize various coalitions whose basic task was to push back when pushed. The state system's requirement to keep the balance could, in other words, be performed by the United States government so long as it could disguise from its own people what it was doing and pretend it was engaged in a noble task. *But could a nation that historically has condemned power politics adapt its outlook and style to a world in which justifying foreign policy in terms of ideological crusades was outmoded; could it "play the game by no other name" in an increasingly multipolar world?* More specifically, how could the United States, disabused of anti-Communism and disenchanted with a world in which the forces of good could no longer crusade against the forces of evil, mobilize congressional and popular support for the continued conduct of its foreign policy? Or would America, no longer believing it had an ideological mission to perform, sway from occasional fits of moral passion and crusadism to moralistic isolationism—or, if that were no longer possible in the late twentieth century—to a major withdrawal from the world? Would the country, having enjoyed its drug of anti-Communism and the resulting "high" of global responsibility and exercise of world power, now swing to the "low" state of reaction and withdrawal?

The incoming Nixon administration in January 1969—which, after the president's resignation from office in 1974 because of the Watergate scandal would become the Nixon-Ford administration—thus confronted a novel postwar situation: how to conduct foreign policy without a consensus. The administration thought it could substitute a policy based on the traditional logic of the state system. This dramatic shift away from a style that stemmed from the nation's domestic values and experiences to a balance-of-power rationale was somewhat surprising because the president, as congressman, senator, and vice-president, had been an exponent of virulent anti-Communism, the "illusion of American omnipotence," and an inflexible moralism that tended to reject having anything to do with Communists lest one be tainted with an "un-American" virus. But as president, he and his national security assistant Henry Kissinger, a German-born Jewish immigrant and Harvard professor, who later became secretary of state after Richard Nixon's reelection, both rejected the traditional American justification for participating in foreign affairs. Indeed, the Nixon-Ford years might well be called the Kissinger era since it was he who primarily articulated and justified the Republican approach to foreign policy, personally carried out much of its behind-the-scenes as well as public diplomacy; and provided an element of continuity amid the transfer of power from a disgraced president to his unelected, or appointed, successor. Kissinger so dominated these eight years that one wag even said of him that he was the only national security assistant and secretary of state ever served by two presidents. His diplomatic exploits earned him widespread admiration and popularity; he was frequently pictured in cartoons as "Super-Kraut," a pudgy figure decked out with a cape as he flew through the sky from one set of negotiations to another. His successors in the Carter administration continued to feel his presence, if only because national security assistant Zbigniew Brzezinski, a former Harvard colleague of Kissinger and at the time of his appointment a Columbia University professor, as well as Secretary of State Cyrus Vance, were constantly being compared with Kissinger—usually unfavorably.

The philosophy underlying American foreign policy during the Kissinger Republican years from 1969 to 1977 began with the assumption that international politics was not a fight between the good side and the bad side. All states had the right to exist and possessed legitimate interests, a right as true for Communist as for non-Communist states. A nation, therefore, did not launch crusades against an adversary on the assumption that differences of interests represented a conflict of virtue and evil. The better part of wisdom was to learn to live with other states, defend one's interest if encroached upon, but also attempt to resolve differences and build on shared interests. Nor would such differences be easily or quickly resolvable, for when states held conflicting views of their interests these views were usually deeply held and not easily relinquished. Summit meetings were important as part of a negotiating process, but one summit did not all problems solve, and to raise false hopes that it would was to produce the cynicism and disillusionment that would endanger diplomacy itself. Good personal relations among leaders might smooth this process, but they were not a substitute for hard bargaining; accords basically reflect the ratio of power between the nations the leaders represent.

And what about dealing with a Communist dictatorship whose values and practices were abhorrent to us? The most the United States could expect was to influence its international behavior in a responsible direction; American power was too limited to transform another nation's domestic structure, and to make agreements dependent upon such a transformation would be counterproductive and raise tensions. American demands would be resisted, and this, in turn, would jeopardize accords on international issues that might otherwise have been resolvable. The United States was not omnipotent and had to abandon its habit of crusading to democratize adversaries. Negotiating with a Communist regime such as that of the Soviet Union was not a matter of morality requiring an internal purification preceding discussions; it was a matter of dealing with a powerful state with which the United States had to discuss issues if peace and security were to be preserved. The key, of course, was the balance of power, but within the parameters of that balance it was necessary to try and accommodate the legitimate needs of the principal disturber of that peace. Power neutralizes countervailing power, and satisfying the interests of other Great Powers would be more likely to produce acceptance of the present international system than continued frustration and hostility to an international system in which they had little vested interest. No state could be completely satisfied, but it could be relatively satisfied.

Kissinger's view, then, concentrated on the powerful actors. Although the rhetoric and style of American foreign policy were to be different and were to reflect more candidly and publicly the operational norms of the international system rather than domestic values and experience, there was to be an essential continuity in policy. The Soviet-American balance remained the preoccupation; it was still the Soviet Union, as a Great Power, whose influence needed to be contained and behavior moderated. This unity of rhetoric and action—the explanation of United States policy in terms of power, balances, spheres of influence, prestige, national interests, and the limits of American power, as well as the specific rejection of ideological justifications and crusades— represented the socialization of American foreign policy by the state system. The United States now explained its actions on the international scene in the same terms as all Great Powers before it—that is, in terms of the logic of the balance of power.

The Carter administration did not always share Kissinger's preoccupation with the balance of power and American-Soviet rivalry. Particularly in the beginning, its concern was to lower America's profile in the world, to ensure that there would be "no more Vietnams," which it attributed to the global containment policy. President Jimmy Carter questioned whether this policy had not been the product of an exaggerated fear of the Soviet Union and, therefore, had represented an overreaction; he asserted that his administration would not be driven by "an inordinate fear of communism." Indeed, even more fundamentally, the Carter approach to foreign policy questioned the entire postwar policy of his predecessors, both Democratic and Republican. Had Vietnam, in the final analysis, not just been the end product of containment but also of the whole "realist" approach? Was the critical problem not the immoral—or at best, amoral—"power politics" philosophy upon which operational, as distinct from declaratory, American foreign policy since World War II had been based?

Carter was, indeed, to be president of the only administration after 1945 that repudiated much of the traditional way of looking at international politics and to embrace a new vision of a more "interdependent" world, which emphasized not security issues but economic or welfare issues, not superpower competition but closing the gulf between the rich and poor nations, not on an international hierarchy based upon power and the use of force but a general egalitarianism among states and the disutility of force, not on conflict in which each nation acts primarily in terms of its national interest but on cooperation among nations seeking to advance the collective interests of mankind.*

Nevertheless, both Carter and his predecessors had to face a world in which certain changes had occurred. One was a domestic one within the United

*See Chapter 10 for an elaboration of interdependence.

States. The nation was weary of its foreign policy burdens and wary of accepting new commitments; it appeared reluctant even to carry out existing obligations. This mood, often portrayed in this post-Vietnam era as being neoisolationist and against national security, was reflected by the attacks on the "imperial presidency," by the later War Powers Resolution, and by restrictions on the Central Intelligence Agency (CIA) covert operations. The president was to be restrained by a more assertive and watchful Congress; his freedom to use his principal instruments of overt and covert intervention abroad were to be limited. In the pre-Vietnam era of containment, Congress had rarely questioned the president's authority to use the armed forces or CIA to carry out U.S. policy. But after Vietnam, the criticisms of America's "global policepower" role were widespread and emphasis was placed on the nation's "limited power," suggesting a more restricted role in what was popularly regarded as the post-cold war era. The Carter administration, coming to power shortly after the final collapse of Vietnam in 1975, by and large regarded the cold war as over. While Nixon and Gerald Ford were to be constrained by the public mood of pseudoisolationism, Carter himself represented that mood until the 1979 Soviet invasion of Afghanistan. In these circumstances, a relaxation of tension, or *détente,* became necessary. For Nixon and Ford, it was necessary until the nation could "recover its nerve" and once more play the leading role they felt was required to protect U.S. interests against Soviet expansion; for Carter, it was necessary because the United States was living in a more complex post-cold war era in which an activist anti-Soviet policy would needlessly rekindle the superpower conflict.

A longer-term reason for *détente* was that by 1970 the balance of power had changed. The Soviet Union had attained strategic parity. The balance between the two superpowers had long been between the U.S. Strategic Air Command, later supplemented by the navy's nuclear submarines, and the Red Army. The American bombers and missiles deterred the Soviet Union by threatening to destroy its cities; the urban population was hostage for the Kremlin's restraint. By contrast, the Soviet Union did not gain an intercontinental capability and capacity to destroy the United States until the massive build-up that began after 1964. From the 1950s to the middle 1960s, America's strategic power was balanced not so much by Moscow's bomber and missile force, which was small in comparison with that of the United States, but by the Red Army. It was Western European forces and American forces stationed in Europe that were hostage to Washington's restraint. The powerful Soviet army, it was believed, would overrun Western Europe; North Atlantic Treaty Organization (NATO) forces could be quickly defeated.

In brief, the American-Soviet balance had been an asymmetric one; the United States held strategic superiority and an intercontinental reach; the Soviet Union, conventional superiority and a regional reach. However, by 1970 the balance had become symmetrical; the Soviet Union's strategic power had caught up with that of the United States, and the Soviets could now hold

America's population—no longer just Western Europe's—hostage. Moreover, this Soviet build-up, which had begun after the Cuban missile crisis when Leonid Brezhnev took over from Nikita Khrushchev, showed no sign of slowing down, not even after the number of Soviet Intercontinental Ballistic Missiles (ICBMs) had surpassed the number of American land-based missiles.

Even during the period of U.S. strategic superiority, Moscow had been willing to risk limited challenges, but it had remained cautious during confrontations: If there was no resistance, it could increase the pressure; if there was resistance, it could retreat and call the challenge off. United States power had set limits to how far the Soviets felt they could push. But in a period in which the strategic balance was shifting and the Soviet leaders had at the very least achieved parity, a continuation of the containment policy by means of threats of force would become more risky and costly. The Soviet leaders had gained a new sense of confidence in their power. The danger was that they might be more willing to challenge the United States, even perhaps expecting the Americans to back down first in a Cuba-in-reverse situation. It became important, therefore, to reduce international tension and try to slow down the arms competition, if it could not be stopped.

Last and most important was the Soviet Union's emergence as a global power. Although its leaders' ambitions might be worldwide—the Soviet Union considered itself the nucleus of a new and more humane postcapitalist world, as well as a Great Power—the reach of Soviet power had been limited essentially to Eurasia. Attempts to extend its power beyond Eurasia had been largely unsuccessful; the Congo and Cuba in 1962, where the Soviet Union, confronted by America's strategic superiority and local conventional (naval) superiority, had to retreat, were painful reminders that the Soviet Union was not, like the United States, a power with a worldwide capacity. The Soviet Union of the 1970s had apparently concluded from Cuba that strategic power paid off politically because it could be used not only to deter but also to intimidate and compel the adversary to retreat. In addition, within the context of this growing strategic power, the Soviet Union had also engaged in a parallel, massive, conventional build-up, particularly of a modern surface navy and airlift capability. This meant that as its ability to neutralize America's nuclear power grew, its capacity to project its conventional power beyond Eurasia grew also. After all, the Soviet naval build-up, which by the late 1970s had produced a navy that exceeded the U.S. Navy in numbers of combat ships (although it did not yet have large U.S.-type aircraft carriers), was hardly a force needed for maritime defense. Soviet allies were contiguous, not overseas as were those of the U.S.; nor was the Soviet Union dependent upon imports of oil and other natural resources, as were all the Western allies. Would the Soviet Union, in these new circumstances, therefore, continue to seek to expand its influence only on land and in territorially nearby areas? Or would it, as a result of its new might, feel a confidence that had been absent before and act more boldly and take greater risks, reopening old issues and challenging the United States in new areas farther away from the Soviet Union? Would the United States, by contrast, now that it had lost its strategic superiority, be more cautious and hesitant to react?

Kissinger used to compare the Soviet Union's emergence as a world power to Germany's development at the turn of the century. In both cases, the challengers were land powers. The symbols of their aspiration and determination to find their "place in the sun" were the navies they built; nothing could have been more symbolic to Great Britain and the United States, the two greatest naval powers in their respective times. Germany's emergence and desire to be a world power resulted in World War I. How could the Soviet Union's newly gained power and its determination to pursue a *Weltpolitik* or global policy and achieve its "place in the sun," as the Germans had called it, be managed peacefully while simultaneously safeguarding American security interests? Should these be jeopardized, the United States might feel compelled to react strongly and risk war. Thus the question of the Soviet Union's massive military build-up raised questions not just about the military balance and its stability but, more fundamentally, about its ultimate intentions and whether the emergence of a peaceful "structure of peace," to use Nixon's phrase, was possible.

Détente *was thus initially adopted as a strategy for managing the superpowers' adversary relationship that would seek to secure American interests at a lower level of tension and lesser cost than those required by the policy of cold war confrontation and frequent crises.* The American-Soviet balance would still be bipolar, but it would be somewhat more complex and fluid than in the earlier, cold war era. And it was here that the stylistic difference was to become more apparent. Nixon's predecessors, while also pursuing a balance-of-power policy, felt compelled to justify their policy in terms of the past crusading style; they were frequently trapped by their own anti-Communist rhetoric and felt forced to be more inflexible and interventionist than they would have been had they not had to pose as the guardians of the true faith against the barbarians from without. For twenty years they had been unable to abandon the fiction that Taiwan was China and to establish a formal diplomatic relationship with the real China on the mainland. The Nixon-Kissinger balance was to include Communist China. As Moscow's bitter rival, Peking could be used to provide the Soviets with an incentive to act with restraint and a greater willingness to compromise if it wished to avoid closer Sino-American relations and cooperation against the Soviet Union. The Nixon tripolarity was thus a tactic devised in order to make the superpower bipolarity work more smoothly and securely.

This balance was, furthermore, to be supplemented by a network of agreements and a set of rules of mutual restraint beneficial to both powers. Cold war bipolarity had been based on the fundamental assumption that what benefited one side would hurt the other and had, therefore, to be prevented by counteraction; this kind of bipolar competition was now to be supplemented by agreements and rules profiting both, thereby presumably enhancing each country's stake in cooperation with the other. The key Kissinger word was "linkage." If a series of agreements and understandings on such matters as arms control and trade could be arrived at, the more expansionist-minded Soviet Union, because of the benefits of these agreements and understandings, would gain a vested interest in good relations with the United States. While the Soviet Union was to be faced, as before, with a continued balance and a strong American military that would provide an inducement for restraint in foreign policy, this "stick" was to be supplemented with enough "carrots" to make that restraint more appealing. Indeed, since employing military sanctions to contain the Soviet Union at a time of strategic parity was becoming riskier, the offer of economic rewards for Soviet restraint or self-containment was particularly appealing.

There was another meaning to "linkage" as well. It referred to the fact that the various issues would be linked together diplomatically. Progress on one front would be tied to progress on another; the Kremlin could not expect to make gains on one issue that interested it but refuse to meet American interests on other issues. If it did so, there would presumably be a penalty exacted in the form of nonprogress on issues of interest to the Soviet Union or the withholding of benefits Moscow was seeking. During the Nixon-Ford periods this linkage was often explicitly declared to exist (although it was not necessarily followed in practice); it was officially denied by the Carter administration (although it was on occasion pointed out that certain Soviet actions could not but affect American public opinion or Congressional support for administration policies). Cooperation and mutual concessions were obviously preferable. The adversary part of the relationship was to be balanced by the partnership element in a new adversary-partnership. The overall purposes were to lower tensions between the superpowers, to confront fewer crises, and to encourage diplomatic negotiations; the new policy did not mean an end of American-Soviet conflict and competition. A *détente* was not an *entente cordiale*.

For Kissinger (as for Brzezinski later, if not always for Carter and Vance), then, *détente* was not only a strategy selected to secure American interests at a lower level of tensions and costs. It was a continuation of containment at a time when the United States had lost its strategic superiority, and the extensive role of this country in world affairs was widely questioned at home. It was to achieve its purpose by exploiting the Sino-Soviet split and relying heavily on American technology and food as nonmilitary "weapons." It should be noted that this political-diplomatic strategy was not utopian; it did not assume that the Soviet Union had become a benign power or that the cold war was over. On the contrary: The Soviet Union was a stronger power than ever before, and it might be tempted to use its power to exploit available opportunities to expand its influence. In brief, *détente* was intended to be a realistic strategy for a time when, because of pseudoisolationism at home, the United States was no longer in a position to compete as vigorously with the Soviet Union as in pre-Vietnam days.

DISENGAGEMENT FROM VIETNAM

Before the relationships among America, the Soviet Union, and China could be reshaped, the United States had to unburden itself of the Vietnamese War. For Vietnam was an albatross around the new administration's neck. But Nixon's and Kissinger's perceptions of Great Power relationships heavily influenced their thinking about acceptable terms for the U.S. withdrawal from the conflict. An option that Nixon had on becoming president, one that would have brought him much public acclaim, was to pull out all American forces immediately on the grounds that the United States had more than magnanimously fulfilled any obligations it had had to Saigon, that after many American deaths and immense amounts of American money, Saigon should stand on its own feet. But in the president's view the central issue was, as he repeatedly pointed out, not getting out of Vietnam—that was a foregone conclusion—but *how* the country would get out. If the United States withdrew quickly, the events it had fought to prevent might well occur; if South Vietnam collapsed and Hanoi unified Vietnam under its control (and presumably Laos and Cambodia as well), the credibility of American commitments and power would be weakened, perhaps gravely so.

Thus the new administration was from the beginning determined not to accept any settlement that was tantamount to a defeat, namely, a coalition government in Saigon controlled by the Communists. For it was Nixon's view that establishing *détentes* with the Soviet Union and China would not be feasible if America's prestige—reputation for power—was badly impaired. It was the president's aim to modify U.S. relations with the two large Communist states, especially the Soviet Union, the more powerful of the two. Why should the Soviet Union, rapidly building up its strategic power, settle for parity and mutually acceptable peaceful coexistence if it sensed that America was weak and could be pushed around? Why should China tone down its revolutionary rhetoric and conduct a more traditional state-to-state diplomacy, and indeed reorient its policy closer to the United States, if it could not count on American strength and determination to resist what it saw as Soviet attempts at hegemony in Asia? In short, the country had to "hang tough" in Vietnam in order to normalize relations with the Soviet Union and China.

Was this policy not contradictory, deciding on the one hand to improve relations with the giant Communist states while on the other hand fighting hard against a Communist pigmy that unlike the Soviet Union and China potentially, could never constitute a threat to the United States? Nixon's answer, like John Kennedy's in 1962, was no. For Kennedy too had won the presidency determined to achieve what is now called *détente* with the Soviet Union. But it gradually had become clear to Kennedy that Khrushchev misread Kennedy's restraint in foreign policy as weakness and lack of resolve to defend American interests. The Cuban missile crisis of October had been only the latest and most agonizing of Khrushchev's challenges to Kennedy; to fail to meet this test and not disabuse the Soviet leader of his misperceptions of the president would therefore be extremely dangerous. Only if Khrushchev gained a healthy respect for Kennedy's will would there be an opportunity to negotiate fairly, compromise on outstanding issues, and relax international tensions.

President Nixon and Henry Kissinger, therefore, devised a twofold strategy. First, American ground troops were to be gradually withdrawn to cut the costs of the war and make further hostilities tolerable for the "silent majority," which Nixon felt was loyal, even though fatigued, and would support him in a search for an "honorable" ending of the war. Thus, in terms of domestic strategy, he would contain his critics. In terms of his Vietnam strategy, the continued involvement of United States forces, especially in the air, he hoped, would provide an incentive for Hanoi to negotiate an end to the war. This incentive would presumably be all the stronger if the president's strategy worked at home, for he would then remove Vietnam as a principal issue in the next election and be reelected. Thus Hanoi, confronted with the prospect of a lengthy war that might last longer than four more years, would have every reason to settle the war diplomatically.

The second part of the president's policy was the "Vietnamization" of the war. South Vietnam's forces were to be trained better and supplied with modern arms so that they could bit by bit take over the ground fighting. Assuming that the South Vietnamese army could hold its own by 1972, although supported by American air and naval power plus economic and arms aid, Hanoi's ability to win on the battlefield would dim and the cost of the war increase. The offer of a negotiated settlement would therefore double its attractiveness.

But could Nixon win the time internally and persuade Hanoi externally? Criticisms and pressures remained strong in the United States. During Lyndon Johnson's tenure, the critics had focused their demands on cessation of the air war against the North to clear the way for what were anticipated to be fruitful negotiations to conclude hostilities; during Nixon's days, the critics concentrated their arguments on the abandonment of the Thieu regime in Saigon, since Hanoi had made it clear that it was not willing to cease fighting unless Thieu was replaced. No coalition government with him was acceptable; indeed, no coalition government, even without Nguyen Van Thieu, in which the Communists did not control the key positions, appeared acceptable. Hanoi remained as adamant as ever in the belief that it was the rightful successor to French power in Vietnam, indeed in Indochina. Thus in Congress, on campuses, and elsewhere, the calls for faster troop withdrawals and forsaking Saigon multiplied. But the president, by appealing to his silent majority, seemed to be quite successful in using Vietnamization to pull the sting out of the peace movement.

The danger inherent in the president's strategy was, however, that as American troops were withdrawn but before the South Vietnamese were ready to meet the enemy in battle, the North Vietnamese would attack. So, for example, in March 1970, Cambodia's Prince Sihanouk, who had tolerated the Communist troops and supply lines in his country, was overthrown by a military regime that wanted Communist troops out of it. The president, aware of North Vietnamese activity in Cambodia and now dealing with a regime that was friendly toward an American presence, decided to expand the war. On April 30, 1970, American and South Vietnamese troops were given a six- to eight-week period and ordered to clean out the North Vietnamese sanctuaries in Cambodia-South Vietnam border areas.

The critics were quick to pounce. The president had not consulted—or even informed—Congress before announcing his move into Cambodia. If the move was indeed short-term, the North Vietnamese could be expected to move right back into the sanctuaries after the troops had pulled out. Dissension spread: within the president's cabinet (the secretaries of state and defense reportedly had been among those opposed); within the State Department; in the Senate; and on campuses, where demonstrations and riots erupted. In one such demonstration, four students were shot to death by the Ohio National Guard. The Cambodian invasion and the shootings at Kent State led to strikes on many campuses, with the complete shutdown of a number of colleges and universities. Protesters once again turned out for a peaceful mass demonstration in Washington. The reaction to Cambodia made it clear that it would be foolhardy for the president to repeat such an action.

Saigon's army was unfortunately the key to the success of the president's strategy. In the spring of 1972 came its first real test when North Vietnam launched an unexpected attack across the DMZ (the demilitarized zone between North and South Vietnam). It was a broadscale conventional assault by almost all of North Vietnam's divisions supported by heavy weapons, including artillery and tanks. American commanders, experts in orthodox warfare, would have welcomed precisely such an enemy onslaught in the days of half a million American troops; but, with some exceptions, the South Vietnamese army performed poorly and, among other results, lost the northern provinces. Only American air support staved off even worse losses.

President Nixon was thus in a quandary on the eve of his visit to Moscow. The Soviets had supplied Hanoi with its modern arms and, whether or not it had been informed of the date of the North Vietnamese offensive, it should—according to Nixon—have restrained its Asian ally if it wished the summit conference to proceed. As a Great Power itself, it must have known that a major South Vietnamese defeat would be humiliating to its adversary on the eve of vital negotiations from which Moscow had as much to gain as Washington. The president was unwilling to negotiate under this shadow of defeat.

"Vietnamization" being in danger, he "re-Americanized" the war by once more initiating extensive bombing of the North and blockading North Vietnam's ports with mines. The point was to stop the supplies from coming in; since the war was now a conventional one, dependent on oil and heavy weapons and large amounts of ammunition, air power might be more effective than during guerrilla operations in halting them. Simultaneously, Nixon also offered

Hanoi just about all it could reasonably expect to be given: "the complete withdrawal of all American forces from Vietnam within four months"—that is, the end of blockade, bombing, and all other American military activities in all of Indochina—if all prisoners of war were returned and an internationally supervised cease-fire were arranged. The Communists could, in other words, keep their forces in the South, a significant concession previously offered only in secret talks. Equally important, the president did not insist on the survival of the Thieu government. Not only did he not mention Thieu, but he specifically said that the United States' withdrawal "would allow negotiations and a political settlement between the Vietnamese themselves." This new set of proposals was, at the very least, a concrete and serious basis for negotiations. But Hanoi rejected the offer. It appeared to want the president to do the one thing he refused to do—guarantee Communist control in Saigon. His proposal, in fact, had seemed to suggest that the North Vietnamese do this job for themselves, if they could do it.

The North Vietnamese thus confronted a dilemma. Despite the heavy bombing and blockade, the Soviet Union had gone ahead with its summit meeting with Nixon. Clearly, Soviet interests were far more important to Moscow than North Vietnam's interests. Communist China too was no longer the fervent advocate of continued revolutionary warfare and opponent of a negotiated cessation to the war that it had been earlier. Moscow and Peking both gave priority to their relationships with Washington. Thus Hanoi was isolated and could no longer count on Soviet and Chinese support for continuing the war. Yet the North Vietnamese leaders had hung onto their goal of unifying Vietnam for so long, paid such a very high price for it, and been so often cheated out of the fulfillment of their dream by their adversaries that they were naturally suspicious of Nixon's offer and resentful of Soviet and Chinese pressures to settle the war. But suddenly in the middle of October, less than a month before the American presidential election, Hanoi signaled its apparent willingness to accept something less than a total victory and by late October negotiated a tentative Indochina settlement. The terms included an internationally supervised cease-fire that would halt all American bombing and mining and bring about withdrawal of all United States forces within two months (two months less than the president's earlier proposal); separate future cease-fires were expected in Laos and Cambodia. Prisoners of war would be exchanged. A series of mixed political commissions, composed of elements from the Vietcong, the Saigon government, and neutralists, would then be established to work out a new South Vietnamese political order leading to a new constitution and the election of a new government.

The Nixon administration felt it had achieved an "honorable peace." The North Vietnamese, after having for years declared that the Thieu government would have to be dismantled as a precondition for a cease-fire, now accepted him as the leader of the government faction; and Thieu remained in control of a sizable army and large police forces with which he administered most of the country and all the urban centers, leaving only minor areas and a small percentage of the population under the control of the Vietcong and the approximately 145,000 North Vietnamese troops. Thus the Thieu faction seemed to have a good chance to compete politically and militarily with the Communists after the fighting ended.

But Thieu stalled against the tentative October 1972 settlement to pressure the United States to demand the withdrawal of the Northern army and recognize Saigon's authority over all of South Vietnam, including areas that Communist forces held. Nixon, however, felt that Hanoi's willingness to allow Thieu to administer the territory he now controlled was a crucial concession; and militarily, he felt that even further prolonged fighting could not compel these forces to withdraw from South Vietnam. Thieu could procrastinate, but he held no veto.

One of the fascinating questions about the negotiations between Hanoi and Washington is why the former was willing to change its mind about Thieu after years of insistence that it would not do any business with him. One suspects that the North Vietnamese did not retreat from their earlier demand and agree to a settlement of the war in order to reelect President Nixon; more likely, they too were familiar with American public opinion polls predicting a landslide victory for the president over his Democratic rival, Senator George McGovern, and they feared that with four more years guaranteed Nixon would raise his demands. Therefore, it would be more profitable to reach a settlement, or at least the outlines of a settlement, before the election. Hanoi thus leaked the terms negotiated during October, thereby seeking to place the responsibility for the continuation of the war on Washington and Saigon; more significantly, it also elicited a public acceptance by the Nixon administration of the basic outlines of a settlement. By the end of the second round of negotiations before Christmas, Kissinger stated that 99 percent of the settlement had been agreed upon; but on that 1 percent the negotiations broke down. Anxious to end the war, or at least American disengagement from the war, Nixon resorted to B-52 bombing of Hanoi—partly to demonstrate to the South Vietnamese government that the United States continued to support it and would maintain a hard line with Hanoi, partly to show the North Vietnamese the kind of heavy punishment they could expect if they did not sign a cease-fire and end the war. In late January 1973, this American disengagement became possible as the war was formally concluded, although this was only a prelude to a continuing political and military struggle among the Vietnamese themselves for control of South Vietnam. But for the administration the disengagement allowed it to concentrate more of its attention on its two large Communist adversaries.

DÉTENTE WITH CHINA

When the Nixon administration came into office in January 1969, Communist China was still outside of the bilateral relationship. The Chinese Communists were opposed to resuming relations with the United States while the latter defended the Nationalist regime, rival to legitimate power over China, on Taiwan, Chinese territory. But the new president recognized the changing circumstances and considered it vital to bring mainland China into the diplomatic constellation. Calling the regime by its chosen name, the People's Republic of China, ending regular patrolling of the Taiwan Straits by the Seventh Fleet, lifting trade and visitation restrictions against China, Nixon opened the way for a visit to China. This visit served in part to symbolize to the American public and Congress, long hostile to dealing with Peking, the dramatic shift of American policy and in part to begin clearing away mutual misperceptions and defining the real nature of some of the more outstanding issues and problems impeding improved Sino-American relations.

Thus, to talk of *détente* and to refer to it as if it encompassed only American-Soviet relations is a mistake. There were two *détentes*, one with China and one with the Soviet Union. Indeed, it may be argued that the *détente* with China was the greater one because of the high degree of hostility that had existed between the two countries since 1950; at least with the Soviet Union, the earlier period of high tension, confrontation, and recurring crises, particularly since the Cuban missile crisis, had been supplemented by an increasing degree of cooperation in the area of arms control. In any event, it is probably correct to argue that *détente* with China was a prerequisite to *détente* with the Soviet Union. At the very least, it would, it was hoped, increase the Soviet Union's incentive for *détente* with America; the purpose was to increase pressure upon Moscow to be more conciliatory on such prominent and substantial issues as arms control of offensive and defensive strategic missiles, *détente* in Central Europe, especially Berlin, and other key issues such as the continuing Arab-Israel hostilities to which the Kremlin had contributed by sending Soviet fighters and pilots, Soviet ground-to-air missiles with crews, and vast military supplies for the Egyptian military training mission.

For the United States, then, the Sino-Soviet split provided an opportunity to pressure the Soviet Union if the latter proved to be diplomatically inflexible and demanding; the clearly implied message to the Soviet leadership was that Soviet obstinacy would compel Washington to align itself more closely with Peking. To the Soviets, already fearful of China, such an alignment and the encouragement it would provide China to be more hostile, as well as renewed tension on the Soviet Union's other front in Europe, had to be a nightmare. Similarly, Peking had for years complained loudly about alleged American-Soviet collusion to isolate and contain China. But as the Soviet Union began to move huge numbers of troops eastward to defend its frontier with China, and on occasion let a rumor slip about the possibility of an attack on China, Peking—apparently convinced that Nixon was pulling out of Vietnam—was interested in detaching Washington from any possible cooperation with Moscow against China. Even more important, better relations with the United States would presumably restrain the Soviet Union from attacking China, for the Kremlin could not be sure that Washington in such a contingency would not support Peking.

In the Shanghai communiqué released at the end of Nixon's historic visit, the United States and China declared their opposition to the hegemony of any power in Asia; it was clear that the power they meant was the Soviet Union. Thus Sino-American relations began despite Taiwan. The Communist position had long been that Peking would not establish any relationship with Washington before the latter ended its official ties with the Nationalist Chinese on Taiwan which, Peking reasserted, was a province of China. Its ties with the rival claimant to power over all of China was, Peking claimed, a domestic matter. The U.S. reaffirmation of its commitment to the defense of Taiwan, therefore, constituted an interference with Communist China's sovereignty. That the People's Republic signed the Shanghai communiqué thus constituted evidence of its fear of the Soviet Union; so was Nixon's signature on a statement in which the United States declared that it would gradually remove all its forces and installations from the island and not interfere in a "peaceful settlement" between the Communists and Nationalists of their differences, including the future of Taiwan, which the administration acknowledged to be a "part of China."

President Nixon's trip to Peking in 1972 symbolized a dramatic change in Sino-American relations and, once and for all, ended the irrationality of a situation in which the United States for almost a quarter-century seemed to ignore the existence of the world's most populated country, a nation with great potential power, a significant stake in Asia's future, and an ideological rival of the Soviet Union. And just as Washington, during the 1950s, had feared the Sino-Soviet coalition, and Peking, during the 1960s, had frequently pointed to an alleged Soviet-American collusion in an attempt to isolate China, so Moscow now became apprehensive of closer Sino-American relations since, among other things, it gave the United States a persuasive lever—if skillfully used—in its negotiations with the Kremlin. The American shift of policy from Taiwan to Peking was long overdue. Domestic politics had too long blocked a rational adjustment and exploitation of the Sino-Soviet conflict, a conflict whose tensions may rise or fall from time to time, but one that is likely to continue despite changes of leaders in both countries, for their quarrels reflect differences of interest more profound than merely differences of personalities, as the death of Mao Zedong in 1976 has amply demonstrated.

Indeed, even as the succession struggle in China continued and President Ford was replaced by President Carter in the United States, progress toward full normalization proceeded. On January 1, 1979, the People's Republic of China and the United States exchanged diplomatic recognition and ambassadors with one another. This was followed almost immediately by an official visit to Washington by China's apparent strong man, Deputy-Premier Deng Xiaoping (Teng Hsiao-ping). The timing of this last step toward normalization had come from Peking which, on the one hand, confronted large modern Soviet forces along its long 4500-mile northern frontier with increasingly obsolete weapons and, on the other hand, had chosen to modernize China and look to the West for economic and technological assistance in everything from building hotel chains and steel mills to exploring China's enormous estimated oil reserves. For the United States, the final shift from Taiwan to Peking meant ending diplomatic recognition of Nationalist China and the mutual security pact, as well as the final withdrawal of the remaining American military personnel. In return, Peking appeared to have accepted the American position that this problem be resolved peacefully, but it continued to express its anger at the United States for continuing to supply the Nationalists with weapons to defend themselves against a possible Communist invasion.

The likelihood of invasion was not great anyway. For one thing, Peking lacked the air and naval capacity to cross 100 miles of water to launch such an invasion. More important, however, Peking, having turned primarily to the United States and Japan to help it modernize, would hardly risk taking an action that would alienate both of these countries—the United States, which it also needed to balance Soviet power, and Japan, which if frightened by such a show of force, might well react with a large-scale rearmament program, including nuclear weapons. That an invasion of Taiwan would be politically counterproductive was further underlined by the fact that Tokyo (which had recognized Peking earlier than Washington) maintained very close and profitable commercial relations with Taiwan; and the United States expected to do the same. In the final analysis, of course, there was nothing to prevent the United States, after it had long insisted on a peaceful resolution of Communist-Nationalist differences, from resorting to force and defending Taiwan should Peking some day change its mind and violate the understanding about the peaceful resolution of this problem.

Thus, having declared in early 1950 that it would no longer intervene in China's civil war, only to do so when the Korean War broke out, the United States had almost thirty years later reverted to its earlier position and taken the final step it had not taken in early 1950; official recognition of the new regime ruling China's mainland. While the United States did not initially sell arms to Peking in order not to provoke Moscow, it was willing to let its European allies sell China the arms China wanted, such as jet fighters and antiaircraft and antitank missiles. The United States limited its own sales to dual-purpose equipment such as radar, trucks, and transport planes, which could be put either to civilian or military use. But the Reagan administration, in its effort to forge stronger links with China against the Soviet Union, did offer to sell Peking arms. The significance of this move was less military, since China had limited funds to buy arms on a large scale, than political. For it signaled the Soviets that the Chinese-American alliance they feared was a little closer to being realized. The United States and China were already cooperating in jointly operating an electronic intelligence-gathering station in China to monitor Soviet missile tests.

The new China connection was not, however, without risk. Clearly, the hostility between the two largest Communist states was preferable to a united Sino-Soviet bloc. A strong China, dividing the Soviet Union's attention between East and West, could not but benefit NATO. Washington therefore had a vested interest in supporting the new post-Mao Chinese leadership, which opposed Moscow and looked toward the West and Japan. Fundamentally, the United States was taking advantage of its adversaries' dilemma and resorting to the time-honored tactic of "divide and rule." Indeed, historically, the United States has always had to choose between China and Japan. When it was friendly to China before World War II, Japan became the adversary; and when during the cold war Nationalist China collapsed, the United States became an ally of Japan and enemy of the new China. Now the possibility of closer Washington-Peking-Tokyo cooperation appeared increasingly possible. The danger was that the United States would align itself too closely with China. Such alignment would be regarded as unfriendly and provocative by Moscow; that, of course, would be also true for Peking, if, in seeking to improve its relationship of *détente* with the Soviet Union, Washington pulled too close to the Kremlin.

One dramatic example of this dilemma occurred shortly after the United States had officially recognized the People's Republic of China and its deputy prime minister had toured America vehemently denouncing Moscow. Peking, concerned with what it saw as increasing Soviet-Vietnamese collaboration to the south—which it interpreted to be part of a growing Soviet influence and attempt to encircle China—struck at Vietnam. Angered by Vietnam's expulsion of almost 200,000 ethnic Chinese, border conflicts between the two countries, and especially by Hanoi's signing of a friendship treaty with the Soviets in late 1977, followed by its invasion of China's friend, Cambodia, China decided to punish Vietnam and "teach it a lesson" by invading the border areas and inflicting heavy casualties on them. The resulting border war demonstrated once again that a common ideology was not enough to prevent conflict between those sharing the same faith and that nationalism was as divisive a force within the Communist sphere as in the rest of the world. The danger for the United States was the possibility of a Soviet military reaction. An attempt "to teach China a lesson," if it was more than a limited incursion into China, could affect American interests and would draw the United States more deeply into the Sino-Soviet quarrel. Moscow already considered Washington's normalization of its relationship with Peking as collusion and tacit support of China's military action, even though Carter explicitly opposed this invasion of Vietnam, as he had opposed Hanoi's earlier invasion of Cambodia. Thus, the possible advantages of "playing the China card" against Moscow were matched by the dangers of China's "playing its American card"; and the possibility of Moscow's someday "playing its China card" against America could not be completely excluded. Yet on the whole, the United States and the People's Republic of China were driven together by their respective security interests and shared fear of rapidly growing Soviet power. Geopolitics prevailed over ideology.

One other factor needs to be noted: Japan's nervousness as the United States moved closer to the mainland regime. America had long believed itself to have had a relationship of friendship and support with China but had not generally had good relations with Japan before the cold war. A principal reason was Japan's long-standing ambition to dominate China. During World War I, President Wilson had opposed attempts by Japan, then an ally, to realize this ambition; Japan's determination to realize it, which had started with her conquest of Manchuria in 1927 and her attack on the rest of China in 1931, resulted in growing American opposition to Japanese domination of Asia in general and finally to the bombing of Pearl Harbor. The United States, regarding itself as China's protector (more in words than in deeds before World War II), shifted its position as an ally from China to Japan only after Japan's defeat and the Chinese Communist victory over the Nationalists.

But Japan, formerly a tough foe, was not anxious to play a major political and military role in Asia anymore, even though she was virtually completely dependent on imported oil, much of it from the Persian Gulf. After Hiroshima and Nagasaki Japan, naturally enough, suffered from a "nuclear allergy"; but she was also averse to any conventional armament beyond a minimal self-defense force. Over the years a prosperous Japan had been spending less than 1 percent of its sizable and growing gross national product (GNP) on defense. Japan appeared to be the first nation in history to attempt to be a Great Power without military strength or a defined political role; essentially, Japan limited herself to commerce. Indeed, it would be fair to say that Japan was less a nation than a corporation; perhaps a more appropriate name for Japan would be Sony Incorporated. By and large, Japan made only minimal efforts to respond to American urgings to raise defense spending and play a larger Asian role. She was content to rely on the American deterrent for her protection against the Soviet Union. Thus, although Japan was now a democratic country and had the world's third largest GNP—right behind the United States and the Soviet Union—her reluctance to play a role commensurate with her economic capability (unlike West Germany) was an additional factor accounting for America's shift *back* to China. In the long run, China, an antidemocratic nation with a population by the 1980s of over a billion, just beginning its drive to industrialize, might not be a reliable and stable partner; Japan might be, especially as the Japanese in the middle 1980s began increasingly to perceive a growing Soviet military threat in the waters around them. For the time being, however, the Japanese, who had signed a peace treaty with China and apologized to her for their past invasion soon after President Nixon's 1972 visit to China, remained somewhat nervous and kept a watchful eye on the developing American-Chinese relationship.

THE SALT PROCESS

At the center of *détente* with the Soviet Union stood the Strategic Arms Limitation Talks (SALT). They were seen in Washington as an attempt to slow down the arms race and stabilize the nuclear balance. The Soviets had begun a steady, large-scale military build-up in strategic and conventional weapons after the Cuban missile crisis. By the time Nixon became president, the Soviets had overtaken the United States in the numbers of deployed missiles. A new arms competition loomed. Perhaps it could be avoided by negotiating mutually acceptable ceilings on strategic missiles. Indeed, given the strong antimilitary feelings in this country in the wake of Vietnam, an agreement became all the more necessary because Congress was in no mood to appropriate the funds necessary to keep up with the Soviets. Public opinion was overwhelmingly against increased defense spending.

Second, the deterrent balance was not only threatened by the continuing Soviet quantitative strategic growth but also by technological innovations in weaponry that were widely believed to be undermining the stability of American-Soviet deterrence. One matter of concern was the development of a new defensive weapon. The Soviets had deployed an Antiballistic Missile (ABM) around Moscow, and were presumed to be working on a second-generation ABM. If such ABMs could shoot down enough incoming American ICBMs and reduce the destruction inflicted on the Soviet Union to an "acceptable" level of a few million casualties, they would undermine U.S. deterrence, which depended upon its capacity to impose "assured destruction."

In turn, this defensive weapon stimulated the United States to improve its offensive technology, specifically, the development of the Multiple Independent Reentry Vehicle (MIRV). MIRV was an ICBM with multiple warheads that could separate in flight, change trajectory, and fly independently to assigned and dispersed targets. The advantage of MIRV was that the sheer numbers of warheads would be able to overcome any ABM defense. But MIRV held its own danger, as Washington quickly noted when it looked at the Soviet SS-9 missile. Unlike the Minuteman, whose warheads were relatively small and intended to destroy Soviet society by destroying its industry and urban population centers in a retaliatory or second strike if deterrence failed, the big SS-9 missile reportedly could carry one twenty-five-megaton or three five-megaton warheads. It was on the basis of this information that the Nixon administration concluded that the SS-9 was a first-strike counterforce weapon aimed at America's land-based missiles, endangering the Minuteman's survival.

Technology, then, might upset the stability of the deterrent balance. For this stability depended upon the invulnerability of American retaliatory or second-strike forces. The danger was clear as the United States made plans to respond to the Soviet SS-9 with its own generation of MIRVs that, fitted with larger and more accurate warheads, would also constitute a first-strike weapon. Once both powers possessed first-strike MIRVs, their mutual fear of a preventive war, and especially of a preemptive strike during a crisis, would make both jittery. Neither might want to attack the other, but with vulnerable forces neither could afford not doing so. Each would fear that if the other struck first, he would be unable to retaliate with sufficient forces to destroy the other; the very vulnerability of the opponent's forces were therefore an incentive to attack first. Thus, the United States and the Soviet Union had arrived at a critical moment as their deterrent forces—but especially U.S. forces—were believed to be increasingly vulnerable to first strikes.

A third reason for SALT was its relation to *détente*. On the one hand, only a relaxation of tensions could provide the diplomatic atmosphere that would enable the two nuclear giants to arrive at an arms agreement that would leave them feeling more secure, sanctify the strategic parity between them, and avoid another intensive and costly offensive and defensive arms race; by the same token, a failure to arrive at an agreement, or continue the SALT dialogue, was bound to have a deteriorating effect on their overall political relationship. SALT, in brief, became a symbol of *détente*. With it, *détente* seemed to be blossoming; without it, *détente* seemed to be fading. A SALT agreement or the failure to arrive at an agreement became the barometer of *détente*.

SALT I was signed by President Nixon and Soviet Communist Party leader Brezhnev in May 1972. It had taken two and a half years to negotiate, and it incorporated two agreements. The first, a treaty, limited each nation's ABMs to 200 launchers (later to be reduced to 100 each, although the United States was to abandon the whole system, since such small ABM forces could not prevent a catastrophic strike by either side on the other); the second, a five-year interim agreement, essentially froze the then current number of offensive missiles each side possessed. This meant 1619 ICBMs for the Soviet Union (of which 300 were the very large SS-9s) plus 740 on nuclear submarines and 1054 ICBMs for the United States plus 656 on nuclear submarines. Bombers, in which the United States had in 1972 a numerical superiority over the Soviet Union of 460 to 140, were not included in the accords. Given the American lead in MIRVing, the offensive accord meant that the larger number of Soviet missile launchers was matched off against the technological superiority of American missiles with their larger number of warheads. Each side had the right to make qualitative changes—to improve its weapons—within the overall quantitative agreement, thus preserving parity (or, officially, "sufficiency"). While no on-site inspection to check against violations was agreed on, both sides pledged themselves not to interfere with each other's reconnaissance or spy satellites, which would be the principal means to check compliance with both accords.

In addition, further negotiations were to be held in order to formulate a final, overall offensive-missile treaty; clearly, the nuclear warhead ratios, estimated to be 5700 for the United States to 2500 for the Soviet Union by the beginning of 1973, would change as the Soviets replaced their current missiles, including the SS-9, with even larger missiles capable of carrying more warheads. The offensive freeze was thus intended to be only temporary, giving time to the two superpowers to negotiate a more lasting agreement. SALT I was to be the beginning of a process, a continuing dialogue and effort to control the arms competition. The two nuclear giants appeared to recognize their special obligation for the preservation of peace by complementing SALT I with certain standards of conduct guiding their behavior. They pledged that they would avoid confrontations, exercise mutual restraint, and reject efforts to gain unilateral advantages.

SALT II was thus crucial in the effort to give each side a sufficiency that it felt would be safe and that decreased its fear that the other side had gained a significant enough advantage that it might risk a challenge and seek to intimidate its opponent into making vital concessions. It was President Ford, after Nixon's resignation, who arrived at the guidelines for SALT II with Soviet leader Brezhnev at a 1974 Vladivostok meeting. This time each power would have an equal number of strategic weapons: 2400 missiles and bombers; 1320 of these delivery systems could be MIRVed. Despite this broad agreement, it took another five years to negotiate the specific terms of SALT II. Indeed, it was seven years after SALT I that Brezhnev and Carter signed SALT II on behalf of the Soviet Union and the United States. It was a complex series of agreements, carefully balancing off the varying interests and different force structures of the two powers. Not surprisingly, SALT II became controversial in the United States.

Proponents of the treaty pointed to the fact that it provided for some reduction of strategic launchers from the Vladivostok ceiling of 2400 to 2250. This change meant that the Soviets would have to reduce their force levels by about 150 older missiles; but since this ceiling was still higher than the total of American launchers the United States could, if it wished, build up to the 2250 level. The treaty also provided for equal ceilings for both powers—1320 MIRVs; 1200 of these were to be ICBMs and SLBMs (Submarine-Launched Ballistic Missiles); of this number 820 were to be the total number of land-based missiles. SALT II defenders thus pointed to a small reduction of Soviet forces—setting a precedent for SALT III, whose main purpose was to be a major reduction of strategic forces—and the equal numbers for each side, which contrasted to SALT I's permitting the Soviets to have 40 percent more launchers than the United States. Some SALT critics noted that the SALT II ceilings were so high that SALT II was, in their judgment, the very opposite of any reasonable interpretation of the words "arms control"; others asserted that despite the equal numbers provided for both sides, the treaty would give the Soviet Union strategic superiority because Soviet missiles were considerably larger, could carry more and bigger warheads, and were more accurate. The Soviets would therefore acquire a sizable first-strike force that by the mid–1980s would be capable of destroying up to 90 percent of America's ICBMs. A "window of vulnerability" was opening up over the American deterrent.

Defenders of SALT II argued that SALT could not be expected to undo what technology and prior political decisions have done. For example, having developed MIRV first in order to overcome possible extensive Soviet ABM deployment, the United States still went ahead with MIRV, even after Moscow had agreed to the virtual elimination of ABM. That decision came back to haunt the United States. The Soviet Union's 1400 land-based missiles would not be capable of threatening the vulnerability of the 1000 Minuteman force if each missile possessed only one warhead. The increasing American vulnerability stemmed from the combination of heavy Soviet missile launchers with the large number of warheads they can carry. SALT could at best reduce the consequence of this development, and it attempted to do so by limiting the number of Soviet land-based MIRVs to 820 and the number of warheads on the SS-18 (the successor to the SS-9, which could carry upwards of 30 warheads) to 10 one-to-two-megaton-range MIRVs. The also new SS-19 carried 6 lower-yield warheads. Still, both liberal and conservative critics had their points—liberals, because SALT II was hardly a step toward major reductions, conservatives because the 300 SS-18s and the approximately same number of SS-19s *each* carried potentially more warheads and total megatonnage than the *total* American ICBM force, and each therefore posed a potentially formidable threat to Minuteman's survivability and America's deterrent capability.

SALT II's supporters asserted that the treaty would in fact permit the United States to undertake programs that would both reduce the vulnerability of American deterrence and strengthen this capability. Under the terms of the treaty, the United States could deploy 200 new land-based MX missiles which, because of their planned mobility, decreased the likelihood of their being destroyed in a Soviet first strike. Also, because it was larger than the Minuteman, the MX could carry 10 large, accurate warheads, thereby matching the Soviet counterforce capability. Additionally, the United States could deploy 20 extremely accurate, long-range, subsonic, air-launched cruise missiles (ACLMs) on 120 B-52s (or 28 on Boeing 747s or DC-10s) for a total of 2400 to 3360 warheads at a time when the Soviets did not have a comparable ACLM. Finally, the United States could also proceed with the replacement of its older Polaris submarines with the new Trident submarines, each with 24 tubes (as opposed to 16 on the older submarines); the Trident I missile, with a range of over 4000 miles, would be placed in some Poseidon submarines as well. In the meantime, testing of the more accurate Trident II, with a range of over 6000 miles, would proceed.

These defenses of SALT II only strengthened the critics, liberals pointing out that the arms-control negotiations merely ratified the arms race, rather than stopping it or slowing it down, conservatives stressing that these weapons did not yet exist because the United States had not kept up with the Soviets in the arms race and that the nation would therefore be increasingly vulnerable to a possible Soviet first strike.

The main debate, however, was between the administration and its conservative critics, and it revolved around two main issues. The first issue was whether the real vulnerability of U.S. ICBMs was as great as the 90 percent theoretical vulnerability that the critics claimed. An attack upon the U.S. deterrent force would simultaneously have to hit the ICBMs, SLBMs, and bombers that compose the American triad. Even if all ICBMs were destroyed, they represent only about 25 percent of American strategic power. The two other elements possess an enormous retaliatory capability of their own, one that was moreover growing; and should even 100 to 200 MIRVed ICBMs survive, U.S. retaliatory capacity was greatly enhanced. Would any leader in the Kremlin really take the chance of launching a first strike, gambling that Soviet forces could destroy a sufficient number of America's deterrent forces so that they would no longer be able to inflict overwhelming losses on the Soviet population and damage to Soviet society? Would he, as Carter's defense secretary, Harold Brown, said, gamble on this "cosmic roll of the dice"? The administration claimed not while the critics feared the worst. The Soviets, they claimed, were driving for strategic superiority and rejected parity. Their force development testified to their commitment to a first-strike capability, not a second-strike or retaliatory capability; the Soviets, they asserted, not only rejected the belief that nuclear war was unthinkable but articulated a strategy of fighting a nuclear war and winning it.

The second issue was the Soviet Union itself. If the Soviets had not invaded Afghanistan, President Carter might have gained the Senate's consent for SALT II. A majority of the American people and senators favored the treaty. The stumbling block was the Senate's requirement of a two-thirds approval for ratification of a treaty. The invasion led the president temporarily to withdraw the treaty from Senate consideration. For several years, Carter had argued that SALT was so important that the negotiations ought to continue and that, when concluded, SALT II should be ratified despite repeated Soviet efforts to expand their influence and increasing suspicion of Soviet motives in the United States. But the brazenness of the direct and overwhelming Soviet use of force in Afghanistan led the president to resort to the Kissingerian linkage he had consistently rejected and that his conservative critics had long demanded. It was Soviet behavior—the continued military build-up and the meddling in the Third World—that in the final analysis killed the treaty. Concern about this behavior had all along reinforced more specific fears, such as those about a Soviet first strike.

The failure of Carter's reelection campaign sealed the fate of the treaty since President Ronald Reagan had opposed the terms of SALT II. Like other critics, he felt strongly that his predecessor had not responded sufficiently to the growth of Soviet military strength by rebuilding America's strategic—and conventional—capabilities and that Carter had tended to regard arms control as a substitute for a major defense effort rather than a supplement to it. Reagan therefore shifted his administration's priority to strengthening American military power; strategic arms control negotiations might be resumed at a later date. First, the perceived shift of the military balance toward the Soviet Union had to be halted.

TRADE AND TECHNOLOGY

American policymakers in the early days of *détente* were willing to fortify the incentives for Soviet political and military restraint with economic help; the

Soviet economy as it entered the decade of the 1970s seemed in serious trouble. The industrial growth rate had fallen off from 7 to 4.5 percent in a ten-year period and was headed further down. The economic decline was particularly notable in those branches of industry associated with the Second Industrial Revolution: computers, electronics, and petrochemicals. In short, in those branches most important for the growth of industry in the last part of the twentieth century the Soviet Union was falling behind the West. The implication of this could hardly be ignored in terms of the Soviet Union's appeal as a socialist state in the world in general, its power competition with the United States, and, not least, unrest within the Soviet Union at the continuing shortages of consumer goods. Even in agriculture the growth in production had fallen sharply below expectations and official plans. Workers on the land, like workers in the factory, fell far behind their American counterparts in per capita production. The problem of a superpower experiencing continued difficulties feeding itself bountifully—indeed, in some years just avoiding widespread hunger—was not just the result of weather conditions but the ideologically determined organization of an agrarian economy administered by a rigid bureaucracy. By contrast, the small private plots that peasants were allowed to own produced much of the Soviet Union's poultry, pork, and vegetables. Just as the regime was failing to live up to its promises of more consumer goods for its citizens, it was falling short of its goal of a richer and more balanced diet, including more meat, for its people.

Brezhnev could not forget the part that Khrushchev's promises of a higher standard of living for the Soviet people had played in his fall from power. His raising of popular expectations and then failing to meet them helped precipitate his fall; the same could presumably occur to Brezhnev. Indeed, the poor state of the Polish economy and worker dissatisfaction with food shortages and a lack of consumer goods had in 1970 led to riots in several cities and the collapse of the government which, even in a Communist-controlled state, had to be replaced. (Similar unrest occurred in 1980–1981.)

The Soviet concern about falling behind in the scientific-technological revolution led the Kremlin to look toward the West for a "technological fix" to help stimulate their economy. In the absence of basic structural reforms of the highly centralized and bureaucratic system, Western technology, industrial machinery, food, and the credit to buy them were the only recourse. And such structural reform was unlikely since it would run into basic ideological hostility to such capitalist ideas as private property, the profit motive, and free market, as well as into the deeply vested interests of the economic bureaucracies committed to self-preservation. Importation of Western goods and food was the only alternative to such fundamental reforms; trade with the United States, with its scale of production, high technology which the Soviets envied, and agricultural abundance, was especially desirable to Moscow. In return, since it had little to sell the United States, it offered to let Americans develop and exploit the huge Soviet deposits of raw materials, especially in Siberia; the

American capital to help finance this extraction would presumably be repaid in oil, natural gas, and other mineral resources in the future. The Soviets also looked to America, often called the world's breadbasket, for food in years of shortages, years that seemed increasingly frequent.

These economic problems, the Nixon-Ford administration believed, would give the United States leverage. Trade obviously was also profitable for American industry and farmers; but the main reason for permitting it was political. American industrial and agricultural productivity, it was hoped, would provide a powerful material reinforcement for a Soviet foreign policy of restraint and accommodation made necessary by the desire to prevent closer Sino-American "collusion," achieve strategic arms agreements to stabilize mutual deterrence, and gain American recognition of Soviet parity and equal status with the United States. As Henry Kissinger put it negatively: "Economic relations cannot be separated from the political context. Clearly, we cannot be asked to reward hostile conduct with economic benefits even if in the process we deny ourselves commercially profitable opportunities." But Kissinger's idea of using economic means to achieve political purposes was to be undermined by the Senate, which approved offering the Soviets trade and credits but on the condition, specified in the Jackson-Vanik amendment, that Moscow would allow more Soviet Jews, who felt persecuted and wished to leave the Soviet Union, to emigrate. Considering the amendment to be an intervention in its domestic affairs, the Soviet Union rejected the trade agreement. No Great Power—let alone the Soviet Union, which claimed to be a nation in which class distinctions and religious and other forms of prejudice no longer existed—would publicly admit that it mistreated part of its population and allow itself to be placed on probation by a foreign nation in return for trade. Western Europe was to receive many of the Soviet Union's economic orders subsequently, with the result that a powerful American weapon remained largely useless. And to the extent that the Soviets' motives for *détente* were largely economic, as many observers thought, the lack of payoff reduced their reasons for maintaining *détente*.

DÉTENTE: CHANGE OR TACTIC?

The Jackson-Vanik amendment was an early indication of an increasing American skepticism about *détente* after the high expectations that had attended the 1972 summit conference at which Nixon and Brezhnev had signed SALT I and the 1973 summit at which they had set down the principles to govern the superpower relationship. A number of events were to occur that raised the central question whether the more moderate Soviet behavior in foreign policy was genuine or whether *détente* was more a tactical adaptation to a new international environment but still part of an expansionist policy. Was *détente* for the Soviets merely a continuation of the cold war by other means? Did it reflect a

Soviet willingness to live and let live with the West on the basis of strategic parity, acceptance of the *status quo* (including the same nonintervention with regard to Western Europe that the West had practiced toward Eastern Europe, the Soviet sphere of influence), and mutual restraint? Or, having learned from experience that a hard line and iron fist tended to arouse and unite the West, were the Soviets using *détente* with its summits and smiles as a way of relaxing the West's guard and shifting the balance? Were they using *détente* to gain—slowly but surely—a superiority of power by lowering Western defense budgets, weakening NATO, winning legitimation of the *status quo* in Europe while confronting China, and acquiring Western technology and economic assistance? Was *détente* really a "selective *détente*" in which the Soviet Union reaped general benefits from the lowering of tensions while unilaterally exploiting opportunities that increased its influence?

The situation that first and most dramatically raised this key question was the 1973 Middle Eastern war. Only a few months after the second summit, which had reaffirmed the general rules of conduct between the two superpowers, Egypt and Syria attacked Israel on Yom Kippur, the highest of all Jewish religious holidays, the Day of Atonement. What shocked Washington and other Western capitals was the Soviet role immediately before and during the hostilities, even though the war may have seemed justifiable to the Arabs. Egypt was now ruled by Anwar Sadat, an Egyptian nationalist who had succeeded Gamal Abdel Nasser, an Arab nationalist or Pan-Arabist, upon his death. The country had become increasingly frustrated by Israel's continued occupation of Egyptian territory up to the east bank of the Suez Canal. This territory, captured by Israel in the Six-Day War in 1967, precipitated by Nasser, looked as if it might remain in Israeli hands for a long time since Israel had no incentives to surrender it. After the war in which it had established its independence, Israel had had to fight for survival again in 1956 and 1967. The Arab states continued to be hostile to its existence, and Nasser, the only Arab leader of stature who could have mobilized popular support throughout the Arab world for a compromise settlement recognizing Israel's right to exist, refused to play the role of peacemaker. Even after having lost the war of 1967, he refused to sit down with Israel and negotiate a settlement; Israel's victory did not therefore bring peace, only another cease-fire.

But Israel thought it was a peace of sorts. It was militarily superior and therefore not likely to be attacked. The American-Soviet *détente* also benefited Israel since the United States did not exercise any pressure on it to give up the captured Egyptian and Syrian territories. The Soviet Union, having improved its relations with Washington, was not about to permit Cairo to jeopardize these relations any more than it had allowed Hanoi to do so when the latter had launched its spring offensive. Indeed, having supplied North Vietnam with the arms that had helped it launch the offensive that had almost jeopardized better Soviet-American relations, Moscow made sure that the offensive arms Cairo wanted for an attack on Israel were not delivered; only Egypt's defenses were bolstered. The territorial *status quo* thus became frozen.

But Sadat was unwilling to live with this *status quo*. He was subject to domestic pressures to seek revenge against Israel; external pressures from other Arab states were also severe. Thus Sadat, an unknown figure succeeding the much loved and charismatic Nasser, was in danger of being overthrown; pro-Soviet Egyptian leaders were particularly anxious to replace him as Sadat first reduced and then eliminated their influence and undertook measures to attract foreign, including American, private capital to rescue Egypt's stagnant economy from Nasser's "Arab socialism." Above all, Sadat realized that if Israel was to be compelled to abandon the Arab territory captured in 1967 he had to look elsewhere than Moscow. Only the United States, Israel's friend, could help him achieve this goal; and this emphasis on the return of the 1967 territory suggested a reciprocal willingness to recognize Israel's existence. But Israel, skeptical after its previous bitter experiences, subject to constant guerrilla attacks, continuously denounced by Arab militants, did nothing; to Israel, Sadat was merely talking, wanting the return of territory that, once returned, would only strengthen him for yet another war. The United States, too, did nothing after Sadat in 1972 threw some Soviet military advisors out, thereby trying to entice Washington to take the initiative in seeking a peace agreement.

Sadat, frustrated, his power endangered, therefore launched the Yom Kippur War, which took Israel by surprise. The Arab armies achieved initial success in crossing the Suez Canal and driving into the Sinai Desert. They could not have achieved these successes without considerable Soviet arms shipments and bridging equipment. While it seems relatively clear that the Soviet Union did not wish to risk *détente* by helping to precipitate another Arab-Israeli war as it had done in 1967, it is also obvious that once informed of the Egyptian-Syrian determination to go to war it was unwilling to risk losing influence in the Arab world by opposing this move and withholding arms and advisors to train the Arab forces. Instead Moscow stepped up its delivery of arms; not only that, it supplied the most modern arms, including ground-to-air missiles and antitank missiles of great accuracy, which would inflict serious losses upon the Israeli air force and armor and greatly improve the chances of an Arab victory.

When indeed, the Egyptian and Syrian armies proved successful in the opening round of fighting, the Soviet Union began a huge airlift of war material and opposed any cease-fire calls that were not linked to a pullback by Israel to the 1967 frontiers; Moscow was proposing a settlement that the Arabs could achieve only by a major military victory, which they had not yet won. Moscow also called upon other Arab governments to join the war against Israel and approved the Organization of Petroleum Exporting Countries' (OPEC) oil embargo against the United States. And when the United States finally began its massive airlift of military supplies (because the Soviet Union refused to match the American restraint) in the face of enormous Israeli fighter plane and tank losses, Soviet denunciations of the United States were stepped up. There could be little question that despite the new code of conduct, the Soviet Union was seeking energetically to exploit *détente* unilaterally in a favorable situation created by its client states.

Once Israel recovered from its shock and had driven the Syrians back from the Golan Heights, however, its forces concentrated on Egypt, crossed the Suez Canal to the west bank, and moved to cut off supplies to the Egyptian forces on the east bank and encircle them. At this point, the United States and the Soviet Union agreed upon a cease-fire resolution in the U.N. Security Council, the United States because it felt that no peace could be arranged if Egypt was again humiliated in war—indeed, the psychological boost derived from its initial successes had to be preserved if it was expected to make any concessions in a peace settlement—and the Soviet Union to avoid an Egyptian defeat that might compel Moscow to enter the war to rescue its client state. But the shooting continued and Israelis drove to encircle and destroy the Egyptian army on the eastern side of the Suez Canal.

Sadat now requested the United States and the Soviet Union to use their own forces to impose their cease-fire resolution. When the United States declined to intervene with its forces and the Soviet Union threatened to do so unilaterally, the two superpowers confronted one another as American military forces were placed on a worldwide alert. Thus Moscow had supplied the arms before the outbreak of the war; had not pressured the Egyptians and Syrians to abandon their plan for war; had not informed Washington that hostilities would occur; had opposed a cease-fire that did not reward the Arabs' initiation of the war; had called upon other Arab states to join the war; had begun a huge airlift of arms to exploit the initial Arab military successes; had endorsed the oil embargo against the United States (and after the war criticized moves for its removal); and had almost confronted the United States over the cease-fire when the Arabs were losing. None of these actions were seen as compatible with the spirit of *détente*.

A second test of *détente* came in Portugal. A year after a military revolt had ended a half-century of a rightist dictatorship in 1974, radical officers led by a pro-Communist premier seized power and made the Communist Party the dominant force in what had been a coalition government with the democratic Socialist Party and the left-of-center Popular Democrats. A general election of a constituent assembly to draft a constitution did occur, but the non-Communist parties were compelled to agree that regardless of the election outcome power would remain with the military. The election demonstrated a lack of support for the Communist Party; it could muster only 12.5 percent of the vote, whereas the Socialists received 38 percent and the Popular Democrats 26 percent for a total of 64 percent. Nevertheless, the Communists in cooperation with the radical officers seized many of the levers of power in the army, national government, municipal governments, trade unions, press, and broadcasting. The Soviet Union reportedly funded and directed the Portuguese Communist Party in its bid for power.

The struggle continued, however, as Catholics, townspeople, and peasants attacked Communist offices and halted Communist activities in the northern part of the country; the Communists also lost some important trade union elections. The country in the meantime suffered from increasing unemployment and inflation and an influx of refugees from Angola (a Portuguese colony about to become independent). The Common Market refused a loan to help out except to a democratic Portugal. Gradually over a period of months, the election results began to be reflected politically as the Socialists led the popular struggle to isolate the Communists. Settlement of the unrest could come only if the cabinet reflected popular sentiment. The pro-Communist premier was dismissed, the moderate officers deposed most of their radical colleagues, and the Communists were limited to one cabinet post. But the Communists and their military supporters were not yet ready to give up and used huge antigovernment demonstrations to try to paralyze and subvert the government; radical military units refused to obey the government, openly supporting the opposition. Loyal commando troops finally went into action and resolved the issue of whether Portugal's new government would be democratically chosen or a radical dictatorship of the left. It had been touch and go.

What is remarkable about the Soviet role in the Portuguese affair is the Soviets' open support of a small minority's efforts to seize power in a country that was a NATO member. The whole point of the earlier cold war had been to draw lines, or "frontiers," between the Western and Communist spheres of influence, which were to be off-limits to the other side. As perceived in the West, the basis of *détente*'s peaceful coexistence was the mutual acceptance of this arrangement. This had already been American policy during the cold war. The United States had not interfered in Eastern Europe in 1953, 1956, or 1968. And the Soviet Union had certainly left no doubt that it expected the West to continue keeping its hands off this area. Yet Moscow, espousing *détente* and seeking to benefit from it, again saw an opportunity to extract a unilateral advantage in a key strategic area close to the mouth of the Mediterranean. For Moscow, *détente* again seemed to be a selective affair as it intervened in the domestic affairs of an American ally in a manner that it would not have stood for had the United States similarly interfered in Poland, Hungary, or Czechoslovakia.

The third example of selective *détente* came in 1975 in Angola, a country rich in oil and mineral resources and geographically dividing "white supremacy" Africa—Rhodesia and South Africa, which controlled South-West Africa or Namibia—from black Africa. As a Portuguese colony, it had helped protect the two racist states from black liberation movements. But as Portuguese colonialism came to an end with change of regimes in Portugal, the interim government composed of three factions, each based on tribal allegiances, began to compete for power. This rivalry continued after Angola became independent. The different factions attracted outside support. Some claim that the large-scale and decisive Cuban military intervention occurred after repeated South African military strikes into Angola, as well as intervention from Zaire (formerly the Congo, now governed by a pro-Western leader) on behalf of two of the rival factions. But the Ford administration did not see the initial Soviet military shipments and Cuban advisers, and the later Soviet air-and-sea lift of jet fighters, mortars, rockets, armored cars, and ground-to-air missiles, along with Soviet military advisers and a Cuban military force of over 12,000 men to help the third pro-Soviet faction, as merely a rescue effort of this "national liberation" movement from probable military defeat. Rather, it viewed the Cubans as proxies acting on behalf of the Soviet Union, and the attempt to impose one of the three contending factions for power in Angola on that country as an expression of "Soviet colonialism."

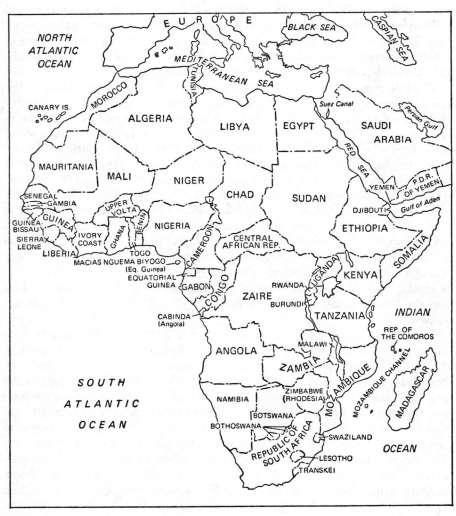

Africa

The result was to reintroduce a measure of Great Power rivalry and possible confrontation into southern Africa. While rejecting any military reaction, Washington denounced the Kremlin's and Havana's acts but limited itself to covert arms aid, purportedly to strengthen the two rival factions, make it impossible for the Soviet-backed movement to win, and compel a negotiated settlement in which power would be shared. But this effort not only did not match that of the Soviet Union but was cut off by the Senate, fearful of another Vietnam in an area that did not constitute a vital American interest. Rejecting the contention that Angola might become another Vietnam, Ford and Kissinger conceded that Angola was not a significant American interest. They emphasized, however, that Soviet behavior could not for that reason be ignored. Angola might be far away, but, in their view, it was a test case of the superpower relationship. Soviet actions were simply incompatible with *détente;* it was another case of selective *détente,* of the Kremlin's seeking unilateral advantage from the general relaxation of tensions. The secretary of state asserted that America could not be indifferent to the Soviet Union's attempt so far from home and so distant from traditional Soviet concerns to impose a government favorable to Soviet interests.

Angola was probably a turning point in *détente.* The Soviets had been virtual allies of the Egyptians since 1955; it was understandable that they would not wish to risk a two-decade investment of political prestige, economic aid, and military assistance by not shipping Egypt offensive weapons, let alone informing Washington of the impending attack in 1973. But to Kissinger, Angola was far beyond any Soviet sphere of influence, and the Soviet action constituted a military intervention to impose a regime of Soviet choice. The Soviet Union's response was to defend its behavior by asserting that support of national liberation movements, including armed intervention, was not incompatible with *détente. Détente* did not mean the end of the antiimperialist struggle. "What's mine is mine, what's yours is negotiable," President Kennedy had once said in summing up the essence of Soviet foreign policy. Had things really changed, *détente* notwithstanding?

The Carter administration, unlike its predecessor, was torn between the "globalists" and the "regionalists." For the former, the prime concern remained Soviet-American rivalry; a gain of influence for the Soviets was a loss of influence for the United States. For the latter, these types of local quarrels among indigenous states in an area were local in origin and had to be resolved locally in terms of the causes that had given rise to them. The globalists maintained that Soviet-Cuban intervention added the element of a superpower competition, which could be ignored only at the eventual great cost to American prestige and the credibility of American power, as well as strategic position in some instances. The regionalists countered that if these conflicts, which had ethnic, racial, regional, or nationalist origins, were resolved on their merit, they would deprive the Soviets of opportunities to meddle; but for the United States to intervene with military assistance and advisors on the anti-Communist side, which often did not have sufficient popular backing, would be to escalate the conflict, needlessly embroil a local problem in a global contest, and thus follow the pattern of Vietnam and risk another long, and losing, war. Political problems, they asserted, could not be solved by the use of force.

Vietnam haunted the Carter administration. Some of the senior officials, including the secretaries of state and defense, had been participants in the decisions leading to the U.S. intervention and had since declared that they had been mistaken; they felt a deep moral responsibility for their past roles. At the assistant secretary level were a number of officials, some former foreign service officers, who had resigned over the war and supported the Democratic presidential candidate, Senator McGovern, in 1972. All shared the sense that the United States had given too much priority to the East-West conflict, and they held the containment policy responsible for the nation's past overcommitments and follies in foreign policy.

But even if President Carter had not rejected the "inordinate fear" of Communism which he said previous presidents had held, Moscow's activities in Africa did not halt. More specifically, another opportunity came in 1977 as Somalia, the Soviet Union's closest African ally, a country in which it reportedly had a naval base at Berbera and which it had well supplied with arms, supported a Western Somali Liberation Front in the Ogaden region of Ethiopia (Somali troops were fighters alongside the Front). Somalia had long claimed that this area, populated by people of Somali origin, was part of Somalia. Ethiopia, already facing disintegration as it confronted other rebellions and secessionist attempts, especially the attempt by Eritrea to establish itself as an independent state, rejected the claim. Like other African and Third World nations, it recognized the borders existing at the time of independence—that is, borders drawn by the colonial powers—as its legal national boundaries. Because Ethiopia is about ten times as large as Somalia with its population of just over 3 million, the Soviet Union supported Ethiopia with an estimated $1 billion of military supplies, 1000 advisors, and 20,000 Cuban advisors and troops to squash the Ogaden rebellion. It was willing to risk alienating Somalia and lose its naval base and some air facilities facing the Indian Ocean because the stakes were great in Ethiopia, greater than in Angola.

There was an irony in a Soviet-supported Marxist regime attacking another Soviet-supported Marxist regime, which the Ethiopian government had become after the overthrow of Emperor Haile Selassie; as relations with Washington worsened, Moscow saw its opportunity to enhance its influence in the strategic Horn of Africa, the eastern tip of the African continent. Across the Gulf of Aden lay Saudi Arabia. Washington's fear was that the Soviet Union might gain control of the southern entrance to the Red Sea, which led to the Suez Canal as well as Israel; and that it would in addition pose a threat to the important oil routes from the Persian Gulf to the West.

The Carter administration's reaction was schizophrenic. Brzezinski, like his predecessor Henry Kissinger, tended to see the Soviet-Cuban intervention to help crush the Ogaden rebellion and long-time Eritrean secessionist effort in the context of the American-Soviet rivalry. So did the Defense Department, which wanted to send military aid to Somalia to displace Soviet influence. The department argued that American inaction, as in the failure to respond in Angola, would be viewed by Moscow and Havana as a sign of weakness and loss of nerve, thereby encouraging further Soviet-Cuban efforts and discouraging resistance by pro-Western states, who felt left in a lurch. Among the states urging American help for Somalia, a Muslim country, were Saudi Arabia, the Sudan, and Egypt, all worried by the expansion of Soviet influence and the need to protect the oil routes through the Suez Canal or around the Cape of Good Hope.

Secretary of State Vance and the State Department's African desk, however, tended to see the problem as essentially an indigenous one in which American intervention could only be counterproductive and lead to deeper involvement, which would be costly and tarnish America's reputation. In a continent where national boundaries, drawn by the colonial rulers, lacked geographic and ethnic logic and where virtually every state had its tribes with separatist hopes, the United States—which in the early 1960s had supported the U.N. effort to prevent Katanga (now Shaba Province) from splitting away from the Congo (now Zaire)—could hardly intervene to help Somalia without alienating most African states. Short of preventing Cuban and Ethiopian troops from crossing over into Somalia after recapturing the Ogaden, this country could do little. The situation, as it existed, simply favored Moscow. Moreover, the Ethiopian government had specifically asked for its help, as numerous governments in the past had asked for America's help. In the long run, it was contended, Soviet efforts to establish a foothold in this situation would fail owing to the strength of African nationalism, even in Marxist-oriented countries.

In short, while the U.S. government could or should do nothing, history would make sure that the Soviet foothold was but temporary. Egypt and other countries in which the Soviets had once possessed influence, only to be ejected later, were cited as proof. And since Egypt had turned toward the West, this citation seemed a particularly strong argument for the Carter position that U.S. interests, while not requiring any action, would nevertheless not be jeopardized. This position, of course, overlooked the problems that had resulted during the years of Soviet preeminence in some of these Third World states. In the specific instance of Egypt, the years from 1955 to 1974 had witnessed three Arab-Israeli wars, which the Soviet Union had helped precipitate with its supply of arms and its failure to restrain Egypt (1956), Syria (1967), and Egypt (1973). Each conflict, moreover, had seen the possibility of American-Soviet intervention grow, and in 1973 a superpower conflict was barely avoided. And these were only the most dramatic events during these two decades.

The Carter administration's division between the globalists and regionalists continued in the following years and the president alternated between them. On occasions he would denounce Moscow and Cuba and declare, as Kissinger had, that the Soviet Union could not benefit from and exploit *détente* simultaneously. Linkages existed, Carter would declare, as he pointed out that the chances for Senate approval of SALT II would be endangered if the Soviet Union continued its African adventures (indeed, Brzezinski would later say that SALT II was buried in the sands of Somalia). After Cuba's alleged involvement with old Katanganese rebels, who had invaded Zaire's Shaba Province (formerly Katanga Province) from Angola in 1978, Carter ordered the air force to help airlift Belgian and French troops to the area. The year before, however, the United States had not assisted French and Moroccan troops when they intervened to counter the earlier invasion of Shaba by the same self-styled Congolese National Liberation Front. But the basic administration position remained that African problems were indigenous and that the American response should be to resolve these problems on their merits, particularly by encouraging other African states to help in their solution. In short, Soviet-Cuban efforts could best be discouraged by removing the opportunities for intervention instead of supporting the anti-Communist side and thus being either identified with the conservative, if not reactionary and sometimes racist, forces or associated with the losing side if they lost because they attracted little popular support.

Not until the Soviet invasion of Afghanistan did the split within the administration end. The 1978 Soviet coup in Afghanistan had been overlooked, but 85,000 Soviet troops, which were sent in during the Christmas holidays in 1979, were hard to ignore. The Soviet-installed Afghan leaders quarrelled and murdered one another, and fierce resistance by Muslim tribesmen to radical and antireligious reforms created a situation in which it looked as if the Soviet-supported regime might fall. Perhaps the Soviets feared that the Islamic fundamentalism then sweeping Iran and Pakistan might also engulf Afghanistan, which lay between these two countries, creating an insecure situation on the Soviets' southern border where it might affect the approximately 50 million Soviet Muslims living in the area. In any event, Moscow invoked the Brezhnev Doctrine, that once a nation had become Socialist, it was not again to be surrendered to counterrevolution (as the Soviets defined these terms). The march of history toward Socialism was inevitable and so irreversible. But this doctrine had previously been asserted only in Eastern Europe, in Hungary in 1956 and Czechoslovakia in 1968. Now the Red Army was to assure history's progress outside of the Soviet sphere in a Third World country.

The Soviets probably expected no more of an American response than in Angola or Ethiopia—that is, words condemning Soviet action as "deplorable," but no action. Clearly, they believed vital security interests to be at stake and did not give much thought to American reactions. Admittedly, there was little to lose. *Détente* hardly survived. SALT II was dying in the Senate; Carter, in order to rescue the treaty, had promised to increase defense spending and to build the new MX missile and was intent on matching Soviet Intermediate-

Range Ballistic Missiles (IRBMs) aimed at Western Europe with U.S. IRBMs in Western Europe (where, to Soviet consternation, they could reach the Soviet Union). The Soviet Union had received little of the trade, technology, and credits it had expected (China, by contrast, had received the most-favored nation commercial status denied to the Soviet Union). Nevertheless, such disregard for American reactions, implying a degree of contempt for American power, was rather new.

For Jimmy Carter and Secretary of State Vance, who had pinned so much of their hope in *détente* on the SALT treaty and restrained themselves from countering Soviet behavior in the Third World in order not to jeopardize American-Soviet relations further, the Soviet invasion was a shock. Carter publicly confessed his previous optimistic views when he said that the Soviet action had "made a more dramatic change in my opinion of what the Soviets' ultimate goals are than anything they've done in the previous time I've been in office." No president in the postwar era has more dramatically testified to his naiveté. Brzezinski, to whom this type of Soviet behavior could not have been much of a surprise but who had not until then influenced Carter's policy toward the Soviet Union too much, began to gain influence; Vance's star, once bright, faded quickly and he resigned a few months later.

The president, swinging with events, now became a "hard-liner"; he halted high-technology sales, embargoed feed grain shipments, and imposed a U.S. boycott on the Olympic Games scheduled for Moscow in the summer of 1980. Most important of all, in the context of growing Soviet influence in the Horn of Africa and the collapse of the pro-Western Shah in Iran and his replacement by a militant anti-American regime (see Chapter 10), Carter announced his own doctrine. Even if Soviet motivations for the invasion of Afghanistan had been basically defensive, the consequence was nevertheless a major advance of Soviet military power toward the vital Persian Gulf-Indian Ocean oil line to the West. After three years of nonresistance to Soviet moves in Ethiopia and after coups in 1978 in both Yemen (on the Arabian peninsula) and Afghanistan, the president suddenly became fearful of a Soviet pincer movement on Saudi Arabia and the other oil kingdoms on the gulf. Having previously denounced those still primarily concerned with the East-West conflict as "globalists" and "cold warriors," Carter shifted gears toward the end of his term and embraced the approach he had previously rejected.

Détente thus appeared to have come to an end. Carter had undoubtedly been correct that not all regional conflicts were tests of superpower strength and credibility; but events had demonstrated that some became so because of Soviet intervention. Few purely regional quarrels existed, in fact; Afghanistan brought that home to Carter. Ironically, then, *détente* collapsed because of a series of regional conflicts that the administration had tried to isolate from American-Soviet rivalry—only to find that it could not do so. Soviet activities in the Third World were evidence that the Soviet Union did not consider this rivalry over, quite the contrary, as it sought to take advantage of American reluctance to act and the illusion that Third World problems could be separated from the superpower competition.

THE COLLAPSE OF U.S. ALLIANCES

Détente was bound to pose several problems for the United States. Alliances are normally drawn together by common perceptions of an overriding external threat. But what cements the bonds of such relationships when that threat is no longer seen as great—indeed, as vastly reduced—by the principal members of the coalition? Is it not inevitable that the strands of such entangling alliances become untangled? In Europe, among America's most important allies, that appeared to be the situation.

In the days when all members of the alliance had perceived the Soviet threat as serious, the individual members had subordinated their national interests to the collective interests of the group. In the era of *détente*, however, the various nations were no longer so willing to give priority to alliance interests. Washington, for example, now negotiated directly with the Kremlin on key issues, as relations with Moscow became in some respects more important than those with NATO members. Not surprisingly, the European states also went their own way. Economic issues proved especially divisive within the Atlantic community. Whereas in the immediate postwar era economic policies such as the Marshall Plan had been consistent with and supported American political-military policy, economic relations were now at odds with the other strands of policy.

The enlarged Common Market emerging in the 1970s was an increasingly powerful economic competitor. During the cold war, the United States had been a leading proponent of European union. A strong United States of Europe would clearly be a significant contribution to the U.S. balance with the Soviet Union. The competitiveness of an economically unified Europe was thought to be worth the risk. In a period of *détente*, however, as the European unification movement stalled, and differences between the United States and Europe grew (including U.S. resentment of European discrimination against U.S. agricultural and other products), past policy often appeared counterproductive because of the economic losses it entailed.

In addition, by the late 1970s, as America was increasingly disillusioned with *détente*, the allies were intent on preserving it. Western Europe had greatly expanded its economic relations with the Eastern bloc, especially the Soviet Union. As European industry had become increasingly uncompetitive in the international market, Western Europe had looked more and more to the East for markets. Western Europe viewed Eastern Europe and the Soviet Union as an economically complementary unit to Western Europe. It had the industrial goods and high technology; the Soviet bloc had natural resources. Each needed the other. Thus Western Europe's economic stake in *détente* was larger than that of the United States, whose trade with the Soviet Union sharply declined.

Politically, too, the Europeans were content with *détente*, in contrast to the Americans, who had increasingly become concerned with the growth of Soviet military power and the expansion of its political influence in the Third World. Europeans virtually ignored Soviet activities outside of their continent, as if relieved that Soviet energies were directed away from Europe. By contrast, compared with the confrontations and frequent Berlin crises of the cold war, the decade of the 1970s had been a period of peace and calm in Europe. For West Germany especially, the period had seen the stabilization of the European territorial *status quo*, the four-power settlement of the Berlin issue, and the mutual recognition between West Germany and East Germany, with increasing trade and person-to-person contact across their boundary; the West Germans saw this situation as the nearest thing to reunification they were likely to achieve. Thus while the United States wanted less *détente*, Europe wanted more. Europeans, therefore, sought to maintain a *détente* separate from U.S. policy and to balance preserving America's military protection with preserving *détente* with the Soviet Union. They did so by distancing themselves from the new harder-line, anti-Soviet rhetoric and actions emerging from Washington.

Carter's economic boycott of the Soviet Union after the Soviet invasion of Afghanistan therefore received little enthusiasm or support; nor did the rather painless boycott of the summer Olympic Games in Moscow. Whereas in 1962 during the Cuban missile crisis, America's allies rallied to its side despite differences of policy over the issue of West Berlin and the continuing Soviet threat to that city, after Afghanistan the French and German leaders journeyed eastward. They sought to salvage *détente* with the nation that had violated another country's neutrality with force, and to disassociate themselves from the nation seeking only to punish the Soviet Union for this aggression. As Soviet military strength in Eastern Europe grew, Western Europe appeared to become more accommodating.

Indeed, the fundamental question raised in the post-Vietnam period was whether Western Europe, with approximately 300 million people, very large industry, and a long military tradition, had the will to defend itself. World War II had ended in 1945 but it still depended upon America with a somewhat smaller population against the Soviet Union with about the same population—in turn in conflict with China with a population of one billion. Too long defended by the United States, had Europe become too used to being defended? It had the resources; did it lack the resolve? The mood of accommodation was strong, and pacifism and neutralism were gaining respectability. The British Labour Party, out of power and under the strong influence of its left wing, favored unilateral nuclear disarmament and declared its opposition to American nuclear bases in Britain; it almost came out for Britain's withdrawal from NATO. On the Continent, governments—with the major exception of France—were also sensitive to public opinion, including the pacifism of youth and some

Protestant clergy (in West Germany especially). Thus, these governments had difficulty supporting a proposed American deployment of 572 IRBMs intended only to respond to the growing Soviet bomber and missile forces aimed directly at Western Europe. Formal endorsements by the NATO governments of this proposal did not end strong opposition to a measure designed to enhance the security of countries that should have been worried that the strategic stalemate among the superpowers might provide Moscow with the opportunity to use its "Eurostrategic" forces and superior conventional forces to intimidate Western Europe.

Symbolically, European defense budgets did not exceed—if they ever met— the 3 percent of gross national product (GNP) the alliance members had agreed to spend in response to extensive Soviet military build-up in Eastern Europe. They pleaded economic problems of inflation and unemployment as a result of rising oil prices, and more benign interpretations of Soviet intentions than Washington, as reasons for not doing more in their self-defense. The latter in fact had to follow from the former, for to admit that the Soviet Union was more than an occasional bad neighbor would have required higher defense spending and the cutback of extensive domestic welfare systems. Nevertheless, the Europeans could not shift attention from the basic question whether they still possessed the will to protect their security interests. Thus Western Europe's increasing inability to compete industrially and increasing military weakness relative to the Soviet Union reinforced one another, as did Europe's growing pacifism, neutralism, and tendency either to be accommodating toward Moscow or to attempt to take a position between Moscow and Washington. Europe's growing vulnerability in an era of strategic stalemate and increasing strength of Warsaw Pact countries in conventional weapons such as tanks and artillery (as well as chemical warfare) could not be denied; but blaming the United States for raising international tensions, trying to separate itself politically and psychologically from American policies, and depending upon the United States for its defense while being more conciliatory toward Moscow hardly appeared feasible long-run policies. Unfortunately, such attitudes created mutual resentments and recriminations. Above all, they clarified that the critical bond of the alliance, a common perception of great external danger to its security from the Soviet Union, was no longer shared. One had to wonder, if the United States faltered or did not exist, would the Europeans do what had to be done to enhance their security or would they become vassals of the Soviet Union?

Other events outside of Europe besides Afghanistan were also divisive. This was especially true of events in the Middle East and Persian Gulf area. The Yom Kippur War of 1973 brought the alliance almost to the breaking point. The Europeans, almost totally dependent upon Arab oil for their well-being, were reluctant to antagonize the Arabs and bring an oil embargo upon themselves. Thus, although the Syrians and Egyptians initiated the hostilities, there was little backing for the United States in its support of Israel. Only the then still right-wing Portugal permitted America to land its aircraft on Portuguese soil (the Azores islands) for refueling during the American airlift. Washington, deeply angered, castigated its allies, and the Europeans responded by complaining about the lack of consultation, especially about the worldwide American alert for a possible confrontation with the Soviet Union without even warning them. The subsequent quadrupling of oil prices, which confronted all Western industrial societies with economic crisis, strained the alliance even further.

This erosion of NATO bonds was not to be eased by subsequent events. While Europe supported American efforts to seek a comprehensive peace among Israel and its neighbors after the 1973 war, the deadlock on the Palestinian and other issues after the Egyptian-Israeli peace treaty (see Chapter 10) led the Common Market countries to take their own independent stand. Moved by the fear of an oil cut-off, as well as by a recognition of the legitimacy of Palestinian demands for self-determination, the European Economic Community (EEC) took a more favorable position toward the Arab states and the Palestinians. While declaring the need of Israel to be secure, the Europeans also recommended the "association" of the Palestinians in the peace process. The Europeans' sensitivity and vulnerability on the question of oil supplies was also in evidence during the period following the seizure of the American hostages in Iran (also see Chapter 10). They remained very cautious in applying economic sanctions as fully and quickly as Washington wanted them to do. Iran's oil shipments, far larger to Europe than to the United States, were not to be risked lightly. Thus on neither Afghanistan nor Iran did Western Europe follow the United States' lead, except reluctantly and only when unavoidable. Some sanctions were invoked, largely for symbolic purposes but not because of any painful effect they might have on the parties to whom they were applied. They were primarily intended to assuage America, which felt that Soviet actions in Afghanistan and the humiliation of the United States in Iran demanded more than verbal protests as a response.

While transatlantic relations were sometimes in doubt, the European Economic Community seemed to be changing its character. With the admission of Greece in 1981 and the prospective admission of Spain and Portugal, the Common Market grew to ten and would eventually have a membership of twelve countries. But the newer members were all less-developed in contrast to the more highly industrialized states that constituted the Common Market's nucleus. This was likely not only to place a strain on EEC's resources and institutions as, among other things, questions of distribution of these resources had to be settled, but also on the original key issue of achieving political unity. The Common Market was always to be more than a profitable economic organization; its central aim had been the formation of a united Europe. The more members, however, the harder this goal would be to achieve; it would have been difficult enough with the original "Inner Six." Thus, the reason for admitting yet three more states, all of whom could at best be called only semiindustrialized, suggests a new rationale for EEC: the defense of democracy. With the fall of the fascist regimes in Portugal and Spain and of the right-wing colonels in Greece, the Common Market countries saw it as their task to help lay the foundation for democratic societies on the "fringes" of Western Europe in countries whose future was, after all, closely tied to all three of these nations. While the United States through NATO remained the principal provider of Europe's security, therefore, the Europeans were apparently going to give more of their attention to the enlargement and stabilization of democracy.

Greek-Turkish-American relations, however, disrupted NATO's southern flank because of a highly emotional and politically explosive situation on the island of Cyprus, an independent state, whose population was both Greek and Turkish. When the colonels then ruling Greece attempted in 1974 to make the slogan "unity with Greece" into a reality, Turkey became concerned for the Turkish minority on the island and invaded the island for the latter's protection from the Greeks. In the ensuing fighting, Turkey was victorious, and the colonels, facing the possibility of a Greek-Turkish War, fell to be replaced by a democratic civilian government. But both Greece and Turkey were also upset with the United States. The Greeks were angry because Washington had not restrained Turkey from invading the island. The Turks were angry because Washington had not used its influence in Athens to head off the attempt at unification and because in retaliation against the Turkish actions, Congress, pushed by the Greek-American lobby, cut off all military assistance to Ankara (assistance was not restored until 1978). Turkey was now demanding about half the island for the Turkish minority; and it refused to budge diplomatically. The southeastern flank of NATO was thus weakened as Greeks and Turks became embittered toward each other and the United States.

While this tension among three supposed allies was going on, the Southeast Asia Treaty Organization (SEATO) collapsed completely. In 1975 it formally dissolved itself after South Vietnam had unexpectedly disintegrated earlier in the year and the North Vietnamese had finally won power in the South. The collapse of Indochina began with another of the many military clashes between North and South Vietnamese troops that had occurred since January 1973. All expectations were that Hanoi would, as in 1968 and 1972, make its big push for victory in 1976 during the American presidential campaign. But a rather routine fight turned into a rout as President Thieu of South Vietnam, allegedly short of military equipment and quickly depleting his stockpiles as a result of Congressional cutbacks of funds for South Vietnam, sought to withdraw troops from the northern part of South Vietnam and concentrate them in the more populated areas. Hanoi, undoubtedly as surprised as Washington at the sudden collapse of Saigon's army, quickly sent its troops southward to help keep up with the retreating South Vietnamese. Thieu had made his decision to pull back in mid-March; Saigon fell April 30. The many leaders of the Saigon governments, who had inherited France's colonial legacy, had been too concerned with their own power, and had relied too much on American assistance and forces instead of developing a social strategy to mobilize the morale and support of its population, now reaped their reward.

The war was finally over. The collapse of an ostensible ally in whom the United States had invested so much in energy and resources could not but fail to affect the politics of the area. Despite a show of force to recoup its perceived loss of prestige when the Cambodians seized the American merchantman, *Mayaguez*, leading to the recovery of the ship and its crew, there was no way to halt the erosion of American influence in Southeast Asia. Shortly after its victory, Hanoi announced plans for the early unification of Vietnam; Cambodian Communist troops also won in that country, and the Laotian Communists gained power politically shortly thereafter in their country. Everywhere in East Asia the result of what was seen as an American defeat in Vietnam was anxiety and nervousness. South Korea was highly agitated as North Korea clearly wished to exploit the American humiliation by invading the South, but China and the Soviet Union reportedly discouraged such a plan. Japan too was apprehensive. The United States tried to reassure all these countries of its steadfastness, especially Japan. This reassurance was later weakened by President Carter's announcement that American ground forces would be withdrawn from the Korean peninsula. Tokyo considered South Korea's security integrally related to its own and later the United States did halt its troop reduction.

It was in these circumstances that SEATO did the only thing it could do—bury itself. No one wept at the funeral. It had been an alliance that, unlike NATO, lacked the principal indigenous nations as its members and was organized against a threat that the countries of the area did not recognize. Its principal members were Western and white, two of whom had been colonial powers in the area. At best, SEATO had provided the United States with the justification for unilateral intervention, but the treaty forming the alliance had hardly proved itself to be what Secretary John Foster Dulles had once called it, the Monroe Doctrine for Asia. It had been another exercise in overstatement, so characteristic of the rhetoric of crusadism; unfortunately, it had also led the country into a disastrous war.

The Central Treaty Organization (CENTO) died more slowly. First, with the splitting off of Bangladesh from Pakistan, which had also been a SEATO member, India emerged as the dominant power on the subcontinent. Pakistan, which had joined both alliances primarily to receive U.S. arms for its adversary relationship with India, thus no longer had much interest in either alliance. In the meantime, it had moved close to Communist China, a regional rival of India. Turkey, at the other end of the alliance's geographical area, was still nursing its wounds after the embargo and suffering from increasing domestic instability. In between, Iran was now the only reliable friend of the West in the area of Southwest Asia.

After Britain had withdrawn from "East of Suez," Iran had become America's local policeman in the Persian Gulf because the United States, given its own isolationist mood, was incapable of filling the vacuum left by the disappearance of British power (as it had done shortly after World War II in Turkey and Greece). The Shah, who, after fleeing his country, had been placed back on his throne in 1954 by the CIA, was a strong supporter of U.S. policy. He had, among other things, sent oil to Israel during the 1973 war, backed Egypt's efforts to make peace with Israel, and not embargoed oil shipments to the United States in 1973–1974. In return, the Nixon-Ford administration had supplied him with all the weapons he requested for building up large and modern Iranian armed forces. But the Shah, who, as an absolute ruler, seemed so safe as the guardian of Western interests in the region, collapsed in late 1978 and early 1979. Traditional Muslim religious leaders inspired their flock to protest against the Shah's rapid modernization and the accompanying Westernization (which was destroying the traditional, religiously oriented society, as well as eroding their own status and influence). They, together with secular left-wing forces and constitutional forces, protested the Shah's despotic rule and pro-Western policy. The Shah was widely perceived by Iranians as a tool of the United States, doing its bidding. And so he fell, and his "foreign" regime was replaced by a more orthodox Islamic republic. Iran quit SEATO, to be followed shortly thereafter by Muslim Pakistan.

The whole area was suddenly in crisis. The overthrow of the Shah and his replacement by a fundamentalist Islamic, anti-American regime; the increasing insecurity felt by the Saudis, who had watched the United States stand by helplessly as another monarchy fell; the spread of Soviet influence in Ethiopia and South Yemen on the Arabian peninsula; as well as the Soviet invasion of Afghanistan, amounted to a collapsing American position throughout the area and a greatly increased danger to the vital oil supplies upon which the United States, and Western Europe and Japan even more, were dependent. Thus in the irony of ironies, President Carter found himself forced to declare that the United States would fight to guard these oil resources. The United States under the Carter Doctrine was now committed to the defense of the Persian Gulf countries.

The lessons were two-fold: one, that no local power, suffering from internal weaknesses, can substitute for American power; and two, that no matter how strong its preference to play a lesser role in the world, the United States as a superpower has extensive interests that it cannot run away from. The world will not sit still while the United States decides whether it wants to play international politics or not. These lessons had to be learned again in the post-Vietnam era in which the United States was left with only one major alliance in Eurasia—NATO—and its power and resolve were questionable.

DISILLUSIONMENT WITH *DÉTENTE*

Any evaluation of *détente* reflects expectations. In the context of America's national style, it is not too surprising that views of *détente* swung from euphoria in 1972 to increasing disillusionment as early as 1973–1974. The national mood tended to think in terms of opposite and mutually exclusive categories: isolationism or intervention; peace or war; diplomacy or force; harmony or strife; optimism that the United States can reform the world or cynicism about an evil world that resists reform and, in the process, corrupts the country—a course that suggested withdrawal from the world as a solution. Thus *détente* was widely believed to be the opposite of cold war even before Carter.

The Nixon administration's initial public overselling of *détente*, and slogans like "negotiation, not confrontation," reinforced the expectation that the cold war was over and that the two superpowers had put their conflicts and crises and the danger of war behind them. Overselling and raising public expectations too high is bound to lead to disillusionment when recorded facts do not live up to original expectations. The problem is that each administration tends to package its foreign policy in slogans that emphasize how its policy differs from that of its predecessors; and, anticipating the next election, it wants to make that policy look appealing and successful. Thus, despite the high degree of continuity of American foreign policy, the United States has rhetorically indulged in containment, liberation, frontiersmanship, and *détente*.

In addition, *détente* as a state of existence that combined both conflict and cooperation was harder to understand than the cold war had been. Both sets of political relationships were a mixture of confrontation and negotiation. The difference between *détente* and cold war was the proportions of the mixture. In the former there is more negotiation; in the latter more confrontation. It is easy to explain a relationship that is essentially one of conflict or cooperation. They are opposite, clearly one or the other, and unambiguous, quite contrary to the more mixed relationship of *détente*. The cold war aroused people, *détente* relaxed them, as if *détente* were the same thing as *entente*, meaning friendship. In fact, *détente* meant a reduction of tensions, not an absence of tensions or superpower rivalry. To regard it as if it were such an absence was bound to produce a cynical reaction.

Indeed, in its conception, *détente* was intended to be containment for a period of domestic pseudoisolationism, superpower parity, and Sino-Soviet schism. The cold war stick was to be supplemented by the carrots of *détente* and issues were to be linked, explicitly or otherwise. The Soviet Union was to be constrained from foreign adventures with force, or the threat of force, plus the withholding of agreements it desired; but, it was hoped, Moscow, enticed especially by Western economic goods, technology, and credits, would restrain itself to avoid the loss of such benefits, as well as other agreements such as SALT. In other words, Moscow would be given the incentives to practice self-containment!

But this U.S.-Soviet adversary-partnership was not static; the mix of these two elements would vary with time and circumstances. In 1972, the Soviets wanted Western, especially American, trade, technology, and credits, a slowdown of the American-Chinese rapprochement, a strategic arms agreement, plus millions of tons of American wheat to help feed their population. But in 1973, the harvest was good, SALT I had been signed but there had been little progress toward SALT II, the Senate had not yet decided what terms of trade and credit to offer the Soviet Union, and, perhaps most importantly, President Nixon's authority was rapidly eroding as the Watergate scandal unraveled. Whereas in 1972 Moscow withheld the offensive arms Sadat wanted and, as a result, suffered the humiliation of having its advisors thrown out of Egypt, 1973 turned out to be a year the Soviet Union did not need the United States for food and was still waiting for the economic payoff of *détente*. The Soviet Union may also have been unsure whether it should still sign any arms agreements with Nixon and felt that he might be unable to react to any challenges; therefore, Egypt received not only the arms with which to launch its war against Israel but the Kremlin's hearty political endorsement. In short, *détente* is not one thing that stays the same year after year. It changes—as one should have expected—with conditions.

We emphasized earlier that one of the basic reasons why the United States initially adopted *détente* as a diplomatic strategy was the pervasive mood of withdrawal in this country after Vietnam. This attitude made containment of the Soviet Union very difficult at the exact time that the latter had become a global power. *Détente* was not a set of self-denying rules. If the Soviet Union is faced with unexpected but favorable situations to exploit, should it shun this opportunity just because the United States is in no mood to resist? Self-restraint as a policy is asking a lot of any major power. Nixon and Ford felt largely restrained by public and Congressional forces, although Nixon did oppose the potential Soviet intervention in the Yom Kippur War and Ford attempted to resist Soviet-Cuban moves in Angola. The Jackson-Vanik amendment also made it more difficult to wield the economic "weapon." Carter, however, shared many of the attitudes of the middle 1970s: that the United States had overextended itself in the world; that it had overestimated the Communist danger and overreacted; that American power had, especially in Vietnam, been misused on occasions; that the cold war had ended and it was time to play a lesser role in the world.

As the 1970s were passing, Americans were increasingly reluctant to use American power because of their sense of guilt about its uses in the past. It was as if the exercise of *American* power, not the expansionist efforts of the Soviet Union, were the main problem. If the United States acted in a more restrained manner, it was said, the world would become a more peaceful place; the Soviets would then follow our example. The Carter administration's constant refrain was "the limits of American power." The phrase made good sense if it was intended to say the obvious, that the United States was not omnipotent and could not indiscriminately commit itself everywhere. It made less sense if it meant—as it often appeared to—that the United States was virtually impotent and could not, therefore, influence events or resist adverse trends. Deeply embedded in the administration's attitude was the old American feeling of shame about the use of power in a morally ambiguous world, as if using it had made us wicked. Vietnam seemed to be obvious evidence of evil.

While the Carter administration was a reasonably accurate reflection of the mood of the country when it took office, another fundamental issue has to be considered, namely, whether the American political system is suited to carrying out a policy of cooperation and confrontation that relies upon an ever-changing mixture of sanctions and incentives (sticks and carrots). How can it be so when the Senate attached a provision about Jewish emigration to a commercial agreement with the Soviet Union or cut off funds for arms being sent to the anti-Communist factions in Angola? How can it be so when the president refuses to use wheat as leverage because he is unwilling to alienate the vote of farmers who prefer cool cash to cold war (or if he does use it, as Carter did after Afghanistan, it is only to find strong farmer resistance); or the president does not want to link, for example, arms control to other issues but there is strong Congressional pressure for him to do so (or vice versa)?

The American presidential and Congressional elections and the frequent conflicts between president and Congress make it difficult to pursue a policy characterized by consistency with flexibility when necessary, as well as the two opposite requirements of opposition to Soviet expansionist efforts and negotiations on issues of common concern. During the cold war, the shared perception of great external threat plus agreement on America's foreign policy aims had generally allowed the president to take the lead and Congress to support him. But in the absence of a clear-cut and overwhelming perception of danger and the presence of intense disagreement about the role and purposes of America in the world, the president and Congress often pulled in different directions (as on the Jackson-Vanik amendment and SALT II). Given the resulting lack of access to America's industrial technology and the failure of significant arms control, even after years of difficult negotiations and America's signature on SALT II, what reason did the Soviet Union have to restrain itself, a Soviet leader might well ask himself, especially at a time when the United States appeared to be in no mood to risk confrontation and the Soviet Union had the opportunities to expand its influence with impunity?

THE SEARCH FOR CONSENSUS AND HUMAN RIGHTS

Perhaps the major problem to emerge from *détente* was that U.S. policy continued to be conducted without domestic consensus. In the absence of external threat and consensus, America has historically been an isolationist country; when it felt provoked, the country has been easily mobilized and united for its foreign policy crusade. As the cold war anti-Communist consensus had disintegrated in Vietnam and the country had tired of its "global policemanship," the Kissinger abandonment of the missionary style and the moralistic justification for foreign policy seemed very much in order. His emphasis on states and their legitimate interests, instead of moral causes and the division of the world into saints and devils, assumed a clear-cut distinction between a nation's foreign and domestic policies. The United States had an obligation to itself to defend its interests and, in doing so against another Great Power, it could use a range of diplomatic, military, and economic tools; it could seek to restrain an adversary with carrots or sticks or a mixture of both.

But it should abandon ideological goals since they spill over into crusades and hinder the diplomatic process by making the recognition of, or compromise with, allegedly immoral states virtually impossible. To make changes in the adversary's domestic structure and ideals a part of the negotiating process and perhaps a prerequisite for other agreements is bound to be unproductive—indeed, counterproductive, since it may well harden the opponent's positions and raise tensions. A Soviet leader, Kissinger contended, may well make some concessions in private diplomacy (as Brezhnev did when he arranged with Kissinger to allow a large number of Soviet Jews to emigrate) but to try and compel a Kremlin leader to change the ways he governs the Soviet Union, a sovereign nation, will expose him to accusations of "coddling capitalism" and selling out "socialist interests" and may even endanger his tenure.

Yet, in asking for the abandonment of America's traditional national style, which had allowed the country to play its foreign policy roles in the past, what was Kissinger substituting? The answer was basically the balance of power, hardly a very exciting idea that would arouse Congress and the mass public. It was therefore hard to sustain support for a policy that involved elements of conflict and cooperation with the Soviet Union and sought to use tactics that offered carrots and sticks in an ever-changing mix as conditions changed. Personal charisma and diplomatic successes gained public attention and support (for SALT, the opening to China, and the attempts to move the Middle East toward peace) and minimized the criticisms. But the increasing public disillusionment with *détente*, the Watergate scandal, Kissinger's own reported involvements with wiretaps, and the succession of an unelected president (and vice-president) with the overall effect of weakening the authority of the presidency eroded support for *détente* and led to increasing attacks on its architect. "Superkraut" had been shot down and American foreign policy continued to operate without a consensus.

Carter sought one in America's self-proclaimed historical role as the defender of democracy and individual liberty. "Human rights" became the platform on which he expected to be able to mobilize popular support; the liberal tradition, which Kissinger was accused of having abandoned in favor of his amoral geopolitics, had been reunited with American foreign policy. The nation, it was now proclaimed, once more stood for something, having reclaimed its democratic heritage and a moral basis for its foreign policy. Jimmy Carter, the born-again Christian, had become the redeemer of the American tradition.

But the policy ran into trouble almost immediately abroad. The Soviets, as

Kissinger had predicted, did not care for Carter's emphasis on human rights, which they felt was specifically directed against them. Moreover, they interpreted political opposition, freedom of assembly, and free speech as an attack upon the foundation of their system; a system that claims that it is based upon an exclusive knowledge of Truth is bound to regard those who disagree with it as "counterrevolutionary." Thus the president's human rights emphasis and his support for Soviet dissidents was viewed in Moscow as a fundamental attempt to undermine the Soviet system. Predictably, it led to a stiffening of Soviet diplomacy on SALT, a postponement of a final agreement from a time when its approval by the Senate might have been relatively easy, an initial sizable reduction of Jewish emigration from the days when Kissinger handled this problem privately with the Kremlin, and a greater crackdown on dissidents.

Similarly, when the president announced the withdrawal of all U.S. ground forces from South Korea, a move presumably heavily influenced by its government's poor human rights record, Japan, the United States' main ally in Asia, felt a greatly enhanced sense of insecurity since the American army in South Korea was seen as the principal deterrent to another possible North Korean attack. In addition, the withdrawal, if it had been carried out, would hardly have improved South Korea's respect for human rights since that government, feeling abandoned by its protector, would have been more concerned with censorship and arresting its critics as its sense of insecurity rose. Thus, on both grounds of American security and the human rights of individuals living under despotic regimes, the wisdom of the Carter administration's strong emphasis on human rights could be questioned.

Indeed, some critics suggested that since the United States could apply sanctions for the violation of human rights more easily to its friends and allies than its adversaries, the policy was applied more frequently to friendly countries who were generally aligned with the United States on foreign policy. It may be admirable of this country to place its weight behind efforts to make countries amenable to its pressure more democratic and more respectful of elementary human rights. In Iran, for instance, the abuse of these rights led the U.S. government in 1978–1979 to give the Shah what at best was only half-hearted support while in effect expecting that his overthrow would result in a more constitutional regime led by Westward-looking democrats. Instead, the result was an Islamic theocracy that was not only militantly anti-American but murdered far more people than the Shah's secret police ever had. The dictator ousted was replaced by an even crueler and more repressive despot. It had happened earlier in Vietnam, after South Vietnam collapsed and Hanoi took over, and in Cambodia, where the Communists slaughtered over 2 million people out of a population of 8 million. Even if one ignored the consequences for American security, could one say that respect for human rights had been improved by these political changes, or, for that matter, by Castro's overthrow of Batista or the shift to the Sandinistas from Somoza? The fact, moreover, that the leaders of these new governments all claim that there has been an improvement in human rights in their societies since the ouster of the American "puppet regimes" suggests that there is no universal agreement on what human rights even are.

A further result of the human rights emphasis was to stress America's double standard of judgment, if not its hypocrisy. One of the early goals of the administration was to normalize relations with Cuba and Vietnam (shortly after the collapse of South Vietnam in 1975, the northern hand behind the origins of the Vietnam War was clearly shown when North and South Vietnam became unified under Hanoi's control). How could that be consistent with "human rights"? Or, how could the president square his human rights stand with normalizing American relations with the most important of Communist countries after the Soviet Union, China, whose government was one of the most totalitarian governments in the world?

Even with non-Communist regimes, human rights came to stand in the way of other objectives. One of the key Carter goals was to stop the further proliferation of nuclear weapons. Brazil, for example, seeking to cut oil imports and find other sources of energy, was buying a complete nuclear fuel cycle from West Germany. This would give Brazil, which also had great power aspirations, the capability with which it could acquire nuclear weapons. American policy vigorously opposed the sale. But instead of seeking to influence the Brazilian-West German deal, the Carter administration condemned the Brazilian government for its human rights violations and further strained American-Brazilian relations. Similarly, when after the Soviet invasion of Afghanistan, Carter embargoed millions of tons of grain shipments to the Soviet Union, one reason for its ineffectiveness was that Argentina made up much of the loss. Argentina had been a frequent target of the Carter human rights criticisms.

Finally, when in order to gain results—as in the SALT II negotiations—the president toned down his denunciations of infringements of human rights, he cast doubts on the credibility of his commitment to human rights and his control of policymaking. The same doubt about Carter's sincerity was also raised by his pre–1979 support for the Shah of Iran. The president publicly praised the man who, while ruling with an iron fist, supplied both the West and Israel with oil and who, the United States hoped, would also help stabilize the Persian Gulf area. And despite his earlier criticism, the president later visited South Korea. Clearly, in all these instances the problem for the administration was one of deciding priorities; failure to decide whether to give priority to human rights or security where these values clashed meant that the pursuit of both enhanced neither. In one sense, the human rights emphasis of the Carter period suggested a kind of cultural arrogance based on the assumption that American values were the appropriate standard for all other societies. The human rights concern, in short, was a revival of the old crusading instinct, and perhaps its timing was not accidental. For its most vocal proponents were also the chief critics of pre-Vietnam America's "global policeman" role. One crusade was simply being substituted for another. In a world of only a couple of dozen or so democracies, this new crusade was bound to run into trouble.

The dilemma of Kissinger and Carter appeared to be how to combine an effective foreign policy with a domestic consensus. Not only does that dilemma remain, but it raises a more fundamental set of questions: Is a consensus still possible? If possible, is it desirable? And if desirable, is it relevant? The answers to all three questions are probably no. It would appear that there is probably no single ideological theme around which the country would again rally in a great burst of enthusiasm. Quite the contrary: An attempt to formulate one would more likely divide the country with controversy rather than unite it in a consensus. It would also seem that even if such a consensus could be formed, it could be undesirable. In the past, when the country had a consensus that mobilized its energies, it engaged in crusades totally to defeat its enemies; and once its mission had been accomplished, it swung back into isolationism. Like a drug addict, the nation swung from its crusading "highs" to isolationist "lows." These kinds of oscillations are hardly desirable in a world that demands a steady, continuous policy. And lastly, the world has become too complex to be managed with ideological slogans. In the security area, how can anti-Communism be invoked when the United States is seeking to use China against the Soviet Union; or democratic slogans be used when some of America's allies and friends are not democratic? And how can the new economic issues of trade and investment be resolved by moral zeal? In a world in which the United States faces not only the Soviet Union but also China, a tangle of indigenous problems in the Middle East and Africa (including the effects of racial problems it had neither created nor could do very much about), and resource problems in the Third World, the issues have become too numerous and too complex to be understood and managed in terms of one or two simple unifying themes. Except in the case of a major war or intense cold war, the days of conducting a foreign policy with a consensus may be over.

Thus, in this more diverse world where the simple foe-friend dichotomy was no longer so applicable as in the earlier era of containment; where the many political, economic, especially energy, racial, and other problems were issues where the United States interests were in conflict not only with its principal adversary but with friends and allies too; and where its own policies were often necessarily contradictory (for example, support of Israel and desire for Arab oil), the conduct of American foreign policy was likely to be more difficult, and subject to greater domestic controversy and criticism, and the leadership potential of American presidents and United States policy options was likely to be more constrained.

Chapter 10

CONFLICT WITH—AND IN—THE THIRD WORLD

THE NEW INTERNATIONAL ECONOMIC ORDER AND NONALIGNMENT

The less-developed countries had benefited from the cold war, even though many of them had criticized the superpowers for their preoccupation with their conflict and neglect of the poorer nations of the world. Far from neglecting them, in fact, the developing countries had received attention and resources from the United States and the Soviet Union wholly disproportionate to the Third World's power. The reason, as we know, was the bipolar distribution of power, which conferred upon these new nations, most of whom were not only poor but also weak, a greater leverage than their own strength and influence warranted. Confronted by two nations competing for their allegiance and loyalty, the Third World countries could first lean toward the East, thus attracting Western economic and military aid and political support, and then toward the West, thereby attracting similar assistance from the East. The increasing replacement of bipolar competition by the newer adversary-partnership meant that their bargaining capacity declined. Nonalignment became acceptable to the United States in these circumstances.

Thus the change in the structure of the international system was the fundamental reason for the decreased American attention and aid to the Third World. Attitudes based on the results of past aid reinforced "donor's fatigue." It had become clear after two decades that the optimistic expectations of "instant development" had underestimated the difficulties and complexities of modernization. Aid seemed never-ending. Additionally, aid had not even been particularly successful in winning friends and gaining influence. In the absence of traditional means of control, the friendship of aided countries was unreliable and frequently fluctuating. American aid, as a consequence of all these changes, had not only been reduced to its lowest point—less than half of 1 percent of the gross national product (GNP)—but the emphasis had shifted from capital development to technical assistance and an increasing role for private enterprise, meaning basically the multinational corporations. In 1979, U.S. aid was only 0.2 percent of the GNP, behind the aid given by such countries as Sweden, Norway, the Netherlands, France, Britain, and West Germany.

Thus, as the decade of the 1970s opened, the lot of the less-developed countries appeared grim. With a few exceptions, they remained less-developed. The optimism of an earlier era that foreign aid would stoke their modernization, or later, that "trade, not aid" would permit them largely to earn their own way and finance their own development, had faded. Actual and potential food shortages in areas of Africa and Asia were a stark reminder of their fate. After years of trying to lift themselves up by their own sandalstraps, they continued to be faced by formidable problems in their attempts to modernize themselves. The hopes of the 1950s and early 1960s had turned into disappointment, even despair, as many of these countries continued to be mired in backwardness. The expectation of the ex-colonial states that they could realize their dream of a better and more rewarding life for their peoples remained unfulfilled. Poverty, illiteracy, ill-health, and overpopulation, among other things, continued to co-exist with dreams of national dignity and material welfare that would provide for the people's basic needs.

The Western states might point out that the causes of the continued poverty of so many of the less-developed countries were of their own making: the continued fragility of nationhood; the low priority given to agriculture and therefore their problems of feeding their populations; the all-too-obvious high birth rate, which tended to defeat the most valiant efforts of economic growth; the large amounts of money spent on arms (including, in the case of poverty-stricken India, a nuclear explosion); and, all too frequently, widespread inefficiency and corruption.

But the non-Western states rejected the argument that the responsibility for the inability of most of them to modernize was internal. They pointed to the external system: the nature of the international economy. In this economy they were the sources of raw material for Western industry. When Western nations' demands declined, or several non-Western suppliers competed with one another for Western markets, or Western industries found substitutes or synthetics, the prices of their resources went down, as did their capacity to earn foreign exchange with which to buy Western industrial products, which have tended to rise in price. In short, their earnings declined while the cost of Western-made goods they needed rose. In addition, when these countries did develop some industry and exported to the West, they often found that Western industry and labor erected protective tariff barriers. In short, even if they worked harder, it was of little help. The structure of the international economy was against them and kept them in a subordinate position, as suppliers of cheap raw material for the rich Western states. Thus Third World countries seemed condemned to continued poverty.

They were, as they saw it, dependencies. They may have gained political independence, but in reality they remained economically chained to foreign— Western, industrialized—economies. Their status remained neocolonial because their own economies were geared not to the needs of their own national markets but the needs of the developed countries' markets. As exporters of raw materials, they were dependent upon Western demand and access to Western markets; thus, they were the victims of Western economic policies, obviously made in the interests of the Western countries who were favored by the law of supply and demand. The international market was stacked against the weak and poor and favored the strong and rich nations. That is why, they claimed, that after decades of working hard and despite foreign aid they remained less-developed and continued to suffer from poverty, unemployment, malnutrition, and inequitable distributions of income within their own countries. For Western nations, the Third World's status as suppliers of relatively cheap raw materials was a matter of self-interest; why should the industrialized world favor their development? Their dependency status in an international economic and political order dominated by the West thus limited, as the Third World nations perceived it, their ability to grow economically; their integration into this global economy has benefited the dominant Western nations with a high standard of living and left them poor.

The less-developed countries, it ought to be emphasized, were not just arguing that the Western-controlled international economic order gave an advantage to the strong over the weak and poor. Their main point was that they were poor because they had been exploited by the West. They had been plundered during the colonial days, and this plunder continued as they sold their resources cheaply on the international market. This plunder was why the Western nations were rich. In this context, their demand for a New International Economic Order (NIEO) was a claim for a redress of past wrongs. Having allegedly used their power unfairly to take from the poor countries what rightfully belonged to them, the rich nations were obligated to make restitutions in the name of social justice and decency. The transfer of wealth from the West to the Third World was thus a moral debt, or conscience money. Whatever the real mix of internal and external reasons, then, for the continued slow development of the Third World, the "revolution of rising expectations" had increasingly become the "revolution of rising frustration." Hence the increasingly strident demand for NIEO, which was essentially a demand for a redistribution of wealth from the rich to poor nations.

It was in this context that during the Middle Eastern War of 1973 that the Organization of Petroleum Exporting Countries (OPEC) raised oil prices fourfold and that its Arab members for a while even embargoed shipments of oil to the United States and the Netherlands, both supporters of Israel. The oil companies, which, according to the imperialist interpretation, were supposed to be such powerful multinational corporations that they dominated the economies and countries in which they operated, were shown to be rather powerless and at the mercy of the governments of the territories under whose soil they operated. And the so-called imperialist states, whose governments were presumably controlled and directed by the capitalists, did not mobilize their military forces to squash the governments that were allegedly their puppet regimes. Confronting a vital threat to their security and well-being from countries that had no military power to speak of, the industrial democracies did not even debate the issue of military intervention. Had this event occurred a few decades earlier, they would not have hesitated to resort to force rather than face the possibility of being destroyed economically. In 1973 they talked of accommodation and acquiesced.

OPEC's action was widely viewed in the Third World as symbolic of a general protest by the less-developed countries against their lot. OPEC was regarded as a kind of "vanguard of the (world's) proletariat," or poorer nations. This mood of anger, resentment, and revolt was clearly directed against the West. Ironically, the effects of the quadrupling of oil prices were felt most in those many non-Western nations that possessed neither large oil reserves nor other mineral resources. Indeed, after 1973–1974, one often talked of the resource-richer less-developed nations as the Third World and the resource-poorer nations as the Fourth World. The sharp increase in oil prices threatened the latter with a slowdown of any plans they had to industrialize and handicapped their efforts to grow more food with technologically intensive, oil-based, agricultural techniques. But whatever their fears may have been for their futures, the less-developed countries stood united with OPEC. Materially and rationally, they should have aligned themselves with the First World, or Western, industrial nations, to compel OPEC to lower its prices to a level more acceptable to them.

But despite their increased suffering, the Fourth World countries did not form a coalition with the United States, Western Europe, and Japan to lower oil prices. This was partly explainable by their fear of irritating OPEC, partly by their hope for promised but largely undelivered OPEC economic help (most of it went to fellow Muslim nations, which used much of it to buy arms), and partly by their desire to imitate OPEC. But the basic reason was that the Fourth World identifies emotionally with OPEC. The latter's action, even though it hurt them the worst, was widely perceived by these countries as "getting even" for past exploitation; it gave them a good feeling that for once the weak had reversed the tables and made the strong suffer. The German word *Schadenfreude* says it best: pleasure received from seeing someone who deserves it really suffer, or "get his." For in this instance, material considerations, which perhaps should have moved them to align with the West against the Third World countries, were subordinated to far stronger emotional and psychological factors, which aligned them with the resource-rich Third World countries against the West. The sight of the rich and privileged nations who had so long ruled them as the "lesser breeds" being humiliated and quaking before their old colonial slaves was just too delicious. While OPEC gained quick immense wealth, the rest of the Third World received an enormously satisfying "psychic income." That was why OPEC's action inspired so much hope. The suppliers, instead of competing against one another and keeping prices low, organized themselves into a producer-cartel to control access to the oil and its price. Perhaps OPEC had provided the example to the other less-developed countries of how they could raise their commodity prices and earn the funds they needed.

Among the things the less-developed countries demanded were higher and more stable commodity prices; indexing those prices to Western inflation rates; more foreign aid; and preferential tariffs so that they could sell their products on Western markets. Basically, the less-developed countries felt they had the resources Western industry needed; without them, Western industry and society would be in serious trouble. The rich nations appeared vulnerable and the poor nations had finally seemed to gain real leverage. Increasingly, observers noted the new First-Third World confrontation and asserted that it was becoming at least as important as the First-Second (Soviet-led) World conflict.

This coalition held into the 1980s, even after the over 100 percent oil price increase in the year or so after the Shah's collapse, the decline of Iranian oil production (although some of the decline was made up by other Persian Gulf countries), and the resulting tighter supplies in a world in which the demand for oil had continued to rise. Bitterness at the West intensified and, as the less-developed countries' frustration and anger grew, their nonalignment increasingly appeared to be alignment with the Soviet Union and its ideological friends against the West. The Soviets had charged all along that the poverty and misery of the non-Western world have been the results of Western capitalism and imperialism. Still, it seemed odd to find Vietnam, Afghanistan, North Korea, and Cuba accepted as nonaligned nations and odder still that their 1979 conference was held in Havana. It seems oddest of all that, when Vietnam was cruelly driving its Chinese population out of the country, usually in boats that would not survive long ocean journeys, its behavior was not condemned as racist, and that neither Vietnam's invasion of Cambodia nor the starvation of the Cambodian people in order to gain diplomatic recognition for the Vietnamese puppet regime in Cambodia was condemned as aggression or a crime against humanity. The Soviets and the less-developed countries would not have hesitated to use such phrases had the United States acted in similar ways. Nevertheless, this coalition between the Soviet Union and the nonaligned nations was by and large tactical. The latter were nationalistic, and they had not fought for national independence only to lose it to Soviet imperialism. Yet it was a sign of the temper of the times that this coalition existed and that only a minority of Third World governments criticized the direction of the nonaligned movement and defended American policies.

OIL AS A "WEAPON"

The quadrupling of oil prices in 1973 and the even sharper rise of prices in the wake of the Shah's collapse in Iran left no country untouched. In the United States and among its principal industrial allies, high oil prices stoked Western inflation; brought on unemployment; created a stagflation, a simultaneous inflation and recession; slowed down economic growth; lowered standards of living; brought about the largest redistribution of wealth in history from the West to the OPEC nations; created large Western imbalances of trade; and sharply lowered the value of the dollar. The "energy crisis" of the 1970s did not merely cause occasional inconveniences such as long lines of cars waiting to "fill up" or higher prices to be paid at the gasoline pump. It profoundly upset entire economies and life-styles, of which smaller cars and lower speed limits in the United States were only two of the more prominent signs; and it raised rather quickly the question of the extent to which Western states, which in the past had paid for welfare programs by means of rapidly growing economies, could still afford such programs and whether to do so, they would have to lower defense expenditures. Or would they be able to maintain strong defenses only by cutting social expenditures? Plenty of "guns" and "butter," as in the past, no longer appeared affordable.

Mao Zedong once said that "power grows out of a barrel." He had, of course, meant a gun barrel. But he had been right in the sense that it also seemed to grow out of a barrel of oil. By organizing themselves into a producer-cartel, the petroleum-exporting countries were rejecting the open market that the less-developed countries had been claiming favored the consumers and not the producers; each producer, seeking to enhance his sales, maximized production, causing an excess of supply and keeping prices low. The cartel gained power by seeking to control both the levels of supply and prices; if it could control enough of the world's supply of oil, so that supplies outside the cartel could not make up for a cutback in the cartel's total production or meet the expanding needs of consumer countries, it would clearly hold the bargaining chips. A second condition was also important, namely, that the resource the cartel controlled was of such importance to the consuming nations that they could not do without it or a readily available substitute. Their demand, in brief, was intense. Thus it was less painful to accept higher prices than to tell OPEC "to drink its oil." The presence of these conditions gave the producer of a barrel of oil "power."

Oil is a vital commodity and is irreplaceable. It cannot be recycled; it takes large-scale capital investments and many years to explore, find, and drill for new oil. Similarly, new sources of energy such as solar energy or shale oil also require enormous investments, lead times, and new technologies. Finally, such older sources of energy as nuclear power are considered unsafe or, as with coal as well, to have undesirable environmental effects. Thus no short-run substitute for oil is readily available for economies that have long depended on relatively cheap oil, neglected research and development of alternate sources of energy, and thus become "hooked" on oil.

No wonder that the developing countries were delighted and held high hopes in the wake of 1973. Not only did the once-powerful suddenly appear vulnerable and weak and the formerly weak powerful, not only did the former colonial masters now quake before their former colonies, but OPEC's actions gave rise to two hopes: one, that OPEC would use its leverage to raise the prices of natural resources from the other Third World countries; and two, that the other producers of resources could follow OPEC's example by organizing their own producer-cartels, limiting supplies and raising prices. Maybe, finally, the less-developed countries could acquire the large-scale financial funds for investment in modernization that foreign aid and free trade had not raised.

The former expectation of a resource coalition against the West did not emerge, and First-Third World negotiations on changes in the economic rules of the game were not very fruitful. The fact is that if we use the rather over-simplified distinction of rich and poor nations, in the 1970s the former were becoming the "declining rich" while the OPEC and a few other Third World countries were becoming the *noveaux riches*. The latter's fundamental interest lay basically with the richer nations. Even more radical states such as Libya, Algeria, Iraq, and lately Iran, all of them "price hawks," have not withheld oil at their nation's cost in order to advance the collective welfare of all Third World states, although all were generally hostile to U.S. policies.

Conversely, OPEC has not refrained from raising its prices because of any social conscience and concern about the devastating impact these raises have on other less-developed countries. OPEC's foreign aid for some less-developed countries remained puny in comparison with what the rising prices have extracted from these nations in funds that could no longer be invested in their own development. Third World unity was, in fact, fragile, if it existed at all. It was a handy term to describe countries characterized by certain social and economic conditions and common emotions and attitudes about past colonialism and modernization, which often vote together in the United Nations. But on material issues that affect each of them differently, there was division. The OPEC countries followed their national interests, even if the cost was great injury to the other less-developed nations.

Nor has OPEC's example been of much relevance for most of the less-developed nations with other resources. Nonoil mineral resources possessed less leverage: There were more readily available substitutes; industrial scraps could be recycled; conservation, stockpiling and new sources of minerals, including beds under the sea, were available options. Furthermore, there are barriers. First, in many areas producing raw materials there are a larger number of producers than in OPEC, which could complicate the task of organizing a united front. Second, the less-developed countries that would benefit from a cartel were obviously those already better off because they were had a product in demand; the poorer nations, less blessed by nature, would not benefit and, given the higher commodity prices that they had to pay, would be worse off. Third, the most difficult barrier to other Third World producer-cartels was the fact that the role of the less-developed countries as the suppliers of raw materials for the industrial world is in part a myth.

Western countries produce most of the world's resources. The ironic fact is that most less-developed countries are net importers of raw materials! Of the nonfood, nonfuel commodities, the Western industrial nations in the mid–1970s supplied 60 percent, the Communist states 10 percent, and the less-developed countries 30 percent. And most of the world's food exports, as repeated Soviet imports of wheat and the threats of starvation in certain areas of Africa and Asia during the 1970s showed, are from the rich countries, especially the United States. Therefore, there would not be a straight transfer of wealth from the rich to poor. Thus, it was not only unlikely that the West would soon confront a series of nonoil OPECs, but even if other producer-cartels were organized they might not do much to help lessen Third World poverty.

Such conclusions were, however, not of much comfort in the West while OPEC retained its key position as an oil producer. For the economic effects of rising prices was not the only matter of concern; the possibility that a political price might be exacted by the oil producers was also worrisome. How much longer would Saudi Arabia maintain high oil production and restrain prices to some extent if the United States could not fashion a solution of the Palestinian problem satisfactory to the Arab states and obtain Israeli withdrawal from Arab lands captured in 1967? If the United States supported South African domestic and foreign policies towards its neighbors, would Nigeria—second only to Saudi Arabia as an exporter of oil to the United States in the 1970s—refrain from exploiting its oil weapon? Indeed, had not America's more even-handed policy in the Middle East since 1973 been partly the result of the fear of the Arab OPEC's use of another oil embargo? Were the Western European countries not influenced by the possibility of an oil cut-off when in 1980 they recommended that the Palestinians be "associated" with the Middle East peace process, or earlier, when many of them received Yasir Arafat, head of the Palestinian Liberation Organization (PLO), as if he were already a head of state, thereby conferring upon the PLO a degree of legitimacy?

Economics is, of course, not a new instrument of state policy. Indeed, during the cold war, economics had become a well-known means of advancing American interests, especially the Marshall Plan for Western Europe and the various foreign aid programs for the less-developed nations. The United States had on other occasions resorted to embargoes, such as cutting off Cuba's sugar quota to this country to punish Castro in his early days in power for moving closer to the Soviet bloc; in Chile, the United States cut off loans from international agencies and prevailed upon American banks not to support Salvador Allende; and after the Iranian seizure of U.S. hostages and the Soviet invasion of Afghanistan, it attempted to use economic coercion either to change the targeted nation's behavior or to exact a price for that behavior.

But economic means are usually of limited effect in gaining at least short-to-medium-range goals. Foreign aid has won few reliable friends; cutting off access to American markets or embargoing food cannot be too helpful if other markets or other sources of supplies are available. Fidel Castro, finding his American market cut off, found a market for Cuban sugar in the Soviet bloc; after Afghanistan, the Soviets bought much of the grain they needed from other countries once the U.S. embargo took effect. In addition, publicly announced sanctions such as these usually have the opposite effect: They unite the targeted nation, mobilize popular support for its regime, and provide a scapegoat for the latter's failures. Oil seemed unique after 1973, because OPEC controlled so much of the world's oil supply and because of the unavailability of sufficient alternate energy sources and the intense need for oil by the consuming countries (although by the 1980s it seemed that even this uniqueness might not last as the demand for oil dropped significantly and more non-OPEC oil became available).

But if in the 1970s OPEC provided the world with a stark reminder of how devastating and influential economic instruments can occasionally be in international politics, it is striking that in the United States the intellectual impact of OPEC's actions was the suggestion that world politics were in a state of change. The oil embargo and quadrupling of prices were not viewed as reinforcing traditional interstate relations because of oil's potentially coercive effect; instead, these events produced an image, widely shared in academia, government, and the mass media, of a more interdependent world, dedicated to enhancing the material welfare of its peoples. Thus the shock of the energy crisis was seen as fundamentally beneficial. Interdependence among nations would transform the very nature of international politics.

INTERDEPENDENCE: GLOBAL TRANSFORMATION OR POST-VIETNAM ESCAPE FROM "POWER POLITICS"?

In one sense, the interdependence of nations—if it meant mutual impact, if not vulnerability—was obvious. The multiple and profound effects on the West of OPEC's actions have already been listed. This interdependence involved the non-OPEC nations of the Third World as well. Recession in the West reduced the demand for raw materials, which lowered their prices, which in turn produced less foreign aid and increased the prices of Western machinery and other goods. With smaller earnings of foreign exchange, the ability of these countries to import high-priced oil declined too, unless they borrowed heavily from Western banks to buy the oil they needed.

Another consequence of this interdependence was that national planning by itself could not lead to full economic recovery. For example, American attempts to cope with stagflation depended on the stability of OPEC's oil price rises and increases of oil production. The price shocks of 1973 and 1979 taught that lesson in the most painful way.

The OPEC countries were also deeply enmeshed in this interdependent world. Without the industrial countries, they could not sell their oil; ruining the Western states was presumably not in their self-interest. If they were interested in modernizing themselves they needed Western assistance, for the West possessed the industry and technology to help them. It could also supply a country such as Saudi Arabia, which believed it had a major security problem, with the most modern weapons and the men to train its forces. In addition, American political support for the Saudi government was desirable because the regime was conservative and concerned with political stability. The government was staunchly anti-Communist and always worried about radical Arab regimes that leaned toward Moscow.

Thus, in a rather obvious sense, the nations of the world had become more interdependent. Price rises, production cuts, inflationary forces, and recession all cut across national frontiers. No nation was any longer "an island unto itself." In an interdependent world, nations could obviously hurt one another. But why were broader conclusions drawn, suggesting that the entire nature of international politics and the historical pattern of state behavior would be replaced by a new world politics whose characteristics would be quite the opposite of the old "power politics?" Why were so many observers, mainly American, so optimistic about this growing international interdependence? Why did interdependence become the new wisdom during the 1970s and possess such a wide appeal among Carter policymakers, news commentators, and academicians?

First, because these authorities claim that in an ironic paradox, nuclear weapons have ensured the peace. The superpowers' strategic nuclear arms are weapons of denial and deterrence; and their existence makes the use of conventional arms less likely because of the danger of escalation of hostilities. The likelihood of major war among them, even among their allies and friends, is therefore not great. When wars occur, however, the conflict may, as in the case of Vietnam, last a long time and be expensive to wage in terms of lives lost, money, and social divisions—in short, the costs may be excessive in relation to the goals to be achieved.

Second, as a result, attention turned from security to economic or welfare issues. The latter have become increasingly salient not only because security seems more assured but also because the democratic societies of the West have become more and more preoccupied with economic growth rates, consumerism, and ever-higher standards of living, while the less-developed countries are bent on modernizing and on satisfying their own people's expectations for a better life. The key issues are thus economic and social rather than military and involve values such as social justice and human dignity rather than violence and destruction.

Third, nations cannot fulfill their socioeconomic goals by themselves. Western societies, for example, run largely on imported oil. The non-Western countries, in their turn, seek Western technology and food. No nation any longer completely governs its own destiny; and no government can, by itself, meet the aspirations and needs of its people for a better life. Thus, worldwide cooperation is not just desirable but a necessity if such goals as peace, political stability, human welfare, and individual dignity are to be achieved on earth.

Fourth, whereas on the traditional issues of security, the state system assumes the separation of states and conflict among them, on these bread-and-butter or welfare issues only cooperation will enhance each nation's prosperity. Whereas in international politics one nation's increase in power and security is seen by its adversary as a loss of power and security for itself, on economic issues each country's welfare was perceived to depend on the existence of prosperity in other countries as well. Economically, they gained or lost together; one did not gain at the other's expense. Thus, precisely because in an interdependent system nations are vulnerable to one another, they need to work out problems together; such cooperation requires a greater willingness to resolve disputes peacefully, if not also a higher degree of mutual understanding and international harmony. Unlike cold war security issues, which were bilateral, the issues of oil or other resources or population or environment require multilateral negotiations. Many nations are affected—indeed, usually different nations on different issues. By "the logic of interdependence," they have to find collective solutions to their common problems.

Fifth, and very important, force and the threat of force are said to play a minimal role on these welfare issues, again in strong contrast to the primary role they play on security issues. The downgrading of force is largely attributable to the fact that countries with whom the United States would negotiate on these issues are allies and friends. Saudi Arabia and Iran (until 1979) were not, like the Soviet Union, America's enemies. Even if the threat or application of force was effective once or twice, invoking or applying it frequently could only alienate countries that are needed on these social and economic issues. Although many of the nations with which the United States must deal on these prosperity issues are comparatively weak militarily, they are hardly helpless and without leverage of their own. They possess commodities that, if production were shut off, would hurt the consuming nations. Militarily weak states such as the major oil-exporting nations thus have formidable bargaining power, which the traditional way of calculating power, by means of adding manpower, industrial capacity, military strength, and other factors, would not reveal. The old hierarchy of states based upon military strength was therefore increasingly irrelevant, and the new emerging world order would be a genuinely more egalitarian one.

At least, power politics would be less relevant. The emphasis would be on cooperation among nations and their common interests, and the prime values to be sought would be human welfare and dignity. While nations clearly continue to exist, their military fangs are to be drawn and their aggressiveness subordinated to the task of building a better future for all peoples. The national interest could be satisfied by serving the human interest. Interdependence, in brief, supposedly restrains national egotism and enmeshes nations in a web of interdependence that compels them to cooperate for the "good of mankind." Interdependence is thus unquestionably in part a description of current reality, but it is *also*—usually implicitly—a cry to move "beyond the nation-state" to a "world without frontiers" by dissolving, so to speak, power politics in welfare politics and "planetary humanism." In short, without denying the reality of existing economic problems of Third World poverty and hunger, the emphasis on interdependence is to some degree an attempt to escape from the structure of the present state system with its inherent conflicts and dangers; it is a plea for mankind to cooperate despite national differences to make "spaceship earth" a truly decent and fit place for all people to live and enjoy life in freedom from oppression and want.

Indeed, what could be more characteristic of America's national style than interdependence, with (1) its distinction between economics, which is thought of as good because it is identified with social harmony and material benefit, and politics, which is equated with conflict, destruction, and death; and (2) the normative commitment to a better future for humanity, to be achieved by a rational response to the allegedly inexorable forces of economics and technology? At one time, free trade was thought to be the answer to war and a unifier of nations because commerce would benefit all of them and presumably give them a vested interest in peace; then economic development was advocated as the key. Is interdependence not just another idea in search of a more peaceful and harmonious world, since the previous proposals have *not* done away with power politics?

Moreover, is the timing of the idea of interdependence not coincidental with, as well as a reaction to, Vietnam and the profound moral revulsion of many policymakers and analysts to that war and "realism" as a way of understanding and conducting American foreign policy? There is certainly an irony of sorts to advocating interdependence. Vietnam created a strong reaction to globalism, which was dismissed as an overreaction of the cold war. Yet, under the guise of interdependence, globalism has been resurrected as the best way for nations to coexist and resolve not security issues but welfare or prosperity issues—population, resource depletion, energy, food, and the maldistribution of wealth.

It is not surprising that this new philosophy of global change strongly influenced the Carter administration's policy. Carter came to power just after South Vietnam's final collapse when the country was sick and tired of the war and the power politics that had allegedly been responsible for the country's involvement. Many of the administration's top officials, who as leaders or members of the bureaucracy in the Johnson or Nixon administrations had participated in the decision making about the war, shared the widely felt sense of shame about the war; they felt guilt about this abuse of American power, as well as other misuses (such as covert political interventions). Kissinger's balance-of-power approach was, therefore, dismissed as increasingly dated; the world had moved beyond the days when this allegedly older or "European approach" seemed relevant. The new administration claimed that it would be more sensitive to the supposed new realities of a more complex world and no longer a prisoner of the old cold war myth of superpower competition and confrontation, which had in the past supposedly imposed a strategic importance they did not possess and had led the United States to support right-wing dictatorships in the name of freedom. The administration, therefore, would move beyond the balance-of-power politics of East-West relations to "world-order" politics and a focus on North-South relations (between developed and less-developed countries).

East-West matters, then, were no longer regarded as of central concern except in the sense of working together for arms control—SALT, balanced reductions of forces in Europe, nonproliferation of nuclear arms, and demilitarization of the Indian Ocean (at the very moment this area was becoming destabilized and demanded a projection, not a withdrawal, of American power!). American-Soviet relations "were a kind of residual atavism, increasingly at odds with the forces gaining ascendance in the new global system. . . .The hierarchy that formerly marked the international system could no longer have anything approximating the salience and significance it once had. The Great Powers could no longer expect to play their traditional preponderant roles and to enjoy their once customary advantages."*

This image of the post-Vietnam War world with its distaste for national egotism and use of power and the reassertion of an older and allegedly more moral American approach to foreign policy—nicely disguised as interdependence and a transformation of world politics—testified to the strength of that approach and its set of attitudes and ways of perceiving the world. Yet the emergence of interdependence as the new intellectual fashion together with the disutility of force as the new wisdom came, contradictorily enough, at the very moment that the Soviet Union became a global power, American strategic superiority vanished, and the "imperial presidency" was weakened. Thus, at the same time that the new administration wished to deemphasize the East-West balance-of-power conflict while focusing on North-South world-order cooperation, the Soviet Union saw opportunities to exploit and expand its influence militarily—in the Third World!

Thus the East-West struggle was not just an old and bad memory. It was still very much alive, even if the United States preferred not to compete actively and told itself that containment no longer seemed wise or relevant since history, the nationalism of the new nations, plus the shift in emphasis from na-

*Robert W. Tucker, "America in Decline: The Foreign Policy of 'Maturity.'" *Foreign Affairs* annual year-end issue entitled *America and the World 1979*, 1980, p. 463.

tional security to global welfare, would limit and defeat such old-fashioned expansionism. The Soviets showed that they shared neither the belief that the nature of international politics had changed nor the view that force had become an increasingly inept, if not irrelevant, instrument of policy. At the time, the Soviet Union was outspending the United States by at least 25 percent, perhaps by as much as 50 percent, on its military forces. Given an economic base about half that of the United States, this very heavy emphasis on "guns" at the cost of "butter" for the Soviet people suggested that these forces were intended for more than just defense. With its simultaneously increasing political-military involvement in the Third World, the Soviets taught the United States once more what it should have learned from earlier experience this century: that there was no escape from the world of Great Power conflict.

Undoubtedly, the United States had, on occasion, as had often been pointed out, made mistakes by giving too much emphasis to East-West relations; but experience showed that ignoring or downplaying these relations also led to grave—if not graver—errors. It is one thing to learn from the past and correct errors; it is quite another to reject the very nature of international politics, whose chief characteristic, one might argue, was its strong sense of continuity. Soviet behavior—the continuing growth of Soviet military power, interventions in the Third World by proxies (Cubans especially), and the outright use of the Red Army in Afghanistan—made one question inevitable: Had Kissinger and preceding administrations been so wrong in granting priority to American-Soviet competition and placing a strong emphasis on military power or in thinking that the East-West struggle sometimes intersected with North-South issues?

FROM GLOBALISM TO REGIONALISM AND BACK AGAIN

The Carter administration's emphasis on the creation of a "new world order" with its central focus on the relationship between the Western industrial world and the less-developed nations left no doubt of its answer to that question. It was precisely this preoccupation with American-Soviet competition that had led to Vietnam. By overlaying the superpower struggle on regional and even domestic rivalries, the United States in the past had become needlessly involved in situations it should have stayed out of and had become identified as a reactionary power supporting the *status quo* rather than needed changes. The Carter administration cited two examples from the Nixon era to support its contention that regional issues should be seen as such and solved in terms of the local forces that had given rise to them and that the United States would be better off not transforming regional quarrels into global ones if it wished to avoid aligning itself with the sides opposing democratic values and nationalism in the Third World.

The first example was Pakistan's breakup in 1971. A nation divided in West and East with 1000 miles of India lying between the two parts, Pakistan had been born in a burst of communal hatreds in which hundreds of thousands of Hindus and Muslims slaughtered one another. It confronted the issue of survival only twenty-four years after its birth, during a period in which India (already hated for its seizure of Kashmir) had tried on several occasions to humiliate Pakistan and destroy it as a possible military threat.

What was to be the breaking point began when Pakistan, ruled for many years by a military regime, held a free election. A majority in East Pakistan voted for autonomy, because under the West Pakistan-dominated government the East had received less than what it considered a fair share of the national wealth (such as it was) and felt itself treated as a colonial appendage. West Pakistan attempted to crush the movement for autonomy with great brutality. The army killed and raped at will, burning village after village; almost 10 million refugees streamed across the border into India to escape this ravaging. The result was the growth of a full-fledged armed independence movement for the establishment of a Bengali Nation, or Bangladesh.

The United States during this period did not utter a single official word of public condemnation against its Southeast Asia Treaty Organization (SEATO) partner's brutal behavior. In part, America's silence and continued shipment of arms to Pakistan appeared to be the result of Pakistan's help in opening new relations between Washington and Peking; and in part this support apparently was reinforced during the sensitive period preceding President Nixon's 1972 visit to the Chinese People's Republic by China's strong diplomatic backing of Pakistan. Alone, India supplied arms to the East Pakistan forces and provided sanctuaries for the rebels. India also turned for support to the Soviet Union and received it in the form of a twenty-year friendship treaty intended to deter a Pakistani attack.

This move away from India's historic policy of nonalignment was also presumably intended to deter American support for Pakistan and give India the confidence to move against Pakistan. While denying that the new treaty represented a departure from nonalignment, India did have a good short-term reason for wanting to go to war, quite aside from the longer-range aim of once and for all eliminating Pakistan as a rival on the Indian subcontinent. This more immediate objective was to end the burden of the millions of refugees, a cost sufficiently great to slow down India's rate of economic growth. In a real sense, a war was cheaper than continuing to support the refugees.

Thus, under circumstances in which both sides claimed the other shot first, war erupted. Pakistan lost its eastern half; Bangladesh attained statehood. India's policy of dismemberment succeeded, the Soviet Union reaped the rewards of India's victory, and its influence on the subcontinent reached new heights, while the United States—and to some extent China—lost prestige by siding with its weaker, military-ruled rival, whose soldiers' brutality had undermined the legitimacy of its cause in the eyes of almost all the world's nations.

The second example was Chile. In Latin America, American-Soviet rivalry—

despite *détente*—had been even more conspicuous. American policy showed a strong continuity with a policy that had historically regarded the Southern Hemisphere to be America's sphere of influence, and while Washington had gradually been accommodating the increasing nationalism of its Latin neighbors, it remained very sensitive to what it perceived to be radical left-wing revolutions and regimes that might bring Soviet influence into America's so-called backyard. Thus, when in 1970 Chile elected Marxist Salvador Allende to the presidency, the Nixon administration, while publicly acting correctly, sought first to prevent Allende from becoming president and, after that failed, to make life difficult for him and encourage a military *coup d' état*. Thus, in a subtler way than John Kennedy at the Bay of Pigs or Lyndon Johnson in the Dominican Republic, the new Republican administration used the Central Intelligence Agency (CIA) for the same anti-Communist reason as preceding administrations. Yet the reasons for the Chilean coup, when it came, stemmed essentially from Allende's own actions and the domestic reactions these precipitated. The CIA may have helped shorten the time until the coup occurred, but the causes of the crisis were internal; by 1973 Allende's end was merely a matter of time. Indeed, Chile provided a most persuasive example of why the United States should *not* intervene in this type of situation.

While not excusing the intervention, it is important to stress this point because Allende has become something of a martyr, frequently portrayed as the revolutionary who was fairly elected to seek reforms and better the lot of the poor and underprivileged, only to be blocked and finally overthrown by a fascist conspiracy on behalf of a reactionary ruling class in league with capitalist America. Had he in fact lived, Allende's reputation would have been stained by the failure of his political leadership; his suicide at the time of the coup elevated his reputation to a level he could never have achieved had he lived and remained as leader of Chile's "road to socialism."

Allende came to power having won 36 percent of the vote, two points ahead of his next competitor in a three-way race. In the runoff vote in the Congress, he received the support of the centrist Christian Democratic Party. At the start of his rule he possessed opposition support for much of his program, including the nationalization of the American-owned copper mines, banks, and major industries and land reform. While it thus seemed possible to work within Chile's constitutional norms with a democratic consensus, Allende believed in class struggle. He deliberately pursued a policy of polarizing Chileans, which did more to consolidate the professional middle and lower-middle classes in opposition to him than to broaden his worker-peasant base of support. As he pursued his program, his vow to maintain constitutional rule fell by the wayside. Representing a sizable minority, but hardly "the people," he could have governed only if he had gained the majority support in the Congress, which he did not possess. In a parliamentary system he would have fallen quickly; in Chile's presidential system he survived by increasingly bypassing the Congress and the courts. The Christian Democrats then joined the rightist opposition, and class polarity was then matched by executive-legislative polarity. Allende had eliminated the middle ground of Chilean politics and emasculated the spirit of the constitution.

The nucleus of Allende's opposition came less from any privileged ruling class than from the lower-middle class, which was deeply affected by an inflation of over 300 percent by 1973, shortages of all kinds in the shops, and worries that their small businesses might be wiped out by inflation or government takeovers. In 1972 and especially in 1973, small truckers, who owned one or two trucks, went on strike and were joined by shopkeepers, doctors, lawyers, engineers, bus and taxi drivers, and airline pilots (between the strikes even the workers in the largest copper mine struck).

The military during this period became increasingly politicized. Asked by Allende at several points to participate in his cabinet to reassure those worried about law and order in the midst of strikes, the street marches of Allende's supporters and opposition, and illegal seizures of land by the president's followers, the military initially served Allende as it had his predecessors (it even crushed one attempted revolt by some military units). What precipitated the military's intervention after forty years of staying out of Chilean politics was the rapid growth of paramilitary forces among Allende's extreme left-wing followers, who had always believed in armed confrontation with "reaction," and the public call for an insurrection in the navy by a close Allende friend and party co-leader; both events apparently occurred with Allende's complicity. The country was on the verge of civil war when the military struck. It did not need American urging.

Not that the United States had not been hostile to Allende from the start. After the expropriation of American property without compensation, Washington cut off American credit and pressured international financial institutions to follow suit. But Allende more than made up his American losses with credits from Communist states, other Latin American countries, and West European countries. Chile also had rich copper mines. Had Allende been a Gamal Abdel Nasser, he would have survived American pressure and hostility by arousing his people's nationalist ardor. But that was why Allende did not survive; he rejected a role as president of all Chileans. He declared himself to be president of only some Chileans—against other Chileans. Such polarization of society, a galloping inflation, and increasingly unconstitutional rule were hardly recipes for political success. Had the CIA practiced abstinence, responsibility for the Chilean coup would properly have fallen on Allende; he destroyed himself politically before he did so physically. The CIA meddling drew attention from this and reaped the blame for Allende's difficulties and fall for the United States. Whatever it says for or against American intervention in its sphere of influence—if such a sphere can still be considered important and relevant in areas far beyond the nearer Caribbean-Central American area in this intercontinental age—Chile, like the earlier Bay of Pigs, makes a persuasive case for nonintervention.

Americans, perhaps because of the democratic nature of their society, seem on the whole rather clumsy at covert intervention and feel morally uneasy about it. Perhaps most reprehensible and in some ways symbolic were the several attempts to assassinate Castro, involving the Kennedy administration, the CIA, and Mafia figures—certainly an immoral alliance to murder in the name of national security. And, unlike in a television play, this unholy alliance failed in all of its attempts. In Chile, a country as far away from the United States as the Middle East, the question is surely whether the United States had the right to try to upset the election of any political figure who was elected according to constitutional processes either in the name of American national security or for the broader consideration of the preservation of democratic values—values Washington did not insist on in Chile after Allende or in other parts of this increasingly nondemocratic globe. One major result has been that the United States reaped widespread condemnation for its intervention and that Chile became for many liberal people a *cause célèbre,* as the Spanish civil war before World War II had become a symbol of the conflict between fascist and progressive forces in the world.

The Carter administration, in any event, had no wish to emulate these efforts. These were local problems that could have been handled more appropriately on a local basis. This meant above all support for those domestic or regional forces that were identified with nationalist aspiration. Symbolic of the new attitude were the negotiations and the acceptance of a change in the status of the Panama Canal Zone, negotiations begun in the 1960s, carried on throughout the Nixon-Ford administration, and finally concluded under Jimmy Carter. For Latin America, the disposition of this issue was critical. This was not a strictly American-Panamanian issue. For all of the Latin American states—left, centrist, and right—supported Panama in its determination to assert its control over a piece of territory that America treated as if it were America's. Would the United States seek to preserve its control of the zone, which would lead to violence between the American forces in the zone and the Panamanians, or would it accommodate itself to the nationalism of not only Panama but all the states to its south?

Theodore Roosevelt had created Panama in order to build the canal for the growing American navy at the turn of the century; the 1903 treaty between the two countries had granted the United States "in perpetuity the use, occupation, and control" of a ten-mile-wide zone to build, run, and protect the canal, although the sovereignty of this territory was to remain vested in Panama. The result was a virtual colonial situation. The American role in that small country became dominant. The Canal Zone cut Panama in two and was run by the U.S. Army. Panamanians in the zone were subject to American law administered by American courts. All business enterprises were operated by the United States; Panamanians were denied the opportunity to compete. And the American government held large tracts of zonal land and water needed by Panama's rapidly growing population. What all this amounted to is that the United States acted as if it were sovereign in the zone when in fact it only possessed certain treaty rights over a piece of Panamanian territory.

The Panamanians also felt that they had received rather scanty economic benefits from the canal; fair or not, the contrast between the standards of living in the zone and outside it was grating and humiliating. Political discontent had become so high by 1964 that nationalist frustrations burst into riots when Panamanian students tried to fly their country's flag next to the American one at the zonal high school. American students resisted, and twenty-one Panamanian and three American students were killed in the subsequent explosion. The confrontation had been a symbolic one and a sample on a minor scale of what faced the United States should it seek to preserve its control "in perpetuity."

By the middle 1970s time was running out. The canal's economic benefits to the United States were declining with shifting world trade patterns and the increasing use of supertankers and container ships too large to pass through the canal; even its military value was being reduced by a two-ocean navy with huge aircraft carriers, which could not go through the canal, and nuclear submarines, which would have to surface to pass from one ocean to the other (providing intelligence to the Soviets of their whereabouts.) The Canal Zone issue, like the flag issue, had become primarily symbolic. American liberals recognized the need for change to meet Panama's aspirations for territorial integrity and real instead of nominal sovereign control; if denied, Panama might become "another Vietnam." But American conservatives, very strong in Congress, bitterly resisted a new treaty, which would restore the zone to Panama by the end of the century while ensuring America's right to continued use of and protection for the waterway; if granted, the "American Canal in Panama" would become "another Suez," an indication of a retreat of American power, another instance of a once-powerful America groveling before a tiny country. Common sense in the end did prevail, although not without a struggle in Washington.

The canal could obviously be better protected with the Panamanians' consent than without—or against—it; the latter situation would produce sabotage and violence, which would compel the United States to send large military forces to the zone to protect it from "the natives." The pictures of American troops shooting Panamanians would make ugly headlines. So would the public confrontation in the United Nations, the international forum to which Panama had said it would take the issue rather than to the Organization of American States, which it considered an appendage of the United States. In the world organization, the United States would stand virtually alone against a solid bloc of less-developed countries. Thus the symbolism of the issue was domestic and international. While for many Americans, and not just some in Congress, the Canal Zone was "American," anything less than eventual Panamanian control over its own territory was equally unthinkable. A new treaty would therefore be a symptom of change in American attitudes toward the nationalist aspirations of its southern neighbors; it would also constitute a recognition of an American reassessment of its formerly dominant position in this hemisphere. Already

Peru, Venezuela, Bolivia, and Argentina had asserted themselves strongly against the United States, and American influence throughout Latin America was clearly on the wane. The area was less and less of an American "sphere of influence." The real stake in Panama, in brief, was America's new global image and role. In April 1978, by only one extra vote over the two-thirds required for a treaty, the Senate ended thirteen years of negotiations and a lengthy national and Senate debate by voting to turn the canal over to Panama by the year 2000.

This became part of a new pattern in Latin America. Where President Johnson had intervened in the Dominican Republic to stop left-wing forces from taking over the government, Carter pressured the Dominican generals who tried to oppose the election of a left-wing president to desist. And in Nicaragua, he opposed the dictatorship of Anastasio Somoza, and it eventually collapsed; his predecessors had frequently supported other despotisms. Carter thus ended up by supporting the Sandinistas, who during Somoza's days were domestically supported by such elements as the Catholic Church and the business community, even though they were externally supported by Cuba. These policies were characteristic of the administration's attempt to be sensitive to the nationalism of Third World countries in its pursuit of world-order politics with the primary emphasis on the North-South relationship; the risk that such successor regimes to the conservative, pro-American predecessors would turn toward Cuba and the Soviet Union for friendship and eventually repress all domestic opposition forces, including genuinely democratic ones, was accepted.

In Africa, this attitude meant that U.S. policy moved away from identification with the white supremacy regimes of Rhodesia and South Africa and toward a closer alignment of American positions with the black states of the continent. Fear of the Soviet Union was admittedly present, for the United States worried that if the guerrilla wars in South-West Africa (Namibia) and Rhodesia (Zimbabwe) could not be ended by political settlements, the Soviets and Cubans might not only provide arms and training for the guerrillas but send Soviet advisors and Cuban troops to help. The West would then be helpless since it would be identified with white racist regimes. But the fundamental purpose was to align U.S. policy with the prevailing African sentiments that were obviously strongly opposed to the white-dominated governments.

The United States therefore sought to promote South-West Africa's independence from South Africa, which had governed the former German colony since World War I, and bring about a cease-fire in its guerrilla war and majority rule under U.N.-supervised elections. Rhodesia was, however, the more critical situation. Its leader was Ian Smith, who had broken Rhodesia away from the British Commonwealth in order to maintain the rule of 300,000 whites over almost 7 million blacks. After years of resisting any change, Smith was compelled by the increasing cost and drain on manpower imposed on Rhodesia by the black nationalist guerrilla war, as well as by economic sanctions, to shift his position. Proclaiming his willingness to accept "majority rule," Smith said free elections would be held. As a token of his intent, he formed a transitional government, which included several moderate black leaders, including Bishop Abel Muzorewa, who were believed to have popular appeal. Smith hoped that the "internal settlement" would end the war by attracting black support at home and isolating the guerrillas in their bases in neighboring Mozambique. Presumably, such a settlement would also gain American and British approval and lead to a lifting of economic sanctions.

The externally based Patriotic Front rejected the internal settlement as a fraud, asserting that it was a clever device to preserve white privilege and power. Virtually all black African states backed the Patriotic Front, led by Joshua Nkomo and the more militant, Marxist-oriented Robert Mugabe. In these circumstances, the Carter administration argued that Anglo-American support for the internal settlement and lifting of economic sanctions would be disastrous and would end the attempts to arrange for talks among all Rhodesian leaders, including the guerrillas. But sentiment for the internal settlement was growing in the United States, where the Senate voted for the lifting of economic sanctions, and in Britain. It appeared to be a solution to the civil war without risking the possibility that the guerrilla leaders would capture power.

The newly elected, Conservative British government, however, decided to make one final effort to reach an overall settlement. Despite a widespread belief that a conference including black domestic and guerrilla leaders, as well as the white representatives, would fail, the British succeeded in bringing the various factions to agree to forego a military solution and abide by the results for a free election. More surprises were in store: The election was won by the more radical Mugabe and not, as expected in London and Washington, by Nkomo; and Mugabe showed himself initially to be a pragmatist and did not dispossess the white farmers and businessmen, whom the newly named Zimbabwe needed if it was to remain prosperous. The Carter administration was thus saved by the British from choosing to alienate either the black states of Africa or the U.S. Senate. (In 1984, however, Mugabe declared that Zimbabwe would become a one-party, Marxist-Leninist state.)

One problem remained, however: The Soviet Union was determined to exploit Third World situations in order to expand its influence. For Moscow, the less-developed world was a natural place to enhance its power. "National liberation" meant the erosion and overthrow of pro-Western regimes—that is, regimes it saw as capitalist, reactionary, and (white) racist. This was all part of the continuing "ideological struggle" that the Soviet Union had never claimed would stop during the era of *détente*. The class struggle to free the exploited and the poor was ordained historically. Thus, as the Soviets saw it, seizing opportunities for undermining the Western position throughout the less-developed world was legitimate and would serve the cause of social justice. Not to do so would be a betrayal of their cause and progressive mankind.

The Soviet Union did not, of course, create these opportunities, which included the collapse of Portuguese colonialism in southern Africa or the white minority governments in Rhodesia and South Africa, or the Somali-supported insurgency in the Ogaden. But it did try and enhance its influence in these situations. In short, the political situation appeared to favor Moscow, and its newly acquired military capability allowed it to act in a way that it could not in Zaire and Cuba in the early 1960s. The Soviet Union now had a sizable surface navy and airlift capacity, so that in Angola it flew in thousands of tons of arms and over 12,000 Cuban troops; and in Ethiopia the Soviets delivered even more arms, 20,000 Cuban troops, plus Soviet technicians and several generals to determine the strategy to drive the Somalis out of the Ogaden.

In a way, it was an old pattern. Already during the cold war the problems of the Third World had affected the superpowers and led to several conflicts. Soviet political strategy after Joseph Stalin's death had been to support the first generation of nationalist but non-Communist leaders of the newly independent countries. They might be bourgeois but their nationalism was directed against the West. Thus a coalition could be forged to weaken the West. But by the early 1970s many of these leaders had either died or they or their successors had turned against the Soviets, who had often made enormous political, economic, and military investments in the Nassers of the Third World. Moscow lost positions of influence in the Sudan and Egypt, which turned toward the West; earlier, it had watched in dismay as Indonesia's Sukarno had turned from the Soviet Union to China before he was overthrown and Indonesia turned to the West.

Thus, while this policy of support for anti-Western nationalist regimes was not abandoned where it could still be pursued as, for example, in Iraq and Syria, the Soviets increasingly turned to helping Marxist or pro-Communist factions gain power and then defending them. Thus the Soviets helped the North Vietnamese with arms supplies during the last phase of the Vietnam War; helped its friends capture power in Angola; assisted Marxist officers to seize power in Ethiopia; helped bring pro-Moscow Marxist regimes into power in Afghanistan and South Yemen; and, by extending a treaty of friendship and cooperation to Hanoi, allowed the former to invade Communist Cambodia and replace the pro-Peking regime there with a pro-Soviet one.

These "pro-Soviet communist regimes in Africa and Asia, imposed by force and backed as they are by Soviet power," to use Donald Zagoria's words,* may of course not necessarily enhance Soviet influence. Communist states, like non-Communist states, have increasingly been divided by nationalism, a force stronger even than Communism—witness, in Asia, the conflicts between the Soviet Union and China, China and Vietnam, and until it invaded Cambodia, Vietnam and Cambodia. In the meantime, however, Soviet intervention had two disturbing effects. The first effect was a rise of regional tensions. In Southeast Asia, the Vietnamese conquest of Cambodia and imposition of a Hanoi-controlled government led to China's punitive invasion of Vietnam, which, had

*"New Soviet Alliances," *Foreign Affairs*, April, 1979, p. 739.

it advanced toward Hanoi or lasted longer, might have led the Soviet Union to punish China by a similar limited border crossing. The dangers were—and remain—obvious. So is the increased danger of Vietnam's expansion and dominance throughout Indochina and other Southeast Asian countries.

In West Asia, in the area from the Horn of Africa to India, the combination of domestic instability, regional conflicts, and growing Soviet influence had also created a dangerous and unstable situation. Brzezinski called the area an "arc of instability." Soviet-Cuban influence in Ethiopia and South Yemen on the Arabian peninsula especially worried the Saudis. Their anxiety about Soviet influence was, moreover, paralleled by anxiety about their internal stability, as they saw the Shah, who, like them, had been using his enormous oil funds to modernize rapidly, overthrown by an opposition led by a clergy upholding traditional Islamic society and opposed to Westernization. The Soviet invasion of Afghanistan and the continued unrest in Iran only worsened the situation.

Fear in the area was thus widespread. Pro-Soviet Iraq, seeking to take advantage of Iran's weakness and domestic preoccupation, attacked Iran, attempting to replace it as the primary Persian Gulf power; it also sought to become the preeminent Arab state and strengthen its role as spokesman for the Arab cause now that Egypt, traditionally the leading Arab power, was isolated as a traitor to that cause. The war, however, divided the Arabs, Syria and Libya supporting Iran and Jordan supporting Iraq; this division increased the rivalries in the area. Saudi Arabia and the other oil kingdoms became fearful of possible airstrikes against their oil fields because they too supported Iraq. And Pakistan, which sent troops to Saudi Arabia to help defend the royal regime, worried over what the Soviets might do as almost 2 million Afghan refugees fled to Pakistan; many of them returned to their homeland to fight with weapons bought (and some, no doubt, supplied by the CIA) in Pakistan.

Always fearful of India, the Pakistanis were rumored to be developing a nuclear bomb to match India's; rumor also had it that Libya, the most radical, anti-American and anti-Israeli Arab state, was financing this development in return for a bomb! Iraq too appeared to be seeking the bomb, a matter of great worry to the Israelis, who presumably already possessed a number of them, as they watched the Iraqis organize the Baghdad front, which rejected Arab peace negotiations with Israel, and Iraq's leader's attempt to become the new Nasser. The Middle East seemed even more of a potential tinderbox than before. And because of its close relationship with Israel and even more because of its dependence on Middle Eastern oil, America could hardly abstain from becoming involved as the superpowers' rivalry was superimposed upon these regional problems. The Carter Doctrine was simply open recognition of the vital interests at stake for the United States in this critical region.

The second effect of Soviet intervention was the impact on *détente* itself. The Soviet Union continued to fish in the troubled Third World waters because the potential gains were high and the costs virtually zero. The problems in Africa or Asia might well be regional, but Soviet-Cuban military interventions in Angola and Ethiopia and involvements in coups in Afghanistan and South Yemen had transformed these local disturbances into aspects of the wider Soviet-American competition for influence. Yet before the invasion of Afghanistan in 1979, no penalties were imposed, and so long as the Soviet Union believed that the United States was paralyzed by the memories of Vietnam, Moscow had no reason to desist. Thus, while the Carter administration abandoned the virtually automatic response to Soviet involvement in the less-developed areas, which characterized American foreign policy during the earlier, bipolar, cold war days and first few years of *détente*, the lack of understanding of the consequences of Soviet-Cuban interventions for American interests and the perception of American power and will as weak by an observing world were very harmful. Increasing sensitivity to the nationalism of the Third World and sympathy for the social struggles and causes involved, while clearly desirable, thus appeared to be an insufficient response. The East-West context continued to intrude. Nowhere was this more vividly demonstrated than in the Middle East, the region that had within a few years become of critical importance to U.S. security and prosperity.

THE MIDDLE EASTERN LINCHPIN

By the 1970s the Middle East with its unstable governments, militancy, and high emotions, and its ability to suck the superpowers into its regional quarrels, increasingly resembled the Balkans at the turn of the century. Even before Carter, the Nixon, and later the Ford, administration resolved to avoid the past pattern in which the Israelis won the military victory but were unable to translate that victory into a political settlement, leaving the Arabs humiliated and resentful, more determined than ever not to accept the right of Israel to exist and willing only to prepare for another round in the struggle. The 1973 war had, in the American evaluation, shown a number of things: the fact that Israel could be caught by surprise, the ability of Arab armies to learn how to use modern weapons effectively, the intolerable cost in manpower losses to Israel of a war lasting longer than a few days, the grave difficulties for the Israeli economy when much of its manpower is mobilized, and the political isolation of Israel in a world in which even the Europeans (except the Dutch) feared the Arab oil weapons and cowered before the people some of whom shortly before they had governed. All these factors spelled further trouble for Israel, whose only friend in the world was now the United States; but in the face of oil embargoes and ever higher energy costs, could Israel continue to count on American support—not for the existence of an Israel within its 1967 borders but for an Israel still holding the territories it had captured?

For Henry Kissinger, the urgency of attempting to reach a Middle East settlement was obvious. And the moment also seemed more favorable than at any earlier time. Anwar Sadat had declared his willingness to accept the existence of Israel and make peace with it on the basis of the 1967 frontiers. Sadat had also been able to organize Arab support for the Egyptian war effort from regimes spanning the spectrum from the ultraconservative to the revolutionary left. Of the former, Saudi Arabia, even wealthier now that oil prices had quadrupled, was the most influential. Anti-Israeli but also anti-Communist and pro-American, the Saudis bankrolled more-moderate regimes such as that in Egypt and made even militant regimes such as that in Syria more dependent upon Saudi money, especially for weapons. Egyptian leadership in the Arab world plus Saudi money made a potent combination, one that the Nixon administration wished to exploit. Finally, the Arab armies for the first time had shown bravery and skill and recovered some Arab self-esteem; diplomatic concessions in these circumstances might be easier. Defeat had only led to inflexibility.

Peace for Israel would also have other desirable consequences. One was avoiding an American-Soviet confrontation that could escalate into a superpower war. Each of the Arab-Israeli wars had harbored the possibility of such a confrontation; in 1973, that possibility had come frighteningly close. Would it be avoidable in yet another Arab-Israeli war? Would the Middle East be the incendiary device initiating the conflagration of World War III, as the Balkans had provided the match for World War I? Another and closely related consequence was the reduction of Soviet influence in the area and its replacement by American influence. American support for Israel had been a principal reason for this Soviet influence. The Soviet Union was a source of weapons and political support for the Arabs. Playing a more even-handed role and arranging for peace, which would achieve security for Israel as well as satisfy Arab territorial and political purposes, would enhance America's position in the area. This was desirable for its own sake, but peace would also have a third consequence, the securing of a reliable source of oil, which was particularly critical at a time when the United States was becoming an oil importer.

Kissinger's strategy for peace was a step-by-step approach. There were too many issues to be settled. To attempt to solve them at one time with all the parties present would be impossible. In a public conference to meet at Geneva, co-chaired by the United States and the Soviet Union, the most extreme Arabs would set the pace; to take a moderate position would in this atmosphere seem to betray the Arab cause. The presence of the Soviet Union was likely to lend support to the militants, because it profited from continued turmoil in the area; without turmoil, the Arabs would perhaps not need the Soviet Union much. And such a conference would openly bring out Israeli-American differences. A step-by-step approach would start with the easier issues and proceed gradually to the hardest ones. The initial task was the disengagement of the Israeli forces and the Egyptians and Syrians after the war; next would be a further Israeli withdrawal in the Sinai and then on the Golan Heights; the last two issues would be the hardest and most emotional—the establishment of a Palestinian state, a cause espoused by the terrorist Palestine Liberation Organization, with whom the Israelis would not even talk directly, and the control of the old city of

Jerusalem. By successfully resolving the initial issues, a momentum would be established to help resolve the more difficult ones; and success would divide the moderates from the more militant regimes, strengthening the former and weakening the latter.

Kissinger was successful in achieving two unprecedented interim agreements—first the disengagement of the hostile forces on the Egyptian Sinai and Syrian Golan fronts, and later a further withdrawal by the Israelis from two strategic passes and an oil well in the Sinai. Throughout, the Soviets denounced Kissinger. Becoming cooler toward the Egyptians, who expected the Americans to pressure the Israelis to leave, the Soviets threw their support behind the more militant Syrians and the PLO. As the Israeli government, which opposed virtually any concessions to the Arabs, became increasingly inflexible, and Egypt became more isolated in the Arab world for having signed the second interim agreement, this strategy promised to permit the Soviets to recoup their influence. Egypt by its agreement had, as the Syrians saw it, left them to face Israel all by themselves; it had agreed to let Israeli-bound cargo on non-Israeli ships pass through the reopened Suez Canal, and it had given general pledges to use diplomacy, not force, in the settlement of Egyptian and, more broadly, Arab-Israeli differences. To the Syrians and many Arabs, these acts were tantamount to a betrayal of the Arab cause.

The Carter administration, upon coming into power, viewed this situation with alarm. Carter, and particularly Brzezinski, believed therefore that the step-by-step approach had reached its end. It had, in their view, some fundamental liabilities. One, Israel was required in each step to give up territory for promises that when all steps had been taken it and its neighbors would sign a peace treaty and Israel would be accorded legitimacy. But by then, it would no longer have any bargaining cards to trade. Two, the incremental approach avoided the central problem of the Palestinians, whose grievances would have to be met if a genuine peace were ever to be established; the Kissinger way of trying to deal with the easy problems first, and then hopefully gaining sufficient momentum and trust among the negotiating parties to resolve the difficult issues later, frittered away precious time and might thereby jeopardize the possibility of peace. The greatest danger was that if the key differences between Israel and the Arabs were not resolved, Sadat would either be outflanked by militant anti-Israeli, pro-Soviet, anti-American Arabs; be overthrown within his own country by a militant; or, in order to survive politically, if not physically, be forced to play the role of the new Nasser. Time, in brief, was not on the side of the United States.

The Carter administration therefore proposed that all parties resume negotiations at Geneva; such a meeting, in Kissinger's mind, would only have taken place at the end when all steps had been successfully taken and would then have symbolized the end of Arab-Israeli hostility. This proposal had at least two serious handicaps. The first was the Palestinians. Who would represent them? How would they be represented? Indeed, would they be represented? It was clear that the Arab states would not even go to Geneva unless the Palestinians were there and that meant the PLO. The PLO, however, was not a state, even if it considered itself a state-in-waiting, and Israel had no intention of dealing with the PLO; it considered the organization to be a gang of murderers dedicated to the elimination of Israel as a state. With these attitudes, it would not permit the establishment of a Palestinian state.

The second handicap was the Soviets. Kissinger had fashioned his strategy to exclude them; only at the final conference would the Soviet Union attend as the co-chairman. Carter, determined to call a Geneva conference and to do so before the end of 1977, decided to approach the Soviets and enlist their cooperation. Moscow had influence with the more militant Syrians and the PLO, and it therefore had the capacity to cause a lot of trouble and block negotiations. If, on the other hand, Moscow helped the peace negotiations, it would presumably retain a degree of influence in the Arab world if and when a peace treaty between Israel and the Arab states was signed, reduce the possibility of a superpower clash, and help strengthen *détente* with the United States.

Neither Jerusalem nor Cairo was happy with the Soviet-American accord in late 1977. Even though it excluded any reference to a Palestinian state or a total Israeli withdrawal to the 1967 frontiers, both of which the Soviets favored, and committed both powers to a peace in which all Middle Eastern states were to have secure boundaries, the Israelis objected and the Egyptians were unhappy. It was probably because of this that Sadat, who had broken his ties with the Soviet Union, decided to strike out on his own and that the Israelis were recep-

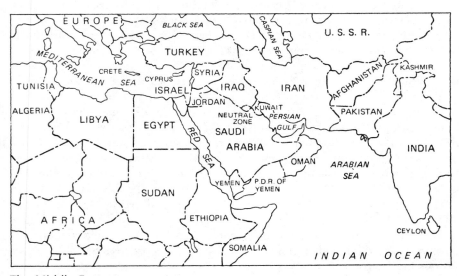

The Middle East

tive to his proposal to bypass Washington and negotiate directly. In a dramatic and internationally televised visit to Jerusalem in November 1977, during which he addressed the Israeli Parliament, Sadat, the leader of the Arab world's strongest nation, in effect extended recognition to the Arabs' archenemy. He expressed his hope that there would be no more war. The impact was euphoric as a comprehensive peace—a peace with all of Israel's Arab enemies—seemed near.

The mood did not last long. Sadat apparently believed peace was easily and quickly achievable since he had taken the significant psychological step to reassure the Israelis that his peace offer was genuine, not a trick. Israel would withdraw to its 1967 frontiers from the Sinai, the West Bank, Syria's Golan Heights, and Jordan's East Jerusalem and would recognize the Palestinians' legitimate rights; and, in return for their land, the Arabs would sign a peace treaty and Israel would gain the legitimacy and peace with security it had sought since birth. The Israelis had long publicly asserted that if only the Arabs would negotiate with them directly, implying recognition, they would be willing to return the territories taken in 1967. Israel had specifically disclaimed annexationist ambitions. The Labor government after the 1967 war had accepted U.N. Resolution 242 committing Israel to the withdrawal from the captured land (or, given some adjustments for security reasons, from almost all).

But the new coalition government led by Prime Minister Menachem Begin, who had spent his parliamentary life in opposition, had other ideas. He proposed to withdraw from the Sinai desert, but he offered the Palestinians on the West Bank and in the Gaza Strip only autonomy, or self-rule, not self-determination. They could elect their own representatives and govern their own affairs but Israeli security interests remained preeminent. The army would therefore remain, and Israel would retain a veto over the question of Palestinian immigration (the return of the Palestinian refugees displaced by the 1948 war and now living in other lands, such as Lebanon). Begin referred to the West Bank by its ancient Hebrew names, Judea and Samaria; the prime minister claimed that they were not occupied territory to be returned but liberated territory to be kept as a part of the Greater Israel of which Begin had long dreamed. The most he would concede was that Israel would recognize that there were other claims to sovereignty over the West Bank and Gaza Strip, that the issue would be deferred for five years and could then be negotiated by the interested parties. But he left the impression that he was irrevocably committed to keeping Judea, Samaria, and Gaza and that he expected to establish Israeli sovereignty over both areas, each of which contained several hundred thousand Arabs. In the meantime, the Israeli government announced that Jewish settlements in the Sinai and West Bank would remain and encouraged more settlements.

To Sadat, Begin's plan for the West Bank and Gaza meant the perpetuation of Israeli military occupation under the guise of autonomy. And without a settlement of the Palestinian issue satisfactory to the Palestinians and withdrawal of Israel from the conquered Arab territories, he could not sign a separate peace with Israel. To do so would be to brand himself as a traitor and become isolated in the Arab world. Indeed, after his trip to Jerusalem, Syria, Libya, Iraq, Algeria, South Yemen, and the PLO had condemned him and formed a "rejectionist front." Sadat, in turn, had broken diplomatic relations with the five states. But there were limits to his freedom of maneuver. He therefore insisted that the first order of business was to agree to a declaration of principles regarding Israeli withdrawal from all Arab land and self-determination for the Palestinians, which would open the way for Jordan and the Palestinians to negotiate the issue of the West Bank's and Gaza's futures themselves. Having gained such commitments from Israel for his "Arab brothers," Sadat felt he could then sign a separate peace with Israel and relieve his country, which had done most of the fighting in four wars, from the burden of heavy defense spending and concentrate on improving the domestic economy and doing something for the people of Egypt.

Since Begin's offer fell considerably short of the concessions Sadat needed, the bilateral negotiations broke down. The fear of what might happen next brought the United States back into the negotiating process. American interests were clear. First, the United States was committed to the security of Israel. But from the American point of view, another war would be even more costly in lives for Israel than the 1973 war, and, as before, Israeli victory would not bring with it a favorable political settlement; it would only lead to more Arab resentment and humiliation. Second, and of even greater concern, was the fear that it might also bring about a Soviet-American clash, as had almost happened in 1973. Third, the United States, Western Europe, and Japan needed oil to preserve the political, social, and economic viability of their societies. If no Arab-Israeli peace accord could be reached, and if a fifth war should erupt, another and longer oil embargo was expected to be very damaging even if an American-Soviet military clash were avoided.

But war or no war, if Sadat, who had turned away from Moscow toward Washington, failed to achieve a peace that the Arabs would consider fair and just and that could therefore enlist the support of other pro-American, moderate Arab states such as Jordan and Saudi Arabia, they would all feel compelled to turn against the United States. In such circumstances, Saudi Arabia would not be able by itself to hold out against the course adopted by the other Arab states once more to seek resolution of the Israeli problem through confrontation. Access to oil and the price of oil would clearly become a weapon in this struggle, particularly because its successful use in 1973 had demonstrated how vulnerable the West was and how much it feared the use of oil as a means of pressuring it. Not only did the Carter administration, therefore, feel that another war was to be avoided but also that progress toward a settlement was imperative.

The effect of American intervention as a mediator in the stalled Israeli-Egyptian negotiations, however, was to bring into the open what Kissinger had expected to put off with his step-by-step approach but had himself not been completely able to avoid during the negotiations of the second interim agreement—namely, American-Israeli differences on how to achieve peace. Carter, like Kissinger, felt that Sadat was offering Israel for the first time in its existence the security and peace it had so long sought, and if this opportunity was not seized the result would be disastrous for Israel and the West, as the Arabs might use their oil weapon and turn again toward Moscow. Israel was already basically isolated diplomatically. Even before the 1973 war, the West Europeans had become increasingly sympathetic to the idea of an end to Arab-Israeli hostilities: recognition by the Arabs of Israel's right to existence for a return of the territories seized in 1967. The war and the oil threat made them even more sympathetic to the Arab position. The United States had thus become Israel's sole source of diplomatic support internationally, providing sophisticated military equipment, especially fighters, and economic aid. In 1976, for example, public assistance amounted to $2.34 billion, which meant that the American taxpayer was paying each man, woman, and child in Israel $700! And the Israeli government now proceeded to alienate Washington as well.

The Carter administration had, upon coming into power, quickly made known what it thought were the ingredients of a solution in the Middle East. One, U.N. Resolution 242 meant the return of most of the Arab territory Israel had captured in 1967. Only minor adjustments for security reasons could be allowed. Two (and in this respect the administration went far beyond any of its predecessors), it boldly asserted that the key to peace was the Palestinian issue. More specifically, it said that the Palestinians had the right to participate in the peace-making process and Carter himself soon publicly declared that the Palestinians had a right to a "homeland" (a term that was deliberately left vague, but nevertheless the use of the term was symbolically significant). Three, in return for such Israeli concessions, the Arab states had to commit themselves not only to ending their state of hostilities with Israel but also to signing a peace treaty followed by such things as diplomatic exchanges, trade, and tourism. The Israelis had been insistent upon this point and the Arabs were balking at such normalization, declaring that it would take a whole generation for this to occur after so much bitterness and anger.

The first two positions were clearly at odds with those of Begin, who had proceeded to reinterpret U.N. Resolution 242, accepted by his predecessors, to mean that Israel was not required to withdraw from the West Bank and Gaza. He was also opposed to a Palestinian state which he, and indeed most Israelis, felt would constitute a danger to the existence of Israel. The issue that symbolically played the role of highlighting these differences between Israel and the United States was the settlements policy. Ever since 1967, the United States had consistently opposed Israeli settlements in the occupied lands as illegal. The Carter administration repeated this while it watched with disbelief as the Israeli government actively encouraged new settlements on the land the Arabs were reclaiming. It appeared as if Israel was deliberately setting out to destroy the one chance it had ever had to gain legitimacy and peace; it certainly impressed Washington, as it did Sadat, as an act of bad faith to plant such settlements in the midst of peace negotiations. Secretary of State Cyrus Vance, a diplomat's diplomat who was careful in his choice of word lest he offend, expressed the administration's anger when he declared that Israeli settlements were not only illegal but an "obstacle to peace."

Repeated American efforts to halt this policy and encourage the Israelis to hold out more hope to the Arabs for the eventual recovery of the West Bank and Gaza were all in vain. Consequently, Israeli policy was increasingly perceived by much of the world as annexationist, using Israel's genuine security needs as a disguise for seizing Arab land. For Washington, therefore, the issue was not what Begin accused it of doing—attempting to dictate Israeli policy—but how much longer the American people ought to finance an untenable stalemate that, when it exploded, would hurt not just Israel but the United States and all of its major allies.

By contrast, Sadat appeared reasonable and conciliatory. He had with great courage provided the psychological breakthrough with his trip to Jerusalem. He had shown characteristic sensitivity to Israel's security needs by being willing to listen to various ideas for demilitarizing or thinning out forces in certain areas, placing U.N. forces between Israeli and Arab armies, and phasing in agreements over five, ten, and fifteen years as Israeli trust in the Arabs' good intentions grew; and he had been willing to accept Israel's demands for a peace treaty and the subsequent normalization of relations not after twenty-five years, or even five years, but immediately. As an indication of his sympathies for Sadat and Saudi Arabia, without whose support the Egyptian leader could not have survived politically in his solo attempt to achieve an Arab-Israeli peace, Carter tied the sale to Israel of American fighters to the sale of fighters to Egypt and Saudi Arabia. Not only had modern and sophisticated American fighter planes not been shipped to these countries before, but never had arms for Israel been tied to a shipment of arms for Arab states. Senate approval of this package deal was indicative of American disapproval of Israeli policy and support for Sadat's offer to make peace essentially on terms declared acceptable by previous and less Zionistically zealous Labor governments.

Nevertheless, the stalemate continued. As the three-year, second interim Sinai agreement was about to run out in October 1978, Sadat began to sound more ominous about a settlement. President Carter therefore took a gamble and invited Begin and Sadat to meet with him at Camp David. It was a gamble because had this summit meeting produced no results, the president's prestige, already low, would have been even more seriously impaired, American mediating attempts would have run their course, and Israeli-American relations would have been set back even further. But the president, for perhaps the first time in his administration, showed persistence and skill and emerged after twelve days of patient negotiations with a series of agreements, including a commitment by the two men to sign a peace treaty within three months.

Sadat made most of the concessions. He did not gain a commitment to an

eventual Israeli withdrawal from the West Bank and Gaza Strip, or full Palestinian self-determination. Begin was still sticking to his formula for autonomy for
the Palestinians. Sadat did gain an Israeli commitment, however, to recognize
"the legitimate rights of the Palestinians," a pledge that the West Bank and
Gaza Palestinians would participate in future negotiations on these areas and
ratify or reject a final agreement, and a temporary freeze on Israeli settlements
on the West Bank. But Israel kept a veto power over the participation of the
PLO leaders in such negotiations or the establishment of a Palestinian state.
Thus the Israeli position had remained intact. Yet Israel gained a separate peace
treaty with the strongest of its Arab neighbors; the others could not by themselves take on Israel without Egypt. Thus for a seemingly small investment
Israel gained the enormous dividend of a real sense of security, since Jordan or
Syria alone or together were too weak to wage war against Israel. That was why,
in fact, Syria had opposed Sadat's journey to Jerusalem and the subsequent
bilateral negotiations. Once the threat of war with Egypt had ended, there
would be no reason why Israel should return the Golan Heights to Syria.

Sadat, however, had taken a gamble. Rather than having sold out, he appears
to have felt that a momentum could be built up because the West Bank and
Gaza Palestinians would gain representation and a degree of power. The Palestinians, who could, after all, elect pro-PLO representatives, would also gain a
voice with which to state their legitimate aims. This momentum would start
with an Israeli withdrawal of the Sinai settlements, an Egyptian-Israeli peace
treaty, and a subsequent total Israeli withdrawal from the Sinai. Sadat also
hoped that Jordan would join the negotiations about the future status of the
West Bank and that the Saudis would continue to support him. In brief, as the
peace process began in earnest with the initial Israeli pullback from the Sinai,
an irreversible process would begin.

The first Arab reaction to Camp David was, however, negative. Jordan and
even Saudi Arabia now joined the rejectionist front of Syria, Iraq, Libya, and
Algeria in condemning Sadat. Thus, instead of widening his base of support in
the Arab world, Sadat was more isolated than ever. Under these circumstances,
President Carter's personal intervention by making a trip to Egypt and Israel
produced the necessary diplomatic breakthroughs and brought peace between
these two long-term enemies.

Yet this treaty did not bring a stable peace to the area. On the eve of the
Israeli-Egyptian peace treaty in March 1979, Prime Minister Begin in a defiant
mood told his parliament—and therefore the Arabs—that Israel would never
withdraw to its 1967 borders, Jerusalem would remain Israel's "eternal capital,"
and that there would never be a Palestinian state on the West Bank and Gaza.
Thus the prospect for regional peace remained somber. For a stable and long-
run peace could be created only if the peace process continued after Israel and
Egypt signed a peace treaty. If, on the other hand, Israel, with Egypt now
neutralized, was unwilling to accommodate the grievances and aspirations of
the Palestinians, Jordanians, and Syrians, the peace treaty would be subjected

to great strain. As it was, in the wake of the peace treaty, Egypt's fellow Arab states, including Saudi Arabia, suspended Egypt's membership in the Arab League and established an economic boycott; most of them broke diplomatic relations with Egypt.

Thus, the Carter administration, having initially rejected Kissinger's step-by-step approach for a comprehensive peace treaty, ended up embracing Kissinger's approach. His idea had been that by resolving easier problems first, a momentum would be built up that would eventually resolve the more difficult problems. Brzezinski's rejection of his predecessor's diplomatic strategy had been based on the grounds that it postponed the critical Palestinian issue too long and that time might not be on Sadat's side. How ironic that his predictions might yet prove correct as the administration, fearful of the immense domestic battle that might occur if it really exerted great pressure on Israel to be more conciliatory, returned to the incremental approach and, instead of creating the momentum to resolve the issues of the West Bank and Gaza, the Golan Heights, and Jerusalem, made the urgency of resolving them far greater and the likelihood of so doing much smaller!

The ink on the Israeli-Egyptian peace treaty was hardly dry when Israel announced the formation of new settlements on the West Bank. Israel was clearly making sure that the West Bank would belong to Israel. Not long afterward, the Israelis began to dispossess the Arabs of their land. Since resistance to this policy enhanced pro-PLO sentiment, the military occupation became increasingly repressive and the censorship tightened as Israel appeared bent on annexing Arab land with a sizable Arab population which, given its high birth rate, would threaten the future of Israel as a Jewish state.

American policy often appeared to be the prisoner of Israeli policy. If any state was dependent upon another it was Israel. America was about the only state left that still supported Israel diplomatically, militarily, and economically, almost without reservation. The United States had a long commitment to the defense of Israel. The United States, a world power, also had two other interests: avoiding a Soviet-American confrontation if another regional war occurred and assuring future oil supplies for itself and its allies. America did not mean to achieve these goals at Israel's expense. Rather, American policy was intended to help Israel achieve peace and security, but Israeli policy often seemed self-defeating, short-sighted, and increasingly annexationist. Yet America exerted no pressure on Israel to be more accommodating; instead it continued to finance and militarily support an increasingly untenable political situation.

The Arabs, of course, held the United States responsible for a peace treaty that omitted resolving the key Palestinian problem and for an Israeli policy that was calculated to make a comprehensive peace impossible. Symbolic was the unilateral Israeli decision to incorporate East Jerusalem into Jerusalem and declare that the city would never again be divided. The action aroused great anger through the Arab lands. The Arabs attributed Israeli policy to American acquiescence. American efforts to be more evenhanded after 1973 appeared to have ended in a return to the pre–1973, one-sided support of Israel, regardless of how provocative Israeli actions were. Did the United States not know its own interests? This question was particularly asked in Saudi Arabia, upon whose oil the United States now greatly depended and whose position in the Arab world had been endangered by Washington's stance.

Saudi Arabia, strongly traditional and conservative, as well as pro-Western and anti-Communist, was naturally pro-American as it sought U.S. help for its modernization and defense. A small country in population, it could not by itself continue to support Sadat's peace efforts after the failure of the Camp David agreement to tackle what the Arabs saw as the central problem of Palestinian self-determination; the royal family feared for its security, threatened among other enemies, by the millions of foreign workers, many of them Palestinians and other Arabs, whom Saudi Arabia needed in its drive to create a more modern society. The Saudis did not like the position in which they were placed by American Middle East policy: a separation from Egypt, which, under Sadat, was also a moderate, pro-Western and anti-Communist state; a "distancing" from the United States in order to avoid too close an identification with it and consequently being labeled a traitor by the rest of the Arab world; and a fear that if the peace negotiations stalled, Soviet and radical Arab influences would again rise while the influence of the United States, to whom Arab moderates had looked for help in gaining a peace that would satisfy Arab needs, would decline once more. In these circumstances, Saudi Arabia might be called upon by the other Arab states to use its oil weapon against the United States; and the Saudis might feel compelled to go along. American policy appeared to be counterproductive if it wished to assure steady oil supplies.

Thus, while the Saudis were being asked to raise oil production to meet American needs and restrain the "price hawks" among the oil producers, their confidence in the wisdom of U.S. policy and American leadership declined. This lack of confidence was reinforced by the perception of an increasing lack of credibility of American power as Iran's Shah was overthrown; the Soviets, whose influence was already established in Ethiopia and neighboring South Yemen, invaded Afghanistan; and the Saudis, along with the rest of the world, watched the new Islamic Republic of Iran humiliate the United States by seizing American diplomats in their embassy in Teheran while the United States for fourteen months appeared impotent and incompetent to deal with the situation.

IRAN AND THE END OF THE VIETNAM SYNDROME

The year 1979 witnessed, as noted earlier, the crumbling of the American positions in Southwest Asia. Deterioration began in Iran, second only to Saudi Arabia in non-Communist world oil production, with the overthrow of the Shah. Iran's oil production fell off sharply and the resulting tightening of world oil supplies led to almost a 100 percent increase in the price of oil by early 1980 (130 percent by the spring of 1980), with devastating effects on inflation and unemployment in the industrial world, especially in the United States. Most important of all, however, was the spectacle of a disintegrating American position in an area of absolutely vital importance for the United States.

The event that came to symbolize the iow level to which American resolution and power had fallen was the invasion of the American embassy in Teheran in November 1979 by a mob of militant students, who seized American embassy personnel. This outrage occurred after the deposed Shah, suffering from cancer, had been admitted to the United States for medical treatment. (He died a few months later in Egypt.) The revolutionary authorities gave the unprecedented action—not even Hitler or Stalin had tried to seize enemy diplomats—their blessing and support. The subsequent efforts by the Carter administration to gain the safe release of the Americans became high public drama. Under the watchful eyes of the cameras of the three major U.S. television networks, the American public was repeatedly exposed to pictures of crowds, like well-rehearsed choruses, chanting their hatred of America, the "Great Satan," as it was called by the Ayatollah Ruhollah Khomeini, Iran's chief religious leader. "Death to America," the crowds screamed constantly. In frequent television interviews Khomeini and other Iranian leaders lectures the American public on its wicked ways for America's past support of the Shah and spoke mockingly of the U.S. naval power gathering in the Indian Ocean. They virtually dared the president to use it.

In the 444 days following the taking of the hostages, the world watched as the Carter administration tried one means after another to gain their release: appeals to the United Nations and the International Court of Justice, both of which were ignored by Iran, and a series of economic sanctions, which were largely ineffective since Japan and Western Europe needed Iran's oil more than the United States did. All was in vain, for the holding of the hostages was a symbolic act, both of defiance and revenge, for the Shah was seen by the new regime as an American puppet who had cruelly exploited Iranians on behalf of U.S. interests. As the administration's patience wore thin, it attempted a rescue mission in the spring of 1980. Its failure, caused by a series of helicopter malfunctions and the crash of a helicopter into a refueling aircraft at a desert stop, at which time the mission was abandoned, dramatically symbolized the humiliation and apparent helplessness, clumsiness, and impotence of the United States, as well as the low level of readiness, competence, and reliability of its armed forces.

Two events finally helped gain the hostages' release on January 29, 1981. The first was the Iraqi attack on Iran in the fall of 1980. The war suddenly made the U.S. economic sanctions, especially the freeze on Iranian money in U.S. banks, painful because Iran's military forces were largely American equipped; the need for spare parts and the cash to buy them and other goods grew as oil production in Iran fell to almost nothing. The second event that spurred negotiations to gain the hostages' freedom was the November victory of California Governor Ronald Reagan as the next president. Since he had run on a tough foreign policy platform and denounced the Iranians as "barbarians" and "kidnappers," the Iranians had every right to expect harsher measures, including military ones, after January 20. In these circumstances, diplomacy finally proved successful, and symbolically, the actual release of the fifty-two diplomats and marines (black and female personnel already had been released) occurred just after Reagan's inauguration. A humiliating chapter in American history had ended. In the exuberance of the welcome that the ex-hostages received upon their return to America one could almost hear the refrain "never again." For in a real sense, America itself and the U.S. government had been taken captive and held hostage.

Until Vietnam, the United States had been extensively involved in the world, and it had justified its role as being anti-Communist. As in the two wars against Germany, the cold war was a moral cause: democracy versus dictatorship. After Vietnam, the reaction set in. The American pattern had long been one of swings from isolationism to crusading and back again. Thus the mood of disillusionment and disengagement from the burdens of more than two decades of American-Soviet conflict—plus the accompanying sense of shame and guilt about the uses to which American power had been put—found their outlet in the Carter administration's rejection of the "inordinate fear of Communism"; the emphasis on America's "limited power" and restraint in its exercise; the avoidance of force or covert intervention in the domestic affairs of other states; a preference for North-South cooperation to erase poverty and broaden human rights—or, at least, reduce the worst abuses of them; a distaste for East-West relations, except for arms control; and a repudiation of old-fashioned power politics in favor of reorienting U.S. policy toward the forces said to be transforming world politics.

Interdependence as a theory fitted the temper of the 1970s like a glove. If balance-of-power considerations were indeed becoming less critical and economic forces and global welfare more important, there was little reason to worry about the Soviet Union despite its steadily growing military power. The reasons advanced for not worrying were many: The Soviets were just catching up with the United States; they had to worry over China as well as the North Atlantic Treaty Organization; and, given the frequency of past invasions, they were just insecure. But, it was forecast, once they had achieved parity with the United States, they would stop. When they did not stop, new explanations said it did not really matter: Nuclear weapons were suicidal and conventional ones too costly to use; the Soviets were just wasting their money; the Soviet leaders were clearly in need of education for thinking that past patterns of behavior would be as useful in the future as in the past.

In any event, whatever the level of Soviet military capability, there was little need to worry about Soviet intentions. By the middle 1970s, it was commonplace to regard the cold war as over. The Soviet Union was said to be a *status quo* power; it might still mouth ideological slogans and revolutionary global aims, but these had about the same practical effect on Soviet policy as most Western churchgoers' Christian beliefs had on their everyday behavior. At worst, Soviet Russia—like Tsarist Russia—might still harbor imperial ambitions like those of other Great Powers throughout history; but these were of a limited nature, not at all comparable to the universal goals of revolutionary powers. The Soviet Union in the 1970s was no longer considered a revolutionary power. Nationalism in the Third World, the determination of the ex-colonial countries to assert their identity and interests, would insure that they would not become Soviet colonies.

The upshot of this unwillingness to face fully the "real world," to explain away continued superpower competition, to minimize concern for the results of this competition while it remained largely one-sided, and the reluctance to assert American power was predictable. The Soviets sensed that they could defy the United States without fear of retaliation. Perhaps indicative of this state of affairs was President Carter's handling of the issue of the Soviet combat brigade that U.S. intelligence had discovered in Cuba in the summer of 1979. The president first declared that this *"status quo* was not acceptable." When Moscow rejected Carter's claim that Soviet troops in Cuba constituted a combat force and said that they were there merely to train Cubans, Carter accepted this reassurance and accepted the very *status quo* he had a few days earlier found unacceptable. Moscow refused to budge on this issue, even though it might—and did—hurt the chances of SALT II's passage through the Senate; rather than risk a confrontation or a delay of SALT II, Carter changed his mind.

Clearly, a few thousand troops in Cuba were not equivalent to the Soviet missiles of 1962, and the president would have been better off not to have precipitated a confrontation over this issue. But once he had, much of the world did remember 1962 and saw the United States in 1979 as a country no longer so strong militarily nor so willing to employ its power (and not just military power) in support of its commitments or declared interests. Is it any wonder that shortly thereafter, having seen the United States frequently change its mind, hesitate, or remain passive since Angola in 1975, the Soviet Union felt it could invade Afghanistan without fear of U.S. retaliation? Or that Iran thought it could seize American diplomatic personnel with impunity and that the sizable U.S. naval forces gathered in the Indian Ocean after the seizure were only a bluff?

Yet the capture of the hostages and invasion of Afghanistan dispelled much of the post-Vietnam atmosphere as the pendulum of public opinion swung once more to a demand for a more assertive and vigorous policy that would guard the nation's interests and preserve its sense of self-respect. Khomeini and Leonid Brezhnev may have done the United States a favor, for it took a German submarine attack on U.S. ships (World War I), a Japanese attack on Pearl Harbor (World War II), and a Soviet coup in Czechoslovakia (cold war), to mobilize the nation when the public mood was one of disengagement and relaxation. After years of pseudoisolationism, the two successive slaps in the face in November and December of 1979, may have been necessary to demonstrate that impotence can only result in national shame. President Carter sensed this shift of mood as he himself took a harder line toward the Soviets. But it was to be the Republican candidate, Ronald Reagan, who received the full measure of the benefit of this shift of mood. He had long taken a hard line toward the Soviet Union; and while the U.S. inflation and weak state of the economy in general may have been the primary factors in accounting for Reagan's election as president in 1980, the fact remains that because of OPEC and the collapse of the Shah, the domestic economic issue was inseparable from American foreign policy and the U.S. position in the world. As on earlier occasions when America had felt provoked, its reaction was predictable. The pendulum of public opinion swung back part of the way to a recognition of the continuation of American-Soviet rivalry and a more vigorous reassertion of American interests and power.

Chapter 11

REAGAN AND COLD WAR II

PRESIDENTIAL IDEOLOGY AND ANTI-COMMUNISM

By the time Ronald Reagan came into office, the national disillusionment with *détente* was widespread. The term "cold war II" was more and more frequently being used. The president's long-term hostility toward Communism in general and, more specifically, the Soviet Union as the strongest of the Communist states, fitted the new post*détente* mood. The Soviet threat became the center-piece for the Reagan administration. No more was to be heard about "world-order politics," the cold war being over, North-South issues taking priority over East-West issues, or the limits of American power. Quite the opposite: The president often sounded like an old evangelist rather than a reborn Christian. The president never indicated that he thought American power had been abused or that the United States should feel ashamed or guilty about the past exercise of American power. Vietnam had been an "honorable" war. He denounced Soviet Communism as "the focus of evil in the modern world." "There is sin and evil in the world," the president said, "and we are enjoined by the scripture and the Lord Jesus to oppose it with all our might." Opposition to the Soviet Union was therefore a religious as well as political imperative. Often Reagan sounded like a crusader, even if in practice he also showed tendencies toward pragmatism and caution.

President Reagan clearly thought of the American-Soviet conflict as not only the critical struggle in the world but also as one of good versus evil, right versus wrong. The president was probably more of an ideologue than any of his prede-cessors. In that respect, he most resembled John Foster Dulles, President Eisenhower's Secretary of State. Reagan talked of the march of freedom and democracy leaving "Marxism-Leninism on the ashheap of history;" of the "great revolutionary crisis" of the Soviet political-economic system and the "decay of the Soviet experiment;" and of Eastern Europe he said, "Regimes planted by bayonets do not take roots"—that is, the Communist's regimes had no legitimacy. He stated that the United States could not accept the "permanent subjugation of the people of Eastern Europe"; Yalta during World War II had not divided Europe into Soviet and American spheres of influence (which was true since the Soviets had promised free elections in the countries of Eastern Europe at Yalta, and then placed Communist regimes in power at bayonet point). In making the point that democracy and freedom were the waves of the future, rather than Communism as the Soviet leadership constantly claimed, the President was in a sense giving the Soviets a dose of their own medicine of denunciations of the U.S. and forecasts of the "inevitable end" of Western capitalism; but, more important, he was questioning the legitimacy and longevity of Communism as a social and political system, not only in Eastern Europe but also in the Soviet Union itself. That really irritated the Soviets.

In his first four years in office, Reagan held no summit meetings with the Soviet leadership. He did not meet Brezhnev and when Brezhnev died, Reagan refused to attend his funeral; neither then nor afterward did he meet the new Soviet leader, Andropov, or his successor, Chernenko, after Andropov's death. Reagan's three predecessors had held at least one such top-level meeting during their administrations. Nixon had held summits annually after 1972.

Symptomatic of Reagan's strong anti-Communism was his attitude toward Communist China. The reconciliation of the United States with China was the product of the Soviet Union's growing power; that is, the reason for their moving closer together from positions of mutual dislike and hostility was a strategic one. But the president's ideological sympathies were with the Nationalist Chinese on Taiwan. His administration, therefore, initially appeared to downgrade Communist China's military strength and political influence, even though she held down about fifty Soviet divisions along her long frontier with the Soviet Union. Simultaneously, by pursuing a tough anti-Soviet policy (more often in rhetoric than in practice), the president offered Peking few reasons to be more accommodating toward Washington. Why should China offer concessions to the United States when its president was so strongly hostile to the Soviet Union? Chinese concessions would be far more likely if Washington were also negotiating meaningfully with Moscow, and Peking wished to prevent the establishment of closer relations between the two superpowers.

During the *détente* of the early–middle 1970s, the United States had gained leverage when both Communist states were negotiating with it and each wished to avoid the other's gaining greater influence in Washington and benefits from its "American connection." Whereas Nixon had positioned himself between the Soviet Union and China to try and play the "China card" against the Kremlin, Reagan's hard line against Moscow allowed China to place itself in the middle and encouraged it to distance itself somewhat from Washington and play its "American card" to try and achieve a *détente* of its own with Moscow.

Admittedly, there were limits to which such a *détente* could go because the Soviet Union was unwilling to meet basic Chinese demands and China could not go too far in breaking with the United States lest the Soviet preeminence that had originally driven China toward America be reestablished. Still, a major relaxation of Sino-Soviet tension could complicate, if not weaken, American policy. In any event, Reagan's anti-Communism made it unnecessary for Peking to be more accommodating toward Washington, as the president discovered on his journey there when his hosts censored his anti-Soviet remarks on television.

Yet the United States could not really afford a break with Peking either, and once more face, as during cold war I, an alliance of the two Communist states. The president was thus torn two ways. Clearly, Reagan's "heart" lay with the defunct Nationalist regime on Taiwan. At one time he even talked of upgrading the United States mission there to a full-fledged embassy, even though the United States had officially recognized the People's Republic in 1979 and transferred its embassy to Peking from Taiwan. Reagan's policy thus bordered on the edge of the old "two Chinas" solution despite the fact that the 1972 Shanghai communiqué issued at the end of President Nixon's visit had stated that there was only "one China." On the other hand, after frequent expressions of Chinese irritation over American arms sales to the Nationalists so that they could continue to defend themselves against a possible invasion by the Communist regime to reunify all of China, the Reagan administration did sign an agreement in 1982 in which the United States for the first time agreed to cap the quality and quantity of arms sales to Taiwan and phase out these sales. Peking, in turn, restated that its basic policy was to seek peaceful reunification with Taiwan. Ideology and pragmatism thus struggled with each other in the Reagan administration, strongly reflecting the president's own inner conflicts. While Taiwan once again almost became an obstacle to maintaining the more critical strategic relationship of the United States and the People's Republic of China, the president's visit to China in the spring of 1983 was a concession to strategic reality. It was also an attempt, like Nixon's in 1972, to enhance his image as a statesman in the upcoming presidential election year. Given his lack of any dramatic foreign policy successes and great public concern that he might get the country into war somewhere—in Central America, if not with the Soviet Union—the president needed a successful trip to China to show he was a peacemaker and superpower leader. Reagan's domestic needs seem to have been a stronger reason for the trip than the country's strategic ones, although both were enhanced by this journey.

Reagan's anti-Communist feelings were, simply put, very deep, even if in practice he had to focus them primarily on the Soviet Union. In his early days as president, he had said that the Soviet leaders would lie, steal, cheat, and do anything else to advance their goals. When critics questioned this and other blanket condemnations, arguing that the United States and the Soviet Union had to live together in the world and that the president's constant denunciations of Moscow would make productive arms negotiations less likely and nuclear war more so, the Soviets did something to make the president's characterization of them look almost moderate. They shot down a South Korean Boeing 747 airliner flying home from Alaska. Some 269 people were killed. The affair was an extraordinary commentary on Soviet behavior for two reasons. First, the Soviets lied about it for a week. Initially they disclaimed any knowledge of the affair; then they said that a Soviet fighter had intercepted the plane but that it had flown out of the Soviet airspace into which it had strayed; then they admitted that the fighter had shot tracers to warn the airliner, after which it had flown away; and finally they confessed that the intruding airplane had been "downed." Second, the Soviets blamed the United States for their act. They claimed that the Central Intelligence Agency had used the South Korean plane as a spy plane. In fact, the Soviets later admitted that they had believed that the civilian airliner was an American reconnaissance plane (a Boeing 707), whose silhouette is a lot smaller and quite different from that of a 747. Quite apart from the questions this raises about Soviet pilot training, the lying, the shifting of responsibility, the refusal to admit that they had made a bad mistake, the fact that the Soviets would shoot down an unarmed plane, regardless of what it was, instead of escorting it out of Soviet airspace or forcing it to land on Soviet soil, aroused an enormous furor in the West.

> What can we think of a regime that so broadly trumpets its visions of peace and global disarmament and yet so callously and quickly commits a terrorist act to sacrifice the lives of innocent human beings?
>
> What can be said about Soviet credibility, when they so flagrantly lie about such a heinous act? What can be the scope of legitimate mutual discourse with a state whose values permit such atrocities? And what are we to make of a regime which establishes one set of standards for itself, and another for the rest of human kind?

The president's words seemed heartfelt. Soviet behavior had confirmed his view of the Soviet regime as brutal and uncivilized. (This was to be reinforced when, shortly afterward, an Italian government prosecutor in an official report strongly suggested that the Soviet secret police, whose head at the time had been Andropov, Brezhnev's successor, had been behind the Bulgarian secret police's hiring of a Turkish terrorist and his attempted assassination of the Pope in Rome. The Soviet leaders apparently were fearful that the Pope, a Pole and a living symbol to Poles of their Catholicism and nationalism, would intervene in Poland, where the Communist Party's monopoly of power was in danger [see below]. This, in turn, threatened the Soviet hold on Poland and, should the revolt in Poland against the Party inspire imitation elsewhere in Eastern Europe, the Soviet grip on the entire area. Thus the Pope had to be "removed.")

Ironically, just before the Korean airliner incident occurred, the administration had appeared to be moving toward the inevitable center of American politics. The upcoming presidential election seemed to be prodding the administration toward more flexibility in arms-control proposals and in other areas as well; for instance, a new long-term grain agreement with the promise of no future embargoes, regardless of Soviet behavior, was signed. But after the shooting down of the 747, American-Soviet relations took on a new chill. Responding to the president's words and reasserting that the plane had been sent on a spy mission by the United States, Andropov, Brezhnev's successor, used some of the harshest language that any Soviet leader had used in a long time.

> In their striving to justify in some way their dangerous, inhuman policies, the same people pile heaps of slander on the Soviet Union, on socialism as a social system, with the tone being set by the President of the United States himself. One must say bluntly—it is an unattractive sight when, with a view to smearing the Soviet people, leaders of such a country as the United States resort to what almost amounts to obscenities alternating with hypocritical preaching about morals and humanism.

The heat of the rhetorical denunciations and insults matched the chill in American-Soviet relations. No wonder the Soviet Union, seeking revenge for America's withdrawal from the 1980 Olympics—which Moscow had intended to exploit as a glorification of Soviet Socialism and Soviet superpower status—boycotted the Olympics held in Los Angeles in 1984 and that it did so in a presidential election year in which the Soviet Union intended to underline the message that President Reagan's anti-Communism and militarism were the sole source of the new superpower chill.

The Korean airline incident could not have resulted in this chill all by itself, however, had the trends of American-Soviet relations not been so bad to start with; the airliner was, after all, not American-owned, and it *was* flying over Soviet territory. For the President, however, the incident, coming on top of Soviet expansion in the 1970s, the invasion of Afghanistan, and the increasing repression of dissidents in the Soviet Union, strengthened his view that the Soviet Union was a wicked power; he also seemed to be suggesting that it was perhaps wrong to have good relations with such an evil country. Confrontation and containment were a more appropriate relationship.*

THE CONCERN ABOUT SOVIET MILITARY POWER

Still, the president's concern over the Soviet Union was not only, or even mainly, the result of personal ideology. The fact remains that Reagan was elected at a time when the American public had grown cynical about *détente* and angered by America's recent humiliations in foreign policy. The stronger anti-Soviet rhetoric and more assertive post-Vietnam American role had, in fact, started with Carter; but Reagan was the chief beneficiary of this mood.

*Strobe Talbott, *The Russians and Reagan* (New York: Vintage Books, 1984), p. 70.

Carter was too identified with the past, especially Iran and his confession of error about Soviet intentions after the Soviet invasion of Afghanistan. Any president by 1981 would have been concerned about Soviet intentions as well as the growth of Soviet military power. Carter's defense secretary had said: "As our defense budgets have risen, the Soviets have increased their defense budget. As our defense budgets have gone down, their defense budgets have increased again." Reagan had once asked, "What arms race? We stopped, they raced." During the 1970s American defense expenditures had fallen to the 1950 (pre-Korean War) low of 5 percent of the nation's GNP at a time when the Soviet Union, despite having an economy only half the size of that of the United States, was spending substantially more than this country on defense. From 1950 to 1969, Congressional cuts in defense budget requests had averaged only $1.7 billion annually, compared with $9.2 billion for non-defense programs. The six Nixon-Ford defense requests were cut by an average of $6 billion annually while the non-defense budget was increased by an average of $4.7 billion. The 1970s were the days of antimilitary sentiment, pseudoisolationist hopes, and cries for "domestic priorities" and for reductions of the defense budget; they witnessed "the most substantial reduction in American military capabilities relative to those of the Soviet Union in the entire postwar period."* Any administration coming into power after a decade and a half of Soviet efforts to exploit America's post-Vietnam mood of withdrawal from the world and the weakening of the American presidency to act would have been concerned with the growing Soviet first-strike capability against an increasingly vulnerable U.S. deterrent force, the shifting military balance as the Soviet strategic and conventional build-up continued, and the increasing Soviet capability to project power beyond Eurasia. It would also have had to be worried about such related matters as the Soviet eagerness to exploit Third World situations to increase its influence, Soviet ability to find and use proxies such as the Vietnamese in Cambodia and the Cubans in Africa to do this, and the Soviets' willingness to use their own military advisors and arms in Third World countries.

It appeared to the administration in 1981 that the Soviet Union continued to view its relationship with the United States as one of rivalry; that while the reasons for Soviet actions in Africa and Southeast and Southwest Asia differed, there appeared to be an increasing emphasis on the use of military power as the primary instrument of Soviet policy; and that Soviet respect for American interests and power was declining. Indeed, the heavy Soviet emphasis on military strength seemed in part to be a reflection of its lack of attractive alternatives, such as economic aid; it also suggested the greater political opportunities to use the threat of force as a means of intimidation as the strategic balance was changing. United States strategic superiority had in the past placed limits on how far the Soviets could safely escalate a challenge; it was prudent to act with re-

*John Lewis Gaddis, *Strategy of Containment* (New York: Oxford University Press), pp. 320–322.

straint. Parity, however, offered greater opportunities and fewer risks since the increase in the possible costs of opposing a Soviet move might, in Moscow's eyes, make the United States prefer not to offer any resistance or desist after initial resistance once it realized the risks were too great.

The Reagan administration therefore rejected an assumption that had become widely accepted during the decade of *détente*: that force no longer had much utility in international politics. The enormous growth of Soviet military power and Moscow's willingness to use it to support its diplomacy suggested otherwise. Force was a useful instrument of policy, whether it was applied or merely threatened as a means of pressure or just provided the background for diplomatic negotiations. The widespread belief in the disutility of force appeared to the new administration to be the result of two decades of deterrence by strategically superior U.S. forces. Ironically, therefore, this view had come into vogue in the United States at the very moment that the deterrent balance was shifting and force seemed once more to have political and military utility. It was therefore time to abandon this myth. The lesson of the 1970s, as the administration read it, was the wisdom of the old-fashioned adage that unwillingness to invoke the threat of force or to actually use it in defense of the nation's interests encourages an opponent to try to expand his influence, for it eliminates any risks or penalties for his behavior; the advantage, in short, goes to the party willing to threaten or actually use violence. Were the latter confronted by the possibility of military opposition—and thus given an incentive for restraint—he might moderate his aims.

More specifically, the administration was especially worried about the state of America's deterrent forces. Their basic rationale had always been that if the enemy knew that after launching an attack he would be destroyed, he would not strike. Thus once the United States had enough missiles to absorb a Soviet first strike and had a sufficient number left over to hit the Soviet Union's major cities and destroy most of its urban population and industries, no more would be needed. Any more would be "overkill" and unnecessary. This logic had provided the rationale for some of the lack of concern about the Soviet strategic forces as they passed those of the United States in numbers of Intercontinental Ballistic Missiles (ICBMs) and Submarine Launched Ballistic Missiles (SLBMs), megatonnage (the total amount of explosive force they could carry), and—potentially—numbers and size of warheads. Tight post-Vietnam defense budgets had made this rationale even more acceptable.

Once it was believed that Soviet forces might strike at U.S. deterrent forces, doing something about the vulnerable Minuteman land-based ICBMs and the aging B-52 bombers and Polaris submarines (all weapons systems built in the 1950s and early middle–1960s, and thus becoming twenty to thirty years old by the early 1980s) was judged to be a key task. American strategic forces needed to be modernized in order to assure their continued deterrent capability against the Soviet Union's growing first-strike ICBM capability, almost all of which had been deployed since the 1972 SALT I agreement. The Reagan administration therefore gave priority to the build-up of American strategic forces, although it also sought to strengthen the nation's conventional power which, at least for missions outside of Europe, had been neglected as part of the "no more Vietnams" mood of the 1970s. A 600-ship navy, including 15 (instead of 12) carrier battle groups, plus several restored World War II vintage battleships, were particularly high on the administration's list of conventional military goals.

At the center of the administration's rearmament program was the MX (Missile Experimental) ICBM, a missile as large as the Soviet SS-19 and carrying ten warheads like the even larger Soviet SS-18. The MX aroused enormous controversy for two reasons. First, the administration rejected the expensive Carter decision to deploy MX in a mobile mode in Utah and Nevada (Republican states in 1980 that did not want such deployment). In doing so, however, it deprived itself of the strongest argument for the missile's deployment: namely that at a time of growing American ICBM vulnerability, MX would decrease the likelihood that the Soviets would strike first because they would not be able to destroy enough American land-based missiles to prevent a devastating retaliatory strike. The administration proposed several alternative ways of deploying MX, including placing them in Minuteman silos (which the administration admitted were vulnerable to a Soviet first strike) and a closely based scheme called "dense pack." Congress, and even most members of the Joint Chiefs of Staff, were dubious that any of these schemes made MX more survivable than Minuteman.

MX, like the proverbial Flying Dutchman, became a missile in search of a mode of deployment. Its critics all argued that its accuracy, which made MX capable of hitting Soviet silos, meant that if deployed in vulnerable Minuteman silos MX would attract a preemptive Soviet SS-18 and/or SS-19 first strike— especially in a crisis—if only to forestall a possible American first strike. Thus the United States would either have to "use them or lose them." In short, a mutual hair trigger situation would follow MX's deployment, and this in turn could lead to a nuclear war that neither side wanted. But each would feel that it had to take that risk because it feared that if it failed to strike first, its ICBMs would be destroyed. To put it another way: The stable deterrent balance, which had gradually been becoming less stable as the Soviet deployed their SS-18s and -19s, would become even less stable with the deployment of MX. Or so the critics argued. Anyway, arms control appeared to have failed.

The second and even more critical reason why MX aroused enormous controversy was the administration's talk of "limited nuclear options," "protracted nuclear war," and "war-fighting." These phrases did not mean that the United States was no longer committed to deterrence. It was. But what if deterrence failed? The reason why the United States had to think of this possibility, according to administration spokesmen (and, it must be added in fairness, according to the secretaries of defense in the Carter and Nixon-Ford administrations) followed from the Soviet deployment of large numbers of accurate warheads on its big missiles. What if, in a crisis, the Soviets attacked only or primarily American ICBMs? Was not the retaliatory capability of American submarines and bombers still so enormous that the Soviets would not dare a first strike? Would not the second-strike threat still deter a first strike? The administration feared not.

Why? A Soviet first strike aimed at ICBMs, generally deployed far away from large cities, would leave the vast majority of Americans alive and most cities still standing. An American second or retaliatory blow with the remnants of the U.S. deterrent forces, bombers and SLBMs, however, would destroy much of the Soviet Union's population and many of its cities because these were inaccurate weapons, usable mainly against urban-industrial areas. Only ICBMs were sufficiently accurate to be used to strike back at Soviet military targets, especially its remaining ICBMs. So? What did it matter if we struck back at cities or missiles? The key question was what would happen if the Soviets, after their initial blow, announced that they had carried out their attack with 30–40 percent of their strategic forces and that, if the United States struck back at Soviet cities, they had enough missiles left to retaliate by striking the American cities they had deliberately avoided attacking before? In short, would a Soviet threat of a *third* strike not deter the American second strike? Would a president order a second strike, knowing that if he did so he would be signing the death warrant of most of America's population? Or would he, faced with that possibility, do nothing?

No one could say. He might retaliate regardless of the consequences. But should any president be confronted with this awful choice? This choice would occur even in the absence of an actual Soviet attack since in a crisis involving the vital interests of both sides, a president would know that the Soviets possessed sufficiently accurate warheads and the United States did not. Thus Moscow could stand firm, increase its pressure if needed, while Washington would have to retreat in future "Cubas-in-reverse." (Indeed, this possibility of nuclear blackmail was thought far more likely than a Soviet attack.)

MX was the means chosen to avoid having to cope with such a situation. Should deterrence of a "limited nuclear attack" fail, then the United States could respond in kind in order to punish the Soviet Union in equal measure, prevent further escalation, and compel it to desist. Most of all, it was hoped that MX's existence would deter the possibility of such a limited strike, thereby avoiding future crisis confrontations in which Moscow could intimidate Washington into submission. MX would provide extra insurance in case Soviet leaders thought that they could resort to a first strike or use the threat thereof. MX—first thought of during the Nixon-Ford administration and first proposed for deployment by the Carter administration—was intended to strengthen deterrence.

Critics, however, thought the whole scenario either bizarre or unlikely, given the past record of Soviet caution and unwillingness to risk the survival of their homeland. And they pointed out further that nuclear weapons were far too destructive to be used discriminately against military targets only. In any event, the momentum of an initial nuclear exchange would inevitably escalate to a full-scale war. What was truly frightening about the Reagan (and previously, Carter) limited nuclear war scenario, they said, was the possibility that the policymakers might really believe that such a war could be waged and that society, suffering "only" a few million casualties, would survive; if they thought this they might be tempted to resort to a nuclear war. The likelihood that this might occur was increased by the fact that MX was basically a first-strike weapon and when aimed at Soviet ICBMs would create a hair-trigger situation that might in itself precipitate a nuclear war. The critics argued that mutual assured destruction was unavoidable and MX was therefore unnecessary. In the final analysis, they contended, plans for a limited nuclear war and MX were based upon the claim that Minuteman had become 95 percent vulnerable to destruction. But this figure was based on simulated computerized war games; in a real-life operation, the Soviets could not achieve such a high kill rate and thus count on a lack of American retaliation, including retaliation by U.S. ICBMs.

Given the uproar over MX, the president appointed a distinguished bipartisan commission, under the chairmanship of Brent Scowcroft, Kissinger's successor as national security assistant to President Ford. It recommended the deployment of MX, mainly as a bargaining chip in arms-reduction talks with the Soviets. At the same time, it urged the nation to abandon MIRVed missiles and return to the pre-MIRV era of stable mutual deterrence. It recommended the development of a small, mobile, land-based missile with a single warhead; such a "Midgetman" would not be as vulnerable to attack as the immobile and increasingly vulnerable Minuteman and MX. It also suggested persuading the Soviets to deploy a similar ICBM while dismantling its SS-18s and -19s, whose multiple warheads constituted a potential first-strike capability. The upshot was that Congress changed its mind and voted for funding MX, hoping—perhaps against hope—that the president, whose skeptical views about arms control were reflected in his appointments, would now negotiate seriously about arms reductions and that the Soviets would become more accommodating to avoid the deployment of MX.

Ironically, the votes for America's biggest missile ever came shortly after the Democratically-controlled House of Representatives had voted in favor of a freeze on the production and deployment of all nuclear weapons! Still, most of the Reagan arms-control proposals, because they were aimed at a vast reduction of the Soviet ICBM force, which threatened U.S. ICBMs, remained unacceptable to Moscow. Why should Moscow give up something it already had to avoid an American missile not even deployed yet? The time for a bargain did not seem ripe. The best that could be achieved was that the two superpowers observe SALT II; despite his frequent criticism of it as "fatally flawed," the president committed the United States to live within its terms. He even accused the Soviets of violating this agreement, which the United States had refused to ratify! Perhaps that was as much as could be expected during a period when the American emphasis was on an arms build-up. The Reagan administration's management of the domestic politics of arms control was, however, inept and kept it in trouble throughout its term, trouble from which it was only partly rescued by the Scowcroft Commission.

The administration's very expensive $16-trillion, five-year rearmament program thus raised enormous controversy, even though much of defense spending went for pay and for weapons that were needed: conventional weapons to modernize the nation's nonnuclear forces and strategic weapons to supplement or replace increasingly obsolete delivery systems with newer ones at a time when almost all of the Soviet Union's strategic forces were less than ten years old. But the administration's harsh anti-Soviet rhetoric, its seemingly reckless talk of limited nuclear war—which suggested that it was shifting U.S. policy from deterring nuclear war to getting ready to fight one—its concern with increasing defense spending over that already scheduled by its predecessor while simultaneously cutting social services, all strengthened the impression that it relied too much on military strength and looked for military solutions to political problems and that it was the United States that was largely responsible for the "arms race." Thus when the president proposed a strategic defense against incoming missiles—thereby saving lives, as the president put it, rather than avenging them in a retaliatory strike—his proposal was quickly dubbed "Star Wars" and he was accused of extending the arms race into space, thus confirming in the eyes of the critics that Reagan was not sufficiently concerned about the danger of nuclear war. The momentum of an uninterrupted twenty-year Soviet program of arms acquisition across the board that was threatening to shift the earthly balance of nuclear and conventional forces to the Soviet Union often seemed to be forgotten. Moreover, the fact that this program had included several years of testing antisatellite satellites, which pose a potential danger to the satellites upon which the U.S. depends for early warnings of attack, communication with its forces worldwide, and verification of arms agreements, tended to be played down.

In an ironic twist of fate, President Reagan thus inspired a widespread "peace movement" in the early 1980s. Its adherents ranged from academia to religious institutions, especially the Catholic Church, whose bishops questioned the morality of nuclear deterrence, a policy based on the threat to use nuclear weapons in order to prevent their use. The bishops accepted the *possession* of nuclear weapons, pending complete disarmament, but not the *use* of these weapons. Yet if they could not be used even in retaliation, how could deterrence be made credible? Was the goal of peace moral but the means of preserving it so immoral that it was preferable to submit to enemy demands? Would a nonnuclear deterrence be moral, even if it failed to prevent war? This was unclear. The bishops did not advocate large-scale conventional rearmament. In the meantime, antinuclear books and films became popular.

Besides the immorality of nuclear deterrence, the second major theme of the "peace movement" was the old one that nuclear war would mean the end of civilization, the "last epidemic," as a doctor's organization phrased it. This theme was given strong support by new scientific arguments that the smoke produced by the many fires burning in cities attacked with nuclear weapons would absorb sunlight, plunging the world into darkness for several months, and causing a prolonged freeze or "nuclear winter," leading to the extinction of most plant and animal life. Even if the attacker had successfully eliminated most of his opponent's retaliatory capability, climactic catastrophe would follow and spread all over the northern as well as southern halves of the globe. Thus the aggressor might be a winner—but for two weeks only. Not surprisingly, most of these antinuclear writings and films, whose stress was on "the day after," concluded that if mankind were to survive, nuclear weapons had to be eliminated and, if possible, a world government established that would end national rivalries. The public mood, which had initially favored the Reagan rearmament program, appeared to have shifted.

Yet there was really little that was novel about these antinuclear books and films. Their emphasis on the horror of nuclear war had been common knowledge by 1980 for thirty-five years; that was, after all, why the United States had adopted a deterrent strategy to begin with. And it was the suicidal nature of these nuclear arms that had encouraged the belief that nuclear deterrence would prevent an all-out Soviet attack on this country and preserve peace among the superpowers. After all, while deterrence could fail, it *had* a historical record. The superpowers had not as much as exchanged a rifle shot in Europe where they confronted one another. Their nuclear power and their mutual fear of suicide had given them forty years of peace, Europe's longest in this century. But Congress, especially the Democratic House, reflected the new antinuclear mood, and after coming within one vote of endorsing a nuclear freeze in 1982, it did endorse a modified version of the freeze in 1983. Proposals for a freeze on the testing, production, and deployment of nuclear weapons to stop the arms race were passed (or almost passed) by many town-hall meetings and voters in ten of eleven states on whose ballots it appeared at the mid-term 1982 election. All Democratic Presidential candidates but one came out in favor of a freeze, although they all remained vague on the specifics.

This mix of concern, unease, and occasional pacifism was not appeased by the administration's professions of peaceful intent. What particularly hurt the administration as it rebuilt American military strength to prevent a shift of power resulting from two decades of Soviet military growth was its arms-control policy, or rather, its lack of an arms-control policy. For the Reagan administration deliberately delayed arms-control negotiations on strategic weapons. Not only was it, like most observers, unsure of what kind of arms-control agreements were desirable—if any were—in the wake of SALT II's burial in the Senate, but it did not want to become engaged in arms-control negotiations until the strategic military rebuilding program had gotten well underway. It was determined to show the Soviet Union that America had the will to match

Soviet power and that it did not consider arms control a substitute for defense efforts. For this was how the new administration saw the preceding SALT process and why it was critical of the SALT II treaty and had no intention of resubmitting it to the Senate for its consent (although, as noted, it said it would abide by its terms if the Soviets did).

Arms control was originally conceived of as supplementing the defense effort. Military strength was the basis of a peaceful superpower relationship; arms control was to ensure the stability of the deterrent balance. But during the 1970s, popular and Congressional opinion resisted large increases in defense expenditures. The military, it was charged, "had plenty"; the services' emphasis on the growing Soviet threat was self-serving, intended only to increase their budgets; if the United States had more arms, it would only get involved in another Vietnam, for the danger was not so much the Soviet Union, but we ourselves! Arms control, therefore, became a means for succeeding administrations to attempt to slow down Soviet quantitative growth and arrange for the best possible balance under circumstances in which the United States focused on qualitative improvements of its strategic weapons (more accurate MIRVs, longer-range SLBMs, and ALCMs to be placed on bombers).

By the time of SALT II, therefore, some senators were saying that they would vote for the treaty only if promised that there would be regular annual increases of defense spending and the deployment of MX. For the impression was widespread that arms control had become an alternative for an expensive defense build-up as a means of keeping up with the Soviets. Indeed, such deployments were often said to undermine arms control! These impressions, whether they were fair or not, were strengthened by President Carter's cancellation of the B-1 bomber (intended to succeed the B-52), the postponement of the production of a "neutron bomb" as a tactical or battlefield weapon, and Carter's general reluctance to commit himself to MX and larger defense budgets for conventional forces until forced to do so by the SALT II debate in the Sentate. The new administration, determined to turn things around, thus focused on American military strength rather than arms control.

Postponing arms control talks proved difficult to do, however, for much of public opinion equated arms control with disarmament and even more so with a sincere search for peace. When negotiations did finally start in 1982, their emphasis was not on limitations but major reductions and the name shifted from SALT to START (Strategic Arms Reduction Talks). But the administration argued that fruitful results could be expected only if the Soviets saw the United States as willing to match Soviet efforts; MX was critical in this respect. Why should Moscow negotiate seriously and agree to arms reductions unless it calculated that future American strength and an American counterpart to their SS-18/19 made it futile to continue its own building program? All this may have been true in the context of a negotiating strategy. But the administration's conviction that arms control had in the 1970s weakened the United States and was therefore a dangerous policy was by now widely perceived. And when it did make arms-control proposals it always appeared as if it were making such proposals reluctantly, to appease public pressures, not because it really had faith in arms control.

The lesson was clear: A president can arm the United States if he believes that necessary, but only if the public also sees him making a genuine effort to control the arms competition and improve the superpower relationship. The Reagan administration had not learned that lesson. MX, always a weapon of controversial merit, had been politically acceptable during the Ford and Carter administrations. The only problem seemed to be its manner of deployment. But when Reagan suggested various options for its deployment, he created enormous opposition, and for the first time since 1945 Congress initially refused to fund a major new weapon requested by a president. Only the Scowcroft Commission temporarily rescued the administration and the missile, precisely because it came up with a long-range program combining the modernization of the U.S. deterrent and arms control. But a great deal of opposition to MX remained, especially in the House; and in 1984 Democratic presidential candidate Mondale said he would cancel MX if elected. Defense, like foreign policy, generated considerable controversy and not much bipartisanship.

THE REAGAN INTERVENTION IN CENTRAL AMERICA AND THE CARIBBEAN

If the Reagan administration refocused American foreign policy on the competition with the Soviet Union and concentrated on American rearmament in order to make American power credible once more, it was also to demonstrate this power in the Central America-Caribbean area. Virtually from the day Reagan took office, his administration placed the spotlight on the small Central American country of El Salvador, a country with a population of 5 million living in an area the size of New Jersey, within the context of superpower conflict. The roots of El Salvador's problems were—as in Nicaragua, Guatemala, Honduras, and even democratic Costa Rica—largely domestic. All except Honduras have been rapidly modernizing since 1960, but their economic growth has benefited mainly a small elite of landowners, businessmen, and generals while leaving the mass of the urban population and peasantry poor. In addition, a rapid birth rate weakened the semifeudal structure in the countryside and forced many peasants, many of whom did not own land, to move to cities where they were exposed to new goods and ideas and consequently experienced rising expectations. Unable to meet these expectations, these countries suffered rising social discontent and tensions. Oil imports only worsened the economic and political situation because of their inflationary effect. In short, economic modernization was undermining the traditional, conservative political systems. Military regimes or militarily supported regimes prevented social reform and political change. Peaceful change being impossible, the authoritarian governments in

Nicaragua, El Salvador, and Guatemala increasingly faced the opposition of leftist guerrillas.

The first result of guerrilla action, the collapse of the Somoza regime in Nicaragua in 1979 and the Sandinistas' victory, led to increased disturbance throughout the region, as the extreme left and right sought to achieve or preserve power through violence. For the shock of Anastasio Somoza's fall after the Somoza family, friends of the United States, had virtually run the country for four decades, encouraged armed, left-wing forces to make a military bid for power. The traditional right-wing authoritarian governments (except in Costa Rica) responded fearfully with force. Each side attacked members of the other side, the right even assassinating nuns and priests, including an archbishop in El Salvador. Even moderate political leaders who advocated peaceful reform and change, such as some of the Christian Democrats who came to power in El Salvador, were targets for assassination. They had difficulty controlling right-wing death squads and factions of the military who, while fighting against leftist guerrillas, also tried to eliminate the center. In Guatemala, government-controlled murder squads carried out thousands of political killings after 1979; victims included Christian Democratic leaders, trade union leaders, and priests. Such action further polarized societies.

The Reagan administration made El Salvador an international issue because after years of Soviet-Vietnamese-Cuban successes in the Third World, it was determined to send Moscow a message: Stop expanding Soviet influence by means of proxies. Asserting that the Duarte government in El Salvador was a moderate one, which had the best chance of succeeding in carrying out domestic social reforms while preventing a radical left-wing assumption of power, the Reagan administration authorized extensive shipment of military equipment plus U.S. advisors to the Salvadoran government forces. This assistance, it was claimed, was necessary to counter weapons sent to the Salvadoran guerrillas by Cuba, Ethiopia, Libya, and Vietnam at Soviet direction; most of these arms were alleged to have been shipped via Nicaragua, which was punished for its complicity by a cut-off of American economic aid. Besides providing arms, the Communist states were also said to be helping the Salvadoran guerrillas with money, training, and advice. The war in El Salvador, the State Department claimed, was a "textbook case of indirect armed aggression by Communist powers." The war thus received widespread international publicity because of Washington's determination to call early attention to and draw a line against Soviet-Cuban expansion in the Third World, especially so near to the United States. The concern was that if, after Nicaragua, El Salvador also fell to left-wing guerrillas and established a second Marxist regime, the rest of Central America would follow, posing a danger to the Panama Canal and to Mexico, and thus eventually to the United States itself.

Whether El Salvador was the right place to take a stand against Soviet Communism and its proxies or whether the revolution should have been allowed to follow its natural course was energetically debated. The critics argued that the

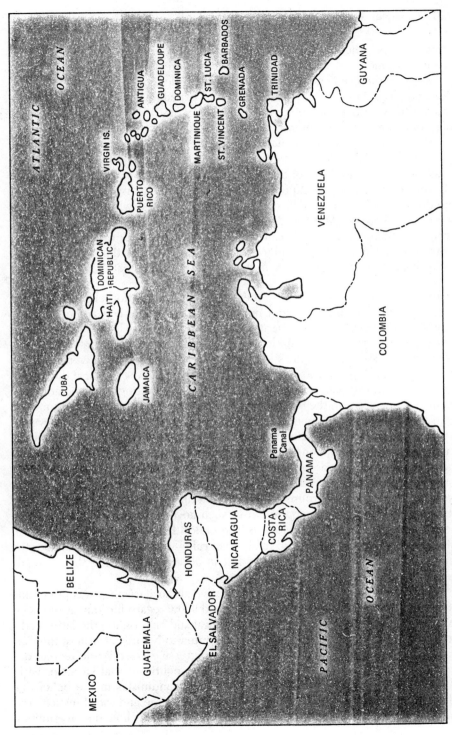

Central America and the Caribbean Basin

arms were not the principal cause for the civil war; the appalling social and economic conditions and political repression were. The United States should not support the privileged few who had long exploited the poor. Social justice demanded nonintervention; so perhaps did expediency, if the United States wished to avoid being identified with the losers, as it had been so many times before. Vietnam was frequently cited as a reminder of the dangers of supporting the wrong side: an unpopular political elite whose vested interest lay in the preservation of the *status quo*. In any event, no purely military solution was possible. Much was made of the violation of human rights in El Salvador. The United States, which is supposed to stand for human rights if it stands for anything, it was said, should not be backing a regime whose security forces were so murderous. Moscow could be the only winner. In Western Europe, as well as in many Latin American countries, especially Mexico, El Salvador's northern neighbor, the Salvadoran guerrillas were also thought to deserve more support than the government because they would create a more equitable society.

In rejecting these arguments, the Reagan administration claimed that the United States was in El Salvador not to help a right-wing government but the Christian Democratic government of Napoleón Duarte, which was committed to peaceful reforms but was under attack by militant left-wing forces who were seeking to destroy the nation's economy and bring down the government. In addition, the administration declared what in its view was a critical distinction between authoritarianism and totalitarianism. Admitting that violations of human rights occur in the midst of a civil war and that authoritarian regimes do repress criticism of and opposition to their political rule in order to preserve the *status quo*, the administration asserted that such governments do not stifle all criticism and jail all opponents. In areas of religion, family, culture, and economics there remained considerable freedom for individuals to pursue their own lives as long as they refrain from political criticism. Thus, when there exist no alternative political groups to support at a time when the Soviet Union and its friends back the main opposition to such governments, these regimes deserved American help; for victory for the radical left meant not only an extension of Soviet influence but also totalitarian rule—that is, total control over the individual's life, not only in politics but in all areas, including those usually regarded as private.

For the Reagan administration conservative authoritarianism was preferable to left-wing totalitarianism. If the former had a low regard for human rights, as America understood them in terms of political and civil rights, the latter had a total disregard for them. Reagan officials pointed to Nicaragua, where the Carter administration, wishing not to block a "progressive Third World revolution" and preferring to be on the "right side" of the political-social struggle, withdrew support from Somoza and supported the Sandinistas in the belief that they would bring Nicaragua a more democratic regime and social justice. Yet, once in power, the Sandinistas began to consolidate their hold on government, gradually suppressing the voices of criticism as counterrevolutionary. They also postponed general elections while building an army larger than Somoza's and establishing relations with Cuba and the Soviet Union. The question was not how Marxist the regime would become as it increasingly turned on the Catholic Church and the business and professional communities, which had helped it depose Somoza, but how dictatorial it would become and how close it would move to Havana and Moscow. While the Sandinistas claimed that they had declared a state of emergency, allowing them to impose censorship on opposition papers and suspend all activities by political parties, only as a temporary reaction to American efforts (which were made) to destabilize the regime, the original Sandinista commitment to political pluralism was very much in doubt; and of its international sympathies, there was no doubt. Despite the Carter administration's initially favorable attitude, its withdrawal of support from Somoza and extension of foreign aid, Nicaragua was soon aligning itself with Cuba and the Soviet Union, causing Washington to reassess its policy even before the arrival of the Reagan administration.

In any event, the Reagan administration did not intend to repeat in El Salvador what it regarded as Carter's error in Nicaragua. Yet American opinion was not enthusiastic about becoming involved in that tiny country. Economic and military aid, but no military intervention, appeared to be the limit it was willing to tolerate; and even that aid Congress made contingent upon an improvement of the Salvadoran regime's human rights record. This left the administration little choice but to support the Salvadoran government while encouraging it to further social reforms and to discipline its own army and security forces for killing civilians whose political leanings were suspected of being left of center. A key aspect of American policy was to legitimate the regime by holding general elections; if the left was willing to participate, such an election might even end the civil war and provide for national reconciliation.

The left, however, opposed participation and the guerrillas threatened those who would vote. Nevertheless, to the surprise of American and other observers watching the election for fraud and intimidation, over 80 percent of the electorate turned out to vote. The results of the 1982 election were ironic. The Christian Democrats, who were in power, received the largest vote of any single party; but the several right-wing parties together polled a larger vote and organized a coalition government. Those who had opposed the Christian Democrats and the reform-minded military officers, both supported by the United States, were therefore the beneficiaries of the American-sponsored free election! The election did, however demonstrate that the former strong support for the guerrillas among peasants, students, and workers had eroded. But the fighting continued, despite the desire of Salvadorans for peace.

As the civil war continued in 1982, it was briefly overshadowed by the Argentinian seizure of the British-owned Falkland Islands in the South Atlantic. Even though the Organization of American States largely supported Argentina, the United States, after failing to mediate the conflicting claims to sovereignty over the islands, supported Britain in the subsequent fighting because it felt that such blatant aggression should not be rewarded, even by a regime with which the administration had been trying to improve its relations. With attention diverted by this undeclared war, the new government in El Salvador proceeded to reverse earlier land reform programs and replace reform-minded military officers, believing that the United States had no choice but to support it, since the alternative was "another Nicaragua."

Thus the war went on. The army was poorly led and trained. As death-squad killings of civilians, mainly moderate centrists interested in democratic reforms, continued and not one government official or soldier was ever convicted of the thousands of murders, Salvadoran politics became further polarized between right and left. But President Reagan wanted to send in more military advisers and greater military assistance. Congress, still haunted by memories of Vietnam and questioning whether the Salvadoran army could win the war, no matter how much aid it would receive, opposed the president on sending in more advisers and only reluctantly supported him with funds for military and economic assistance. The fundamental problem remained political for most of the critics. For them, the decisive issue was not the flow of foreign arms to the rebels, as the administration asserted, but the nature of El Salvador's society, which made people pick up guns. Just as first in China and then in Vietnam, "our" Chinese or Vietnamese never fought as well as "theirs," so "our" Salvadorans did not fight as well as "theirs." "Ours" lacked motivation. For the administration to succeed, the United States would have to exert greater control over the Salvadoran right, strengthen the moderates and build public support for the center, rebuild an economy deliberately ravaged by the guerrillas to force the government to its knees, and transform the military into an effective army. This formidable task would take years, if feasible at all.

The president, however, persisted because he was unwilling to lose. For he saw the stake as a "domino" whose loss would greatly affect American interests. "If guerrilla violence succeeds," Mr. Reagan said, "El Salvador will join Cuba and Nicaragua for spreading fresh violence to Guatemala, Honduras, even Costa Rica. The killing will increase and so will the threat to Panama, the Canal and ultimately Mexico." America's strategic stakes were too high in Central America "for us to ignore the danger of governments seizing power there with ideological and military ties close to the Soviet Union." However strongly the president may have believed this domino analogy and tried to use El Salvador as an issue with which to alert the American public on Soviet-inspired expansion in the Third World, including now in our own hemisphere, he managed to arouse mainly memories of Vietnam.

America did not want to see El Salvador "go Communist," but it was reluctant to use American forces to prevent this, and Congress remained worried that the increasing commitments of money and arms to El Salvador might lead to direct intervention. It was also concerned that the administration's covert help for anti-Sandinista forces—whom the president called "freedom fighters"—

would escalate. Even in its more assertive post-Iranian hostage mood, public opinion remained cautious about military intervention—"another Vietnam"— in the Third World. The bipartisan Kissinger Commission, appointed by the president to mobilize more Congressional and public support for policy in Central America, did not fundamentally alter this caution. Nor did it eliminate the suspicion that the key problem in the area was less Nicaraguan-Cuban-Soviet intervention than fundamentally repressive *status quo* regimes uninterested in alleviating the social, economic, and political grievances that threatened to undermine them even if there were no outside attempts to exploit these grievances.

The United States, in search of a moderate center, appeared trapped between reactionary forces whose rigid commitment to the *status quo* only intensified revolutionary sentiment and endangered American interests, and radical forces that tended to be Marxist and to look to Havana and Moscow, again jeopardizing American security. It was rescued from this trap by the Salvadoran presidential election, which brought the reformer Napoleón Duarte back to power and strengthened the Reagan case for assistance to El Salvador because it could rightfully claim that the United States was not supporting the right wing as an alternative to the radical left.

The dilemma that the United States faced was how to avoid either intervening militarily or losing. Hence the debate between the administration, which emphasized military aid, and the critics, largely Democrats, who emphasized domestic reforms without which, they claimed, all the military assistance in the world could not win the war. It was also clear that everyone was looking for a course that would avoid another Cuba in Central America while simultaneously also avoiding another Vietnam. Yet the possibility of direct U.S. armed intervention was of course present, and it was to remind America's enemies in the region that this possibility was perhaps not as remote as they might think in this post-Vietnam period that the administration put on a show of force in Grenada, a tiny island of 110,000 people lying in the southern Caribbean.

Governed by a self-styled Marxist regime that had achieved power by means of a *coup* several years earlier, Grenada's leader was overthrown and murdered by a more militant pro-Soviet faction in late 1983. Washington sent in the military, professing concern about the safety of 1000 American medical students, amid the political turmoil and about their possible seizure as hostages, as in Iran in 1979. It also stated that U.S. forces were sent in response to a request by the virtually unknown Organization of Eastern Caribbean States, composed of a group of small, formerly British colonies who were becoming increasingly anxious over Grenada's leftward direction and ties to Cuba, which lay at the northernmost point of this island chain. While most Latin American countries, moved by memories of past interventions, opposed the American action, and while the United Nations condemned it, Grenada's island neighbors, who sent token forces to Grenada to give the intervention the appearance of a collective action, were clearly worried about their future security. In fact, the growing

Cuban-Soviet presence on Grenada had been of concern to the administration earlier. Grenadians, it ought to be added, overwhelmingly welcomed the intervention, which rescued them from Cuban control and domestic repression.

As it turned out, many of the several hundred Cuban construction workers resisted the American landing, which the president called a "rescue mission," not an invasion. Soviet military personnel, North Koreans, and East Germans were also present on the island. Large caches of arms were found, as well as documents showing that larger shipments of arms were to be sent in the future, presumably to be shipped to leftist rebels in Latin America or used for training guerrillas. For Cuba, the invasion of Grenada was certainly a blow. Castro lost a bridgehead and influence in the Caribbean (where, for example, the leftist government in Surinam, a former Dutch colony, immediately expelled the Cuban ambassador) and Central America (for Castro announced that he would not be able to help Nicaragua if it were invaded). The American action undoubtedly was aimed at Nicaragua. American pressure against the Sandinistas had been increasing for some time with the support of the antigovernment insurgents and the stationing of sizable American naval forces off both the Atlantic and Pacific coasts of Nicaragua. These pressures had for the first time led the Sandinistas to sound more interested in a possible diplomatic solution of the Salvador problem. Grenada was intended to escalate this pressure and demonstrate to the Sandinistas, Cubans, and Soviets that the United States would once more use force if the administration felt this to be necessary to protect its interests. They might mock the United States for attacking such a mini-state, but presumably they would exercise more restraint in the future—at least in Central America and the Caribbean.

In the broader context, the Reagan administration's policy in El Salvador, Nicaragua, and Grenada was an attempt to reverse what it saw as a one-sided Third World contest that had taken place in Angola, Ethiopia, Yemen, Afghanistan, and Cambodia after Vietnam. The Soviets and their allies had been using force as an instrument of statecraft; they had been allowed this monopoly because of the widespread feeling in the United States that the use of force had become counterproductive, that it was so clearly immoral that short of an attack on the United States itself or its allies in Western Europe it was not a legitimate means of protecting or advancing American interests. Quite the contrary. "Force will not solve political problems" became the commonplace phrase. In this atmosphere of American nonintervention, neither Moscow nor Havana were penalized for intervening; the absence of sanctions, indeed, provided them with an incentive for exploiting favorable political opportunities. The Reagan administration had been skeptical from the beginning about the notion of the disutility of force. Grenada was intended to raise the risks and the costs for the Soviets and Cubans should they continue to try and extend their political and military control in this hemisphere, as well as elsewhere. Asserting that it had intervened just in the nick of time to prevent Grenada from becoming a "Soviet-Cuban colony," the administration called Grenada a "warning shot."

But Grenada could not resolve the key problem to which the Kissinger Report had drawn attention, namely, that American policy overseas had always assumed the security of America's own borders. The nation's ability to project power to Europe, Asia, or the Middle East, all far away from the United States, had always assumed this hemispheric peace. By contrast, this strategic luxury had been denied to the Soviet Union, which has had to be concerned first with the security of her long frontiers. It was to enhance her sense of security that Stalin transformed Eastern Europe into a Soviet buffer zone and that Brezhnev later formalized the Soviet right to intervene in that area to prevent "counterrevolutions" jeopardizing Socialism in Eastern Europe. The Brezhnev Doctrine, announced at the time of the Soviet intervention in Czechoslovakia in 1968, had already been practiced in East Germany in 1953 and Hungary in 1956. The Monroe Doctrine had historically reserved this hemisphere as America's sphere of influence; if it was anything, the Monroe Doctrine was a Caribbean Doctrine, making that area America's buffer zone (the southern tip of Argentina was, after all, farther away than Western Europe). The Kissinger Commission, like the Reagan administration, certainly defined the Caribbean-Central American area as America's "strategic rear" or "soft underbelly." The unstable political conditions throughout the area and the rise of Soviet-Cuban-Nicaraguan influence was therefore a matter of great concern. For it confronted Washington with three undesirable options: much larger defense spending to guard against future efforts to expand Communist influence and the stationing of larger military forces, including carrier battle groups, in the area; a reduced role and reduced capability to defend more distant areas, including Western Europe; or military intervention in El Salvador, if not eventually also in Nicaragua, if the Salvadoran army could not defeat the guerrillas. But such an intervention would hardly be like Grenada, but more like Vietnam. Yet Korea, and Vietnam even more, had shown the political unpopularity of lengthy limited wars. Only short, successful interventions with little loss of life against much weaker opponents, as in the Dominican Republic in 1965 and in Grenada, won either public approval or acquiescence. Thus the administration had no alternative but to hope that Salvadoran domestic reforms plus military aid to the Salvadoran army would allow Washington to avoid the choice between losing or intervening.

NATO, DÉTENTISM, AND DISENGAGEMENT

The more activist Reaganite containment policy met with little enthusiasm in Europe. Western Europe appeared determined to cling to *détente* as if it were a life raft. Having complained during the Nixon-Ford administration of American-Soviet collusion and during the Carter Administration of American vacillation and insufficient firmness, it now charged that American policy was too rigid and continued to attempt to preserve its own separate *détente* with the Soviet

Union. Two events were to demonstrate rather quickly how great was the gap separating Europe from Reagan's United States. The first one was Poland, where domestic changes had occurred that threatened the Polish Communist Party's monopoly of power and control. It was highly ironic that it was in Poland, a so-called people's democracy and a Communist state, allegedly representing and protecting the interests of the working class, that a truly spontaneous Marxist workers' revolution against their exploiters (the Communist Party!) occurred in 1980. Stimulated by a failing economy as a result of poor political leadership, bureaucratic planning and mismanagement, the workers demanded the right to form their own independent trade union, including the right to strike. The workers were driven by the shortages of consumer goods, especially food, as well as by outrage against the privileges of those who governed Poland. Such a demand was unheard of in a Communist country where the Party claimed to embody the workers' aspirations. In fact, in wanting their own union, the Polish workers were rejecting this claim and challenging the basis of the Party's legitimacy.

Strikes, which virtually brought to a standstill an economy already in debt to Western banks and governments for $27 billion by the early 1980s, brought the government down, as they had in 1970 when the ship workers had managed to replace another set of leaders who had mismanaged the economy. This time, however, the economic conditions were far more severe. The political leadership was again changed, and the right of the workers to form their own union, called Solidarity, was recognized. In effect, this meant a loss of the Party's monopoly of power and a sharing of power with Solidarity whose demands from the beginning were not only economic but also political. Mass was to be televised on Sundays; Solidarity meetings were to be broadcast as well; censorship was to be restricted; corrupt officials were to removed from office; and a farmers' union was to be accepted. As the Party-controlled government retreated before each demand, the demands increased and the Party withdrew further in the face of strikes and threats of strikes. It was a heady experience for a still very Catholic and nationalistic people, who hated the Soviets and who had been denied freedom so long. The taste of a little freedom only fed that taste and the demands for reforms spread.

With its successes, Solidarity grew more militant. At its first national conference, it publicly asserted that it was "the authentic voice of the working class" and announced support for other Eastern European workers who might wish to form independent unions; domestically, sentiment favored free parliamentary elections and free speech and a voice in government policy, including the running of the economy. Despite what to the Soviets was provocative behavior—they accused Solidarity of seeking "political power"—they continued to refrain from invading Poland.

This restraint contrasted sharply with Soviet behavior in Hungary and Czechoslovakia, where the Soviet Army had intervened when the Party's monopoly of power had been threatened. And Poland, the nation through which every Western invader of Russia had marched and through which the Soviet Union had projected its power into the center of Europe since 1945, was geographically far more critical than those two countries had been. On the one hand, the situation therefore became increasingly intolerable in Moscow's eyes. The danger of the Polish example spreading to other Eastern Europe states, and perhaps some day even to the Soviet Union if its economy suffered an expected decline in the 1980s, made it all the harder to stand by and do little but launch verbal criticism and hold very visible Soviet-Warsaw Pact military maneuvers in order to frighten and restrain the Poles. The Soviet Union could afford neither a weakening nor a collapse of its hold on Eastern and Central Europe nor a dilution of totalitarian controls at home.

But the risks and costs of intervention were also great. The Soviets recognized that Solidarity was not just a narrow trade union movement seeking better working conditions but, unlike Czechoslovakia in 1968, represented a well-organized mass movement. Thus there were the possibility of a clash with units of the Polish army, the costs of occupation, difficulties of pacifying the population, and difficulties getting the people to work. In addition, the cost of paying off Poland's debt to the West at a time when the Soviet Union's economy was having its own difficulties would be a drain; harm to future relationships with most Western Communist parties was likely; maintaining the separate *détente* with America's European allies would become more difficult; and the establishment of a better relationship with the new U.S. administration would be jeopardized. For President Reagan could exploit a Soviet invasion of Poland to rally the North Atlantic Treaty Organization (NATO) allies and obtain the military appropriations from Congress he wanted for America's rearmament. It was to avoid these results and give Reagan a pretext for his anti-Soviet policies that Moscow for over a year demonstrated remarkable restraint (just as one suspects that administration officials must have hoped deep down for a Soviet invasion despite their frequent warnings to Moscow not to intervene if it wished to improve its relationship with Washington). When the strike against Solidarity finally came, it was the Polish military and police who arrested the union leaders and imposed martial law on Poland.

Whether Moscow ordered the intervention or the Polish government acted to forestall Soviet action, there can be little doubt of increasing Soviet pressure on the Polish authorities to crack down on what the Soviets called "anti-socialist" and "counterrevolutionary" elements. For any movement that weakened the Communist Party's monopoly of power as the self-acclaimed representative of the workers in any Communist country was unacceptable. Solidarity, by winning the sympathies of almost 10 million members, about one-third of the population, was a living refutation of this claim and symbolized the bankruptcy of Communism. Unable either to produce a decent standard of living or to tolerate a minimal degree of freedom, Communism in Poland had lost legitimacy; force was therefore necessary to maintain the Party in power (in reality, it was the army that was in power and had replaced the Party). Poland, it was said, was occupied by its own army! In response, the United States imposed some economic sanctions on both Poland and the Soviet Union; they were less punitive than symbolic of American displeasure. But in Western Europe, one almost heard a collective sigh of relief that the Red Army had not invaded Poland. The Polish army's crackdown was considered a domestic affair, not a matter over which *détente* was to be sacrificed.

Europe's attempt to preserve its separate *détente* with Moscow, including its profitable trade relationship, also ran headlong into Washington's determination not only to rebuild American power and contain efforts to expand Soviet influence but also to squeeze the Soviet Union economically. In contrast to the *détente* policy of the 1970s, which had attempted to balance the military stick with the economic carrot to provide the Soviet Union with incentives for greater self-restraint in foreign policy, the Reagan policy concluded that the proferred trade, technology, and credits had not worked. The Soviet civilian industrial and agricultural economies continued to be weak, except in the military sector. Why should the West help strengthen the economy of a hostile state? Lenin had once said the capitalists in order to make money would even sell the Communists the rope with which they would hang the capitalists. Was the West, in its eagerness to trade and sell its latest technology, not selling the Soviets that rope and even providing the money for its purchase as low-interest credit? And would the chief beneficiary of this Western "subsidization" of the Soviet economy not be the Soviet armed forces? By putting up trade barriers instead, the West could increase Soviet economic difficulties and compel the Soviet leaders to switch resources from the military sector to the civilian one in order to prevent their people's standard of living from declining even further, which would cause social unrest. Only by increasing the Soviet quota of "pain" might the Soviet Union be compelled to relax international tensions and moderate its behavior.

Given the different European-American perspective on American-Soviet relations, and the role of trade, it was not surprising that soon after the Reagan administration took office, conflict erupted over the construction of a Soviet pipeline which was to be built from Siberia and carry Soviet natural gas to Western Europe. Europe, overwhelmingly dependent upon imported energy, was trying to diversify its energy sources and become less dependent upon the Arab members of OPEC. The Reagan administration fiercely opposed the pipeline, to be built by the Soviets but financed by the Europeans. The principal reason was the fear that Western Europe would over the years become more and more dependent on the Soviet Union for its energy and that this would grant the Soviets the political leverage to gradually undermine NATO by turning off the tap. Another reason was that the pipeline would allow the Soviets to earn hard currencies with which it could buy Western technology. Thus, instead of cutting back on its investments in the military area in order to help general economic growth, Moscow would be able to continue its sizable investment in military technology and production.

The Europeans denied that their energy purchases would make them dependent upon the Soviet Union or politically amenable to Soviet pressure. Moreover, they argued, the Soviet leadership had never hesitated to starve the consumer sector of the economy so as to afford the military hardware it felt it necessary to possess. Indeed, economic sanctions, argued America's allies, had generally failed as instruments of punishment. The Reagan administration's idea of cutting Western economic links to the Soviet Union in order to compel its leaders to behave with greater restraint would do just the opposite by producing resentment and anger, which would reinforce Soviet hostility toward the West. Indeed, greater Soviet moderation was more likely to be produced by an extensive network of economic relationships.

To force the Europeans to comply with American policy, President Reagan ordered American companies in the United States, and then their branches in Europe and European firms producing American technology under license from American corporations, not to sell to Moscow the items needed for the building of the pipeline. These items were for the most part large turbines. The emotional and political fallout that resulted led the European governments to order their firms to comply with national policies. Washington responded by imposing sanctions against these firms! Thus President Reagan became the first president to impose sanctions against this nation's allies (the companies, rather than nations, were penalized to lessen the level of resentment in Europe, but there was no doubt at whom American anger was aimed).

Secretary of State Haig had opposed the president's course on this issue. He had predicted that the Europeans were determined to go ahead; to oppose them, therefore, was to risk dividing members of the alliance even further at a time when they should be closing ranks. The pipeline was one of the issues over which Haig resigned, and initially his successor spent much of his time trying to defuse it. The pipeline controversy was a symptom of the increasing divisiveness among NATO members which, in this instance, hurt the alliance more than the Soviet Union, the intended target.

By the early 1980s, indeed, it had become commonplace to say that the Western Europeans wanted to pursue an independent political policy while still counting on the United States for its defense; they wanted, it was said, to "uncouple" themselves politically from Washington but to remain "coupled" to it militarily. Even this military "coupling" was called into question when Western European opinion appeared to go back on a decision, collectively agreed to by the United States and Western Europe, on how to meet the threat of the new, mobile, and powerful Soviet SS-20 Intermediate Range Missiles (IRBMs) with three warheads each. It was the West German government that had first raised the issue of the SS-20 deployment and requested the United States to counter the new Soviet missiles aimed at Western Europe. The proposed American force of 572 missiles to deter the over 300 SS-20s was to consist of 108 Pershing IIs (with one warhead each) whose range was sufficient to hit western Russia, plus 464 subsonic Ground-Launched Cruise Missiles (GLCMs).

Since the beginning of NATO, the Europeans had wanted the alliance strategy to emphasize deterrence. Europe had had its bellyful of wars in this century. The NATO army, therefore, was to serve as a "plate glass" which, once the Soviet invasion occurred, would sound the alarm and call in the United States strategic forces. The army's purpose was not to fight a long war like World War II, even when it was reinforced by some 200,000 American soldiers. Europe wanted its defense on the cheap; nuclear weapons were to be a substitute for a lot of manpower. The army's function was to ensure that American bombers and missiles would respond and attack the Soviet Union; the presence of American troops was to guarantee this result. Once American soldiers were killed, would the United States not retaliate? In short, the army's role was to "couple" Europe's defense to American strategic forces. It was the fear of nuclear retaliation by the latter that would presumably deter the Soviet Union from invading Western Europe.

The Soviet SS-20s threatened to uncouple Europe's defense from the American deterrent. NATO ground forces, it was claimed, were no match for the Warsaw Pact forces. Nor could NATO's tactical nuclear forces any longer compensate for NATO's lack of manpower, especially reserves. The SS-20s would deter a NATO escalation from conventional to tactical nuclear weapons. But were the American strategic forces not still the instrument of last resort? Perhaps they were, but perhaps not. Ever since the first Soviet missile test in 1957, the key questions had been: Would the United States risk its own survival for the defense of Europe? Some had answered this question with a no; most had been uncertain, although United States strategic forces at the time had been superior to those of the Soviet Union. Even if it were uncertain that these forces would be used, could Moscow take the chance and risk an attack on Western Europe? Probably not. Since the 1970s and the emergence of strategic parity, however, the answer to this question had grown even more doubtful. It was one thing for the United States to attack the Soviet Union when the latter could not yet attack this country or when America had possessed a vast strategic superiority; it was quite another to do so when the Soviet Union could retaliate fully. Was America's strategic deterrence still credible? Washington's standard reply was yes, but in Western Europe there was more doubt than ever that this was so.

The Pershing IIs and GLCMs were supposed to reassure the allies. Since the Pershings could strike targets in the Soviet Union itself, the Soviet Union would presumably consider such a strike as an act of American aggression and would retaliate against American missiles in Europe *as well as* the United States to forestall an all-out attack. The Pershings were thus to tell the Soviets that any attack on Western Europe could not be limited to that area while the strategic forces of both sides guarded their respective homelands. In other words, the Pershing's capacity to hit targets in the Soviet Union, was intended to reassure the allies that their defense was still "coupled" to the American deterrent.

Instead of being strengthened, however, the NATO "marriage" came close to a divorce. Huge crowds throughout Western Europe (except in France) protested the proposed deployment of the American missiles; the greatest opposition was in West Germany. The accusations were many: America was stoking the arms race; America intended to fight a war limited to Europe; America was the aggressive party in the cold war. And on it went. The Soviet Union, its strategic build-up, the growth and improvement of its conventional forces facing NATO, and the continued deployment of SS-20s were hardly mentioned; or, when mentioned, hardly seemed critical. Nor were Afghanistan and Poland. Moscow was not seen as the chief threat. It was Washington, which had defended Western Europe since 1949 and had not yet deployed a single Pershing II, which was regarded as the bigger menace to peace! Indeed, the more SS-20s the Soviets deployed, the greater their threat to Western Europe, the shriller became the protests against the United States counterdeployment, which— few Europeans wanted to recall—they had initially requested. Much of European opinion seemed to want to remove Western Europe from the "super-power struggle," a phrase that appeared to suggest that their own destiny as democratic societies was somehow not involved in this struggle and that this conflict concerned only the two Great Powers, both interested only in expanding their power and morally equally bad. In short, Western Europe had no stake in the outcome, and the United States, Europe's protector, was considered little or no better than the Soviet Union (Grenada was widely viewed as equivalent to Afghanistan).

The antinuclear demonstrations that took place in Western Europe, which frequently had anti-American overtones, did not help advance American-Soviet negotiations on these IRBMs. If the protests might prevent the American deployment, why should Moscow make any concessions to stop the Pershings and GLCMs emplacement? Further, by repeatedly saying that they were eager to negotiate the issue, the Soviets appeared reasonable while placing the United States on the defensive. The president thus felt compelled to respond to the demonstrations in Europe and to the Soviet initiative. So he proposed a "zero option" whereby the United States would not deploy any of its Pershings and cruise missiles if the Soviets dismantled all of their IRBMs, including the SS-20s. It sounded good. All intermediate range missiles were to be eliminated; what could be more beneficial for peace and more moral than doing away with a whole class of dangerous weapons? For a while, it stilled the protests. But after Brezhnev's death, the new Soviet leader, Andropov, launched further initiatives. Among them was a proposal to reduce the number of SS-20s to the numbers of nuclear missiles possessed by Britain and France.

Both countries protested; their missiles were not part of the superpower balance, and France declared again that its missiles were an independent force and not part of the NATO alliance. The United States agreed with all these points, but America's rejection of the Soviet initiative again placed Washington on the defensive. European leaders began to talk of an "interim solution." Zero missiles could still be the ultimate objective. European governments were clearly worried about the mass demonstrations and how their own position would be weakened if they accepted the American missiles. Especially Chancellor Kohl of West Germany, who during the 1983 election campaigned on loyalty to the Western alliance, had cause for concern if no American-Soviet agreement could be negotiated. For the Protestant churches, the universities, the left-wing of the Social Democratic opposition party, and a new party, which called itself the Greens, were all opposed to the deployment, the latter militantly so. A mixture of environmentalists (against all things nuclear), pacifists, neutralists, and just antiestablishment figures, the Greens were the party of the streets, although they had won some representation in the West German parliament in 1983. As in the United States, the lack of productive arms-control negotiations strengthened the "peace movement."

But Western Europe's clinging to *détente* after Afghanistan and Poland and years of Soviet military growth, and its constant cry for arms control suggested something more than a natural concern to take measures to lower the risks of war. These actions had about them a sense of desperation—not because the situation was desperate—but because the Europeans wished to avoid taking the measures necessary for their own defense. *Détente* and arms control were therefore offered as substitutes for making that effort. After being defended for over three decades by the United States, the European allies, whose combined population and industrial output exceeded that of the Soviet Union, were still unwilling to raise the size of their forces and relied not only on the American strategic deterrent but also on 300,000 Americans to bolster their own forces; none of the major allies, except France, was meeting the agreed-upon NATO defense budget increases. This was at a time when the Soviet forces opposite NATO had grown in numbers and, more important, had been equipped with large numbers of much more sophisticated weapons. In tanks, for example, the Soviets vastly outnumbered the NATO forces.

The Warsaw Pact armies were generally considered superior in numbers of men and in equipment; the Soviet Union now also possessed SS-20s to deter a Western attempt to even the odds by resorting to tactical or battlefield nuclear weapons; and the superpowers strategically neutralized one another so that the threat of using the American strategic forces was no longer as credible as it had once been as a deterrent to a Soviet invasion of Western Europe. One obvious response by NATO in these circumstances would be to field adequate conventionally armed military forces, including sufficient ground forces, to hold a Soviet armored thrust and blunt it without resorting to nuclear weapons unless the enemy used them first. But the European allies were unwilling to significantly upgrade their defense efforts; to pay more for defense, especially at a time of unemployment; or conscript more men for military service. In the final analysis, they were unwilling to sacrifice the high benefits of the American nuclear-protected welfare states they had created. It was easier to try to preserve a *détente* separate from their major protector, to talk with Moscow regardless of its behavior, not to take any actions (as they accused the Americans of taking) that might provoke the Soviets, and to emphasize arms control instead of strengthening their own defenses and shifting public expenditures from the social to the military sector.

Western Europe, in short, appeared even less prepared to build up its conventional forces to deter Moscow than it had been thirty years earlier, when Europe's economic condition after World War II had at least provided a reasonable excuse. So it looked to nonmilitary policies to compensate for its lack of military muscle. The end result could only be increased demands in the United States for the withdrawal of American forces from Europe. Most of the American defense budget allocated for hardware and maintenance was not spent on strategic forces; half went for the upkeep of conventional forces whose primary mission was the defense of Europe. Could an American president continue to justify this tax burden when its allies (except for France) taxed themselves at a lower percent of the gross national product to defend themselves, not even meeting the figures they had agreed to? These were, after all, *their* countries. Yet in Western Europe in the early 1980s, public opinion seemed increasingly polarized between the neutralists—those who preferred to keep their distance from both superpowers, and appeared more worried by American missiles than Soviet missiles—and the NATO supporters, who were clearly on the defensive. French Foreign Minister Cheysson likened this growing NATO rift to a "creeping divorce."

Thirty years after its formation, NATO thus reached its greatest crisis. The alliance had witnessed many policy disputes throughout the years, but none had threatened the disintegration of the alliance, as the crisis over the deployment of the American Pershing IIs and GLCMs had. Even if the deployment were successful and the formal structure of the alliance survived, its health was very much in question. When the alliance had been formed, the Europe nations vividly remembered the failure of appeasing a totalitarian regime, the defeats and suffering of World War II, their postwar collapse, and the need for American protection against the new threat from the East. Europe in the 1980s was basically prosperous; none of its countries appeared willing to slow down welfare spending in order to spend more money on strengthening themselves militarily; the memory of having appeased Nazi Germany was fading after fifty years, and this appeasement was not even a part of the history or consciousness of the new generation that had grown up in a peaceful Europe.

Europe, protected by the United States, seemed to be forgetting the realities of international politics. Only in France, which had fielded forces that had been withdrawn from the integrated NATO structure and was deploying a growing independent French deterrent force, were there no massive antinuclear and anti-American demonstrations. And it was French Socialist president François Mitterrand who in 1983 said that "I'm against the Euromissiles (the SS-20s aimed against Western Europe). But I notice two terrible simple things about the current debate: Pacifism is in the West and the Euromissiles are in the

East. I consider this an unequal relationship." Such an imbalance, he pre-dicted, would ensure war, not avoid it. Except in France, however, the popular historical association of national independence and pride in the nation's armed forces appeared no longer to exist. Otherwise, except in a few instances, as when British forces were pulled out of NATO and used to win a victory against the Argentinians in the Falkland Islands, to great popular acclaim in Britain, NATO's armies—always commanded by an American—aroused little national enthusiasm.

Europe's defense had become, it seemed, an American responsibility. After thirty years of American stewardship, with Western Europe not having to shoulder the primary obligation for its own defense, it appeared to many Euro-peans that it was the American plans for deployment that jeopardized the peace; and parties that were formerly stalwart defenders of NATO (the British Labor Party, which had fathered containment and proposed NATO originally, and the German Social Democrats, which had first requested the deployment of the new American missiles to counter the SS-20s), now literally deserted the alliance. Given that circumstances vastly differed from when NATO was founded, one had to wonder whether if NATO were being proposed in the 1980s there would be an alliance at all, and if so, which countries would join it?

By the mid–1980s one thing was very clear: The intermediate-range nuclear weapons issue, which had started out as a strictly military issue, had become a political one. The military issue no longer seemed important; the question of whether the alliance would survive—and was worth rescuing—was para-mount. The decision to deploy the Pershing IIs and GLCMs had been an alliance decision. Attempts to negotiate with the Soviets a reduction of their constantly growing SS-20 force against a smaller U.S. deployment had been fruitless. Moscow refused to accept any American deployment and rejected the principle of superpower equality. The Soviet purpose was clearly political: to exploit Europe's fear of war in order to drive a wedge between the NATO allies, especially between Europe and the United States. The Soviets had no reason to compromise in separate arms-control negotiations on this issue; they had every reason to see whether European public opinion would abort the American deployment, leaving the alliance with, as President Reagan worded it, "Warsaw Pact, 300 SS-20s, NATO, zero!" The Soviets could deploy their missiles and target every European capital, but the United States could not deploy missiles which could hit the Soviet Union. "What Moscow has is not negotiable, what NATO has is," was the message.

In brief, could NATO, having made a key decision, stick with that decision? Or would it show itself to be incapable not only of sticking with its defense and diplomatic strategy but of resisting pressures from within that were abetted by shrewd Soviet political propaganda? If the Soviets had been genuinely con-cerned about the U.S. missiles, especially the accurate Pershing IIs, which could strike at Soviet military targets in western Russia more quickly than missiles from the United States, they could have prevented their installation through genuine negotiations. But Moscow sought to avoid their installation without making any concessions. It was determined to test the strength of the Western "peace movements." That is why the alliance itself was at stake on this issue. And the gravity of the situation was magnified by the fact that in Britain and Germany, governments had recently been elected that had campaigned in favor of the American deployment. So not only was the alliance at stake but the democratic process. Would governments elected by clear majorities give in to the constant "peace marches"? Was the alliance and the viability of democratic elections to be negated by the politics of the street?

The SS-20 Pershing II issue was for Moscow a means of destroying the alliance by accelerating the growing split between the United States and Western Europe that had started with the decline of *détente*. No such serious issue had confronted the alliance since German rearmament in the early 1950s and the Berlin crisis after 1957. For these two issues had involved the future of NATO, its ability to face down intimidation and remain united. Above all, they had involved a struggle for West Germany, NATO's strongest member, without whose territory the alliance could not defend itself. Moscow obviously wanted to detach it from NATO and destroy the alliance and Washington to keep it within the alliance. Given the political stakes for each superpower, should it have been a surprise that American-Soviet relations reached a low point in the early 1980s, regardless of who their respective leaders were? Neither side was willing to compromise in what it regarded as a critical test of wills; and when the United States began its deployment during the cold winter months of 1983– 1984, was it really a surprise that Moscow walked out of all arms-control negotiations in order to raise European fears of war another notch and stampede Western Europe into an even greater neutralism and pacifism, and that the chill in American-Soviet relations continued? The "Euromissiles" issue, then, was as good a test as any of whether Europe still had the will to withstand Soviet pressures, and it left to the future the other issue of whether it would assume more of the burden of its own defense.

Indeed, the key question was whether the Europe of the Common Market would ever gain the economic and political influence it could have if it marshaled its political will. It is perhaps not entirely coincidental that the years of the missile crisis were also the years that would decide whether the Common Market would survive. Originally, a bargain between agricultural France and industrialized West Germany (and later, Britain), the Common Market was producing lakes of milk and wine and mountains of butter because agriculture was protected and subsidized; the industrialized countries, who contributed much of the Market's budget, wanted these subsidies reduced and the funds invested in industrial development and technology. Thus the fundamental deal that had led to the foundation of the European Economic Community appeared to be in danger, a symptom of Europe's continued lack of will to organize itself, to transcend its nation-state basis as was originally envisioned, and to find a new direction in which to go in this postcolonial superpower age.

THE MIDDLE EAST AND THE
ANTI-SOVIET STRATEGIC CONSENSUS

The oil in the Arabian peninsula and in some of the nearby countries clearly had made this area critical for the United States and the West in general since the early 1970s. But, as already noted, the area was both threatened and unstable. With a sizable army in Afghanistan on the border of Pakistan, a recently dismembered nation that was caught between the Soviet sphere and unfriendly India, and with the use of air and port facilities in Ethiopia and South Yemen, the Soviet presence in the area and its threat to the oil and shipping lines—lifelines for the West—were real. The increasing nearness of Soviet power and influence frightened Saudi Arabia and the other oil kingdoms, which were already confronting the possibility of domestic instability as a result of the presence of workers of foreign nationality (such as Palestinians) and fundamentalist Islamic groups opposed to Western-style modernization. The Carter Doctrine was a symbol of America's vital interest in the area. The establishment of a Rapid Deployment Force (which in 1984 was still basically neither rapid, deployed, nor a force); the search for bases in Kenya, Somalia, and Oman; the modernization of the base on the island of Diego Garcia in the Indian Ocean; the sizable U.S. fleet in the Indian Ocean-Persian Gulf area; and the discussions of possible military cooperation with Egypt (with whose forces the United States held common exercises)—these were all part of an American effort to establish an American presence and balance Soviet power in the area. The superpower rivalry was thus imposed on top of the potential and actual internal instability of key countries, as well as on regional rivalries such as those of India and Pakistan and of Iran and Iraq. And, of course, the politics of the area could hardly be separated from the Arab (minus Egypt)-Israeli quarrel, with which they often intersected. Arab unity was shattered by the Iraqi-Iranian war; Libya and Syria supported non-Arab Iran, while former adversaries of Iraq such as Jordan helped it; even Egypt, the target of Iraq's Rejectionist Front, sent arms. The area was a veritable tinderbox.

An assassination of a few oil kingdom sheiks; unstable political conditions in countries such as Iran and Iraq; overthrows of pro-Western conservative regimes (like that of the Shah in Iran); more wars between Arabs and Israelis, and among Arabs, Arabs and non-Arabs; further extensions of Soviet influence—all these threatened the price and security of future oil supplies. These supplies were abundant in 1981 mainly because Saudi Arabia produced 2 million barrels of oil per day more than its normal production before Iran's revolution and the later Iraqi-Iranian war; the West's economic recession had also substantially decreased the demand for oil.

The Reagan administration pursued a twofold foreign policy strategy in order to reduce this insecurity. First, based upon the assumption that Saudi Arabia, the key oil country, kept its distance from the United States because of its lack of confidence in American leadership and power, the new administration decided to upgrade the U.S.-Saudi relationship by agreeing to sell the Saudis the fuel tanks and air-to-air missiles they requested for their F-15 fighters as well as five Airborne Warning and Control System (AWACS) aircraft—Boeing 707s with large disklike antennas mounted on them—even though the Israelis worried about the threat these aircraft posed to them because of their ability to collect information on Israeli air force movements. President Reagan vowed that "we will not permit [Saudi Arabia] to be an Iran," thereby upgrading Carter's commitment to protect Persian Gulf states against external forces. For this statement implied that the United States would protect the Saudi government even against internal insurrection.

If reassuring Saudi Arabia of its special relationship with the United States and America's ability and willingness to protect the kingdom's security was fundamental U.S. political strategy, what about the Arab-Israeli conflict? Reagan administration officials were fond of stating that the region's various rivalries and domestic instabilities were only marginally related to the Arab-Israeli struggle, suggesting thereby that if the United States could establish its power in the area and the pro-Western regimes then felt more secure, the oil supplies for the West would also be more secure. The key issue was American leadership and the credibility of American power, not the self-determination of the Palestinians, the critical issue blocking a more comprehensive Arab-Israeli peace.

The second part of the Reagan strategy was therefore to stress the anti-Soviet nature of its policy. Fundamentally, this attempt to forge an anti-Soviet "strategic consensus" was intended to overcome the Arabs' resistance to joining forces with the United States because of their resentment of Israeli policy; specifically, its purpose was to gain the cooperation of countries such as Egypt, Jordan, Saudi Arabia, and Pakistan, as well as Israel. They should all give priority to containing Soviet influence, subordinating their local quarrels to this more important task. This approach amounted to downplaying the central Arab-Israeli conflict and postponing a settlement of the most critical problem preventing a settlement, the Palestinian problem.

It was not a successful strategy. The Israelis continued to be very anxious about any weapons sold to any Arab state, and Saudi Arabia, as an Arab state, could hardly ignore the Palestinian and other issues. In fact, the Saudis argued strongly that the increasing frustration and anger about the lack of progress on the Palestinian issue was the *main* danger to the U.S. interest in keeping the oil flowing and that *all* Arabs, not just Israel's neighbors, felt the same way. Only the establishment of a Palestinian state would eliminate much of the regional anti-U.S. feeling, which made it impossible for any Arab state to be closely linked to the United States or cooperate with it fully on oil or military issues. In short, the countries in the area continued to give priority to their quarrels while the United States continued to search for ways of resolving both the oil and the Arab-Israeli problems, problems that refused to be divorced from each other.

The administration received four lessons early. The first came in Lebanon,

Israel's small northern neighbor, which several years earlier had disintegrated into civil war between Christians and Muslims. The former, long the wealthier and politically the more influential, sought to retain their position by suppressing the Palestinians, whose presence had become sizable after Jordan's King Hussein had driven them out of his country during the early 1970s. Sympathetic to their fellow Arabs and their aspirations for a greater say in Lebanese affairs, which would reflect their rapidly growing numbers, the Palestinians, heavily armed, constituted a threat to the integrity of Lebanon. They upset the agreement of the Christians and Lebanese Muslims for a domestic redistribution of power because the more militant left-wing forces felt that they could militarily defeat the Christians with the help of the Palestine Liberation Organization (PLO) and win most of the political power. Syria, however, was opposed to a solution that would probably have led to a Christian secession from Lebanon and the establishment of two states, one Christian and one Muslim. It therefore sought Lebanon's survival and political integrity, first through political mediation and, when that proved unsuccessful, through military intervention. Syria did so for several reasons: to boost its prestige; to prevent creation of a Muslim neighbor with a more radical and militant leadership than Syria's own; to avoid being dragged into a war with Israel by such a leadership at a time of the latter's choosing; and mostly, to establish its dominance in Lebanon, essentially incorporating it into Syria's sphere of influence.

An uneasy peace, frequently violated, prevailed as the Syrians tried to keep the peace. But this Christian-Syrian alliance was an unnatural one. The Christian-Israeli alliance was a better partnership since the two groups shared an interest in containing, indeed in weakening, PLO influence. Close cooperation followed. After an Israeli invasion of southern Lebanon to destroy PLO bases, the Israelis let the Christians take over the area and supplied them with arms in order to provide a buffer zone between themselves and the PLO; they also secretly committed the Israeli air force to defend the Christians against Syrian airstrikes. The Syrians, in their turn, were sympathetic to the Muslim majority fighting the Christians. Lebanon was slowly disintegrating in a civil war in which each side was supported by an external power.

One of these incidents in 1981 escalated quickly when Israeli fighters shot down two Syrian helicopters during a fight with Christian forces blocking the road from Beirut, Lebanon's capital, to Damascus, Syria's capital. Subsequently, the Syrians brought ground-to-air missiles into Lebanon. The Israelis were determined to destroy the missiles if Syria refused to withdraw them because they threatened Israeli air superiority over Lebanon and therefore Israeli ability to strike at PLO bases. Because a military clash between Syria and Israel might realign the Arab states with Syria and again link the United States with Israel; and because it would also place the Soviet Union, with whom Syria had a treaty of friendship, on the Arab side, the Reagan administration mediated the issue. Thereafter the issue faded for a while; nevertheless, it demonstrated dramatically once more that the Arab-Israeli conflict provided the powerful political and emotional context through which most other problems, including oil, were filtered.

In the midst of these negotiations, the Reagan administration received the second lesson, an even more dramatic reminder that the Arab-Israeli conflict could not be subordinated to an anti-Soviet strategic consensus. Asserting that Iraq, an oil-rich nation, would use its new nuclear reactor to produce nuclear bombs, which it would then drop on Israel, the Israeli air force attacked and destroyed the reactor just before it became operational. Whether Iraq, which had signed the nuclear nonproliferation treaty, would have produced such bombs or used them to destroy Israel, which had not signed this treaty, is of course unknown. Israel's claim was based upon Iraq's possession of a reactor; Iraqi leadership of the Arab states rejecting the Camp David peace process; and an Iraqi leader whom Israeli Prime Minister Menachem Begin claimed was a "tyrant" and "crazy." Presumably, this description meant that he would produce and use the bomb against the "Zionists" and that the two dozen nuclear bombs that the Israelis were said to possess would not suffice to deter the Iraqis (although a former defense and foreign minister said that Israel only had the capacity to produce A-bombs and needed a "short-time" to manufacture them). Clearly, the Israeli idea of self-defense was a very broad one and included the right to attack a potentially hostile neighbor who might develop nuclear arms and attack Israel with them.

Despite Israel's claim that its action had reduced chances of nuclear proliferation, Washington viewed this airstrike as politically damaging. It revived the perception of Israel as the prime Arab foe, set back U.S. efforts to portray the Soviet Union as the chief threat to the area and forge an anti-Soviet alliance with moderate Arab states, and endangered further peace efforts toward achieving a broader Arab-Israeli peace. The airstrike also confronted the president with an unpleasant dilemma: If the United States acquiesced in the Israeli action it would risk alienating the moderate Arab states, including Saudi Arabia; if it punished Israel, it would stir domestic opposition. Thus it joined Iraq in the United Nations in condemning Israel, but the condemnation had no teeth in it, for the United States insisted that no sanctions be applied, although it temporarily withheld several jet fighterplanes from delivery. This mild slap on the wrist was viewed by the Arabs as confirmation on America's one-sided attitude, regardless of how extreme or provocative Israel's actions were.

The third jolt to the Reagan strategy of subordinating the Arab-Israeli conflict to an anti-Soviet strategy was the reelection of Begin as Prime Minister of Israel. Begin, having made peace with the only Arab state that had potential power to be a threat to Israel, saw no reason to be accommodating on other issues. Washington had hoped that the Labor Party would win the election and take a more flexible approach when the peace process was resumed. Instead, the most right-wing government in Israel's existence came to power. Begin appointed a foreign minister who had opposed the peace with Egypt, a defense minister who as an earlier agricultural minister had been in charge of an aggressive policy of settling the West Bank, and—symbolic of Begin's annexationist policy before and after the election—an *interior* minister who was in charge of the Palestinian autonomy talks! Begin had always pursued Israeli interests, as he defined them, regardless of American preferences, offering occasional demonstrations of the natural order of things turned upside down—of a small country manipulating its far stronger protector (and able to do so because most U.S. presidents were genuinely concerned about Israeli security as well as fearful of domestic repercussions if they pressured Israel).

As if to underline his determination to act independently, Begin followed his attack on Iraq's nuclear reactor with a powerful air attack on the Palestinian headquarters in Beirut, which caused a sizable loss of civilian lives. Washington reacted in anger, denouncing Begin and continuing the suspension of delivery to Israel of U.S. jets. But the Reagan administration's preoccupation with the Soviet threat to the area weakened any resolve to pressure Israel to be more accommodating; for Israel, as the strongest military state in the area, appeared in that context as a valuable ally.

This fourth blow was the biggest one of all to the administration: the assassination of President Sadat in October 1981. While both Israel and Egypt immediately announced that they remained committed to carrying out the remaining provision of their peace treaty—the final Israeli withdrawal from the Sinai in April 1982—uncertainty over the future increased. The Camp David peace process would have been endangered at that point anyway, even had Sadat lived, for Israel remained bent on annexing the West Bank. Sadat's whole policy had been based from the beginning upon the belief that the United States would pressure Israel; in that respect, the United States had clearly failed him. No American administration had been willing to take that domestically political risky course. None had been willing even to speak out publicly about what had been the U.S. interpretation of Camp David and how the peace process was supposed to evolve, or to say that Begin's policy was the reason for Egypt's isolation in the Arab world, criticism of—and opposition to—Sadat at home, and the increasing perception in the region of the United States as either one-sided or an ineffective mediator.

The Palestinian issue was not the only question on which Washington and Israel differed, as Begin quickly demonstrated when, unexpectedly, and without consulting the United States he annexed Syria's Golan Heights. As in his attacks on the Iraqi nuclear reactor and Beirut, Begin again showed his willingness to act unilaterally, his concern only for Israeli interests as he interpreted them, and his total disregard for the interests and concerns of the United States, his principal source of protection and military and economic assistance. When the United States, feeling that cooperation between the two countries was a two-way street, voiced its displeasure, Begin characteristically lashed out, viciously accusing the administration of practicing anti-Semitism, breaking its word, and treating Israel like a "banana republic." Begin clearly thought that Israel should be able to do whatever it wanted and that America should support Israel, regardless of the consequences its action had on American interests;

even if the United States thought that Begin's moves jeopardized the peace process, increased Egypt's isolation, and weakened America's position in the area, it should keep quiet. In short, while Israel could be insensitive to American interests, America should be sensitive to Israeli interests; to do less was to be disloyal, even anti-Semitic.

What the Israeli action did, however, was to raise the key question of whether Israel and the Unites States could work together for peace. The American assumption had always been that a Middle East peace could be built upon an exchange of the 1967 Israeli-conquered Arab territories for Arab acceptance of Israel; the Israeli withdrawal from the Sinai suggested that Israel shared that belief. But increasingly since the peace treaty with Egypt, it had become clearer that Begin's Israel preferred the expansion of territory to peace with its neighbors based fundamentally on the 1967 borders. Negotiations were replaced by annexation—of East Jerusalem, the Golan Heights, and, for all practical purposes, the West Bank and Gaza. Could the United States in these circumstances still assume that Israel would withdraw from these areas in return for Arab acceptance of Israel, and more fundamentally, that American and Israeli interests coincided?

The 1982 Israeli invasion of Lebanon to crush the PLO and solve the political problem of the Palestinians by purely military means, dramatically underlined this critical question. The reason given for this invasion was the danger to Israeli citizens in northern Israeli settlements from PLO artillery and rocket fire. The stated purpose was to drive the PLO back from the border and establish a rocket-free zone. The immediate cause for the invasion was the assassination of the Israeli ambassador to England by, the Israelis claimed, the PLO. The PLO denied the charge. Clearly, the Begin government was looking for a pretext to set in motion detailed plans for an invasion long planned. Once the invasion began, it also became very clear that the Israeli goal was more than the security of its citizens living along the border with Lebanon. No immediate danger to their lives existed; the American-negotiated truce had held over nine months. The very fact that the Israeli forces hardly stopped for refueling once they were twenty-five miles deep into Lebanon but continued their rapid advance toward Lebanon's capital of Beirut suggested that West Beirut, the Moslem half of the city where the PLO had its headquarters, had been the principal goal all along. If the Israeli forces could militarily defeat the PLO and politically humiliate it, they would be doing more than ensuring the safety of Israeli citizens from PLO terror; crushing the PLO would, it was hoped, destroy Palestinian nationalism on the West Bank. Once the Arabs there could no longer look to the PLO for leadership in establishing a Palestinian state, they would be more likely to submit to the inevitable Israeli annexation of the area; demoralized and without hope, what else could they do but accept the inevitable? Another principal aim was to place Lebanon more firmly in control of the Christians, who were friendly to Israel, and thus enhance Israeli security on its northern border.

But the siege of Beirut was to turn events upside down and once more demonstrate that a military victory cannot always be transformed into a desirable political settlement. Every night for several weeks, the television showed Israeli warplanes, tanks, and artillery pounding West Beirut, bringing destruction and human misery, and world criticism of Israel grew. Even though it was the PLO that decided to fight in the city among the civilian population, the heavy Israeli fire greatly damaged Israel's reputation in the West. In its previous three wars, it had attacked only after an attack on it appeared certain or had in fact occurred. No such danger to Israeli security had existed before the invasion of Lebanon. The invasion was therefore widely viewed as an unprovoked offensive action, and none of the ever-changing, publicly stated reasons given for it had much to do with the real reasons why it was launched. Israel not only shocked many of its admirers by the transparency of the rationales it offered but also by the disproportion between the means it used and the limited ends it claimed to be seeking. The massive use of force did, however, achieve the central Israeli aim: the expulsion of the PLO from Beirut. Abandoned by their fellow Arabs, as well as their Soviet friends, the PLO finally gave in and accepted an American-negotiated truce that kept Israeli forces out of West Beirut and provided for a multinational peace-keeping force composed of Italian, British, French, and American troops to supervise their exit mainly via ship to the twenty-odd Arab countries.

Yet, ironically, in victory the Israelis defeated themselves. Seeking to crush the PLO and thereby Palestinian nationalism, they made the Palestinians a central political issue. Initially, the Israelis shamed everyone: the Arab states not neighboring on Israel that did not lift a finger to help the PLO (and only reluctantly accepted their "freedom fighters" after their defeat); the front-line Arab states, including Syria, whose Soviet-equipped and -trained army in Lebanon was badly mauled by the Israelis; Egypt, whose peace with Israel seemed even more of a betrayal of the Arab cause (and whose only action, short of violating that peace, was to recall its ambassador from Israel); the Soviets, who said that they were not going to bail out the PLO when the Arabs themselves stood by; and the United States, which in Arab eyes had tacitly approved the Israeli invasion because it had failed to stop it. However, the pounding of West Beirut angered President Reagan and tested his strong pro-Israeli feeling, which had already been eroding as a result of Begin's earlier actions.

It now appeared to the president that the Palestinian problem could not be subordinated to regional anti-Soviet policy; that the Arab-Israeli problem was a separate issue; and that the key to resolving that conflict, as well as establishing closer and more cordial relationships with the Arab countries, including the oil producers, was resolving the future of the Palestinians. The Israeli government, insensitive to American interests in the area while heavily dependent upon American aid and weapons, expecting Washington to acquiesce in the invasion of Lebanon and the *coup de grâce* delivered to the PLO, now found itself alienated from the United States and faced by an American initiative it had neither expected nor welcomed. Clearly separating himself from Begin's policy, President Reagan proposed a new peace plan whose basic features were genuine autonomy for the Palestinians living on the West Bank and Gaza and the association of the West Bank with Jordan. In short, there would be no Palestinian state, which Israel constantly declared was unacceptable because it would pose a security risk despite Israel's obvious military superiority over any Arab state. But there would also be no Israeli annexation of the West Bank; instead, Israel was expected to withdraw from most of the West Bank. While the initial Arab and PLO reaction was one of interest, the immediate reaction of Prime Minister Begin was a swift, abusive, and total rejection.

Israel appeared to be isolating itself in the world, even among Jews. The always loyal Jewish community in the United States largely supported the president in his peace efforts. The World Zionist Congress, meeting in Israel at the time, denounced Begin's efforts to annex the West Bank. And then came the real shock, a human tragedy that placed the Israeli invasion, Prime Minister Begin, and his defense minister, Ariel Sharon—the man largely responsible for Israel's policy on the West Bank and the invasion of Lebanon—in the global limelight. In Lebanon, a country deeply divided between Christians and Moslems, whose hatred for one another had grown during the bloody civil war, the newly elected pro-Israeli leader of the Christian, or Phalangist, militia was assassinated on the eve of becoming president. Begin and Sharon immediately sent Israeli forces into West Beirut in violation of the truce (the multinational peace-keeping forces had already been pulled out). Ostensibly they did so to protect the Muslim population from Christian revenge; but the real aims appear to have been to gain control over West Beirut and to make the United States (which had arranged the truce, which was supposed to keep the Israelis out of West Beirut) look helpless. This, in turn, would undermine the support the president needed from the moderate Arab states for his peace plan. Once in West Beirut, the Israelis called on the Christian militia, the Phalangists, to go into the Palestinian refugee camps to rout out any remaining PLO terrorists. The purpose was to save the lives of Israeli soldiers. But the Christian forces then proceeded to slaughter several hundred Palestinians, mainly women, children, and older men.

The worldwide shock registered even in Israel. To what extent were Israel's leaders and army implicated? At best, knowing of the hatred and past killings between Christians and Moslems, the Israeli authorities should have known better than to send the Phalangists into the Palestinian camps in the wake of their leader's death, presumably at the hands of Muslims. Begin, hardly taking the time to express his sorrow at this turn of events, denied any responsibility and harshly denounced the critics. But the strength and decency of Israeli democracy insisted otherwise. Begin refused to establish an impartial judicial commission of inquiry. The president of Israel, however, normally a symbolic figure, intervened and publicly called for such an inquiry as a moral necessity. Street demonstrations also occurred. Jewish leaders in Europe and America too protested Begin's decision. The prime minister was compelled to change his mind. How could a Jewish state, composed of people so long persecuted themselves, do otherwise than investigate this tragedy, even if direct responsibility for the massacre lay with Lebanese Christians? How could a country that arose out of the slaughter of 6 million Jews by the Nazis not feel that Israel's moral reputation had been stained? How could Israeli officials be held blameless, especially after they had sent Israeli troops into West Beirut allegedly to protect the Muslim population?

For many Jews in Israel and outside, Begin and Sharon had squandered Israel's most precious asset, its self-respect and the respect of the world. The subsequent report by the judicial commission did, indeed, hold Israel "indirectly responsible." It issued separate reports on Begin, Sharon, Israel's foreign minister, the chief of staff, and the commanding general in Beirut, among others, assessing their responsibility. Specifically, it recommended Sharon's dismissal as defense minister and, by implication, from the government. Characteristic of Begin's general insensitivity and refusal to accept any blame for Israel, he asked Sharon to give up the Defense Ministry but kept him in the cabinet, thus accepting the inquiry's recommendation but violating the spirit of the recommendation.

If Begin and Sharon appeared morally callous and Israeli policy too eager to use force to resolve problems, Lebanon also showed the Arabs to be lacking in foresight and courage. While neither the Arab states nor the PLO completely rejected the president's plan, they soon reaffirmed their commitments to an Israeli withdrawal to the 1967 borders, a Palestinian state, and the PLO as the representative of Palestinian nationalism. Despite words to the effect that they were willing to accept co-existence with Israel, and despite several meetings between King Hussein and PLO leader Arafat during which the two men explored the possibility of Hussein's negotiating on behalf of the PLO, nothing happened. Little attention was given to Hussein's reported warning that if the Reagan initiative were allowed to die, Israel would determine the West Bank issue once and for all with its settlement policy. There was little time left for the Arabs to negotiate, reverse the Israeli policy of annexation, and gain American backing. The time may have passed for a Palestinian state, and the Reagan plan might be the most that could still be achieved to advance Palestinian goals.

But the PLO remained divided between moderates and rejectionists who sought the destruction of Israel. As in earlier years, Arafat was unwilling either to crush the extremists or to split the organization in order to get the best deal possible before time ran out. The Arab leaders were also unwilling to seize the initiative. This included Jordan's King Hussein, who would not proceed without PLO consent. Despite its military defeat, the politically weakened PLO was allowed to exercise a veto to prevent the moderate Arab states from exploring the Reagan plan. There was, in short, no Sadat who was willing to seize the opportunity, and announce that he was willing to accept Israel and negotiate with it on the basis of the American formula; and who, had the Israeli government rejected this offer, would have placed Israel on the defensive, isolated her diplomatically, especially from the United States; divided Jewish opinion within and outside of Israel; and stimulated a serious debate within Israel about the wisdom of once again exchanging territory for a secure peace versus the wisdom of annexing the West Bank, a course opposed by both the Arabs and the United States, a course that also risked transforming the character of Israel (the addition of another 1 million Arabs, whose birth rate was higher than the Jewish one, would someday threaten Israel's Jewish character, its democratic character if it denied them the vote, and its humane character if it uprooted most of them and drove them out). With the PLO defeated, its "freedom fighters" scattered over many Arab countries, all of whom exercised tight control over them, its "armed struggle" against Israel no longer a real option, and Arafat's control contested by Syria—and with a global "oil glut" rendering the Arab "oil weapon" impotent—was there an alternative to a diplomatic solution? With the United States having distanced itself from Begin (who quit office in late 1983) and having advanced a peace plan more sympathetic to Palestinian aims than any previous American plan, the enormity of the Arabs' lack of political imagination and courage to seize this fleeting opportunity was startling. American officials were especially disappointed that the Saudis, the recipients of so much political and military assistance from the United States in recent years, were unwilling to use their influence to urge the PLO and/or Jordan to negotiate within the Reagan framework. As for Arafat, by allowing the PLO rejectionists to block negotiations, he condemned the PLO to political irrelevance.

Nor did the United States escape from Lebanon unscathed; it too was to blunder there as a result of Lebanese politics and regional rivalries. Lebanon, as noted, had long been divided between the wealthier and politically powerful Christians and the poorer and politically less influential Arabs (Druse, Sunni, and Shiite Muslims). As the latter grew in numbers and the demographic balance between Christians and Arabs changed, the Arabs demanded a domestic redistribution of power reflecting the new population distribution. The PLO, settling in Lebanon after being ejected from Jordan, had in the 1970s backed this demand with support and arms. The PLO's defeat by the Israelis in 1982 thus shifted power to the Christians and led to the formation of an Israeli-supported, Christian-dominated government. But this did not settle the fundamental constitutional problem of how Lebanon could end its civil war and govern itself peacefully; quite the contrary, it fired up the domestic war among the various political and religious factions, all of whom had their own armies.

The Israelis also demanded a normalization of Lebanese-Israeli relations; in short, they demanded a peace treaty as the price of withdrawing their troops. This, it was widely assumed, would then lead to a simultaneous Syrian troop withdrawal, allowing Lebanon once more to govern itself. The reason Israel demanded more than security arrangements for its northern border with Lebanon—the original pretext for the invasion—was that the Israelis had suffered high casualties and the war had for the first time led to domestic protests. The government therefore needed to justify these losses and pacify the opposition.

Peace with another Arab state appeared to be a prize worth Israeli sacrifices. Lebanon's fragile Christian-dominated government was reluctant to accede to Israeli terms, however; it knew that most of its Arab population would refuse to go along. But it finally accepted an American-mediated agreement because it appeared to be the only way to get the Israelis and Syrians out of Lebanon.

Not only were Lebanon's Arabs thus opposed to the government because it was Christian-dominated, but there was now the added factor of the peace with Israel. Most important, Syria, which had opposed the earlier Israeli-Egyptian peace, opposed the terms of this peace as well and refused to withdraw its 50,000 troops. As Israeli forces, tired of the continued losses of lives, pulled back to southern Lebanon, Syrian influence grew. During the months that the Israelis had refused to pull back and had pressured the Lebanese government to accept the normalization agreement, the Soviets had reequipped the Syrian armed forces, badly defeated by the Israelis in 1982, and had sent along 7000 military advisers to Syria. This strengthened Syria's resolve and its hand in settling Lebanon's future. Besides helping the PLO dissidents to destroy Arafat, the Syrians now supplied the military hardware the various Arab militias needed to attack the Lebanese government and its small, new, and poorly trained army.

In the midst of this escalating and fiercely fought civil war, the multinational peace-keeping force no longer had a peace to keep. The approximately 1500 U.S. marines, even with the fleet offshore, were in no position to impose domestic peace. There were only two possible ways of doing so: an Israeli attack on the Syrian army in Lebanon, if Israel wished to preserve the pro-Israeli Christian government and the peace agreement; or an American attack on Syrian forces or Druse and Shiite forces around Beirut. Only if Syria or its Lebanese friends were bloodied and weakened would they have reason to be more accommodating in negotiations with the Christians about Lebanon's domestic political power distribution and Lebanon's withdrawal from the Arab confrontation with Israel. But Israel had wearied of the war it had started; and Washington could not politically send sizable U.S. forces to Lebanon to battle Syria. Much of American public opinion was not persuaded that preventing Lebanon's partition between Syria and Israel was a vital interest of America. Israel had always had a keen sense of its own security and acted accordingly; let it do so now if it felt its security threatened.

Nevertheless, without ever announcing it, President Reagan changed the marines' mission. He judged it to be important to preserve the Lebanese government from its domestic opponents and their Syrian supporters. Their victory over the government, whose jurisdiction at the time did not extend beyond Beirut's city limits (if that far), was likely to result in a basically anti-American, anti-Israeli government controlled by Syria; and Syria had close relations with Moscow, as well as with Libya and Khomeini's Iran. The role of the marines and the fleet was thus shifted from keeping the peace to enforcing it on behalf of a pro-American and pro-Israeli government. It should be clearly understood that this meant that the United States was supporting one side in a civil war; the Arab factions were thus bound to see the marines and the navy offshore, no longer as noncombatants, but as enemies. They began to fire on the marines' position at the Beirut airport, where the marines had dug in to protect themselves as best as they could. The best tragically proved inadequate as pro-Iranian Shiites filled a truck with gas-enhanced explosives equaling in tonnage an atomic bomb and in a suicide mission destroyed a barracks where the marines were sleeping. Some 241 deaths occurred as a result of this terror attack, which could not possibly have been organized without Syrian knowledge, if not help. The demands to bring the marines back home now increased.

The president resisted these demands, although 1984 was an election year and Lebanon was a political liability for him. Events, however, allowed him to change his mind and pull out the marines as the Syrian-backed Muslim factions defeated the Lebanese army, many of whose Muslim soldiers deserted as the fighting continued. The cabinet resigned. Only then did the Christian president, previously unwilling to make sufficient concessions to achieve "national reconciliation" because of American support, prove more willing to make the government more representative and renounce the agreement with Israel. But the victorious Muslims and Syria now said that these concessions were too little and too late. They were clearly bent on destroying the American-supported government. The Syrians in particular appeared determined to humiliate Washington and show the world who was the victor. Lebanon was in effect partitioned between Syria in the east, Israel in the south, with Syria the dominant influence in Beirut as well. Most of Lebanon thus fell in Syria's sphere of influence, as almost everyone else looked back at the Lebanese quagmire, recalled their original expectations and aims, and then assessed the rather meager results.

For the United States in particular, the withdrawal of the marines and the collapse of the Christian-dominated government and the Lebanese-Israeli treaty was a bitter experience—a defeat, to put it frankly. The Reagan administration had tried to demonstrate to Arab moderates that unlike its predecessor, it would be a staunch friend, someone they could rely on in a crisis. The result in Lebanon suggested the contrary. Apparently, the better part of wisdom might be to keep one's distance from the United States, an unreliable and weak friend with little stomach for a fight with even a small but tough adversary. American prestige, on the line once the marines became civil war participants, suffered a serious blow when they were pulled out and the Beirut government and its army collapsed. For many observers in the area, the friends of America—as in Vietnam and Iran—had lost again. This was surely a warning to America's remaining friends, such as Saudi Arabia and Jordan, which in the wake of the PLO's demise considered whether to negotiate with Israel. Indeed, Jordan's King Hussein abruptly announced that he would not do so.

This was surely the lesson that America's enemies wanted the states in the region to learn. It was Syria, a small, poor country with fewer than 10,000,000 people, that had finished what Israel had started and did so while the whole Arab world stood by meekly—it had humiliated Arafat and asserted its control over what was left of the PLO by militarily supporting the rejectionists in the PLO, who destroyed the remainder of Arafat's forces, once more hiding among civilians (this time in Tripoli); it had outlasted Israel, which had withdrawn its forces to its northern border; and it had forced President Reagan to pull out the marines while Syria established control in Lebanon and simultaneously made itself the powerbroker for any future Middle East negotiations. Syria's friends, like Libya and Iran, whose aim was to destabilize the pro-American oil regimes in the Gulf, could only feel great satisfaction and could perhaps feel assured that they could safely pursue their policies in opposition to the American "paper tiger." Whatever lessons Grenada was supposed to have given about the American willingness to use force and use it effectively beyond the Caribbean-Central America area were lost in Lebanon. When vital interests seem ambiguous, or even when they are starkly clear, if the nation is unwilling to use force on a scale larger than 1500 marines—and use it effectively—less prestige is lost by avoiding involvement altogether than by intervening and failing.

THE THIRD WORLD, THE CASE FOR DEMOCRATIC CAPITALISM, AND OPEC'S DECLINE

While the Reagan administration was very much concerned about the oil-producing countries, its attitudes toward the Third World in general were considerably less enthusiastic and positive—certainly less than those of the Carter administration. First, as already emphasized, during the 1970s the Third World was seen in terms of Soviet activities and the continuing superpower competition for influence. The "globalist" viewpoint prevailed once more. Second, the administration tended to view Third World demands for the New International Economic Order (NIEO) and complaints about Western capitalist exploitation, or "imperialism," with a lack of sympathy. It took a rather similar point of view of the world's poor as it did of the domestic poor, namely, that they were undeserving because they did not work hard enough; thus the less-developed countries should not look for Western "charity" to do for them what they would not do for themselves. From the beginning, the administration emphasized that the less-developed countries were responsible for their own welfare, just as it held individuals responsible for their own personal welfare at home.

Instead of aid—of which the United States in 1979, the last Carter year, gave only 0.20 percent of its gross national product, which ranked it ahead of only Austria and Italy among all Western nations—the stress was on "the magic of the marketplace," private enterprise, investments, and international trade. Selling their goods in the huge American market was, as President Reagan emphasized, the best contribution the United States could make to the less-developed countries' economic progress; in 1980, the non-OPEC countries earned $63 billion with their exports to the U.S. market, over half of these nations' manufactured goods. An improvement of the American economy would presumably help them sell even more of their exports as the U.S. demand for their goods would rise; thus the administration could claim that the priority it had given to the U.S. economy was not only the best domestic course it could pursue, but also the best foreign policy for the Third World.

As it did with regard to the Soviet Union, the administration was quick to react to Third World complaints that their problems were not their own fault and assertions that the West owed them aid and technical assistance because of past and present exploitation. The administration considered these charges unfair and rejected them. It also attacked the Third World's preference for Socialism as a system allegedly superior to capitalism for encouraging development. Not only did the administration argue that those less-developed nations that were most deeply involved in the present international economy were the best off but that it was the policies of the national governments of these self-styled Socialist states that were to blame for the lack of development. There was certainly considerable evidence to support this contention, such as the conspicuous consumption and corruption among the governing elites, the long neglect of agriculture so that many of these nations could no longer feed themselves but had to import food, and the vast spending on military hardware. The administration therefore recommended a course of self-help by means of greater domestic austerity, high savings, and productive investments.

At Cancun, Mexico, in 1981 at a meeting of twenty-two developed and less-developed countries, including China and India, the latter group tried to impress upon the U.S. president their lot and needs; they urged that "global negotiations" between the rich and poor countries deal with such problems as the distribution of wealth, food, and energy. The president, however, continued to stress the virtues of democratic capitalism and the creation of new wealth rather than the redistribution of existing wealth. He also pointedly noted that the Soviet Union's absence from the conference was a tacit admission that it had nothing to contribute, despite its claim that the world's economic problems were the result of capitalism and all solutions lay with Socialism. "Who's feeding whom?" Reagan asked. (The Soviet's response was that they had not cared to attend a meeting of the "civilized plunderers" and "the plundered.") The United States was taking a critical and adversary position and reminding the less-developed countries that the American experience had combined economic development, political freedom, and respect for human dignity.* It was this emphasis on private investments and trade, rather than governmentally provided economic aid, which was the focus of the president's Caribbean Basin plan to assist the non-Communist Caribbean and Central

*The Reagan administration's attitudes to the Third World are well expressed in Peter Berger's "Speaking to the Third World," *Commentary*, October 1981, pp. 29–36.

American nations to combat further domestic radicalization by dealing with their social and economic problems.

The American decision not to accept Third World charges that their poverty was due to an exploitive Western-dominated international economy, or that the West was morally obligated to assist the less-developed countries by creating a NIEO, spilled over into a general critique of their self-professed nonalignment. In October 1981 a delegation from ninety-three Third World nations issued a communiqué harshly criticizing the United States for such things as stimulating the arms race (without mentioning the long Soviet build-up), not granting independence to Puerto Rico (even though in several elections its population had rejected this option), attempting to "destabilize" a number of Latin American countries, committing "aggression" against Libya by downing two of its planes when they attacked U.S. planes, and having a friendly attitude toward South Africa. By contrast, in mentioning Afghanistan and Cambodia, the communiqué referred only to the withdrawal of "foreign forces," not Soviet and Vietnamese forces. Jeane Kirkpatrick, the American delegate to the United Nations, thereupon asked the delegates of forty nations to explain why, professing nonalignment, they had supported such a one-sided communiqué with its "base lies and malicious attacks" upon the United States. Asserting that she could not believe that these statements accurately reflected their governments' views, she asked what the United States was to think when they joined in such charges instead of dissociating themselves from them?

In 1983, at the conference of 101 nonaligned states, things were not that different. Although the conference mood was described as more moderate, the United States was denounced for "aggression" against Nicaragua, but the conference again refused to denounce the Soviet Union for its invasion of Afghanistan, a Third World country, or its use, according to persuasive American intelligence, of poison gas in conducting the war. Once again, the nonaligned states called for the withdrawal of "foreign forces," with no reference to the Vietnamese in Cambodia. Israel and South Africa came in for their by now routine denunciations. Nonalignment was certainly losing credibility as the movement embraced Communist states like Cuba and Vietnam (which, like the Soviet Union, boycotted·the Olympic Games in 1984), met in Havana, and accused the United States by name of gross injustices but refused to accuse the Soviet Union. How seriously could these denunciations be taken when most of the Third World's non-Communist leaders do not represent democratic opinion and when many preserve their power with brutality and repression and are hardly innocent of aggression themselves (for example, Iraq against Iran)? How seriously should their accusations be taken of white South African or Israeli treatment of blacks and Palestinians respectively when not a word was said about human rights abuses by Third World states of their own or other citizens (for example, the cruel expulsion of over 1 million aliens by Nigeria in 1983)? In any event, as a symptom of America's mood, the United States in 1984 gave notice that it would withdraw from the United Nations Educational, Scientific, and Cultural Organization (UNESCO) because it had become thoroughly politicized, and constantly attacked Western values, institutions, and interests.

The Reagan administration's vigorous defense of American policies and unwillingness to acquiesce in what it regarded as unjustified and one-sided attacks was symptomatic of a new mood in America not to put up with such hypocrisy. Yet at the same time there could also be no doubt that the Third World was of increasing importance and concern to the United States. The developing countries had become a larger export market for the United States than Western Europe and Japan combined, formerly the recipients of most American exports. The United States also depended on the less-developed countries for tin, natural rubber, bauxite, and other strategic materials besides oil. And, of course, prosperous developing nations were less likely to suffer domestic instability, which might threaten American security interests. Negatively, the enormous $600 billion debt of the less-developed countries to Western banks also demonstrated the growing economic closeness of the First and Third Worlds. The fear was that one or more of these countries might refuse to pay its debt— Mexico, for instance, whose debt was $80 billion—and bring down major banks, if not the entire banking system.

Thus Third World needs could hardly be ignored. In the early 1980s, its nations suffered from the lowest nonoil commodity prices in thirty years; they had borrowed heavily during the 1970s to pay for oil; their earnings were down because of the West's recession; so was Western aid. They could not pay their debts nor earn enough to make a living without going further into debt. And the hope of the 1970s that OPEC would be only the first "resource cartel"— thereby conferring more leverage on the Third World—collapsed as OPEC's future as a cartel appeared increasingly in doubt after 1982–1983. OPEC's huge price escalation after the Shah's collapse in Iran in 1979 proved its own undoing, for it resulted in genuine Western conservation of energy (in 1983, U.S. oil imports from the Gulf were down to less than 5 percent of total oil imports, Europe's to 25 percent, and Japan's to 50 percent); a deep recession idling many factories and workers, which decreased the market for OPEC oil even further; an increase in the supply of non-OPEC oil (for example, from Mexico, Alaska, and the North Sea); and the use of alternate energy sources (for example, coal). The result was an oil glut, and the real price paid for oil fell below the official price of $34 per barrel.

The only way OPEC could ensure its future as a cartel and regain control over oil prices was by cutting production closer to demand. But in general, the countries with larger populations, such as Nigeria, Iran, and Algeria, expected the smaller Arab Persian Gulf countries to absorb most of the cuts. Presumably, the latter, with less expensive development programs, needed less money. Saudi Arabia was expected to accept the biggest cuts. But the cartel members had many conflicts with one another. Libya, for example, accused Saudi Arabia of betraying the Arab cause by being pro-American; Iraq was at war with Iran; and the latter, having to finance this war, refused to accept its OPEC-set pro duction levels. Thus, given the OPEC members' conflicting national interests, production levels were hard to set. Even when OPEC finally did agree to new production levels and lowered the official price to $29 per barrel, its influence remained in doubt, for it depended on the refusal of non-OPEC producers like Britain, Mexico, and the Soviet Union (the world's largest oil producer) to undersell OPEC and on the refusal of OPEC members to seek advantage at one another's expense.

OPEC's declining influence might thus save Third World states billions of dollars but left them in a weak position. Higher prices for their commodities, more aid, and preferential access to Western markets were largely a matter of a renewed Western economic growth. OPEC's lot had confirmed the fact that producers without customers cannot thrive. In the meantime, the world moved toward an increasing division between the few Western "rich" states and the many "poor" ones, which by the year 2000 would hold an estimated 80 percent of the world's population.

THE U.S. ECONOMY AND GLOBAL COMMITMENTS

In a fundamental sense, the critical problem facing the Reagan administration from the day it took office was not the Soviet Union, El Salvador, NATO, or the Middle East but the stagnation of the American economy. No president in the 1980s could put off this problem any longer, for without a growing economy—in the doldrums after 1973, but stagnating even earlier—the United States could not support a global foreign policy. America has long been the world's leading industrial power. It was her enormous productive capacity that was the basis of the victories in World Wars I and II. Most especially, it had been the enormous wealth created by American industry and agriculture that had made it possible for the United States to accept commitments in so many areas of the world and simultaneously to afford sizable deterrent forces and a conventional military capability that fought two long limited wars thousands of miles away from the continental United States.

The key question that American policymakers after World War II repeatedly asked themselves was whether a particular area or country was of vital interest to the security and/or prosperity of the country. If they decided it was, the appropriate policy followed. The question whether the nation could afford it was only rarely asked; that was assumed. Only conservatives on occasion asked whether the nation could afford a Marshall Plan or large deterrent and conventional forces. The Eisenhower administration was particularly concerned with the question of costs, federal deficits, and balanced budgets. But in the words of presidential candidate John Kennedy, the country could afford anything it needed for its security. While funds were obviously not unlimited, the assumption was that the nation was wealthy enough to support a high standard of living at home and a global policy abroad.

The 1950s and 1960s were decades of very rapid economic growth. It became commonplace to refer to the United States as an "affluent society," the "people of plenty." Wages for workers rose rapidly during this period as trade unions grew powerful, expecting sizable annual pay raises. American industry apparently could afford such raises in an increasingly consumer-oriented society while still earning handsome profits. The Kennedy and Johnson administrations vastly expanded the welfare state. Not only were the payments made by older programs such as social security frequently increased but new ones were initiated; some, like Medicare, started small but grew rapidly in cost as more people became eligible for them and the benefits were adjusted to meet inflation. Known as entitlement programs, they were made possible because the economy was growing rapidly and producing sufficient wealth to support both a high standard of living and welfare payments as well as an extensive foreign policy. President Johnson went to war in Vietnam expecting to finance both his Great Society programs and the war (which originally was expected to last two years and involve 200,000 troops) without increasing taxes.

The enormous expense of the Vietnam War, plus the dramatic increase of oil prices, which simultaneously produced a high inflation and large-scale unemployment, put a brake on the economy. Instead of growing rapidly, it stagnated. As a result, the country could no longer afford both guns and butter. It had to make choices: An economy that at best was growing only slowly could not afford constantly rising wages, rapidly rising annual welfare costs and expensive foreign policy commitments. In a growing economic pie, there is more for every program; but when the pie does not grow, increases in one program come at the cost of others. In a democracy these choices are painful: Workers do not gladly accept pay cuts; voters are not too happy with a slowdown in the increase, let alone cuts, in welfare programs; and although defense cuts are often advocated and followed in these circumstances, the nation also needs to guard itself against foreign threats.

President Reagan, asserting that defense spending had been held back during the 1970s, greatly increased military spending and cut back the growth of social programs. Politically, of course, this can only be done for so long. The longer-run solution, according to the Reagan administration, was to stimulate the economy so that it would once more grow as rapidly as it had in the 1950s and 1960s. The policy advocated was supply side economics. Whatever the validity of this approach, the fact was that the American economy had changed greatly over the last two decades. On the one hand, American agriculture remained the most bountiful in the world, and the export of food was a major source of dollar earnings in foreign trade; the high technology sector of the economy was also thriving. But traditional smokestack industries, like steel, and consumer goods industries ranging from high fidelity to automobiles, became increasingly uncompetitive internationally and declined. There were many reasons for this decline, all of which reflected underinvestment in the American economy: high wages in the United States; a desire to be nearer overseas markets; and the Common Market's tariff barriers against imports. American industry therefore tended to go overseas, for there wages were lower, especially in Third World countries (for example, Asia); it could save transportation costs on goods produced in this country; and it could avoid the Common Market's tariff wall by building factories in Western Europe. The U.S. economy lost vitality as it became common to refer to American industry in Europe as the second largest economy in the world, right behind our own. Industry considered its actions rational: Goods could be produced more cheaply outside of the United States, where large-scale markets and opportunities were also opening up. Goods, for consumers both abroad and at home, it was argued, would be less expensive and more competitive with foreign goods and would increase corporate profits.

Industries like steel, which stayed home, foundered; Japanese steel, produced by more modern methods, could be shipped to the United States and still sold more cheaply than steel made in Ohio. The automobile industry, on the other hand, did invest but kept mass-producing the same large gas-guzzling, showy cars year in and year out, expecting customers to continue frequently changing their mode of transportation. When the oil crisis hit, the industry was caught without small, fuel-efficient, well-made automobiles. Japan had them and captured a sizable sector of the market. Even with Detroit's recovery, which resulted from its being far more efficient than before and from a ceiling on Japanese imports (because lower Japanese labor costs continue to make Japanese cars about $1500 cheaper than an equivalent American model), most of the workers laid off during the 1970s recession were not reemployed; robots were more efficient and cheaper.

Can the economy still support a foreign policy that keeps 300,000 men in Western Europe, defends Japan, is committed to the Persian Gulf, and is increasing U.S. commitments in Central America? Can it do all these things *as well as* support ever more expensive welfare programs and higher wages and still find the investment capital necessary to restimulate the growth of the private sector—a process often referred to as the "reindustrialization" of the American economy? Given the expenditures necessary to make the American economy internationally competitive once again, how much can be spent on American commitments abroad and on defense? Should the United States cut back on these commitments and the forces needed to support them—mainly conventional forces that are more expensive than strategic nuclear or deterrent forces? Do these commitments divert funds from welfare programs, including social security, thereby risking domestic dissatisfaction, hardship, and conflict? Should ailing industries be protected with tariffs and subsidies or compelled to become more efficient (assuming they survive), even if that means forcing wages downward? How much should the government become involved, through the investment of tax money, in the reindustrialization of America?

In the 1970s it became apparent that for the first time in the postwar period, the nation was no longer capable of supporting an extensive foreign policy role, maintaining an ever higher living standard at home, and at the same time saving sufficient funds for the regeneration of the economy through a new industrial revolution, which was necessary if the other two aims were to be achieved. How the United States responds to this dilemma will be critical for its future security. The Reagan administration placed great emphasis on the recovery of the economy, above all cutting back the high inflation rate. Not confronted, as it had been during previous administrations, by sharply rising oil prices—in fact, oil prices were lower—the economy did pick up momentum. Whether that recovery will be sustained, whether sufficient capital will be found to invest in new industries that also greatly reduce unemployment, whether wage demands can be restrained, and whether increases in welfare payments can be slowed down, all remain to be seen. It also remains to be seen whether the United States will reduce its commitments, especially if its allies refuse to do more for their defense.

Yet the trend is clear. Anti-Communism, as Vietnam showed, was too expensive a habit. Even before oil prices quadrupled in 1973, the decline of the American economy was becoming apparent. Thus the Nixon rapprochement with Communist China made sense not only in terms of balance of power logic but as an economy move. Since the two principal Communist states had become adversaries, the long overdue exploitation of their differences and hostility toward each other signaled a significant shift—in part, a reversal—of American foreign policy from anti-Communism to anti-Sovietism (which had been its original starting point despite the universal language of anti-Communism embodied in the Truman Doctrine). Even though the Carter administration was initially not preoccupied by the conflict with the Soviet Union, it also moved increasingly closer to the People's Republic as relations with the Soviet Union worsened. Nixon began the shift toward Communist China; Carter made the final move in 1979, officially recognizing the mainland regime. Despite his own strong anti-Communism and his favorable attitude toward the Nationalist Chinese on Taiwan, President Reagan—reluctantly, to be sure—accepted the logic of power calculations and economics. He celebrated the narrower anti-Soviet basis of post-Vietnam cold war II American policy with a visit to China in the spring of 1984. The broader principle underlying this basis did not, however, apply only to China; presumably, other Communist regimes, as long as they were not tied to the Soviet Union, were also now acceptable to Washington. American policy, then, aimed not only at making "the world safe for democracy" but at making it safe for "national Communism." As long as Communist states were independent of Moscow, the United States would protect them from Soviet Communism—a rather new and novel task, to say the least!—if they, in turn, would help this country's containment policy.

Chapter 12

CONTAINMENT: A REAPPRAISAL

THE CONTINUITY OF CONTAINMENT

During the twentieth century the United States has been repeatedly compelled by the changing distribution of power to emerge from its historically isolationist course. In both World Wars I and II, Germany appeared likely to achieve dominance over continental Europe and threaten Britain, whose navy had during the nineteenth century guarded the Atlantic approaches to the Western hemisphere. In 1917, Germany's submarine campaign against all shipping, including American vessels sailing to England, propelled the United States into the war. After Germany's defeat of France in 1940, the United States became engaged in a limited naval war with Germany in the Atlantic as the United States sent war supplies to Britain to keep it in the war; had the Japanese not attacked Pearl Harbor in 1941, Germany would sooner or later have attacked American shipping again in order to bring Britain to its knees. War with Germany had become unavoidable, just as it had thirty years earlier.

In short, the nature of the state system and the changing distribution of power left the United States little choice but to become involved in both wars. American leaders have long considered the dominance of Europe by any power that could mobilize Europe's population and resources to be a potential threat to American security. In neither 1917 nor 1941 did American leaders or public opinion *want* to go to war; the preference was to remain at peace. But as Germany appeared about to achieve a superiority of power and continental control, peace was no longer possible. This pattern was repeated after World War II as Soviet power expanded into Eastern and Central Europe; exerted pressure southward toward Iran, Turkey, and Greece; and constituted a threat to postwar Western Europe.

The need to balance Soviet power was initially recognized by Britain. American recognition came more slowly and occurred only after Britain said it did not have the capability to contain the Soviet Union; until then, the United States thought its primary function was to mediate what appeared to be only a Soviet-British conflict! Again, the American preference was to withdraw from international politics and limit its role mainly to this hemisphere and participation in the United Nations. But the emergence of a bipolar world made that impossible as the Soviet Union, with a very large army and straddling Europe *and* Asia, was seen, like Germany before it, as a threat to American security.

The containment of Soviet power therefore became the centerpiece of postwar U.S. foreign policy. A broad consensus emerged and underlay American policy until Vietnam: the central conflict in the world was the one between the Soviet-led Communist world (which after 1950 was seen as including Communist China) and the American-led "free world"; any Communist gain of influence was a loss of influence for America and its allies and friends; it was the task of the West to oppose such expansion; and since the United States was the only Western country that had the requisite strength, the role of containing the Soviet Union and its allies fell primarily upon the United States. When the cold war was replaced by *détente,* the policy amounted to essentially an adaptation of containment to an era of superpower strategic parity, Sino-Soviet schism and pseudoisolationism in the United States. Given the conflict between the two leading Communist powers, American policy refocused on the stronger Soviet threat and moved closer to China, which was also interested in containing her large northern neighbor.

Détente as the continuation of containment by another name was based upon the assumption that Soviet military power had grown so enormously that the Soviet Union constituted an even greater threat than before, not on any illusions that it had been transformed into a *status quo* state (at least not during the Kissinger phase of *détente*). The aim was to provide the incentives for Moscow to act with greater restraint by an ever-changing mixture of carrots and, when necessary, sticks. *Détente* was thus intended to be a tactic, a holding operation until the American people "recovered their nerve." If President Jimmy Carter sometimes appeared to forget this and genuinely believe that American-Soviet rivalry was a thing of the past, his Henry Kissinger, Zbigniew Brzezinski, tried to remind him; above all, the Soviets reminded Carter when they invaded Afghanistan. Thus from Truman to Reagan, American foreign policy has displayed a remarkable continuity, despite frequent four-year changes of administration (Eisenhower being the last president until Reagan to have served an eight year term), changes of parties in power, and the erosion of the original cold war consensus.

Indeed, during the Vietnam War, even former supporters of containment—indeed, some of its most zealous advocates—became its strongest critics. American power, they asserted, was very great, but the United States was not omnipotent and therefore could not pursue global commitments: It simply did not have the wealth to take care of all possible foreign policy obligations and at the same time handle its pressing domestic needs. Policymakers therefore had to rank carefully the external priorities—usually Europe and Latin America were considered of primary importance—and concentrate on these. By being more selective in commitments, the nation could bring the ends of policy and the means of its implementation into balance. Vietnam was thus seen as a tragic product of an indiscriminate anti-Communism that had led the nation to over-extend itself. It also was seen as a chastening experience that would result in the reduction of American commitments, a concentration on urgent domestic problems, and a generally more sober and restrained international behavior. America was no longer to be "the world's policeman"; its future conduct would reflect its "limited power." A more discriminating policy would commit American strength only to the defense of its truly vital interests, not lesser concerns.

AN INDISCRIMINATE CRUSADE OR PRUDENT POWER POLITICS?

After Vietnam, these broad recommendations were probably useful reminders to policymakers, but had they in fact been ignored in the earlier conduct of foreign affairs? In looking backward over two decades of containment, the first thing that can be said is that American policymakers, during World War II and in the immediate postwar years, had been aware of the nation's limited power, of its need to be selective in making commitments according to some criteria of priorities and to apply power discriminately. Indeed, during the war they had planned no overseas obligations whatsoever. The whole point of Franklin Roosevelt's policy toward the Soviet Union was to overcome Joseph Stalin's suspicions of the West and win his friendship for, and commitment to, postwar cooperation. The expectation was that the United States, the Soviet Union, Great Britain, and Nationalist China would, in a new era of goodwill, jointly keep the peace. America's partners would preserve it in Eurasia; the United States would limit its responsibilities to its own hemisphere. It was the disintegration of these hopes, as Soviet hostility became apparent and Britain and continental Europe collapsed, that left America as the only countervailing power to the Soviet Union. Even then, American responses were limited to those countries and areas where the Soviets challenged the territorial *status quo* left by World War II.

Aware of the need to be selective, the Truman administration decided that priority should be given to Europe, the cradle of the American heritage, the area where an imbalance of power had twice in this century sucked the United States into total wars. This focus on Europe was the chief reason the United States did not intervene in any major way in the Chinese civil war between the Nationalists and the Communists. While the U.S. furnished the Nationalists with some economic and military assistance, limits to its intervention were dictated by the resolve not to become militarily engaged. Similarly, in husbanding the nation's resources and trying to keep a balance between America's commitments and "limited power," troops were withdrawn from South Korea. Continental Asia was strictly of secondary interest, and the American defense perimeter in the Pacific was publicly defined in terms of the island chain, including Japan, off the Asian coast. The Soviets and North Koreans apparently drew the logical conclusion that the United States had written off the Republic of Korea. Consequently, in June 1950, the North Korean army marched southward across the thirty-eighth parallel, and America was suddenly and unexpectedly engaged in its first "frontier war."

A second point about the containment policy, however, was that despite the efforts to arrange American interests on some scale of priorities, the United States as a superpower occasionally became involved in some areas or countries even though it would have preferred not to become involved. Despite a nation's best intentions, commitments were not always determined by *a priori* selection but by contingencies and events over which even a Great Power had little or no control. Thus, twice in this century the United States had become involved in world wars, although no commitment of defense to France and Britain had existed. It had little choice on both occasions if it wished to preserve the balance and guard its security.

A rather quick and painful postwar reminder of this lesson came in Korea when the United States decided to fight a "limited war" in the defense of South Korea after the North Korean invasion. American forces were committed not because the United States had a legal obligation to defend South Korea or because the southern half of the Korean peninsula was a strategic American interest, but because the political and psychological consequences of inaction were believed to affect the global balance. In Asia, reestablishment of a balance after Nationalist China's collapse on the Chinese mainland depended upon creating an American-Japanese alliance; a demonstration of fear or indifference to the fate of a friend would hardly win Japan to an alliance. A nation that permitted Communist power to establish itself 100 miles across the water from Japan was hardly to be relied on. Similarly, the United States had just committed itself through the North Atlantic Treaty Organization (NATO) to the protection of Europe; if Korea were allowed to fall, the newly acquired European allies, who still recalled America's post-World War I withdrawal and isolationism and who still were apprehensive about a recurrence, might disregard NATO and try to bargain for the Kremlin's best terms.

In short, it was believed that the impact of not defending South Korea in a bipolar world would result in the neutralization of Japan and Europe. Suddenly, American security was recognized as very much involved in this area of secondary interest. Thus a noncommitment, deliberately excluded from the defense perimeter because it did not seem vital, overnight became a primary commitment; yet a prior commitment pledging American help in case of attack, supported symbolically by a few thousand troops, might have deterred the

Communist invasion and spared the Americans a costly war. (One need but compare the situation in Europe, including the divided city of Berlin, where the American presence and a defense commitment have kept the peace for almost forty years, even though a spark between the confronting American and Soviet forces might well have erupted into a major fire extremely difficult to extinguish.)

The post-Vietnam period reinforced this lesson about commitments. Despite the longing for relief from the active role it had played during the cold war and the desire to assume a lower profile on the international scene, America was affected, often deeply, by virtually all problems, whatever the origin, wherever they occurred and whether the Soviets sought to exploit these issues or not— be it nuclear proliferation, the race problem in South Africa, the stability of monarchical regimes in Iran and Saudi Arabia, or the border conflicts between new states (such as those between Ethiopia and Somalia). It appeared that regardless of American preferences to play a lesser role, the United States would remain extensively involved in the state system, for the world would not leave it alone; indeed, sometimes it appeared that the nation was even *more* extensively involved than during the days of the cold war and America's frequently criticized role of global policeman. And many of these problems, as in southern Africa, the Horn of Africa, and especially the Persian Gulf area, not only held important consequences for the United States that might lead to commitments far beyond those of the Truman and Eisenhower Doctrines of the 1940s and 1950s, but they could not be easily isolated from the American-Soviet rivalry. Even before the Shah's collapse in Iran and the Soviet invasion of Afghanistan, it had become clear that American and Western interests in oil required a commitment of American power in an area in which the United States had not previously been engaged. Again, it was not so much a question of what it wanted to do but of what it had to do. Symbolically, it was President Carter, who talked constantly of America's "limited power," who placed his name on the doctrine that formalized this new commitment and thereby extended America's global-policeman role to a new area.

A third point about the containment policy is that this extensive American involvement was not due to any "arrogance of power" or desire to dominate the world or quest for capitalist profits, let alone to an unawareness of the need for the nation to order its foreign policy priorities; rather, it was due to the postwar bipolar distribution of power. In a reevaluation of containment, it is worth stressing once more that a bipolar distribution of power is the most sensitive of all balances. In a bipolar balance, each power sees its adversary as its foe; for the opposing power is the only one who can hurt it and threaten its security. The balance is continuously seen as being at stake, since each fears that once the adversary has shifted the balance in his favor and gained a superiority of power, the shift may be irreversible. For reasons of security, therefore, when one side sees the other push, it feels compelled to push back. A bipolar balance is, consequently, one of continuous confrontation and frequent crises and occasional limited wars. Even moves in areas of secondary interest will be opposed since each power fears a domino effect; that if one of its allies, protégés, or satellites is allowed to fall, others will follow and that an accumulation of small losses of power—each one of which would be tolerable—would add up to a major loss of power—which would be intolerable and therefore must be prevented.

The Korean War, the rise of Communist China, and the subsequent Chinese intervention in Korea as American armies advanced toward China's frontier, plus the Sino-Soviet alliance, reinforced this bipolar pattern: the Soviet Union and China extending across most of the Eurasian continent versus the United States and NATO on the western rim of Eurasia and Japan on the eastern rim. Not surprisingly, then, after America first bluffed intervention and then accepted the division of Vietnam in 1954, the seventeenth parallel became part of the frontier drawn between the Communist bloc and "free world." Increasingly thereafter, the defense of South Vietnam was seen as a test of the credibility of American commitments, a domino whose fall would result in the loss of further dominoes. Containment was therefore applied in South Vietnam and not reassessed in the late 1950s and early 1960s when the Communist world showed increasing signs of divisions as nationalism eroded the cohesion of a group of countries that claimed that their unity resulted from sharing a common ideology.

Even after Vietnam, the superpower rivalry continued, although for a while the United States was not in a mood to respond to Soviet moves as frequently or vigorously as before. For the Soviets quickly exploited this postwar weariness and mood of withdrawal by taking advantage of opportunities for expanding their influence. This, in turn, caused increasing American disillusionment with *détente*, which came to be widely viewed as a one-way street. President Ronald Reagan was elected in part because of this disillusionment. His administration refocused American policy on opposition to the Soviet Union. Thus, even in a world that is no longer strictly bipolar, American-Soviet competition remains the central preoccupation of U.S. foreign policy.

A fourth point was that this bipolar distribution of power resulted in the militarization of containment. Although during the first few years the policy of containment was in existence its implementation was mainly economic, the attack upon South Korea and the resulting fear that the Soviets might try something similar in Europe led to vast American and other Western rearmament. After Korea, the concept of deterrence as a drawing of frontier lines and a threat of major retaliation if these were crossed was extended from Europe to the Middle and Far East. Because the rise of nationalism in these areas was frequently accompanied by anti-Western overtones, the alliances formed to support such lines proved relatively useless as containers, caused a great deal of turmoil among the nations of these regions, frequently drew the United States into their quarrels, and led the nation to support some rather despotic regimes in the name of defending freedom. This emphasis on drawing lines of containment of establishing military alliances—multilateral ones such as NATO, the Southeast Asia Treaty Organization (SEATO), and the Central Treaty Organization (CENTO), as well as bilateral ones such as the American alliances with Japan or Taiwan—largely followed from the bipolar division of power. Given the great sensitivity of the superpowers to any changes in the balance, especially of the United States, which saw itself as essentially on the defense against Soviet (and for a while, Chinese) expansionism, the essence of the cold war—in which neither side felt it could advance without risking nuclear war nor retreat without risking political collapse—was the drawing of "frontiers" to mark off their respective spheres of influence, and then defending the resulting territorial *status quo*.

In short, both superpowers formed alliances primarily as a means of delineating the areas of vital interest to them and communicating these to their adversary in order to deter an attack; to maintain the cohesiveness of their respective alliances and prevent defections, even if it required military or covert intervention; and perhaps most symbolically, to engage in an intense arms race spurred by the fear that with rapid changes in the technology of modern weapons the opponent might achieve a technological breakthrough that he would then exploit to gain a perhaps irreversible superiority of power. A bipolar balance in which two powers constantly confront one another, and often push each other in attempts to shift the balance and push back to maintain the balance, is indeed more dependent than any other distribution of power on military strength to preserve an equilibrium.

A fifth point was the gap between declared policy, with its rhetoric of a universal anti-Communist crusade, and operational policy, with its more specific and limited objectives in different situations. This distinction is critical because of the widely held belief that if the United States had not been so passionately anti-Communist after 1945, it would not have undertaken so many commitments. Was American globalism, it was asked, not really the offspring of the nation's penchant for crusading against opponents who had provoked it? The presumption of anti-Communism as a principal motive of postwar American foreign policy assumed that the cold war was somehow different from the typical historical power struggle inherent in an anarchic state system that left each state to be its own protector and therefore compelled it to concern itself with its power relative to other potentially hostile states. The record of U.S. foreign policy since 1945 was, in fact, less that of a crusader than of a practitioner of the ancient art of power politics. The purpose of containment, the label for America's balance-of-power policy, was precisely that: to contain the Soviet Union and, after 1949, Communist China until its break with the Soviet Union, by a central American–Soviet balance supplemented by regional balances where required. The aim of American policy was not the launching of a holy anti-Communist crusade to overthrow the government in Moscow or Peking. Passionate anti-Soviet and anti-Chinese speeches and talk of "liberation" were not translated into policies.

In other words, American policy has been "limitationist" and American power has been used with restraint, as shown for example in Berlin, Korea, Hungary, and Czechoslovakia. It was primarily the anti-Communist rhetoric that had tended to create the widespread public impression of a policy lacking moderation and proportion and pursuing instead an ambitious and often wasteful adventuristic world role. Nonetheless, despite extravagant declarations of intentions, the objective was the containment of Soviet power and, for a period, China. Instead of being a crusade to eliminate the Soviet Union or Communist China, American policy from the beginning accepted the reality of co-existence. Its aim was only to prevent further Soviet and Chinese expansion.

As a nation that had put isolationism behind it and, once it had become actively engaged in international politics, had quickly learned to play power politics as had others before it, the United States was never so blinded by an allegedly indiscriminate anti-Communism that it could not adopt the age-old technique of divide-and-rule. Thus, within a year of the Truman Doctrine, the United States offered help to Communist Yugoslavia after Tito's break with Stalin, demonstrating that American policy was anti-Soviet, not anti-Communist. In China after World War II, the United States first sought to arrange a coalition government composed of the Nationalists and Communists to stop the civil war and unify China; and once the Communists had won the civil war, Washington, foreseeing the possibility of conflict between the Soviet Union and China, expected to exploit this split when it occurred. Even after the Korean War had embittered Sino-American relations, the United States negotiated with Peking whenever Washington felt its interests were involved (as in ending the Korean War and the first Indochina War), while continuing its policy of nonrecognition of the new mainland regime.

Underlining the point being made, it was President Richard Nixon, whose political career had been built upon smearing his political opponents in election campaigns with charges of "appeasement" and "coddling Communism," who moved toward reconciliation with the Chinese People's Republic after twenty-odd years of nonrecognition of its government. In short, in a position of authority he acted rationally, exploiting Sino-Soviet differences; had such action been taken earlier, the Soviet Union might have been compelled to act with greater restraint earlier and the United States might have avoided intervention in Vietnam.

Anti-Communism has thus been less a motive explaining American foreign policy than a tool used by American leaders for mobilizing public support. The United States has traditionally been an essentially inwardly oriented society. Nor is this accidental, for, quite apart from the historic tasks of westward expansion and modernization, a political system in which the people vote and the governors must therefore be responsive to mass preferences is a system that concentrates upon domestic affairs and welfare issues rather than on a burdensome, costly, and distracting foreign policy. To arouse the public to support external ventures, the struggle for power and security inherent in the state system had to be disguised to appear as a struggle for the realization of the highest values. From the beginning of its existence, the United States has felt itself to be a post-European society—a New World standing as a shining example of democracy, freedom, and social justice for the Old World. Anti-Communism fitted beautifully into this traditional dichotomy. America could thus practice *Realpolitik* as long as it could be disguised as *Idealpolitik*, which fitted its national style of conducting foreign policy; power politics needed ideological justification in a nation that had always felt that the use of power internationally was evil. Domestically, power was legitimated by the democratic purposes for which it was used; externally too, its employment had to be justified in terms of American democratic values.

THE PERSISTENT INFLUENCE OF NATIONAL STYLE

A final point about containment is that while the United States was basically concerned with maintaining the balance of power and behaving as other Great Powers had done in the past, this concern did not mean that the influence of national style was negligible. An anti-Communist crusade may have been intended primarily to arouse the public and mobilize popular support for cold war policies—just as such crusades had done during World Wars I and II—while the nation in fact pursued more limited aims. However, once an administration had aroused the public by promising to stop Communism, it laid itself open to attacks by the opposition party in case of setbacks, even if the latter occurred for reasons beyond America's ability to control. The out-party could then seek to exploit foreign policy issues by accusing the in-party of "appeasement" and being "soft on Communism." This in turn made it difficult to recognize a Communist regime, build bridges to Eastern Europe, and especially discriminate between the defense of areas of vital and secondary interest.

Democratic administrations were particularly affected because they recalled that it was their party that had been in power when Nationalist China had collapsed, it was they who had been accused of "treason" and "selling out" China, and it was they who had lost the 1952 presidential election. The desire to avoid accusations of being soft on Communism had affected Harry Truman's decision to advance northward across the thirty-eighth parallel before the 1950 midterm elections; it had made it impossible for Truman to negotiate any settlement of the war that would leave Korea divided; made it impossible for John Kennedy, who had campaigned on a tough anti-Castro platform, to reject the Eisenhower-initiated invasion plan about which the new president had serious qualms; led the Kennedy and Johnson administrations to make their piecemeal commitments in Vietnam, lest the Democrats be charged with the "loss of Indochina" as well as China; influenced Lyndon Johnson to bomb the North and finally escalate the war by sending in the army; and persuaded him to land troops in the Dominican Republic to prevent "another Cuba" from being established.

These examples illustrate the high price the United States consistently paid for the need to moralize power politics: overreaction, diplomatic rigidity, and overt or covert interventions which it might otherwise never have launched. National style, in brief, was a principal reason for the long nonrecognition of Communist China and the failure in general to understand the nature of Asian Communism, including the nature of the war in Vietnam; it was also a major reason, if not *the* reason, for the subsequent intervention. It was because the domestic costs of losing a China or Indochina or any other place were so high that those in power felt compelled to intervene with the Central Intelligence Agency (CIA), marines, or army in order to avoid such losses. The desire not to face accusations of appeasement, of betraying the nation's honor, of weakening its security was keenly felt; the costs of intervention, by contrast, appeared far smaller. This was especially true just before elections—and, of course, there was always an election coming up—than the domestic costs of nonintervention.

These costs should not be underestimated. The president would lose prestige; in turn, this would affect his ability to gain support for the rest of his foreign, as well as domestic, policies. In short, he would be vulnerable to Congressional attacks, and his entire program for the nation, abroad and at home, would be jeopardized. Thus far more than the president's personal reputation, his ability to be reelected, and his party's electoral future were at stake, although these were hardly minor stakes. The basic rule of domestic politics during the cold war years, therefore, was to avoid what appeared as major losses to Communism overseas.

Only conservative—Republican—administrations seemed less vulnerable to such attacks. Dwight Eisenhower was the first president during the cold war to meet the Soviet leaders; he signed the same peace in Korea that Truman could not; nor did he feel compelled to intervene in Indochina in 1954 and, although he supported the new Diem regime in Saigon, he carefully limited United States support; and it was Nixon who could do what a rational foreign policy would have done years earlier—seek a reconciliation with China and try to exploit the Sino-Soviet schism. Neither president could credibly be accused of being "soft on Communism." Their credentials as strong anti-Communists were above reproach. They were "hawks," not "fuzzy-minded liberals." In his first term, President Reagan did not follow in the footsteps of his Republican predecessors because he perceived the necessity of rebuilding American military strength and reestablishing American credibility before negotiating seriously with the Soviet Union. But there is no question that if he wants to negotiate major agreements with the Soviet Union in his second term he can do so. After years of vigorous anti-Soviet rhetoric and posturing, he is hardly likely to be accused of being an "appeaser." Indeed, his denunciations of the Soviet leadership have been so harsh that agreements would be welcomed by most in Congress and the public.

But the main point remains: Liberal Democratic administrations before Vietnam tended to be more interventionist and generally hard-line in policy toward the Communist bloc (with the single exception of Yugoslavia) than Republican administrations which, for all their strong anti-Communist speeches, were in fact less interventionist and more prone to accommodation toward the Soviet Union and China. Ironically, many liberal Democrats were so badly burned by the Vietnamese experience that they became deeply antiinterventionist, finding few vital American interests outside of Western Europe and Israel that might require the threat or use of American military forces or covert intervention. Their model president, ironically, was a Republican: Eisenhower. Having in the past denounced him as a lazy president who had not been vigorous enough in the world, they now praised him for his moderation, his reluctance to intervene, and his careful calculation of the national interest. Eisenhower's nonintervention in Indochina, in Quemoy and Matsu on two occasions, his refusal to escalate the Berlin crisis after 1958, or to be panicked into a new arms race after the first Soviet ICBM test, as well as other actions criticized during the 1950s, now became the very incarnation of wise American policy for liberals.

National style was also evident in the reappearance in American foreign policy behavior of the pendulum pattern—from pre-cold war isolationism to crusading and back again which, after years of cold war interventionism, now showed up as pseudoisolationism or, at the very least, as the desire for a lower American profile in the world. Indeed, it was widely asserted that "the cold war was over"; *détente* was frequently understood publicly as its opposite state. The former was a condition of conflict and confrontation, the latter one of peace and negotiation. This was typical of America's national style with its view of the world in either-or terms: war or peace, force or diplomacy, harmony or conflict. All of this was attended by the guilt and shame America has felt before when it perceived power as being abused and misused. Historically it was thought that since "power politics" is morally bad, the best course is to abstain from using it; but once used, it can be justified only by the nobility of the purposes pursued. The total destruction of the antidemocratic regimes that in two world wars provoked the United States was seen as a worthy goal. The nation was making "the world safe for democracy." American power had to be "righteous power."

But America intervened in Vietnam on the side of an undemocratic regime, and the conduct of war, particularly the massive bombing, was for many Americans at best morally ambiguous, if not downright immoral. Self-accusation followed. The nation was pictured as an evil country whose policies were wicked; it had not just gone astray or made a bad error, courses that could be corrected. The optimism that the United States was a force for good in the world was replaced by disillusionment and cynicism. The United States had better withdraw from the international scene, renew and purify itself by concentrating on its domestic affairs, and build a fully free and socially just society whose example would radiate throughout the world. "Power politics" would be replaced by "social politics"; America's foreign policy would be its domestic policy. In the words of a former chairman of the Senate Foreign Relations Committee, America should "serve as an example of democracy to the world" and play its role in the world "not in its capacity as a *power* but in its capacity as a *society*." Virtue, not power, would be the hallmark of American foreign policy; other nations would be attracted to the United States by the merit of its principles, not by its superior strength.

Expressions of the priority of domestic policy and abstinence from international politics were symptoms of the nostalgia for the old isolationism. "Come home, America" was a slogan that expressed the longing of millions. The consequences were the imposition of restraints upon the presidency and the CIA, the chief arms of overt and covert U.S. intervention, and the cutbacks of military budgets as a percentage of the gross national product to pre-Korean War (1950) levels at a time of unprecedented Soviet spending on arms of all kinds. These measures were clear evidence of this antinational security mood. They were intended to assure America's lesser role in the world, one limited basically to the defense of the democracies in Europe and Japan and security in the Western Hemisphere. Revisionist histories, in the meantime, stressed that the cold war was largely the fault of a U.S. policy to which Stalin, whose aims were only limited, defensive, and legitimate, had reacted in fear. If America, then, reduced its international role, the world would be a more peaceful place. America was the problem, not the Soviet Union. Restraint of the United States, not the containment of Communism, was the chief task.

In these circumstances of pseudoisolationism, self-blame, and self-flagellation, the country was again to be stirred up by its enemies. Just as Stalin's seizure of Czechoslovakia and the Berlin Blockade provoked the United States in the late 1940s, so Iranian and Soviet actions in late 1979 angered and aroused public opinion once more. The retrenchment of American power, the failure of the United States to act like a superpower in defense of its vital security and economic interests, the obvious revulsion many Americans felt about the past employment of American power, and the hesitation and reluctance they betrayed in using power in the post-Vietnam period—these attitudes were visible to the entire world. Instead of praising America for its restraint, many states— allies and adversaries alike—criticized it for loss of a will to act. Not only a superpower such as the Soviet Union but a relatively minor power such as Iran felt that in these circumstances it could act with impunity even if it hurt and insulted American interests.

National impotence was bound to lead to national humiliation. If the lesson of Vietnam was "no more Vietnams" (no more interventions), the lesson of Iran was "no more Irans" (no more being pushed around while we flounder helplessly). That was the mood of the country when it elected President Reagan instead of reelecting President Carter, a late convert who had for most of his term reflected the earlier passivity and guilt, as well as the hopes for a new post-power politics world in which the nation-state, national egotism, security and power considerations, and the use of force would play a lesser role, if not be replaced by a more beneficent world-order. Still, even with Reagan at the helm, the nation continued to sway somewhere between the post-Vietnam and post-Iranian moods—between Grenada on the one hand and Lebanon-Central America on the other.

THE FUTURE OF CONTAINMENT

Thus, in the 1980s, the containment policy—whether still called *détente*, cold war II, or some other name—continues, although in a much more complex world than during cold war I. For one thing, the American-Soviet relationship had itself become more mixed in what might be called an "adversary-partnership." The competitive and conflictual nature of the relationship is clear. The growth of Soviet military power has, indeed, intensified this rivalry since it has been accompanied by a more assertive Soviet foreign policy. In cold war I, the United States held strategic superiority, naval supremacy, and an ability to apply U.S. power rapidly in almost all areas of the world. The Soviet Union, whose superiority was long limited to conventional, land-based forces that held our European allies hostage while it built up its intercontinental strategic forces to gain the ability to strike the United States, therefore had to act with great caution. Essentially, until the 1970s the Soviet Union remained a Eurasian power whose challenges were essentially low-risk operations. She might probe, but if she met effective counteraction, she would desist; above all else, she wished to avoid a conflict with the United States that might escalate, endangering the Soviet Union's survival.

But after 1975 Soviet policy began to exploit opportunities for expanding Soviet influence more actively. Three factors, which occurred almost simultaneously, accounted for this shift in Soviet policy. One was the emergence of strategic parity and the modernization of large conventional forces, including an airlift and sealift capability that gave Moscow the ability to project its power beyond Eurasia. The second was America's post-Vietnam mood of pseudoisolationism, which looked very hard and skeptically at any interventions beyond the nation's borders. Even as the memories of the war faded and the nation became more activist again, the cry of Vietnam continued to be heard loudly and insistently every time a potential or actual new intervention arose. Congress and much of public opinion remained "gun-shy." The third was the decrease in the United States' economic capability to support as extensive a foreign policy as it had in earlier decades.

Such figures as Kissinger, Brzezinski, and Haig, among others, were indeed concerned about Soviet policy, not only because of the Soviet Union's growing military might, but because this growth coincided with an increase in Soviet domestic problems. They felt that these internal factors would act not as a restraint on Soviet behavior but as an inducement to foreign adventures. Among the factors cited were ideological disillusionment at home and the Soviet Union's lack of appeal as a model in the rest of the world; the future minority status of the Russians when later in this century a majority of the

Soviet people would belong to other nationality groups (many of whom have little love for the Russians); and, of course, the economy. Economic growth rates, already declining, might fall even further as agricultural and nonmilitary industrial production continues to face all sorts of problems as a result of too much centralization, too much bureaucratization, too little high technology, a declining incoming labor force, and a general lack of worker productivity (not helped much by high rates of absenteeism and drunkenness). One especially critical problem was that if the Soviet government continued its large-scale investment in military production, even the expectations of small increases in the standard of living by the Soviet people would be jeopardized, thereby increasing social tensions. In fact, the Soviet Union is too top-heavy for its economy.

In addition, the post-Brezhnev years will likely see a series of succession struggles to replace the rather aged leadership with a generation of younger men who may not share their predecessors' sense of vulnerability because they did not fight in World War II; this generation grew up at a time when the Soviet Union was a superpower and rapidly gaining military strength. The main danger of this shift of leadership from one generation to another was that the younger men might be more self-confident and assertive in seeking the Soviet Union's "place in the sun." Given the country's enormous military strength— and, by contrast, the bankruptcy of Soviet official ideology and its weak economic base—the temptation to use the one instrument it had in abundance to expand its influence in the world would be hard to resist. This is especially so for a leadership whose principal constituents besides the Communist Party— heavy industry, the military, and, at least during Andropov's short tenure, the secret police—are generally believed to possess a vested interest in a hard-line foreign policy. The Soviet Union does not have a political-military-industrial complex; it *is* one. This leadership, moreover, in order to legitimate its monopoly of power and crush dissent, must claim that foreign enemies surround the Soviet Union and that their agents are trying to subvert the nation from within. A "garrison state" like the Soviet Union cannot justify itself unless it invents enemies who are laying siege to it.

More specifically, the fear was that when confronted by its domestic problems, to which one could add the hatred for the Soviets by China to their rear and the Eastern Europeans in their front yard, the Soviet leaders might be tempted to unite the nation and mobilize popular support by resorting to adventures beyond Soviet borders. In 1914 *Tsarist* Russia had, along with Austria-Hungary and Germany, attempted to "export domestic dissatisfaction" and unify their countrymen by following highly nationalistic policies. This had helped precipitate World War I. The concern was that Soviet domestic weaknesses in the future might similarly aggravate the international situation and entice the Soviet Union to resort to its formidable military forces.

Whatever the validity of this thesis, a number of things are clear from the experiences of the 1970s. First, as already noted, the newly acquired Soviet conventional military capabilities allowed the Soviet Union in the context of strategic parity to project its power beyond Eurasia. Moscow intervened repeatedly to protect its friends from defeat and produce political results that benefited them as well as itself. Such large-scale "proxy interventions" as in Angola, Ethiopia, and South Yemen had not been possible before. Second, the Soviet Union was willing to use force. The invasion of Afghanistan by the Red Army was the first direct use of force by Moscow outside of its Eastern European sphere of influence and in a Third World country. More frequently, the Soviet Union used military advisers, arms transfers, treaties of friendship, and proxies ranging from Cuban soldiers to East German policemen. Third, in the process of enhancing its influence and exploiting opportunities to do so, the Soviet Union has acquired a number of regionally active and powerful clients: Cuba and Nicaragua in Central America, Vietnam in East Asia, and, to some degree, Syria in the Middle East. These states are less satellites than partners who have interests that often coincide with Moscow's, upon whom they are also economically and militarily dependent. Fourth, the Soviet Union responded less to American expressions of goodwill and appeals for restraint than to firmness. It respected power as much as it harbored contempt for weakness or the failure or unwillingness to exercise power. It did not hesitate to exploit American pseudoisolationism in the 1970s.

This last point was a lesson that every administration has had to learn in its turn: namely, that expectations of unilateral Soviet restraint are bound to be disappointed. As American forces were shifted from Europe to the Far East after Germany's defeat, and, after Japan's defeat, demobilized, the Soviets consolidated their hold on Eastern Europe and began to probe for soft spots from Iran to Western Europe. In 1955, President Eisenhower's efforts to lower tensions with the new post-Stalin leadership at a summit conference were followed shortly thereafter by the arms deal with Egypt, the prelude to the 1956 Suez War. Similarly, a year after the celebration of *détente* at the 1972 summit, Moscow shipped to Egypt and Syria the arms needed to launch their 1973 war and then encouraged the other Arab states to help them, approved the subsequent Arab oil boycott of the United States, and counseled against its lifting in 1974. A few years later, with an administration in power that stated that the cold war was over and that it wished to improve American-Soviet relations even more than had its Republican predecessors, the Soviets did not hesitate to intervene in the Third World, even though they knew that the cost might be the SALT II agreement, which they wanted. And throughout the 1970s, as noted earlier, the Soviet military build-up went on uninterruptedly despite American restraint; if there was an "arms race," only one side was racing.

Possessing military strength was not enough to deter Soviet probes for weak spots into which to expand its influence. That America's atomic monopoly did not suffice in 1945 clearly demonstrated this fact. Only when faced with determined opposition did Moscow show restraint. American power, economic as well as military, had to be linked to a will to use that power. The pattern has been clear since Iran at the end of World War II: Weakness invites challenges, strength deters them and leads to their being called off. This lesson has had to be learned repeatedly. The fact that almost every administration had to do so testifies to America's continuing optimism that if only it could demonstrate its sincerity and desire for peace and friendship, the Soviet Union would reciprocate. The critical task of American foreign policy since 1945 has in fact been to draw lines in order to communicate to the Soviet leadership what the limits were beyond which Soviet efforts to expand would be resisted. And, ironically enough, Moscow has been more comfortable with American administrations that have clearly drawn these lines than those that have left their intentions uncertain; with the former, it has been willing to exercise restraint and arrive at major accommodations, with the latter it has been tempted to probe, which has often resulted in an increase of tensions with the United States. Had Moscow known that Washington would react firmly, it probably would not have acted. The problem is that the Soviet Union cannot resist the temptation to exploit potential opportunities. Thus the chief aim of the United States remains foreclosing such opportunities.

Yet, despite their continuing rivalry—now over forty years—the two superpowers share a common interest in avoiding a nuclear holocaust. Arms-control negotiations have reflected this desire in the past. More specifically, the two countries shared an interest in stabilizing the strategic balance, preventing or slowing down further nuclear proliferation, improving crisis management and, on occasion, cooperating in certain regions to avoid a superpower clash. Every American president before Reagan has been an arms-control president: Truman, with the Baruch-Lilienthal-Acheson plan for the international control of atomic energy; Eisenhower, with the Open Skies plan; Kennedy, with the Limited Nuclear Test ban; Johnson, with the Non-Proliferation Treaty; Nixon, with SALT I; Ford, with the Vladivostok guidelines for SALT II; and Carter, with SALT II. Each president has felt the awesome responsibility of the enormous power that he has controlled, that he could literally destroy the world at the push of a button. And none, regardless of party affiliation, regardless of whether he was a hawk or a dove, as popular terminology would have it, took this responsibility lightly. As the commander-in-chief charged with the defense of the United States, each president confronted the difficult task of protecting the nation's vital interests as he perceived them by preserving the nation's military strength while simultaneously trying to avoid precipitating a nuclear holocaust. And each succeeded. This is also true of Reagan, who has concentrated on rearmament rather than arms control.

An American-Soviet war has not resulted from any of the following crises and limited wars: Berlin (1948–1949), Korea (1950–1953), East Germany (1953), Hungary (1956), Berlin (1958–1961), Cuba (1962), Czechoslovakia (1968), Vietnam (1964–1973), or the Arab-Israeli wars (1956, 1967, 1973). Both the United States and the Soviet Union have acted with a restraint they might not have demonstrated if nuclear weapons had not existed. This in turn reflects the impact of "the bomb"; its enormous destructive power has disciplined the conduct of the superpowers' foreign policy. The age of the "absolute weapon" that can destroy the nations that dare use it is also the age of deterrence, crisis management, limited wars, and wars by proxy—in short, the absence of all-out war. For forty years, the nuclear peace has been kept; this is already twice the time between the first and second World Wars. And despite the strong rhetoric both superpowers hurled at each other during the years of the first Reagan administration, and the Soviet walk-out from arms-control talks in 1983 and the Olympics in 1984, there were no Berlin, nor yet Cuban, crises or Middle East wars that threatened to draw in the United States and the Soviet Union.

In addition, the East-West conflict is no longer the only one. There is also the North-South conflict. The Third World has its own set of attitudes and interests—largely revolving around the New International Economic Order—that it asserts against the North. But the Third World is itself divided in many ways (for example, the *nouveaux riches* Organization of Petroleum Exporting Countries versus the poorer oil-consuming states) and increasingly unstable. Domestic unrest appears everywhere. The increasing frustration at the lack of development; the breakdown of religion and related tradition with whatever modernization occurs (often condemned, as in revolutionary Iran, as alien Westernization); the continuing unequal distribution of wealth, which tends to be accentuated in the early stages of economic development; the lack of legitimate and stable political institutions permitting peaceful change and transfers of power; and the ever-present possibility of national disintegration and territorial claims by neighboring states—all these problems tend to lead to discontent, opposition, and the appearance of revolutionary ideas and regional conflicts. And most startling of all, the Third World will have over 80 percent of the world's approximately 6 billion people by the end of this century. In short, the majority of the globe's people will be nonwhite and poor. The potential for an "international class war," the Marxist class struggle within nations projected worldwide as a struggle between the poor nations and the minority of rich nations, means that the prospects for international stability are not high. Thus the opportunities and enticements for superpower intervention and confrontation are plentiful.

Events during the 1970s demonstrated vividly that the East-West and North-South conflicts cannot be divorced from each other; they interact. Even the regionalists in the Carter administration were concerned with solving issues such as Zimbabwe because failure to transfer power from the ruling tiny white minority to the black majority would have benefited the Soviet bloc; talk of U.S. military intervention in 1973–1974 to seize the Persian Gulf oil fields was usually met with concern about Soviet intervention. Indeed, the fear that the Soviet Union, a "northern" state, might seek to dominate the nearby "southern" oil states was strengthened by the Soviet invasion of Afghanistan and led to the Carter Doctrine. While the Soviet Union's motivation may have had nothing to do with such domination, the fact remains that as a consequence of this invasion Soviet power stands closer to the Gulf. And, of course, many Third World states increasingly voice anti-Americanism, as they did at the 1980 and 1983 meetings in Havana and New Delhi respectively. The nonaligned movement has embraced Communist states such as Vietnam, North Korea, and Cuba. Nonalignment, the declared foreign policy orientation of most Third World members, appeared increasingly to be sheer hypocrisy, as well as on the decline.

THE CONTINUED ABSENCE OF CONSENSUS

Perhaps the most serious handicap for the United States as it faces the future is the continued lack of a foreign policy consensus. The two parties have essentially changed positions. During cold war I, it was the Democratic Party that was the most interventionist and most strongly anti-Soviet (and anti-Chinese during the days of the Sino-Soviet alliance) in its behavior. This reflected, not only the Party's efforts to ward off Republican attacks on the Democrats as the Party of appeasement and the views of its strong Southern conservative anti-Communist wing, but also the Party's essentially dominant liberal orientation. The liberal wing, essentially northern and committed to democratic values and social justice at home, was equally concerned with the protection of democratic values from Soviet totalitarianism abroad. It was because the Democratic Party was essentially liberal that it was also a cold war party. The term "cold war liberalism" was the phrase usually used to describe this pattern of thought. By contrast, with the exception of its eastern moderate wing which supported postwar Democratic foreign policy, the Republican Party, largely conservative, remained to a large extent isolationist, especially toward Europe. Only its rhetoric was fiercely anti-Communist and largely directed toward the Democrats, accusing them of "coddling Communism." In 1952, General Eisenhower ran for the Party's presidential nomination because he feared that if the conservative wing led by Senator Taft from Ohio won the nomination, the Party would abandon the nation's foreign policy commitments should it win the presidency. Eisenhower's main task for eight years was in fact to gain his Party's support for the nation's international role.

Since Vietnam, the two parties have flip-flopped. It is the Republican Party that is now interventionist in foreign policy whereas the Democrats are much less willing to intervene abroad and to use force or the threat of force to support foreign policy objectives. Indeed, they are much more likely to define these objectives very selectively. The old cold war liberals, who belonged to the Hubert Humphrey–Henry Jackson wing of the Party, have essentially disappeared. Liberalism—that is, the commitment to democratic fulfillment, social justice, and egalitarianism domestically—is now to a large extent divorced from a hard-line foreign policy stance. It is ironically in the Republican Party that this stance is on the whole alive and well.

The Republicans, whether during Nixon's *détente* or Ronald Reagan's cold war II, still perceive the world as the Democrats used to: For them, the world remains basically bipolar politically and militarily; international politics revolves mainly around issues of security; the prime focus for American foreign policy is the East-West conflict, including in the Third World; and the principal threat is still the Soviet Union, which remains an expansionist power whose military capability continues to grow beyond any conceivable defensive needs. In short, for the Republicans (except the small and declining number of moderates who are close to the Democratic liberal viewpoint), the key issue remains freedom versus tyranny, democracy versus totalitarianism. Containment of Soviet power cannot therefore be abandoned.

The post-Vietnam or post-cold war liberal Democratic Party defines the world as multipolar. It perceives the Soviet Union as a fundamentally conservative country, primarily concerned with preserving its gains; as militarily powerful but in orientation essentially defensive, if not paranoid about its security, because of past invasions; as willing to exploit opportunities for expansion in the Third World where opportunities arise, but these opportunities could be minimized if the United States were more willing to eliminate some of the causes of Soviet exploitation. Indeed, the Party's focus is not only on East-West issues but North-South ones; in fact, the latter concern may be the stronger. The concern is with poverty, overpopulation, hunger, ill-health, and other social diseases (a concern strengthened by the Democratic Party's large black constituency, which focuses on poverty and racism at home and tends to be concerned with these issues abroad, to the extent that it has much of a foreign policy commitment. The Democrats' Hispanic constituency is also likely to strengthen this Third World orientation.) In short, the Party's focus is very largely on social and economic issues rather than security issues. Once the party of cold war crusaders, it now regards the use of force with a distaste reminiscent of the Founding Father's attitude toward "entangling alliances."

In turn, as noted earlier, this Democratic stance reflects the Party's concern with interdependence—the global issues such as the inequitable distribution of wealth in the world, the population explosion, the scarcity of natural resources, and environmental pollution which cut across national boundaries. These problems confronting all humanity are said to be the critical issues for the future, more important than national and ideological differences among the superpowers and their allies. Building this new world order should, therefore, be the focus of attention and effort rather than the continuation of old-fashioned balance-of-power politics with its undue concentration on national interest, national security, and military power, all of which endanger the survival of the world. Thus, in an increasingly interdependent world, the Democrats are willing to live with self-proclaimed Marxist states; in their commitment to social change in the Third World, they are sympathetic to left-wing forces, hostile to right-wing ones even if they are pro-American, and generally sensitive to Third World claims for social and economic justice, which are allegedly blocked by the democratic-industrial or First World (above all, the United States).

Thus while the Reagan administration saw a Soviet-Cuban-Nicaraguan security threat to the United States in Central America, the Democrats by and large saw the problem in that area as essentially domestic; they viewed El Salvador and Nicaragua as the products of years of American-supported repressive rule. Thus the proposed solution was to bring democracy and the elimination of poverty to El Salvador and to attract Nicaragua away from Moscow and Havana by offering it help rather than opposing it and "driving the Sandinistas into Soviet-Cuban arms." But in both cases, the Party was resolutely opposed to military intervention and was very critical of the Reagan administration's deployment of carrier battle groups on both coastlines of Nicaragua, the covert intervention in that country, and the military assistance provided to the Salvadoran forces. In the 1984 elections, Democratic presidential candidates all promised to end the military and covert interventions and to demand of El Salvador a greater concern with human rights as the price of continued aid. Short of the Soviets' actually deploying missiles or basing their forces in Central America, no Soviet threat was really seen in an area in which American military power, it was argued, was clearly preeminent. The critical issue was social revolution and a desire for social justice within the area. In the context of the 1960s, most liberal Democrats were willing to live with Castro but, as then, drew the line at a Soviet land base in this hemisphere. (Presumably, they forgot the 1962 Cuban missile crisis or, if they remembered, hoped that the Soviets would not do such a foolish thing again. If the Soviets did do it again, however, in the new strategic environment, the Democrats were apparently willing to face a far more dangerous confrontation than in 1962—or retreat from their opposition to a Soviet base when and if it appeared with some proper rationalization.)

By contrast, on the security issue of the military balance, all Democratic presidential aspirants supported some sort of nuclear freeze and were critical of the Reagan military build-up, especially the strategic build-up, promising to stop the production and deployment of the MX missile and B-1 bomber. The problem was not the Soviet Union's military growth and deployments, which included over 300 SS-20s aimed at Western Europe, or its general foreign policy behavior, but America's rearmament programs, lack of arms-control negotiations and agreements with the Soviet Union, as well as President Reagan's frequent denunciations of the Soviet leaders. In any event, the point is clear: an absence of agreement between the two parties on foreign and defense issues,* a disagreement made all the more serious by the moral conviction with which each held its position. Characteristically American, each identified its position with morality: the East-West issue of freedom versus totalitarianism and the North-South issue of social change for the poor and often repressed masses of

---

*In fact, this lack of consensus is somewhat more complex, involving more than just the division between the two parties, or liberals and conservatives, or hawks and doves. See James N. Rosenau and Ole Holsti, "U.S. Leadership in a Shrinking World: The Breakdown of Consensus and the Emergence of Conflicting Belief Systems," *World Politics* (April 1983), pp. 368–92.

the Third World. And also characteristically American, each party tended to view the East-West conflict or the North-South struggle as global.

THE PURPOSE OF AMERICAN FOREIGN POLICY

Although both parties increasingly tend to perceive the world quite differently, including what constitutes a safe balance of power, it is well to remind ourselves in concluding what the chief purpose of American foreign policy is. The balance of power, however defined and whatever its military ingredients, is not an end in itself. It is the means to the end of preserving the security of a democratic America. In turn, successive administrations felt that this end required the maintenance of an international environment congenial to the survival of democratic societies. The fundamental orientation of American foreign policy has been, therefore, to support the democracies, old and new, in Western Europe and Japan through alliances—and to support one state, Israel, which has no formal alliance with the United States (although, for all practical purposes, it might as well have.) Indeed, as the cases of West Germany, Italy, and Austria in Europe, and Japan in Asia suggest, the expansion of American power and influence in the world is by and large associated with the promotion of democracy. Our former enemies, all once dictatorial in nature, are today stable, free societies. This is hardly accidental. Our political leaders reflect the values of American society, and when at times they seem to disregard these values in their conduct of the nation's foreign policy, they are usually criticized by other members of the executive branch, Congress, the opposition party, and the press. America's open society is its best insurance that, by and large, the nation "stays on course"; otherwise, its leaders had better have a convincing rationale for straying.

If we look at the societies liberated by the Soviet Union during World War II, the contrast is striking. No Eastern European country could be described as a "free society"; attempts to move toward greater freedom have been squashed by the Red Army in East Germany, Hungary, and Czechoslovakia and by the Polish army in Poland. East Germany had to build the Berlin Wall in that divided city and a barbed wire fence along its entire border with West Germany to prevent its citizens from escaping. As South Vietnam was collapsing in 1975 before the advancing North Vietnamese armies, much of the population "voted with its feet," fleeing southward; and after the unification of Vietnam, thousands more risked their lives fleeing from their country in small boats (and in the process often dying). In neighboring Cambodia, the new Communist rulers killed over 2 million people out of a total population of 8 million. And when intermittently Cuba allows its people to leave, they do so by the hundreds of thousands.

Admittedly, the United States has on occasions acquired a set of dictatorial allies and friends, usually of right-wing coloration, which appears to weaken Washington's democratic rationale and lay its foreign policy open to the charge of hypocrisy. One reason for this has been, as we just saw in the case of South Korea, that the security of Japan required the defense of the authoritarian regime in the southern half of the peninsula. Similarly in Europe, the desire for air and naval bases to strengthen NATO, composed of the principal remaining democracies in the world, led to the inclusion of Portugal as an ally and Spain as an associated power, both of whom at the time were governed by right-wing authoritarian regimes. It is, of course, preferable to have democratic allies, but in a world most of whose states are not democratic it is not always possible. Security and democracy are therefore bound to appear on occasion as conflicting values; which is to be given priority is a difficult and often agonizing choice. If in the name of security a democracy somewhat indiscriminately picks up a large number of dictatorial allies to enhance its power, acquire strategic position, or play off one country against another, it may indeed corrupt its purposes; on the other hand, if in the name of democracy it refuses to align itself with any undemocratic regimes in order to keep its hands clean, it may remain pure but weaken itself against its principal adversary. Thus, in the real world, a democracy must at times sup with a dictatorship, be it of the Right or Left, although when it does so it should remember to eat with a long spoon.

The question is not whether a democracy should ever ally itself with an undemocratic government or come to its rescue if it sees that its *own* security is involved—as, for instance, Great Britain did when it went to the rescue of an undemocratic Poland attacked by Nazi Germany in 1939 or the United States did when it sought to bolster undemocratic Turkey and Greece against perceived Communist expansionist pressures from the Soviet Union in 1947— but how often, for what purposes, how long, and at what level of commitment such an association should be forged. On these issues, honest men can and do differ vigorously. In the absence of war, it cannot be proven that America's relations with Portugal and Spain, for example, contributed to the prevention of hostilities and therefore the protection of Western Europe; perhaps war would not have occurred without them and we need not have stained our cause. Perhaps the United States could have achieved its diplomatic objective of restraining the Soviet Union even without aligning itself with Tito's Yugoslav dictatorship after 1948 or, after 1972, with the totalitarian regime in Communist China. In any event, given the democratic nature of American society, the pros and cons of aligning with right- or left-wing despotisms when it occurs tends to be debated so that the trade-offs between the values of democracy and security become clear, even if disagreements remain about the exact mix that policy should reflect. This has been particularly true since Vietnam.

It also needs to be added that although not a single Communist state has ever evolved into a Western-style democracy or been overthrown by force from within in favor of a parliamentary form of government—one need but look at the squelching of the first glimmers of freedom in Poland as the 1980s began—

some of America's authoritarian allies and friends, such as Portugal, Spain (which joined NATO in 1982), and Greece, were overthrown, collapsed, or began to evolve in a more democratic direction. This, in turn, suggests that it is not altogether hypocritical to say that there is an essential difference between left-wing Communist totalitarian and right-wing authoritarian regimes in terms of the degree and permanence of government control and oppression of the population, despite such similarities as arbitrary government or the loss of civil and political rights in both types of regimes.

In any event, the principal thrust of American policy since World War II, as before the war, has remained the preservation of a balance of power that would safeguard democratic values in the United States and other basically Western countries. Indeed, this has been a consistent policy since World War I, whether the threat came from the expansionism of the Right (Germany twice) or the expansionism of the Left (the Soviet Union once). American policymakers in the twentieth century have opposed both types of regimes, for they threatened not just our security but, more broadly, the international environment in which democratic values could prosper. And this remains the crux of American opposition to the Soviet Union: that its great power is a threat to Western values and Western-style open societies. Indeed, Communism, as reflected in the organization of all Communist societies, remains the antithesis of societies that believe in individual freedoms, whether of speech or religion, in free-party competition and genuine political choice, and in a distinction between state and society. The basic purpose of American foreign policy, after all, is the protection of a democratic social order in a hostile world, and it is America's counterbalancing power that has protected democratic values; without that power, Soviet power and the Soviet Union's social values and order would have prevailed. Freedom in the world, in short, is intimately tied to American power. As Henry Kissinger, while secretary of state, succinctly expressed it, "If we do not lead, no other nation that stands for what we believe in can take our place."

APPENDIX A

U.S. Alliances in Europe and Asia

Alliance	Date of Origin	Membership
NATO (15 members)	1949	Belgium, Britain, Canada, Denmark, France, Greece, Iceland, Italy, Luxembourg, Netherlands, Norway, Portugal, Turkey, United States, West Germany
ANZUS (3 members)	1951	Australia, New Zealand, United States
Philippine Treaty (2 members)	1951	Philippines, United States
Japanese Treaty (2 members)	1951	Japan, United States
Republic of Korea (2 members)	1953	South Korea, United States
Republic of China (2 members)	1954–1978	Nationalist China, United States
SEATO (8 members)	1954–1975	Australia, Britain, France, New Zealand, Pakistan, Philippines, Thailand, United States
METO (later CENTO minus Iraq), 1955–1979. (Initially 6, later 5, members if the United States is counted, although not a fully fledged member)		Britain (chief sponsor of this alliance) Iran, Iraq (until it pulled out after 1958 overthrow of monarchy), Pakistan, Turkey, United States

The United States also has alliances in all but name with Israel, Egypt, and Saudi Arabia. While no treaties of defense exist, long commitments and/or continued strategic or economic interests have made these countries virtual allies.

Soviet Alliances in Europe and Asia

Alliance	Date of Origin	Membership
Sino-Soviet (2 members)	1949–1979	Communist China, Soviet Union
Warsaw Pact* (7 members)	1955	Bulgaria, Czechoslovakia, East Germany, Hungary, Poland, Romania, Soviet Union

The Soviet Union has in recent years signed a number of treaties of friendship: Angola (1976), Ethiopia (1978), Afghanistan (1978), Vietnam (1978), and Syria (1981). While Moscow has emphasized that the purpose of the treaties is one of consultation, the implication is that they involve defense commitments; the aim is certainly to deter the United States from any actions against these nations.

*The Soviet Union had signed bilateral alliances with Czechoslovakia, Poland, Romania, Hungary, and Bulgaria in the 1940s.

APPENDIX B

SELECTED PRINCIPAL EVENTS

Year
1945   The Yalta Conference seeks to organize postwar world.

World War II with Germany ends.

World War II with Japan ends after two atomic bombs are dropped.

President Roosevelt dies.

Vice-President Truman succeeds.

United Nations is established.

Soviet military forces occupy Poland, Romania, Bulgaria, Hungary, and Czechoslovakia.

1946   United States confronts the Soviet Union over Iran and later withdraws its troops.

Winston Churchill, Britain's wartime prime minister, delivers "iron curtain" speech at Fulton, Missouri, warning of Soviet threat.

1947   Truman Doctrine commits the United States to assist Greece and Turkey.

Marshall Plan for the economic recovery of Western Europe is devised by Secretary of State Marshall, formerly the U.S. chief of staff and architect of victory during World War II.

George Kennan, a Foreign Service officer, provides the government with the analysis that was to be the basis of the containment policy of Soviet Russia.

India becomes independent.

1948   Soviet *coup d'état* takes place in Czechoslovakia.

Soviets blockade all ground traffic from West Germany to West Berlin and the Western airlift starts.

Vandenberg resolution of U.S. Senate commits American support for the Brussels Pact of self-defense.

Marshall Plan is passed by Congress.

North and South Korea are established.

The state of Israel is established and receives immediate U.S. recognition.

President Truman wins upset reelection.

Stalin expels Yugoslavia's Tito from Communist bloc.

1949   North Atlantic Treaty Organization (NATO) is formed.

Soviet Union ends Berlin Blockade.

West and East Germany are established.

Soviet Union explodes atomic bomb.
Nationalist China collapses and Communist China is established.
U.S. troops are withdrawn from South Korea.
Truman announces Point 4 foreign aid program for less-developed countries.

1950   North Korea attacks South Korea by crossing the thirty-eighth parallel.
United States intervenes on behalf of South Korea.
Communist China intervenes after U.S. forces advance into North Korea toward China's frontier.
Soviet Union and Communist China sign thirty-year treaty of mutual assistance.
European Coal and Steel Community is formed.
Senator Joe McCarthy begins his attacks on government for treason and "coddling Communism."

1951   Truman fires General MacArthur in Korea for proposing that the United States attack Communist China.
General Eisenhower is appointed supreme Allied commander in Europe and Truman sends U.S. forces to Europe.

1952   General Eisenhower is elected president.
Greece and Turkey join NATO.
Britain tests its first atomic weapon.

1953   Stalin dies.
Armistice negotiated along thirty-eighth parallel in Korea.

1954   United States explodes first hydrogen bomb.
France is defeated at Dienbienphu in Indochina.
United States threatens to intervene in Indochina.
Vietnam is partitioned at the seventeenth parallel at the Geneva Conference.
Southeast Asia Treaty Organization (SEATO) is formed.
U.S.-Japanese mutual security pact is signed.
U.S.-Nationalist China defense treaty is signed.
Central Intelligence Agency overthrows Guatemala's left-wing government.
Soviet Union intervenes in East Germany to quell revolt.

1955   Communist China shells the Nationalist Chinese-held islands of Quemoy and Matsu.
The Formosa resolution authorizes President Eisenhower to use force, if necessary, to protect Taiwan against a possible Communist Chinese invasion.
Middle East Treaty Organization (Baghdad Pact) is formed.
West Germany joins NATO, and Soviets establish "their NATO," called the Warsaw Pact.

1956   United States withdraws financial aid offer to help build Egypt's Aswan Dam.
Egypt nationalizes the Suez Canal.
Suez War breaks out after Israel attacks Egypt, and France and Britain intervene.

U.N. forces are sent to Egypt to keep the peace between Israel and Egypt.
Soviets suppress Hungarian revolt and almost intervene in Poland.
Khrushchev attacks Stalin at twentieth Communist Party Congress.

1957   Soviet Union tests ICBM.
Soviets launch two Sputniks, or satellites, into space.
British test hydrogen bomb.
Eisenhower Doctrine commits the United States to assist Middle East countries that resist Communist aggression (or states closely tied to the Soviet Union such as Egypt).

1958   United States lands marines in Lebanon and Britain lands paratroopers in Jordan after Iraqi revolution.
Soviets offer to build Egypt's Aswan Dam.
Soviet Union declares it would end the four-power occupation of Berlin and turn West Berlin into a "free city."
The European Economic Community (the Common Market) is established.
First of several Berlin crises erupts.
Communist China shells Quemoy-Matsu again.
Britain tests its first thermonuclear bomb.

1959   Khrushchev visits President Eisenhower for Camp David meeting over Berlin issue.
Castro captures power in Cuba.
Central Treaty Organization (CENTO) replaces the Baghdad Pact.

1960   Soviets shoot down U.S. U-2 spy plane over the Soviet Union.
Paris summit conference collapses over U-2 incident.
The Congo becomes independent from Belgium, causing the first superpower crisis in sub-Sahara Africa.
U.N. forces sent to the Congo to help resolve the crisis there.
France becomes an atomic power.
Kennedy wins presidential election.

1961   Kennedy launches abortive Bay of Pigs invasion of Cuba.
Kennedy proposes Alliance for Progress for Latin America.
Kennedy holds summit conference with Khrushchev in Vienna.
Kennedy sends first military advisors to South Vietnam.
Soviets build Berlin Wall.

1962   In Cuban missile crisis, the United States blockades Cuba to compel the Soviets to withdraw their missiles from the island.
Chinese-Indian frontier conflict erupts.

1963   French President de Gaulle vetoes Britain's entry into the Common Market.
"Hot line" established between the White House and the Kremlin for direct emergency communications.
Atomic test-ban treaty is signed.
President Kennedy is assassinated and President Johnson succeeds him.
Soviets place man in space.

1964   Congress passes Gulf of Tonkin resolution, raising the U.S. commitment to
            the defense of South Vietnam.
            Khrushchev falls from power and is replaced by Prime Minister Kosygin and
            Communist Party Secretary Brezhnev.

1965   United States starts bombing North Vietnam and sends American land forces
            into South Vietnam.
            Protests against the war start.
            United States intervenes in the Dominican Republic.
            War erupts between Pakistan and India.

1966   Communist China becomes nuclear power.
            France withdraws its forces from NATO's integrated command structure but
            remains a member of the alliance.

1967   Six-Day Middle East War between Israel and its Arab neighbors takes place.
            Greek colonels seize power in Greece.

1968   Tet Offensive in South Vietnam escalates demand for U.S. withdrawal from
            Vietnam.
            Johnson withdraws from presidential race.
            Nixon elected president.
            Vietnamese peace talks begin in Paris.
            Nuclear Non-Proliferation Treaty is made.
            Soviet Union intervenes in Czechoslovakia to squash revolt.

1969   Brezhnev Doctrine is proclaimed asserting the right of Soviet Union to inter-
            vene in Soviet sphere to suppress "counterrevolution."
            ABM deployment is narrowly voted by Senate.
            United States tests MIRV.
            SALT talks start.
            "Vietnamization" program starts. South Vietnamese are to do more of the
            fighting while the United States begins troop withdrawal.
            Ho Chi Minh dies.
            United States lands men on moon.
            Lt. Calley stands trial for My Lai massacre of civilians in South Vietnam by
            U.S. troops.
            First of several Sino-Soviet border clashes occurs.

1970   West Germany concludes treaties with Soviet Union and Poland recognizing
            Poland's western border and acknowledging Germany's division into East
            and West Germany.
            Senate repeals Gulf of Tonkin resolution.
            U.S. invasion of Cambodia causes widespread student protests including
            National Guard's killing of four students at Kent State.
            Chile elects a Marxist, Salvador Allende, president.

1971   India and Pakistan go to war over the Bangladesh (East Pakistan) secession
            effort.
            Communist China joins the United Nations.

Four-power Berlin settlement is reached ensuring Western access to Berlin.

1972　President Nixon visits Communist China, beginning a process of normalizing relations after two decades of hostility.

North Vietnam invades South Vietnam.

Nixon retaliates by expanding air war against North Vietnam and blockading the harbor of Haiphong.

Nixon visits Moscow for summit conference with Soviet leaders, signs Strategic Arms Limitation Talks (SALT) I and ABM treaty.

Watergate affair starts with police arrest of five men in Democratic Party headquarters.

Soviets buy enormous quantities of U.S. grains, raising U.S. domestic prices.

Britain, Denmark, and Ireland join Common Market, increasing membership to nine countries.

Paris peace talks, close to success, break down and the United States bombs North Vietnam heavily during Christmas season.

Nixon reelected president (Massachusetts was the only state not to elect him).

1973　Kissinger is appointed secretary of state while remaining the president's national security assistant.

Vietnamese peace agreement is signed.

United States and China establish liaison offices, or informal embassies, in Washington and Peking.

Yom Kippur War breaks out in Middle East.

Arab members of the Organization of Petroleum Exporting Countries embargo oil to the United States because of U.S. support for Israel.

OPEC quadruples oil prices.

U.S.-Soviet Mutual and Balanced Force Reductions in Europe start.

West and East Germany exchange recognition and ambassadors, acknowledging Germany's division into two Germanies.

Congress passes the War Powers Resolution over Nixon's veto.

Vice-President Agnew resigns and Ford succeeds him.

Allende is overthrown by military in Chile.

1974　India explodes "peaceful" nuclear device.

Congress asserts right to veto large arms sales to other nations.

Annual Nixon-Brezhnev summit conference further reduces small numbers of ABMs the United States and Soviet Union are allowed by SALT I treaty.

Kissinger negotiates first agreements between Israel and Egypt and Syria as part of his "step-by-step" diplomacy intended to achieve a comprehensive regional peace.

Nixon visits Egypt, Syria, and Israel.

Nixon resigns and Ford becomes unelected president; New York Governor Nelson Rockefeller becomes vice-president.

Ford and Brezhnev set Vladivostok guidelines for SALT II negotiations.

1975　Soviet Union rejects American-Soviet trade agreement because of the Senate's Jackson-Vanik amendment.

South Vietnam collapses and unified Communist Vietnam is established.

Cambodia too falls to Cambodian Communists.

Cambodians seize U.S. merchant ship *Mayaguez* and the United States re-
acts forcefully to free crew and ship.

SEATO dissolves itself.

Helsinki agreements, including Western recognition of Europe's division
(and thus Soviet domination in Eastern Europe), arrived at by Western and
Eastern states.

Congress passes arms embargo against Turkey.

Lebanese civil war erupts.

Franco dies and King Juan Carlos starts to lead Spain to democracy.

In Angola, three major factions struggle for control as Portugal gives Angola
independence.

1976   Soviet-Cuban forces in Angola win victory for Marxist-led faction over pro-
Western factions.

Syrian forces intervene in Lebanon.

Communist China's Mao Zedong dies.

Carter elected president.

1977   Carter announces U.S. withdrawal from South Korea (to be reversed later).

Carter sends letter to leading Soviet dissident and receives another one in
the White House.

Soviets denounce Carter's human rights campaign as violation of Soviet sovereignty.

Carter submits new SALT II plan to Soviet Union, which quickly rejects it
because it is not based on Vladivostok guidelines.

Carter halts plans to produce B-1 bomber and instead chooses to deploy
air-launched cruise missiles on B-52 bombers.

United States and Panama sign Panama Canal Treaty.

Somalia expels Soviet advisors and denounces friendship treaty with Soviet
Union.

Soviet-Cuban military help for Ethiopia grows.

Begin is elected prime minister in Israel.

Egyptian President Sadat pays historic visit to Israel, offering peace and
friendship. Other Arab states denounce Sadat.

1978   Soviet-Cuban military intervention in Ethiopia's war against Somalia forces
latter to pull out of Ogaden.

Soviet-inspired *coup* occurs in Afghanistan.

Camp David meeting of the United States, Israel, and Egypt arrives at
"framework for peace" between the two former enemies. Other Arab states
denounce framework because it did not provide for a Palestinian solution.

Senate approves sales of jet fighters to Israel, Egypt, and Saudi Arabia.

Panama Canal treaties approved by Senate.

Carter postpones neutron "bomb" (tactical warhead) production.

United States ends arms embargo on Turkey.

Shah leaves Iran.

Rhodesian Prime Minister Smith announces "internal solution" to the race
problem—the formation of a black-led government.

1979   United States officially recognizes the People's Republic of China. It also
        breaks ties with government on Taiwan as official government of China and
        ends mutual defense treaty.

        China briefly invades Vietnam to punish it for the invasion of Cambodia in
        1978, which overthrew a regime friendly to China and replaced it with a
        pro-Soviet and pro-Vietnamese one.

        Shah's regime in Iran replaced by Islamic republic led by the Ayatollah Kho-
        meini.

        U.S. embassy in Teheran, Iran, seized by militant Islamic students after Shah
        is hospitalized in United States for cancer treatment.

        United States freezes Iran's financial assets in United States and boycotts
        Iranian oil.

        Oil prices shoot upward as Iranian oil production drops and world supplies
        tighten.

        SALT II Treaty signed by Brezhnev and Carter at Vienna summit conference.

        Soviets send 80,000 troops into Afghanistan to assure survival of pro-Soviet
        regime.

        NATO decides to deploy almost 600 theater nuclear weapons to counter So-
        viet "Eurostrategic" missile build-up.

1980   U.S. mission to rescue hostages in Teheran ends in disaster before it reaches
        embassy.

        SALT II "temporarily" withdrawn from Senate by Carter after Soviet inva-
        sion of Afghanistan.

        Carter embargoes shipments of feed grain and high technology, and declares
        United States will boycott summer Olympic games in Moscow.

        Carter Doctrine commits United States to security of Persian Gulf oil-pro-
        ducing states if they are externally threatened.

        United States organizes Rapid Deployment Force to back up the Carter Doc-
        trine.

        Iraq attacks Iran.

        Reagan elected president.

1981   U.S. hostages released moments after Reagan assumes presidency.

        AWACs deal with Saudi Arabia is approved by Senate.

        Reagan declares United States will not allow Saudi Arabia to become "an-
        other Iran."

        Begin is reelected in Israel.

        Sadat is assassinated in Egypt.

        Reagan decides on large program to rebuild U.S. military power, including
        100 MX missiles and 100 B-1 bombers.

        Polish government imposes martial law in Poland.

        United States imposes economic sanctions on Poland and on Soviet Union,
        believed to be behind the Polish crackdown.

1982   Reagan announces an economic assistance plan for the Caribbean Basin (the
        Caribbean and Central America) as he continues to support El Salvador's
        government against rebel forces and to isolate the Sandinistas in Nicaragua
        despite much Congressional criticism.

Israel invades Lebanon, attempting to destroy the PLO.

U.S. marines are sent into Beirut as part of a multinational peace-keeping force to supervise the PLO's leaving.

China and the United States sign agreement on the reduction of U.S. arms sales to Taiwan.

Soviet leader Brezhnev dies and is succeeded by Yuri Andropov, former head of the secret police.

Argentina invades the British Falkland Islands, which she has long claimed. Britain reconquers the Islands.

U.S. imposes—and later, lifts—sanctions on U.S. and European companies selling equipment to the Soviets for the building of a natural gas pipeline to Western Europe.

Secretary of State Haig resigns.

1983   Reagan denounces the Soviet Union as an "evil empire."

Bipartisan Scowcroft Commission recommends deployment of 100 MX missiles and eventual replacement of MIRVed missiles with mobile, smaller single-war headed missile. Congress accepts these recommendations.

Catholic bishops in pastoral letter deplore nuclear deterrence for its immorality. French bishops endorse deterrence as "service to peace."

Two hundred forty-one marines killed in suicide truck-bomb attack on their barracks in Beirut.

Soviet Union shoots down Korean 747 airliner with 269 passengers after it strayed into Soviet airspace.

U.S. forces, together with troops from six Caribbean states, invade the island of Grenada. They depose the Marxist government and return Cuban worker-soldiers to Cuba, and then withdraw.

The United States begins deployment of Pershing II and Ground-Launched Cruise Missiles in Europe.

Soviet Union responds by breaking off all arms-control talks.

1984   Bipartisan Kissinger Commission recommends extensive economic and military assistance to Central America to combat both domestic poverty and Soviet-Cuban intervention in the area. But Congress remains critical of administration policy.

The new Soviet leader Andropov dies and Brezhnev's confidante, Konstantin Chernenko, succeeds him.

Reagan is reelected.

A SELECTIVE
BIBLIOGRAPHY

Listed below are books. But for those readers who wish to keep up with contemporary foreign and defense policies, the articles in *Foreign Affairs, Foreign Policy,* and *International Security* are especially relevant and useful.

AMERICAN SOCIETY AND STYLE
IN FOREIGN POLICY

Almond, Gabriel A. *The American People and Foreign Policy.** New York: Praeger, 1960.

Boorstin, Daniel J. *The Genius of American Politics.** Chicago: Phoenix Books, 1953.

Fromkin, David. *The Independence of Nations.** New York: Praeger, 1981.

Hartz, Louis. *The Liberal Tradition in America.** New York: Harvest Books, 1955.

Herberg, Will. *Protestant, Catholic, and Jew,* rev. ed.* New York: Anchor Books, 1960.

Hofstadter, Richard. *The Paranoid Style in American Politics.** New York: Vintage Books, 1967.

Krasner, Stephen D. *Defending the National Interest.** Princeton, N.J.: Princeton University Press, 1978.

Packenham, Robert A. *Liberal America and the Third World.** Princeton, N.J.: Princeton University Press, 1973.

Potter, David M. *The People of Plenty.** Chicago: Phoenix Books, 1954.

AMERICAN FOREIGN POLICY

Alperovitz, Gar. *Atomic Diplomacy.** New York: Vintage Books, 1967.

Aron, Raymond. *The Imperial Republic.** Cambridge, Mass.: Winthrop Publishers, 1974.

*Asterisked titles are available in paperback editions.

Barnet, Richard. *Roots of War.** New York: Atheneum, 1972.
———. *The Giants.** New York: Simon & Schuster, 1977.
Bell, Coral. *The Diplomacy of Détente.* New York: St. Martin's, 1977.
Bloomfield, Lincoln P. *In Search of American Foreign Policy.** New York: Oxford University Press, 1974.
Draper, Theodore, and others. *Defending America.* New York: Basic Books, 1978.
Fleming, D. F. *The Cold War and Its Origins, 1917–1960,* 2 vols. Garden City, N.Y.: Doubleday, 1961.
Fulbright, J. William. *Old Myths and New Realities.** New York: Vintage Books, 1964.
———. *The Arrogance of Power.** New York: Vintage Books, 1967.
———. *The Crippled Giant.** New York: Vintage Books, 1972.
Gaddis, John L. *The United States and the Origins of the Cold War, 1941–1947.* New York: Columbia University Press, 1972.
———. *Russia, the Soviet Union and the United States.* New York: Wiley, 1978.
———. *Strategies of Containment.** New York: Oxford University Press, 1982.
Gilbert, Felix. *To The Farewell Address.* Princeton, N.J.: Princeton University Press, 1961.
Halle, Louis J. *The Cold War as History.** New York: Harper & Row, 1967.
Hilsman, Roger. *To Move a Nation.* Garden City, N.Y.: Doubleday, 1967.
Hoffmann, Stanley. *Primacy or World Order.* New York: McGraw-Hill, 1978.
Kennan, George F. *American Diplomacy, 1900–1950.** New York: Mentor Books, 1952.
———. *Russia and the West under Lenin and Stalin.** New York: Mentor Books, 1961.
———. *Memoirs.* Boston: Little, Brown, 1967.
———. *The Clouds of Danger.* Boston: Atlantic/Little, Brown, 1977.
Kolko, Gabriel. *The Roots of American Foreign Policy.** Boston: Beacon Press, 1969.
———, and Joyce Kolko. *The Limits of Power.** New York: Harper & Row, 1972.
May, Ernest R. *Lessons of the Past.** New York: Oxford University Press, 1973.
Morgenthau, Hans. *A New Foreign Policy for the United States.** New York: Praeger, 1969.
Oglesby, Carl, and Richard Schaull. *Containment and Change.** New York: Macmillan, 1967.
Osgood, Robert, and others. *America & the World.** Baltimore, Md.: Johns Hopkins Press, 1970.
———. *Retreat from Empire?** Baltimore, Md.: Johns Hopkins Press, 1973.
Steel, Ronald. *Pax Americana.** New York: Viking, 1967.
Talbott, Strobe. *The Russians and Reagan.** New York: Vintage Books, 1984.
Tucker, Robert W. *The Purposes of American Power.** New York: Praeger, 1981.
Wildavsky, Aaron, ed. *Beyond Containment.* San Francisco: Institute for Contemporary Studies, 1983.

AMERICAN MILITARY POLICY

Abel, Elie. *The Missile Crisis.** New York: Bantam Books, 1966.
Blechman, Barry M., and Stephen S. Kaplan. *Force Without War.** Washington, D.C.: Brookings Institution, 1978.
Dinerstein, Herbert. *The Making of a Missile Crisis.** Baltimore, Md.: Johns Hopkins Press, 1976.

Epstein, William. *The Last Chance.* New York: Free Press, 1976.

George, Alexander L. *The Limits of Coercive Diplomacy.** Boston: Little, Brown, 1971.

————, and Richard Smoke. *Deterrence in American Foreign Policy.** New York: Columbia University Press, 1974.

Gompert, David, Michael Mandelbaum, Richard Garwin, and John Barton. *Nuclear Weapons and World Politics.** New York: McGraw-Hill (for the Council of Foreign Relations/1980s Project), 1977.

Gray, Colin. *The Soviet-American Arms Race.* Lexington, Mass.: Lexington Books, 1976.

Horelick, Arnold L., and Myron Rush. *Strategic Power and Soviet Foreign Policy.* Chicago: University of Chicago Press, 1966.

Hyland, William, *et al.*, ed. *Nuclear Weapons in Europe.** New York: Council on Foreign Relations, 1984.

Kahan, Jerome H. *Security in the Nuclear Age.** Washington, D.C.: Brookings Institution, 1975.

Kissinger, Henry A. *The Necessity for Choice.** New York: Anchor Books, 1961.

————. *Nuclear Weapons and Foreign Policy.** New York: Harper & Brothers, 1957.

————. *The Troubled Partnership.** New York: Anchor Books, 1966.

Scoville, Herbert, Jr. *MX.** Cambridge, Mass.: M.I.T. Press, 1981.

Smoke, Richard. *National Security and the Nuclear Dilemma.** Reading, Mass.: Addison-Wesley, 1984.

Talbott, Strobe. *End Game.* New York: Harper & Row, 1980.

Thayer, Charles W. *Guerrilla.** New York: New American Library, 1963.

Whetten, Lawrence, ed. *The Political Implications of Soviet Military Power.* New York: Crane, Russak, 1977.

Wolf, Joseph. *The Growing Dimensions of Security.* Washington, D.C.: Atlantic Council, 1977.

AMERICAN POLICY IN POSTWAR EUROPE

Calleo, David P. *The Atlantic Fantasy.* Baltimore, Md.: Johns Hopkins Press, 1970.

————. *Europe's Future.** New York: Norton, 1967.

De Porte, A. W. *Europe Between the Superpowers.* New Haven: Yale University Press, 1979.

Feld, Werner, and John Wildger. *Domestic Political Realities and European Unification.* Boulder, Colo.: Westview Press, 1977.

Hoffmann, Stanley. *Gulliver's Troubles or the Setting of American Foreign Policy.** New York: McGraw-Hill, 1968.

Holborn, Hajo. *The Political Collapse of Europe.* New York: Knopf, 1951.

Jones, Joseph. *The Fifteen Weeks.* New York: Viking, 1955.

Kleiman, Robert. *Atlantic Crisis.** New York: Norton, 1964.

Mally, Gerhard. *Interdependence.* Lexington, Mass.: Lexington Books, 1976.

Mander, John. *Berlin, Hostage for the West.** Baltimore, Md.: Penguin Books, 1962.

Newhouse, John, ed. *U.S. Troops in Europe.** Washington, D.C.: Brookings Institution, 1971.

Pipes, Richard, ed. *Soviet Strategy in Europe.* New York: Crane, Russak, 1976.

Ranney, Austin, and Giovanni Sartori, eds. *Euro Communism.* Washington, D.C.: American Enterprise Institute, 1978.

Willis, Geoffrey. *The Permanent Alliance.* Leiden, Netherlands: Sythoff, 1977.
Speier, Hans. *Divided Berlin.* New York: Praeger, 1961.
Steel, Ronald. *The End of Alliance.** New York: Delta Books, 1966.
Tucker, Robert W., and Wrigley, Linda. *The Atlantic Alliance and Its Critics.** New York: Praeger Publishers, 1983.

AMERICAN POLICY IN ASIA

Barnett, A. Doak. *China Policy.** Washington, D.C.: Brookings Institution, 1977.
———. *China and the Major Powers in East Asia.** Washington, D.C.: Brookings Institution, 1977.
Clough, Ralph N. *East Asia and U.S. Security.** Washington, D.C.: Brookings Institution, 1975.
Clubb, O. Edmund. *China and Russia.** New York: Columbia University Press, 1971.
Cohen, Warren I. *America's Response to China.** New York: Wiley, 1971.
Dulles, Foster R. *American Foreign Policy Toward Communist China.** New York: Crowell, 1972.
Fall, Bernard B. *The Two Viet-Nams,* 2d rev. ed. New York: Praeger, 1967.
Feis, Herbert. *China Tangle.** Princeton, N.J.: Princeton University Press, 1953.
Gelb, Leslie, and others. *The Pentagon Papers.** New York: Bantam Books, 1971.
Gurtov, Melvin. *The First Vietnam Crisis.** New York: Columbia University Press, 1967.
Halberstam, David. *The Best and the Brightest.** New York: Random House, 1969.
Hammer, Ellen J. *The Struggle for Indochina, 1940–1955.** Stanford, Calif.: Stanford University Press, 1966.
Hellmann, Donald C. *Japan and East Asia.** New York: Praeger, 1972.
Hinton, Harold C. *Three and a Half Powers.** Bloomington, Ind.: Indiana University Press, 1975.
Hoopes, Townsend. *The Limits of Intervention.** New York: McKay, 1969.
Lake, Anthony, ed. *The Vietnam Legacy.* New York: New York University Press, 1976.
Lewy, Guenter. *America in Vietnam.** New York: Oxford University Press, 1978.
Meisner, Maurice, *Mao's China.* New York: Free Press, 1977.
Oksenberg, Michel, and Robert Oxnam, eds. *Dragon and Eagle.* New York: Basic Books, 1978.
Spanier, John W. *The Truman-MacArthur Controversy and the Korean War,** rev. ed. New York: Norton, 1965.
Sutter, Robert. *Chinese Foreign Policy After the Cultural Revolution.* Boulder, Colo.: Westview Press, 1978.
Thompson, Sir Robert. *No Exit from Vietnam.* New York: McKay, 1969.
Thompson, W. Scott, ed. *The Third World,* rev. ed. San Francisco: Institute for Contemporary Studies, 1983.
Tsou, Tang. *America's Failure in China, 1941–1950,** 2 vols. Chicago: Phoenix Books, 1963.

AMERICAN POLICY IN THE MIDDLE EAST

"America in Captivity: Points of Decision in the Hostage Crisis," *New York Times Magazine,* May 17, 1981.

Doran, Charles, *Myth, Oil and Politics*. New York: Free Press, 1977.
Golan, Galia. *Yom Kippur and After*. New York: Cambridge University Press, 1977.
Golan, Matti. *The Secret Conversations of Henry Kissinger.** New York: Quadrangle/ The New York Times Book Co., 1976.
Quandt, William. *Decade of Decisions*. Berkeley, Calif.: University of California Press, 1977.
———. *Saudi Arabia in the 1980s.** Washington, D.C.: Brookings Institution, 1981.
Reich, Bernard. *Quest for Peace*. New Brunswick, N.J.: Transaction Books, 1977.
Sadat, Anwar. *In Search of Identity*. New York: Harper & Row, 1978.
Safran, Nadav. *Israel.** Cambridge, Mass.: Harvard University Press, 1978.
Sheehan, Edward. *The Arabs, Israelis and Kissinger*. New York: Reader's Digest Press, 1976.

AMERICAN POLICY IN AFRICA AND LATIN AMERICA

Blasier, Cole. *The Giant's Rival*. Pittsburgh, Pa.: University of Pittsburgh Press, 1983.
El-Khawas, Mohamed, and Barry Cohen, eds. *The Kissinger Strategy for Southern Africa*. Westport, Conn.: Lawrence Hill, 1976.
La Feber, Walter. *The Panama Canal.** New York: Oxford University Press, 1978.
———. *Inevitable Revolutions*. New York: Norton, 1983.
Lake, Anthony. *The "Tar Baby" Option*. New York: Columbia University Press, 1976.
Leiken, Robert S., ed. *Central America*. New York: Pergamon Press, 1984.
Lemarchand, René, ed. *American Policy in Southern Africa*. Washington, D.C.: University Press of America, 1978.
Rangel, Carlos. *The Latin Americans*. New York: Harcourt, 1977.
The Report of the President's National Bipartisan Commission on Central America. New York: Macmillan, 1984.
Sigmund, Paul. *The Overthrow of Allende and the Politics of Chile*. Pittsburgh: University of Pittsburgh, 1977.

THE NEW INTERNATIONAL POLITICS

Atlantic Council Working Group on the U.S. and the Developing Countries. *The United States and the Developing Countries*. Boulder, Colo.: Westview Press, 1977.
Bhagwati, Jagdish, ed. *The New International Economic Order*. Cambridge, Mass.: M.I.T. Press, 1977.
Blake, David, and Robert Walters. *The Politics of Economic Relations.** Englewood Cliffs, N.J.: Prentice-Hall, 1976.
Brown, Harrison. *The Human Future Revisited*. New York: Norton, 1978.
Fishlow, Albert, Carlos Diaz-Alejandro, Richard Fagen, and Roger Hansen. *Rich and Poor Nations in the World Economy*. New York: McGraw-Hill (for the Council of Foreign Relations/1980s Project), 1978.
Keohane, Robert, and Joseph Nye. *Power and Interdependence.** Boston: Little, Brown, 1977.

Lewis, Arthur. *The Evolution of the International Economic Order.** Princeton, N.J.: Princeton University Press, 1978.

Morse, Edward. *Modernization and the Transformation of International Relations.* New York: Free Press, 1976.

Report of the Independent Commission on International Development Issues under the chairmanship of Willy Brandt, *North-South: A Programme for Survival.* Cambridge, Mass.: M.I.T. Press, 1980.

Rothstein, Robert. *The Weak in the World of the Strong.* New York: Columbia University Press, 1977.

Spero, Joan. *The Politics of International Economic Relations.** New York: St. Martin's, 1977.

Tucker, Robert. *Inequality of Nations.* New York: Basic Books, 1977.

Vernon, Raymond, ed. *The Oil Crisis.** New York: Norton, 1976.

Wriggins, Howard, and Gunnar Adler-Karlsson. *Reducing Global Inequities.* New York: McGraw-Hill (for the Council of Foreign Relations/1980s Project), 1978.

MEMOIRS AND BIOGRAPHIES OF AMERICAN STATESMEN AND ADMINISTRATIONS

Acheson, Dean. *Present at the Creation.* New York: Norton, 1969.

Brzezinski, Zbigniew. *Power and Principle.** New York: Farrar, Strauss, Giroux, 1983.

Brown, Harold. *Thinking About National Security.* Boulder, Colo.: Westview Press, 1983.

Bundy, McGeorge, ed. *The Pattern of Responsibility.* Boston: Houghton Mifflin, 1952.

Byrnes, James F. *Speaking Frankly.* New York: Harper & Brothers, 1947.

Carter, Jimmy. *Keeping Faith.* New York: Bantam Books, 1982.

Eisenhower, Dwight D. *Mandate for Change.** New York: New American Library, 1965.

———. *Waging Peace.* New York: Doubleday, 1965.

Ferrell, Robert H. *George C. Marshall.* New York: Cooper Square Publishers, 1966.

Gerson, Louis. *John Foster Dulles.* New York: Cooper Square Publishers, 1967.

Guhin, Michael. *John Foster Dulles.* New York: Columbia University Press, 1972.

Haig, Alexander. *Caveat.* New York: Macmillan, 1984.

Harriman, W. Averell. *Special Envoy to Churchill and Stalin, 1941–1946.* New York: Random House, 1975.

Hoopes, Townsend. *The Devil and John Foster Dulles.** Boston: Atlantic/Little, Brown, 1975.

Johnson, Lyndon B. *The Vantage Point.** New York: Popular Library, 1971.

Kalb, Marvin, and Bernard Kalb. *Kissinger.** Boston: Little, Brown, 1974.

Kearns, Doris. *Lyndon Johnson and the American Dream.** New York: Harper & Row, 1976.

Kennedy, Robert S. *Thirteen Days.** New York: Norton, 1971.

Kissinger, Henry A. *The White House Years.* Boston: Little, Brown, 1979.

———. *Years of Upheaval.* Boston: Little, Brown, 1982.

Nixon, Richard. *RN.* New York: Grosset & Dunlap, 1978.

Parmet, Herbert S. *Eisenhower and the American Crusades.* New York: Macmillan, 1972.

Schlesinger, Arthur M., Jr. *A Thousand Days.** New York: Crest Books, 1967.
Smith, Gaddis. *Dean Acheson.* New York: Cooper Square Publishers, 1972.
Sorensen, Theodore C. *Kennedy.** New York: Bantam Books, 1966.
Stoessinger, John. *Henry Kissinger.** New York: Norton, 1976.
Truman, Harry S. *Memoirs.** 2 vols. New York: New American Library, 1965.
Vance, Cyrus. *Hard Choices.* New York: Simon and Schuster, 1982.

SOVIET FOREIGN POLICY

Byrnes, Robert F., ed. *After Brezhnev.** Bloomington, Ind.: University of Indiana Press, 1983.
Donaldson, Robert H., ed. *The Soviet Union in the Third World.* Boulder, Colo.: Westview Press (2nd ed., 1984.)
Duncan, W. Raymond, ed. *Soviet Policy in the Third World.* New York: Pergamon Press, 1980.
Goldman, Marshall I. *U.S.S.R. in Crisis.* New York: Norton, 1983.
Hammond, Thomas T. *Red Flag Over Afghanistan.** Boulder, Colo.: Westview Press, 1984.
Luttwak, Edward. *The Grand Strategy of the Soviet Union.** New York: St. Martin's Press, 1984.
Nogee, Joseph L., and Robert H. Donaldson. *Soviet Foreign Policy Since World War II*, rev. ed.* New York: Pergamon Press, 1984.
Rubinstein, Alvin Z. *Soviet Foreign Policy Since World War II.** Cambridge, Mass.: Winthrop Publishers, 1981.
Valkenier, Elizabeth K. *The Soviet Union and the Third World.* New York: Praeger, 1984.

INDEX